GOSPEL TRUTH

The Works and Wisdom of Jesus Christ

Curtis Garwood

ISBN 978-1-960903-65-5 (digital)

ISBN 978-1-960903-66-2 (paperback)

ISBN 978-1-960903-67-9 (hardcover)

Publify Publishing

1412 W. Ave B

Lampasas, TX 76550

publifypublishing@gmail.com

GOSPEL TRUTH: THE WORKS AND WISDOM OF JESUS CHRIST

"... we heard about your faith in Christ Jesus. ... Your faith and love have arisen from the hope laid up for you in heaven, which you have heard about in the message of truth, the gospel."

--Colossians 1:4-5, New English Translation

Table of Contents

AUTHOR'S INTRODUCTION

Just a few decades after the death of Jesus Christ, many accounts of his life and ministry were circulating.[1] Today it is safe to assume that more has been written about Jesus than any other historical figure. Why, then, should yet another book about him be published?

This book, unlike some others, has no doctrinal bias or denominational agenda. The main text is purely narrative, free of exposition and commentary. (Exposition and commentary are restricted to footnotes and supplements.) The narrative proceeds in chronological order, as can best be determined from comparing the accounts of Matthew, Mark, Luke and John.. These features, along with informative footnotes and enlightening supplemental material, make *Gospel Truth* unique among books on Jesus Christ.

The book's format will appeal to serious students of scripture as well as to readers who are new to the greatest story ever told. The breakdown of that story into shorter accounts may assist parents and teachers to prepare lessons for their young charges. Passages on which the accounts are based are cited to direct the reader to the gospels themselves. This Bible-based book is by no means intended as a substitute for the Scriptures.

To possess "life that lasts forever" means "to know … the only true God, and to know Jesus Christ." The process of "coming to know" the Father and the Son never ends.[2] (John 17:3, *New Life Version; New World Translation)* If this book aids the reader in attaining that life-giving knowledge, it will have served its humble purpose.

Curtis Garwood

March 2023

THE GOSPEL ACCORDING TO...

Matthew

... is directed to Jewish readers, presenting Jesus as the fulfillment of the Old Testament's prophecies about the Messiah, the "Son of David" (1:1; 9:27; 12:23; 15:22; 20:30-31; 21:9, 15; see "Jesus, A.K.A. ...")

... is explicit in mentions of money, figures and values, consistent with the tradition of its author being a tax collector (17:27; 26:15; 27:3)

... refers to the kingdom of Heaven 30-plus times, more than the other gospels

... is more than 40 percent original, that much material not to be found in the other gospels

Mark

... has for a source (according to ancient tradition) the apostle Peter; Mark was associated with Peter in Babylon (1 Peter 5:13)

... was written primarily for the Romans, using more Latin expressions and idioms than the other gospels (6:27; 15:16, 39) and using Roman money to explain the value of coins commonly used by the Israelites (12:42); also explains Jewish customs and teachings unfamiliar to non-Jewish readers (2:18; 7:3, 4; 14:12; 15:42), translates Hebrew and Aramaic expressions (3:17; 5:41; 7:11, 34; 14:36; 15:22, 34) and supplies information about

geography and seasons that Jewish readers would not need (1:13; 11:13; 13:3)

... frequently records how Jesus felt and reacted (1:41; 3:5; 6:6, 34; 7:34; 8:2, 12; 9:36; 10:13-16, 21; 14:33-34)

... is the shortest of the gospels, a fast-moving dynamic view of Jesus' life and ministry (the Greek word for "immediately" is used 47 times)

... emphasizes the activity of Christ—portraying Jesus as a man of action—rather than his sermons and teachings (recording approximately the same number of miracles as Matthew and Luke but only a few parables); devotes more than a third of its content to the final eventful week of Jesus' human life

Luke

... was written by one Gentile believer (Colossians 4:11, 14) to another (1:1-4)

... is some 60 percent unique; it relates at least six specific miracles and includes many illustrations not mentioned in the other gospels

... provides extra details about the physical condition of some whom Jesus healed, which accords with the tradition that its author was a physician (4:38; 5:12; 6:6; 22:50; Colossians 4:14)

... has a vocabulary larger than that of the other three gospels combined, suggesting the level of the author's education

... was written, not by an eyewitness to the events recorded (unlike Matthew and John), but by a careful researcher and historian (although it has been suggested that Luke may have been the unnamed companion of Cleopas in chapter 24); the author had opportunity to interview many who saw the events of Jesus' life, such as the surviving disciples and possibly Jesus' mother

...gives the matter of prayer special attention—instances in which Luke alone mentions Jesus' praying are 3:21; 5:16; 6:12; 9:18, 28; 11:1; 23:46

John

...is a powerful presentation of Jesus' divine authority and the only gospel to clearly state its purpose to the reader (20:31)

... was the last of the gospels written (after the other three had been circulating for possibly decades) and by a specially loved member of Jesus' inner circle (21:20-24)

... is some 90 percent unique, that much material having no parallel in the other gospels; for example, information on Jesus' pre-human existence (1:1-2, 15; 3:13, 31; 6:38; 8:23, 42, 58; 17:5) and the record of six miracles (including Jesus' first miracle of turning water into wine and his last miracle of the huge catch of fish [2:6-10; 21:6-11])

... records many dialogues with individuals—followers and opposers—and includes Jesus' longest recorded prayer (17:1-26)

... uses the Greek words for "love" and "to love" more often than the other three gospels combined

PROLOGUE
FROM THE BEGINNING...

John 1:1-5, 9-14, 16-18

From the beginning the Word had existed with God.[3] What God was the Word was. God brought everything into existence through him—the life and light of humankind.[4] He came into the world[5] (the world that owed its existence to him) but he was not acknowledged by the world—not even by his own people. However, everyone who did recognize him and believe in him was reborn as a child of God.[6] And so the Word became human and lived with humankind.[7] He possessed all the glory of the Father's one and only Son,[8] and he—his Father's bosom companion—revealed the invisible God to all.[9]

PART ONE
"THE CARPENTER'S SON"
(MATTHEW 13:55)

One Angel, Two Messages
Luke 1:5-56

In Judea, during the reign of King Herod the Great, live an elderly childless couple. (See "Biographical Sketch: Herod the Great") The priest Zechariah and his wife Elizabeth have long prayed for a family.[10] One day, as Zechariah takes his turn burning incense on the altar at Jerusalem's Temple,[11] he is startled by the sudden appearance of the angel Gabriel.[12] The heavenly messenger calms Zechariah and assures him, "Your prayer will be answered: your wife will give you a son, and you shall call him John." Not just Zechariah and Elizabeth will "be thrilled with gladness"; "many will rejoice" over John's birth, because the child will be great in God's eyes.[13] "He will turn many Israelites to their God," continues Gabriel, "by preparing for God a people fit for him."[14]

Gabriel's good news is unbelievable to an old man whose wife is well past her childbearing years. For this lack of faith, Zechariah won't be able to speak until the day when the angel's words come true.

Meanwhile, people outside the Temple have finished their prayers and are wondering, 'Why is the priest taking so long?'[15] When Zechariah finally appears, he cannot speak and attempts to communicate with gestures. The people perceive that he has seen something supernatural in the Temple.

Zechariah completes his duties and returns home. Soon thereafter, Elizabeth becomes pregnant. "How kind of God to look upon me," she sings, "and take away the shame of my barrenness!"[16]

Five months later, one of Elizabeth's relatives also receives a visit from the angel Gabriel.[17] Mary[18] is a young unmarried woman who lives in Nazareth, a city of the region called Galilee. Gabriel salutes Mary: "God be with you, favored one! You will become pregnant and give birth to a son and call his name Jesus." Mary's child, says Gabriel, will inherit the throne of his ancestor King David, and rule his kingdom forever.[19]

Thoroughly shaken, Mary asks, "How can this happen? I'm a virgin!"

"The spirit and the power of the Highest will surround you," Gabriel explains. "And so, the child will be called the holy Son of God."[20] Gabriel then reveals to Mary that her elderly relative Elizabeth, "who was called barren," is in her sixth month of pregnancy. "Nothing is impossible for God," he declares.

Mary, God's humble servant, tells Gabriel, "Let it be as you say."[21]

Gabriel disappears. Mary travels with haste into the highlands, to a city in Judah.[22] She arrives at Zechariah's house, enters and greets Elizabeth, who is instantly overwhelmed with God's spirit. To Mary she says, "Among women you are truly blessed! And so is the child you carry! Who am I to have the mother of my Lord come to me? As soon as I heard your greeting, the child inside me jumped for joy!"[23]

Mary responds with praises to "the Powerful One" for his "great deeds."[24] For about three months Mary stays with Elizabeth.

BIOGRAPHICAL SKETCH: HEROD THE GREAT

"Herod" was the family name of a dynasty that ruled over Israel by appointment from Rome. The Herods and their immediate predecessors ruled in Palestine for many years before, during and after Jesus' lifetime. They were Idumeans (Edomites) and nominally Jewish.

The forefather of the Herods was Antipater, governor of Idumea. Antipater's son Antipas received the governorship of Judea from Julius Caesar. Antipas appointed his sons Phasael and Herod as governors of Jerusalem and of Galilee respectively.

Herod distinguished himself by ridding his territory of robber bands, whom he executed without due process of law. When Antipas was poisoned by a Jewish general, Herod bypassed all legal formalities and had his father's assassin slain. This was much to the consternation of the Sanhedrin, whose authority he openly flouted. Jerusalem's aristocracy tried in vain to persuade Rome to remove Herod.

Because of a successful revolt led by Jewish prince Antigonus, Herod fled to Rome. Herod's brother Phasael failed to escape and was forced to commit suicide. With Rome's help, Herod defeated his enemies in Judea. He deposed Antigonus and executed him and his supporters among the aristocracy. All the Sanhedrin save two were slain at Herod's command. Rome rewarded his victory with more territory and power.

Herod estranged himself from the Jews (whom he hypocritically called his "countrymen") by his enthusiasm for pagan festivities like the Grecian and Roman games and other idolatries. To pacify his Jewish subjects Herod spent much money and many years rebuilding Jerusalem's Temple. (John 2:20) However, he also built many temples in honor of Caesar Augustus, and a temple at Rhodes to the Greek deity Apollo.

Herod's other building projects included a palace for himself on Mount Zion, theaters, amphitheaters, hippodromes, citadels, fortresses, gardens, aqueducts and monuments—even cities named for himself, his relatives or the emperors. He built an artificial harbor city, Caesarea, which rivaled the seaport of Tyre. He rebuilt Samaria, and carried on vast building projects in Tyre, Sidon and in cities as far removed as Athens and Antioch.

Herod the Great was an astute politician but also a ruthless murderer, probably his worst act being the attempted murder of the infant Jesus. The Bible's account of the Bethlehem massacre harmonizes with what is known of Herod's temperament and his resolve to eliminate rivals—real and imagined. (Matthew 2:16) For alleged plots against him, Herod had two of his sons strangled. In a fit of jealousy, he executed his wife, Mariamne. Suspicion led him to murder his wife's grandfather. Envious of the popularity of one of his brothers-in-law, a mere youth whom he had appointed high priest, Herod had him drowned.

To minimize the rejoicing that was sure to accompany his death, Herod ordered that the principal men of the Jews be killed when he died. That edict was not carried out. At the age of 70 Herod succumbed to disease, likely caused by licentious living.

Herod's sons Antipas and Archelaus both claimed to be the new king of Judea. Rome intervened and Herod's domain was divided, half for Archelaus and half for Antipas and Herod's other son Philip. Archelaus proved unpopular with his subjects and masters; Rome eventually removed him and appointed their own governor.[25] In the meantime, Antipas and Philip continued to govern their own tetrarchies. This was the political situation at the start of Jesus' ministry.—Luke 3:1.

THE TEMPLE—CENTER OF ISRAEL'S WORSHIP

The first permanent building in Jerusalem that replaced the portable tabernacle was constructed by King Solomon; 400 years later it was destroyed by the Babylonians. (2 Chronicles 6:1; 36:18-19) After the Israelites returned from exile in Babylon, a second temple was built by Zerubbabel (Ezra 6:13-15; Haggai 2:2-4); it was destroyed by the Roman army in A.D. 70 but not before being rebuilt by Herod the Great.

The Judeans, who distrusted Herod, refused his proposal to rebuild the 500-year-old Temple until he provided materials and labor. Razing of the old was done piecemeal with construction of the new. The work was 40-plus years in progress when Jesus Christ performed his first miracle. (John 2:11, 20) The rebuilding was finished about six years before the Temple was destroyed by Rome.

According to historian Flavius Josephus, Herod doubled the size of the Temple area, building up the sides of Mount Moriah with great stone walls and leveling off an area on the top of the mountain. The Temple Mount, says the Mishnah, measured 500 cubits (729 feet; 223 meters) square. Like the previous temples, this one faced east. Along this side was Solomon's Colonnade, consisting of two aisles with columns of marble pillars. Here Jesus was approached by certain Judeans asking if he was the Messiah. (John 10:22-24) In the north and west were also colonnades, dwarfed by the Royal Colonnade on the south, consisting of four rows of Corinthian pillars—162 in all—with three aisles. The pillars' circumferences were so great that it took three men with outstretched arms to reach around one of them.

There were eight gates leading into the Temple area: four on the west side, two on the south and one each on the east and north. Because of these gates, the first court, the Court of the Gentiles (so called because non-Israelites were permitted to enter it), also served as a thoroughfare for travelers who preferred to go through it instead of outside around the area. From this court Jesus expelled merchants who commercialized worship of the True God.—Matthew 21:12-13; Mark 11:15-18; John 2:13-17.

The Temple was not just one building but a series of structures of which the sanctuary was the center. On the way to the sanctuary there were several courts through which one passed. Each succeeding court was of a higher degree of sanctity. Passing through the Court of the Gentiles, one encountered a wall three cubits (4.4 ft; 1.3 m) high with openings. On its top were large stones bearing a warning (written in Greek and Latin): death to any foreigner who entered![26] The Court of Women, where women could enter for worship, was 14 steps higher. Among other things, this court contained treasure chests, near one of which Jesus sat when he commended a destitute widow's contribution. (Mark 12:41-44; Luke 21:1-4) Fifteen large semicircular steps led up to the Court of Israel, which ceremonially clean men could enter. Then came the Court of Priests, where the altar stood; it was built of unhewn stones and, according to the Mishnah, measured 32 cubits (46.7 ft; 14.2 m) square at the base. The priests reached the altar by an inclined plane. A "laver" was also in use, says the Mishnah. Around this court also were various buildings.

Herod's Temple, like previous ones, consisted primarily of two compartments: the Holy and the Most Holy. The floor of this building was 12 steps above the Court of Priests. Chambers were built on the sides of this building and there was an upper chamber. The entrance was closed by golden doors, each 55 cubits (80.2 ft; 24.5 m) high and 16 cubits (23.3 ft; 7.1 m) broad. The front of the building was wider than the back, having wings or "shoulders" that extended out 20 cubits (29.2 ft; 8.9 m) on each side. Inside the Holy, which was 40 cubits (58.3 ft; 17.8 m) long and 20 cubits wide, were the Lampstand, the Showbread Table and the Incense Altar—all of gold. The Most Holy was 20 cubits long and 20 cubits wide. The entrance was a beautifully ornamented thick veil. At the time of Jesus' death, this curtain was torn from top to bottom. (Matthew 27:51; Mark 15:38; Luke 23:45) In place of the Ark of the Covenant was a stone slab upon which the high priest sprinkled blood on the Day of Atonement.[27]

The Temple area was used as a fortress during the Roman siege of Jerusalem in A.D. 70. A Roman soldier, disregarding orders from Commander Titus, set fire to the Temple. Jesus' prophecy regarding the destruction of the Temple was thus fulfilled.—Matthew 24:2; Mark 13:2; Luke 21:6.

The Forerunner Is Born
Luke 1:56-80

Mary, unmarried and pregnant, leaves for home before people begin arriving for the birth of Zechariah and Elizabeth's child. Eight days after the baby boy is born, neighbors and family members come to circumcise and name him.[28] They want Zechariah's son to be named after his father. Elizabeth objects, "No, he must be called John."

Friends and relatives protest that John is not a family name, and they ask Zechariah what he wants to call his boy. On a tablet he writes,[29] "His name is John." With that, Zechariah's speech is miraculously restored.[30] From the fullness of God's spirit, Zechariah sings a prophetic blessing to the God of Israel:[31] "He has raised up a powerful savior[32] in the house of his servant David[33] to rescue us from our enemies so that we can worship him fearlessly—in holiness and righteousness—all the days of our life."[34]

To John Zechariah says, "You, child, will be called a prophet of the Highest. As the Lord's forerunner, you will impart knowledge of salvation and forgiveness to his people[35]—such is the merciful kindness of our God."

Another Angel, Another Message
Matthew 1:18-25

Mary is in her fourth month of pregnancy; her condition will soon become public knowledge. (Luke 1:56) Her fiancé is a carpenter named Joseph. Chagrined but noble, he decides to end the engagement.[36] Before Joseph can act, an angel appears to him in a dream.

"Joseph, son of David,"[37] says the angel, "don't be afraid to take Mary into your home[38] for this child has been conceived through God's spirit. She will bear a son and you are to name him Jesus, a name that will mean salvation for his people."[39] When Joseph wakes up, he immediately does as the angel directed and takes Mary as his wife.

A virgin will bear a child? Yes, as prophecy foretold: "The virgin ... will give birth to a son and will call him Immanuel[40] (which means 'God is with us')."—Isaiah 7:14, *New Living Translation.*

JESUS' GENEALOGY

The importance of genealogy is evident from the Bible's first prophecy, which foretold a Messiah for humankind. (Genesis 3:15) About 2,000 years later, God favored Abraham with the promise that the Messiah would be one of his descendants. (Genesis 22:17-18) In time, the promise was narrowed down to Abraham's great-grandson Judah, then, further, to King David's familial line. (Genesis 49:10; 2 Samuel 7:12) The genealogical records of Israel testified that Jesus was of the right line of descent—from King David of the tribe of Judah.—Matthew 9:27; Luke 2:1-6; 2 Timothy 2:8; Hebrews 7:14.

There are four primary lists of Christ's line of descent, three of them beginning with Adam, and they appear in the Bible as follows: (1) Genesis and Ruth; (2) 1 Chronicles, chapters 1 through 3;[41] (3) Matthew, chapter 1, verses 1 through 17; and (4) Luke, chapter 3, verses 23 through 38. With one exception,[42] they agree exactly from Adam to David's son Solomon. Parallel to Solomon, Luke lists Nathan, another son of David. To this point Luke traces the genealogy of Jesus from his maternal grandfather Heli, thereby proving Jesus' <u>natural</u> right to the Messiahship as a son of David (for Jesus had no earthly father, being the foster son of Joseph, but the actual Son of God by a miracle; Luke 1:34-35). Matthew traces Jesus' descent in the line of Solomon, through which the <u>legal</u> right to the throne of David ran. Therefore, Matthew and Luke purposely differ on lines of descent from David down to Jesus. Both genealogies make it clear that Jesus was not actually the son of Joseph but was the true natural son of his wife Mary.—Matthew 1:16; Luke 3:23.

Matthew omits some names that are contained in the other listings. To name every link in the line of descent was not necessary. (Compare Ezra 7:1-5 with 1 Chronicles 6:3-14.) Matthew doubtless copied from the public register, if not every name, the ones necessary to prove the descent of Jesus from Abraham and David—just as someone wanting to prove that they were a descendant of someone famous would need only to name a few of the most recognizable, acknowledged descendants of the famous person, and show that their own forebearer was one of them. Matthew also had access to the Hebrew scriptures, which he could consult alongside the official public records.—Compare Ruth 4:12, 18-22; Matthew 1:3-6.

Significantly, none of Jesus' Jewish enemies ever challenged his descent from David; neither did the Gentile enemies attack Jesus' genealogy until after the records were destroyed with Jerusalem. Thankfully, Jesus' genealogy was preserved in the Bible; it is part of the foundation of Christian faith and a testimony to the sureness of the word and promises of God.

The Savior Is Born
Luke 2:1-20

Caesar Augustus, emperor of Rome, decrees that a census of his subjects be taken.[43] (See "Biographical Sketch: Caesar Augustus") Everyone is required to register for the census, and this must be done in the enrollee's hometown. From their home in Nazareth of Galilee, Joseph and Mary travel to Judea, to Bethlehem, where Joseph was born.[44] No lodging in Bethlehem is available so the young couple stay in a stable; there, Jesus is born. Mary swaddles her son and lays him in a manger.[45]

Nearby, shepherds are in the fields, guarding their flocks at night.[46] Suddenly, an angel appears to the shepherds, and God's glory radiates around them. The angel tells the trembling shepherds not to fear, and announces, "I bring you good news of great joy for all people: to you is born this day in David's city a Savior,[47] the Anointed Lord[48]. By this sign you will know him: a babe wrapped in swaddling clothes lying in a manger."

Many more angels appear and sing, "Glory to God in Heaven! Peace to people of goodwill on Earth."[49]

The heavenly entourage disappears, and the shepherds hurry to Bethlehem; they find the newborn Jesus just as the angel said. When the shepherds relate what the angel told them, all who hear it are astonished.[50] These sayings Mary remembers in her heart and cherishes.[51]

BIOGRAPHICAL SKETCH: CAESAR AUGUSTUS

Gaius Octavian was 18 years old when his grandmother's brother, Roman dictator Julius Caesar, was assassinated. This death ignited a power struggle between heir apparent Octavian and Mark Antony, Caesar's chief lieutenant. Thirteen years later Octavian defeated the combined forces of Antony and Egyptian Queen Cleopatra to emerge the undisputed ruler of the Roman Empire. After Antony and Cleopatra committed suicide, Octavian annexed Egypt, and Rome became the preeminent world power.

For fear of repeating his despotic uncle Julius' mistakes and sharing his fate, Octavian announced his intention to turn over control of the provinces to the Senate and offered to resign. This tactic of disguising his monarchy under a republican garment produced the desired effect. The appreciative Senate urged Octavian to retain his position and power. They further bestowed upon him the illustrious title "Augustus." Octavian accepted and thus became the first emperor of Rome, Caesar Augustus.

Augustus claimed to have transformed Rome from a city of bricks into one of marble. What did the emperor do to affect such a conversion? Augustus not only completed buildings left unfinished by Julius Caesar, he restored temples, constructed roads and bridges, established an effective postal system, reorganized the army, created a permanent navy and established an elite band of imperial bodyguards known as the Praetorian Guard. (Philippians 1:13) Under his patronage, such writers as

Virgil and Horace flourished and sculptors created beautiful works in what is now called the classical style. The government of Augustus was marked by a measure of honesty and a sound currency. The Pax Romana ("Roman Peace") that he introduced lasted more than 200 years.

Augustus renamed a calendar month for himself and borrowed a day from February so that August would have as many days as July, the month named after Julius Caesar. After a 44-year reign he died at the age of 76 in the month to which he gave his name and was deified thereafter.

Child of Promise
Luke 2:21-38

Joseph and Mary's son is circumcised when he is eight days old, as God's law requires.[52] On that day it is also customary to give a baby boy his name. (Luke 1:59) As the angel Gabriel had directed, Joseph and Mary call their son Jesus.

Later, Jesus' parents take him to the Temple in Jerusalem. It is time for Joseph and Mary to make a purification offering and to ceremonially present their son to God.[53] "You must devote to Jehovah every firstborn male," God's law commands.[54] At the Temple, Joseph and Mary offer a sacrifice according to their circumstances in obedience to the Law: a pair of birds.[55]

Motivated by God's spirit, a devout man named Simeon comes to the Temple. It has been divinely revealed to Simeon that before he dies, he will see the Messiah.[56] Simeon approaches Joseph and Mary and takes their son into his arms. Holding Jesus, Simeon offers thanks: "As you promised, Sovereign Lord, let your servant die in peace.[57] I have seen your means of salvation for all people. He is a light to reveal you to the nations,[58] and the glory of your people Israel!"

Joseph and Mary wonder at what they hear. Simeon blesses them and tells Mary, "Israel will stand or fall because of this child. He has been sent as a sign from God but will be rejected.[59] Pain—like a sword—will pierce your soul.[60] And the deepest thoughts of many hearts will be revealed."[61]

Also present on this day is Anna, an elderly widow and prophet. Worshiping day and night with fasts and prayers, Anna has spent practically her entire life at the Temple. She comes to Joseph and Mary and sees the baby Jesus. Anna gives thanks to God and speaks about Jesus to all who will listen.[62]

Magi[63] Visit the Messiah
Matthew 2:1-23; Luke 2:39

Stargazers from the East enter Jerusalem and begin asking about "the newborn king of the Jews"; they explain: "We observed his star at its rising and have come to pay him homage."[64]

This inquiry perturbs Jerusalem's populace and eventually comes to the attention of Herod. With nervous interest, the king asks Israel's chief priests and scholars where the Messiah is to be born.[65] Basing their reply on Scripture, the experts answer, "In Bethlehem of Judea."[66]

In a secret meeting, Herod tells the stargazers, "Go, search diligently for the child. When you have found him, bring me word so that I too may go and pay him homage."

After the men leave, the "star" that they had seen travels ahead of them until it stops above a house—the house where Joseph and Mary live with little Jesus.[67] The visitors enter, bow down to Jesus, and present to him gifts of gold, frankincense and myrrh.[68]

In a dream the stargazers are warned not to return to Herod, so they leave for their own country by another route. Joseph, too, receives divine warning by dream; an angel tells him, "Get up! Flee to Egypt with your child and his mother—stay there until I tell you.[69] Herod is going to search for the boy to kill him." Joseph, Mary and their son escape by night.

Meanwhile, Herod learns that the stargazers have tricked him. Enraged, he gives orders to put to death all the boys in Bethlehem and its surroundings who are two years old and younger.[70] (This age calculation corresponds to the time of the star's appearance, which Herod ascertained from the stargazers.[71]) Herod's soldiers carry out his cold-hearted command, and the bereaved mothers' mourning fulfills prophecy: "Thus says JEHOVAH: 'A voice is heard in Ramah, lamentation, and bitter weeping, Rachel weeping for her children; she refuses to be comforted for her children, because they are no more.'"[72]

After Herod dies, an angel appears to Joseph in a dream again; it is now safe for his family to return to Israel. In this way the prophecy of Hosea (11:1) is fulfilled: The Son of God is called out of Egypt.[73]

Herod's son Archelaus succeeds as the ruler of Judea. (See "Biographical Sketch: Herod Archelaus") Warned by God of the danger in another dream, Joseph moves his family to the city of Nazareth in the territory of Galilee,[74] outside Archelaus' jurisdiction. Here, Jesus grows up, which also fulfills prophecy: He will be called a Nazarene.[75]

BIOGRAPHICAL SKETCH: HEROD ARCHELAUS

Herod the Great willed to his son Archelaus the rulership of Judea, Samaria and Idumea. Due to opposition from certain Judeans and one of his brothers, Archelaus could secure from Caesar Augustus no better than the title of ethnarch—tributary prince—a title considerably inferior to that of king (although more honored than that of tetrarch—territorial prince).

Archelaus was unpopular with his Judean subjects. Twice he deposed the high priest. He divorced and remarried, which, for a Jew (albeit a nominal one), was unlawful. Archelaus was an ineffective and cruel ruler. His reign was marred by one violent uprising after another; thousands of subjects and soldiers died. Understandably and providentially, Joseph moved his family to Galilee when he heard that Archelaus had become ruler of Judea.—Matthew 2:22-23.

In response to complaints from Judeans and Samaritans, Caesar Augustus banished Archelaus to Gaul. Archelaus had been in power for about ten years. His territories of Judea, Samaria and Idumea were incorporated into the province of Judea and thereafter ruled by Roman governors.

JESUS' EARLY FAMILY LIFE

When Jesus was about two years of age, his parents Joseph and Mary moved to Nazareth, a small city in northern Galilee. Here Jesus' half-brothers—James, Joseph, Simon and Jude—and half-sisters were born.[76]

Among Jesus' other relatives were his second cousin John the Baptist. John's mother Elizabeth was Mary's first cousin.[77] Mary's sister and Jesus' aunt Salome[78] and her husband Zebedee had two sons, James and John—these first cousins of Jesus eventually became his apostles. Two other apostles, James the Less and his son Judas Thaddaeus, were related to Jesus on Joseph's side. Joseph had a brother named Clopas (also called Alphaeus); he and his wife Mary, one of Jesus' female followers, were the parents of James the Less and grandparents of Judas Thaddaeus.[79]

Joseph, a carpenter, raised Jesus as his own son and taught him his trade.[80] Thus, Jesus came to be called "the carpenter's son" and "the carpenter." (Matthew 13:55; Mark 6:3) The life of Joseph's family centered on the worship of the God of Israel.—Luke 2:41; 4:16.

Jesus in His Father's House
Luke 2:40-52

As Jesus ages into adolescence, he enjoys favor with God and with everyone who knows him. He is also wise beyond his years, made evident by something that happens when he is 12 years old.

Joseph's family, along with friends and relatives, journey to Jerusalem to celebrate the Passover.[81] (See "Passover.") Following this year's observance, Jesus stays behind in Jerusalem, unnoticed by his parents.[82] Joseph and Mary, assuming Jesus is with their group of fellow travelers, do not realize that their son is missing until they are a full day into the return to Nazareth. Failing to find Jesus among their friends and family, Joseph and Mary take their search back to Jerusalem. On the third day, they locate Jesus in the Temple. He is sitting amidst the teachers, listening to them and asking questions.[83] The teachers are astonished by Jesus' comprehension and comments.[84]

"Son, why have you treated us this way?" Mary asks. "Your father and I were frantic, looking for you everywhere!"

"Why were you looking for me?" Jesus wonders. "You must have known that I would be about my Father's business here in his house."[85]

Reunited, Jesus, Joseph and Mary go home to Nazareth. Jesus remains obedient to his parents.[86]

PASSOVER...

... is a celebration of Israel's liberation from Egyptian slavery in the sixteenth century before Christ. God commanded the Israelites to commemorate that event annually on the 14th day of their first month, called Abib (later known as Nisan; corresponding to March-April).—Exodus 12:42; Leviticus 23:5; 2 Chronicles 8:13.

The word "Passover" refers to the last of the Ten Plagues, which killed every firstborn in Egypt. God instructed the Israelites to splash the blood of a slaughtered lamb or goat on their doorways. Seeing this sign, God would pass over their homes and spare their firstborn.—Exodus 12:7, 13, 21-22, 27; 13:15.

How did Israelites prepare for and observe the Passover? On the tenth day of Abib (Nisan), a one-year-old lamb (or goat) was selected and, on the 14th day, slaughtered. The animal was roasted whole and eaten. The Israelites also ate unleavened bread and bitter greens (see "Passover Preparations"). As part of the observance, children would ask their parents questions focusing on the meaning of the event. For seven days after the Passover, the Israelites celebrated the Festival of Unleavened Bread, during which time they did not eat leavened bread.—Exodus 12:3-9, 17-20, 24-27; Deuteronomy 6:20-23; 2 Chronicles 30:21.

As time passed, adjustments were made. Israelites traveled to Jerusalem to observe the Passover. (Deuteronomy 16:5-7; Luke 2:41) Wine and singing came to be included in the celebration.—Matthew 26:19, 30; Luke 22:15-18.

PART TWO
"THE SON OF GOD"
(JOHN 1:34)

A Voice in the Wilderness
Matthew 3:1-12; Mark 1:1-8; Luke 3:1-18; John 1:6-8

Since Jesus at age 12 was questioning the teachers in the Temple, about 18 years have passed. (Luke 2:42; 3:23) Jesus' cousin John, known as "the Baptizer,"[87] is preaching in the Judean wilderness.[88] His message is a call to repentance because, he says, "the heavenly kingdom is near!"[89] John's ministry fulfills ancient prophecies: he is the foretold Messenger and a Voice "who cries in the wilderness: 'Prepare the way of Jehovah; make straight in the desert a highway for our God.'"[90]

John's message and the man himself attract attention. 'Could he be the Messiah?' people wonder. John is not the Messiah; he is God's witness and representative. He eats locusts and wild honey.[91] His clothing is made of camel's hair, and he wears a leather belt around his waist.[92] People from all of Judea—particularly Jerusalem and the Jordan district—come to John confessing their sins. They repent and get baptized by John in the Jordan River.[93]

Religious leaders—Pharisees and Sadducees—come to investigate John's baptizing. (See "Who Were the Pharisees and the Sadducees?") He calls them a "brood of vipers" and asks, "Has someone warned you to run from the retribution that's coming?"[94] He exhorts them to "produce fruitage of repentance,"[95] warning, "Even now the ax lies at the root of the trees. And every tree that fails to bear good fruit will be cut down and thrown on the fire.[96] I baptize in water as a sign of repentance. However, the one who comes after me is greater than I; to untie his sandals I am not worthy.[97] He will baptize[98] in God's spirit and in fire.[99] With shovel in hand, he will gather his wheat but the chaff he will burn in inextinguishable fire."[100]

WHO WERE THE PHARISEES AND THE SADDUCEES?

The Pharisees and the Sadducees were two prominent religious sects in the first century A.D. Their approaches to Judaism could not have been more different, but they shared a determination to destroy Jesus.

The Pharisees—"the separated ones"—were champions of Jewish exclusivity. *(The New Compact Bible Dictionary,* page 453) In the second century B.C. Antiochus Epiphanes, a Seleucid prince of Syria who controlled Palestine, forbade all observances ordained in the Law of Moses and tried to Hellenize the Jews. Some bowed to his edict and to Greek influence. The Pharisees revolted, and for their defiance were persecuted by High Priest Alexander Jannaeus. But his wife and successor Alexandra brought the Pharisees into favor with official recognition.

As authorities on Law and tradition, the Pharisees were influential and held in high esteem.[101] (Matthew 23:2, 6; Acts 5:34) Some of their number, including Nicodemus and Gamaliel, sat on Israel's high court, the Sanhedrin. (John 3:1; Acts 5:34) Because they elevated oral traditions to the level of God's written Word, the Pharisees often ran afoul of Jesus. (Mark 7:8) These religious leaders conspired with politicians to murder the Messiah. (Matthew 22:15-16; Mark 3:6) However, some Pharisees, most notably Saul of Tarsus, became Christians.—Acts 6:7; 15:5; 23:6; 26:5; Philippians 3:5.

Unlike the Pharisees, who were associated with the laymen of Israel, the Sadducees were made up of priests and wealthy aristocrats.[102] (Acts 5:17) Among the Sadducees were a political faction known as the Boethusians, referred to in the gospels as the Herodians. (Mark 3:6; compare Matthew 16:6; Mark 8:15) The name Sadducees is likely connected with Zadok, who was high priest in the days of David and Solomon. (1 Kings 1:32-45; 2 Chronicles 31:10) This class continued to bear the name Sadducee (or Sadducean) even after the high priest line was transferred to the Hasmonean house in the days of the Maccabees.

While the Pharisees claimed authority by virtue of learning and piety, the Sadducees based their prerogative on genealogy and position. They wielded great authority over Temple activities. As regards Holy Scripture, the Sadducees accepted only the Pentateuch, rejected prophecies as speculations, and considered the historical, poetical and proverbial books to be uninspired and nonessential. They rejected scriptural teachings about the resurrection and angels, as well as the Pharisees' oral traditions.[103] (Mark 12:18; Luke 20:27; Acts 23:8) Whereas the Pharisees inclined toward fatalism and predestination, the Sadducees held that humans were free moral agents. But like the Pharisees, the Sadducees opposed Jesus. (Matthew 16:1) Including chief priests Annas and Caiaphas, Sadducees took a leading part in seeking Jesus' death, as well as in trying to stop the spread of Christianity.—Matthew 26:62-66; John 7:32; 11:49-53; 18:3; Acts 4:1-3; 5:17-18, 21.

“You Are My Beloved Son”
Matthew 3:13-17; Mark 1:9-11; Luke 3:21-23

Jesus, now 30 years old, approaches John and asks to be baptized in the Jordan River. John resists. “You come to me for baptism?” he asks. “I need to be baptized by you!”

Jesus insists, “Please, John. It’s good for us to do what God says is right.”[104] John assents.

When Jesus comes up from the water, God’s spirit descends and lights upon him like a dove.[105] As Jesus prays,[106] the heavens open to him,[107] and God’s voice is heard to proclaim, “You are my beloved Son;[108] with you I am well pleased.”[109]

‘If You Are God’s Son …’
Matthew 4:1-11; Mark 1:12-13; Luke 4:1-13

Right after Jesus is baptized, God’s spirit[110] leads him into the wilderness;[111] here, the king of Heaven’s kingdom encounters the prince of this world. Jesus fasts for 40 days and is tempted by Satan the Devil.[112] “If you are the Son of God,” Satan suggests, “command this stone to become a loaf of bread.”

Jesus rejects temptation with a quote from Scripture: “Man is not to live by bread alone; man is to live by everything that comes out of Jehovah’s mouth.”[113]

The Devil next challenges Jesus to throw himself off the pinnacle of the Temple in Jerusalem,[114] baiting him with a quotation from the Psalms: “For He shall give His angels charge over You ....They shall bear You up in their palms, that You do not dash your foot on a stone.”[115]

Jesus’ counter-quotes: “You shall not test Jehovah your God.”[116]

Then the Devil leads Jesus to a mountaintop and shows him the kingdoms of humankind.[117] "They will all be yours,"[118] Satan says, "if you kneel before me just this once.[119]"

Again, Jesus answers with a scripture: "You shall fear JEHOVAH your God; and you shall serve him only."[120] He also orders Satan to leave.

For the moment, Satan gives up. After the Devil departs, ministering angels come to Jesus' aid.

SATAN THE DEVIL—EVIL SPIRIT-PERSON OR EVIL PERSONIFIED?

Jesus Christ was sinless and, therefore, had no evil inclinations to wrestle with. (Hebrews 4:15; 1 Peter 2:22) Jesus was tempted by an evil spirit-person whom he acknowledged to be this world's ruler. (John 12:31; 14:30; 16:11) The Devil's offer to Jesus of world rulership in return for worship would have been meaningless if Satan were not real. (Matthew 4:8-10; Luke 4:5-8; compare the interaction between God and Satan in Job chapters 1 and 2.)

Furthermore, Jesus described the Devil as a liar and a murderer who had once been "in the truth." (John 8:44) Satan "was an angel in God's original creation who, through pride and a twisted desire to supplant God, led a revolt of angels in heaven and successfully tempted Adam and Eve in the Garden of Eden." (Genesis 3:1-19; Isaiah 14:12-15; Jude 6) Consistently, the Bible portrays Satan the Devil as an evil spirit-person, not a personification of evil. "As leader of the kingdom of evil, he continues to tempt us to sin with his many schemes. He used his most potent devices against Jesus, who showed us the way of firm commitment to the will of the Father."—The NIV Topical Study Bible, page 545.

Introducing “the Lamb of God”
John 1:15, 19-51

The ministry of John the Baptist continues to draw much attention. Near the river Jordan at Bethany[121], clergymen from Jerusalem[122] approach John and ask, “Who are you?”

“I am not the Messiah,”[123] John confesses.

“So, then, are you Elijah?”[124] they ask. “Are you the Prophet?”[125]

“No,” John replies.

They become insistent: “Tell us who you are. We must give an answer to those who sent us.”

John identifies himself as a Voice that calls, "Prepare the way of JEHOVAH in the wilderness! Make a level highway in the desert for our God."[126]

“If you’re not the Messiah, nor Elijah, nor the Prophet,” they wonder, “why are you baptizing?”[127]

John answers, “Yes, I baptize; but one among us whom you do not recognize will succeed and surpass me.”[128] The next day, John will identify this surpassing successor.

After 40 days in the wilderness, Jesus returns to John the Baptist. John points out Jesus as he approaches and declares to those present, “There is the Lamb of God, who takes away the sin of the world![129] He’s the one I was talking about yesterday. I am baptizing so that he can be revealed to Israel.” John relates what he saw and heard at Jesus’ baptism: “He who sent me to baptize with water told me, ‘The one who will baptize with spirit is the one on whom you will see my spirit come down and remain.’[130] Now I have seen and borne witness that he is the Son of God.”

The following day, John is with two of his disciples, one of whom is named Andrew,[131] when he sees Jesus again. “Look! This is the Lamb of God!”

John announces. Andrew and the other disciple begin to follow Jesus, staying with him for the rest of the day.

At one point Andrew brings his brother Simon Peter to Jesus,[132] telling Peter, "We've found the Messiah!"[133]

Jesus looks at Peter and says, "Son of John, your name is Simon. But you will be called Cephas."[134]

A day later, Jesus is about to depart for Galilee.[135] Before leaving, he invites a man named Philip to be his follower.[136] Philip then finds his friend Nathanael sitting under a fig tree,[137] and tells him about "Jesus of Nazareth": "He's the one that Moses wrote about in the Law, the one that the Prophets foretold."[138]

Doubtful, Nathanael responds, "What good can come from Nazareth?"[139] Philip urges Nathanael to meet Jesus and see for himself.

Jesus notices Nathanael coming, and says, "See a true son of Israel, a man of integrity!"[140]

"How do you know me?" Nathanael asks.

"Before Philip approached you, I saw you sitting under that fig tree."

Nathanael is amazed: "Teacher, you are the Son of God, the King of Israel!"[141]

"You believe in me because I said that I saw you under the fig tree?" Jesus asks. "You will see things more wonderful than that![142] In fact, you'll see Heaven open and God's angels in the Son of Man's service."[143]

Water into Wine
John 2:1-13

With his newly acquired disciples, Jesus leaves the Jordan Valley and heads for Galilee to attend a wedding reception[144] in Cana.[145] There also is Jesus' mother Mary, who brings a problem to her son. "They've run out of wine,"[146] she reports.

"Is that your concern, or mine?" Jesus asks. "It's not yet time for me to act."[147]

Mary leaves the matter in her son's hands, saying to the servers, "Do as he tells you."

As required by Jewish purification rules, stone water jars are present.[148] Each jar can hold about twenty gallons. Jesus instructs the servers to fill the six jars with water, then draw some out and take it to the director of the wedding feast.[149] What the servers draw out is miraculously produced—to quote the director—"fine wine."[150] This is Jesus' first miracle, and it reinforces the faith of his followers.[151]

After the wedding, Jesus, his mother, his half-brothers and the disciples travel to Capernaum.[152] They do not stay long, however, because Passover is approaching.[153]

Jesus' Passion for His Father's House
John 2:14-22

Upon arriving at the Temple in Jerusalem, Jesus finds dealers in cattle and sheep, pigeon-sellers and money changers sitting at their tables.[154] This use of the Temple as "a market" angers Jesus.[155] He makes a whip of ropes and drives out the sheep and cattle. He also pours out the moneychangers' coins and overturns their tables.[156] Those selling doves he orders out.[157] The sight of Jesus' righteous indignation at work makes his disciples think of Psalm 69:9: "I am on fire with passion[158] for your house"!—*The Bible in Basic English.*

Authorities who see Jesus in action challenge him. "Show us a sign," they demand. "Prove that you have the right to do what you're doing."[159]

"Destroy this temple," Jesus replies, "and I will raise it in three days."

Assuming that Jesus means the literal Temple, the Judean leaders ask, "Will you rebuild in three days this Temple that has taken 46 years to put up?" However, Jesus is referring to his body as a temple.[160] His disciples remember these words when he is resurrected three years later.—See “The Temple—Center of Israel’s Worship.”

“How Much God Loved the World”!
John 2:23–3:21

While in Jerusalem for the Passover celebration, Jesus performs miracles. Many people put faith in him. A Pharisee named Nicodemus visits Jesus—at night.[161] “Teacher, we know that God has sent you,”[162] Nicodemus confesses. “No one could perform the signs you do unless God were with him.”

Jesus teaches Nicodemus “the solemn truth”: no one can see the kingdom of God without being “born again[163].”

“How?” Nicodemus asks. “You can’t mean to re-enter the womb and be born a second time!”

“No one can enter God’s kingdom without being born from water and spirit,”[164] Jesus clarifies. “When the wind blows you can hear it, but you have no idea where it comes from or where it’s going. It is the same with everyone born again by the wind of God, his spirit.[165] I’m telling you the solemn truth.”[166]

Jesus, who has “descended from heaven,” is talking about “heavenly matters.” Although Nicodemus is a respected teacher, this idea of being born again surprises him.[167] Jesus continues, “As Moses lifted up the serpent in the wilderness, the Son of Man must be lifted up,[168] so that everyone demonstrating faith in him[169] may have eternal life.[170] This is how much God loved the world:[171] he gave his only and unique Son[172] so that everyone demonstrating faith in him might not perish but live forever. It was to save the world, not to judge it, that God sent his Son.[173] Whoever demonstrates faith in him is not judged. Whoever does not demonstrate faith in the Son of God is already judged.”—Numbers 21:9.

Jesus closes his conversation with Nicodemus, who has come to him under cover of darkness, by revealing to him “the basis for judgment: Light has come into the world,[174] but those whose works are wicked love the darkness instead of the light. Wrongdoers hate the light and avoid it, lest their wrongs be exposed. But those who live the truth are drawn to the light, to make it clear that their works have been done through God."[175]

Jesus Increases, John Decreases
Matthew 4:12; Mark 1:14; Luke 3:19-20; John 3:22–4:3

After Passover, Jesus and his disciples leave Jerusalem for the Judean countryside. There, under Jesus' direction, the disciples baptize new followers. The parallel ministry of John the Baptist and his disciples is being carried out in Aenon near Salim, where water is plentiful.[176] John's disciples complain to him about Jesus: "Teacher, the man you testified about—the one who was with you across the Jordan[177]—is baptizing people, too. All are going to him."[178]

John, however, rejoices in Jesus' success and reminds his disciples, "You heard me say that I was not the Messiah, but had been sent ahead of him." John illustrates his privilege as Jesus' forerunner: "The bridegroom has the bride, and the bridegroom's friend is happy for him. Such is my happiness—my complete happiness! He must continue increasing, while I continue decreasing."[179]

Sometime after this discussion with his disciples, John is arrested by King Herod.[180] (see "Biographical Sketch: Herod Antipas") Hearing about this and learning that the Pharisees know of his activity in Judea, Jesus leaves with the disciples for Galilee.[181]

"The Savior of the World" and the Woman at the Well
John 4:4-42

As Jesus and his disciples travel through Samaria,[182] they come to the city of Sychar,[183] near a field that the patriarch Jacob gave to his son Joseph. Jesus rests[184] by Jacob's Well[185] while the disciples go into the city to buy food.[186] In their absence, a Samaritan woman carrying a jug comes to the well to draw water. Jesus requests, "Let me have a drink."

Because Israelites usually don't associate with Samaritans (let alone drink from their vessels[187]) the woman says, "Are you, an Israelite,[188] asking me, a Samaritan woman, for a drink?"

Jesus replies that, if she knew who he was, she would ask him for water—"living water."

The woman observes that the well is deep, and Jesus doesn't have a bucket. "Where would you get this 'living water' from?" she asks. "Besides, you surely don't think you're better than Father Jacob, who gave us this well. Can you offer better water than he and his sons and his livestock drank?"

"Whoever drinks this water will get thirsty again," Jesus answers. "Whoever drinks my water will never get thirsty at all; that water will become a fountain springing up within and giving eternal life."[189]

The woman responds, "Give me some of that water, sir, and I won't get thirsty or have to come here to draw." When Jesus tells the woman to bring her husband to him,[190] she answers, "I don't have a husband."

"That's right, you don't have a husband," Jesus verifies.[191] "In fact, you've had five husbands, and the man you live with now is not your husband."[192]

The woman perceives that Jesus is some kind of prophet.[193] "You Israelites insist that Jerusalem is the place to worship," she says, "but our forefathers worshiped here on Mount Gerizim."[194]

"Believe me," Jesus replies, "the time is coming when you will worship the Father neither on this mountain nor in Jerusalem. You Samaritans worship a God you do not know; we worship a God we know, as salvation begins with Israel.[195] Nevertheless, the time is coming—in fact, it is already here—when true worshipers will worship the Father with spirit and in truth—those are the worshipers that the Father wants. God—a Spirit[196]—must be worshiped with spirit and in truth."[197]

"I know this much: Messiah is coming,"[198] the woman asserts, "and he'll make everything plain to us."

Jesus pointedly tells her, "I am the Messiah."[199]

Just then the disciples return from Sychar with food. They are shocked to find Jesus talking with a Samaritan woman, but they keep their feelings to themselves. She leaves her water jug and heads for the city.

The disciples urge Jesus to eat but he replies, "I have nourishment that you aren't aware of." The disciples wonder if someone else has brought Jesus some food. "My nourishment comes from doing the will of the One who sent me and finishing his work," Jesus explains.[200] "Look at the fields—ripe for harvesting![201] Even now the one who harvests is rewarded, gathering fruit for eternal life."[202]

Meanwhile in Sychar, the woman tells people about Jesus. "He told me everything about myself," she relates. "Maybe he is the Messiah!" Because of her testimony, many Samaritans put faith in Jesus.[203] They invite Jesus to stay in Sychar; he remains for two days. As the people listen to Jesus, many more accept him as the Savior of the World.[204]

SAMARIA AND SAMARITANS

Though its exact boundaries are not known today, Samaria lay between Galilee in the north and Judea in the south; it extended west from the Jordan River to the coastal plains of the Mediterranean Sea. For the most part, the district embraced the territories once belonging to the tribe of Ephraim and the half tribe of Manasseh (west of the Jordan).

Jesus occasionally passed through Samaria on his way to and from Jerusalem; however, he told his disciples not to preach in Samaritan cities because their primary responsibility was to fellow Israelites. (Matthew 10:5-6; Luke 9:51-52; 17:11; John 4:4-5) Just before his ascension to Heaven, Jesus directed his followers to carry the gospel to Samaria. (Acts 1:8) When persecution broke out in Jerusalem, some Christians—Philip the Evangelizer, in particular—preached throughout Samaria. Peter and John were later sent there so that the Samaritans could receive God's spirit.—Acts 8:1-17, 25; 9:31; 15:3.

Originally, "Samaritans" were Hebrews who lived in Israel's northern kingdom before it was conquered by the Assyrians. (2 Kings 17:29) The Samaritans' separation from their brothers began earlier when King Jeroboam established idol worship in the northern kingdom. (1 Kings 12:28) After the Assyrian conquest, "Samaritan" came to refer to the descendants of native Israelites and foreign colonists. This mixed population further corrupted worship in Samaria.—2 Kings 17:24, 41.[205]

While claiming devotion to the God of Israel, Samaritans opposed rebuilding Jerusalem's Temple and city walls. On Mount Gerizim they built their own temple, probably in the fourth century B.C. In retaliation for Samaritan aid to Syria in its wars against Israel, high priest John Hyrcanus burned down Mount Gerizim's temple in 128 B.C. However, the Samaritans continued to worship in that mountain,[206] and populated the Roman district of Samaria in the first century A.D. By then the name Samaritan had an ethnic and religious connotation, and Samaritans were treated with scorn by Israelites.—John 8:48.

"God's Kingdom Is Near!"
Mark 1:15; Luke 4:14-15; John 4:43-54

Jesus arrives in Galilee. He teaches in the synagogues,[207] proclaiming, "The time has come: God's kingdom is near![208] Change your ways and believe this good news."[209] Jesus expects no honor in his home country, yet many Galileans receive him well. Some of them were in Jerusalem at the last Passover and saw Jesus perform remarkable signs.[210]—John 2:23-25.

A certain member of the royal court learns that Jesus is in Galilee.[211] This man's son is deathly ill. He travels many miles from his home in Capernaum and finds Jesus in Cana[212] (where Jesus changed water into wine at a wedding feast). "Please, sir," the father urges Jesus, "come at once before my boy dies!"

Jesus responds, "Go home—your child will live."

The man believes what he hears and starts his return trip to Capernaum. On the way he is met by his servants, who have hurried to tell him wonderful news: his son is alive and well!

'When did he begin to recover?' the father wants to know.

"His fever broke yesterday," they answer, "at the seventh hour."[213] The father realizes that this is exactly when Jesus said, "Your child will live." This man and his whole family become believers.

Jesus in His Hometown Synagogue
Luke 4:16-30

In Nazareth, Jesus visits the local synagogue on the Sabbath day.[214] He stands up to read, and the scroll of Isaiah's prophecy is handed to him. Unrolling the scroll, he finds the place where it is written:[215]

The Spirit of the Lord JEHOVAH is on me; because JEHOVAH has anointed me to preach good news to the humble.[216] He has sent me to bind up the brokenhearted, to proclaim liberty to the captives, and release to those who are bound,[217] *to proclaim the year of JEHOVAH's favor...*[218]

When Jesus finishes reading aloud, he rolls up the scroll, hands it to an attendant and sits down. All eyes are riveted upon him as he announces, "These words, in your hearing, have come true today."[219]

People marvel at the winsome words of Joseph's son. Jesus responds, "No doubt you will apply to me the proverb, 'Physician, heal yourself,' and expect me to bestow on my hometown the charity I showed to Capernaum.[220] But for a fact, no prophet is accepted in his homeland.[221] In the days of the prophet Elijah, for instance, there was drought and famine for three and-a-half years. Many widows in Israel suffered; yet Elijah was sent to a widow in Zarephath in the land of Sidon.[222] And in Elisha's time, there were many lepers in Israel; yet Elisha healed, not one of them, but Naaman the Syrian."

Enraged, Jesus' audience rushes him outside the city to the brow of a mountain to throw him off![223] Jesus extricates himself from the mob and escapes.[224]

A TYPICAL SYNAGOGUE SERVICE

Scholars note that Luke 4:16-21 is the earliest known description of a synagogue service. According to tradition, the service usually began with private prayers as the congregants entered the building, after which the Shema, or confession of faith, was recited. The Shema received its name from the first word of the first scripture used, "Hear [Shema], O Israel: Jehovah our God is one Jehovah." (Deuteronomy 6:4, Young's *Literal Translation)* Public prayers followed, after which a portion of the Torah, or Pentateuch, was read aloud according to a schedule. (Acts 13:15) In many synagogues, the entire Law was scheduled to be read in one year; in others, the program took three years. Such reading was done every Sabbath. (Acts 15:21) The next portion of the service was a reading from the Prophets along with an exposition tying the two readings together. The reader customarily stood, and he may have had some freedom to choose his prophetic passage.

"Fishers of Men"
Matthew 4:13-22; Mark 1:16-20; Luke 5:1-11

From Nazareth Jesus goes to the shoreside city of Capernaum.[225] The presence of Jesus—the Light of the world—in Galilee fulfills a prophecy: "The people who walk in darkness shall see a great Light—a Light that will shine on all those who live in the land of the shadow of death."[226]—John 8:12; 9:5.

Near Capernaum Jesus finds some of the disciples who traveled with him in Judea. Peter, his brother Andrew, and their business partners James and John, the sons of Zebedee, are tending to their fishing nets. Jesus speaks to many people along the seashore.[227] The crowd presses in on him, trying to catch his every word. Jesus climbs into Peter's boat and asks him to pull away from land. When Jesus, Peter and Andrew[228] get out a little distance, Jesus resumes teaching the people.[229]

His discourse concluded, Jesus bids Peter to pull out to deeper water for a little fishing. Peter protests, "We fished all night and caught nothing, but we'll do as you say." They lower the nets and catch such a great number of fish that the nets begin to rip! Urgently, the men signal to James and John in a nearby boat to come and help. Soon both boats are filled with so many fish that the heavily laden vessels start to sink. Overwhelmed and astonished, Peter falls at Jesus' feet and says, "Master, go away from me—I'm a sinful man."[230]

Jesus responds, "Don't be afraid. From now on you will fish for souls."[231] Peter, Andrew, James and John abandon their fishing business to become "fishers of men[232]."

FISH AND FISHING IN THE SEA OF GALILEE

In Galilee fishing was a common and lucrative occupation. Brothers Peter and Andrew were in business with Zebedee and his sons James and John. (Matthew 4:18; Luke 5:10) They had employees and more than one boat; their business was prosperous.—Mark 1:20 Luke 5:7.

Of the 18 species of fish in the Sea of Galilee, about ten have been sought by fishermen;[233] among these is the abundant tilapia, a regular part of the Galilean diet. (Luke 24:41-43) The two fish with which Jesus miraculously fed thousands of people could have been dried-and-salted tilapia. (Matthew 14:17, 19; Mark 6:38, 41; Mark 9:13, 16) The tilapia often swims with its young in its mouth. However, when not carrying its young, it may carry a pebble in its mouth, or it might even gather up a shiny coin lying on the bottom of the sea.—Matthew 17:27.[234]

Boats and nets were standard fishing equipment. A boat may have been rigged with a mast and sail(s) and may have had a crew of five—four oarsmen and one helmsman—who stood on a small deck at the stern.

Fishermen on the Sea of Galilee used two types of casting nets—one made of finely woven mesh to catch small fish, and another made of larger mesh to catch bigger ones. Unlike a dragnet, which usually required the use of at least one boat and took a team to maneuver, a casting net could be handled by one person in a boat or standing close to shore. The net was weighted around its perimeter so that it would sink and trap the fish as it drifted to the sea floor. A fisherman might dive in and retrieve fish from the submerged net, or he might carefully draw the net to the shore. It took skill and strength to use the net effectively. Fishing nets were expensive and high maintenance. Much time was spent mending, washing and drying nets at the end of every fishing expedition.—Luke 5:2.

'God's Holy One' Versus the Demons
Matthew 8:14-17; Mark 1:21-34; Luke 4:31-41

The Sabbath after Jesus calls his first full-time followers—Peter, Andrew, James and John—they all go to a synagogue in Capernaum; there he teaches, astounding his listeners. Unlike the religious scholars, Jesus teaches with authority.[235]

A man possessed by a demon is present.[236] Right there in the synagogue, the man shouts, "Jesus of Nazareth, I know you are the Holy One of God![237] What do you want? Are you here to destroy us?"[238]

"Silence!"[239] Jesus rebukes, commanding the wicked spirit to depart. The demon flings the man to the ground in a convulsion, shrieking at the top of its voice. But the demon comes out of the man without harming him.[240] People in the synagogue are astonished. "Even the evil[241] spirits obey his orders!" they gasp. News of the exorcism spreads throughout Galilee.

Leaving the synagogue, Jesus and the disciples go to Peter's family home. His mother-in-law is confined to bed with a burning fever.[242] Standing over her, Jesus rebukes the sickness (as he rebukes demons[243]). Then he takes her by the hand and raises her up. Completely recovered, and with renewed strength, she immediately assumes her duties as host to her visitors.

Later, after sunset, people from all over bring their sick ones to Peter's door.[244] Jesus lays his hands on all of them, 'taking away their infirmities and carrying away their diseases,' as was foretold of him.[245] In addition to curing various illnesses, Jesus expels many demons.[246] As these evil spirits depart, they shout, "You are the Son of God!" But Jesus cuts them off, not allowing them to testify.[247]

On A Tour of Galilee

Matthew 4:23-25; 8:2-4; Mark 1:35-45; Luke 4:42-44; 5:12-16

Early the following morning, Jesus rises and goes out alone. He finds an isolated spot where he can pray. But his privacy is short-lived. Peter and others find Jesus. "Everyone is looking for you," Peter informs him.

The people of Capernaum want Jesus to stay but he is determined to preach elsewhere. "I must declare the gospel of God's kingdom to other cities as well," he explains. "That's why I'm here." Jesus leaves Capernaum, taking his four disciples with him.

Throughout Galilee Jesus teaches in the synagogues and preaches the Kingdom gospel. Crowds of people from Galilee—as well as from Judea, the Decapolis[248] and Perea[249]—follow Jesus. News about him spreads as far as Syria;[250] people from there bring to Jesus those who are demon-possessed, paralyzed, epileptic—and he heals them.

Word of Jesus' deeds reaches one city where there is a man who has leprosy.[251] When Jesus arrives, the man approaches him; on bended knee he pleads, "If you just want to, Lord, you can heal me[252]."

"I want to," Jesus assures him. With compassion,[253] he touches the man and says, "Be healed."[254] The leprosy vanishes! "Don't tell anyone,"[255] Jesus orders the man. "Your actions will speak for you when you appear before a priest and offer the appropriate gift for your healing."[256] But the man cannot keep the miracle to himself—he spreads the story far and wide. Soon Jesus cannot go anywhere in public without being mobbed. Often, he retreats to lonely places for prayer.[257]

"Your Sins Are Forgiven"

Matthew 9:1-8; Mark 2:1-12; Luke 5:17-26

News of Jesus' return to Capernaum travels fast and far. People from everywhere in Galilee and Judea gather at the house where Jesus is staying.[258] Among his visitors are scholars and Pharisees.[259]

Four men carry a paralyzed man on a stretcher to the house. Many people jam the doorway, preventing the men from reaching Jesus. Undeterred, they climb onto the roof, break through it, and lower the paralytic on his stretcher into the house.[260] Impressed by this act of faith, Jesus says to the paralyzed man, "Your sins are forgiven."

The Pharisees and scholars are offended. "What is this blasphemer saying?" they mumble. "Only God can forgive sins."[261]

Jesus discerns his critics' hostility[262] and asks them, "To say, 'Your sins are forgiven,' or to say, 'Get up and walk'—which is easier?"[263] Demonstrating his authority to forgive sins, Jesus turns to the paralytic and commands, "Rise, pick up your stretcher, and go home."

The man stands up before everyone, picks up what he used to lie on, and goes home praising God. The awestruck onlookers likewise give glory to God, saying, "We've seen marvelous things today!"

A Call to Discipleship
Matthew 9:9-17; Mark 2:13-22; Luke 5:27-39

One day while teaching at the Sea of Galilee, Jesus sees a tax collector named Matthew Levi[264] sitting in his custom house.[265] Jesus invites Matthew to follow him, and the tax collector accepts his call to discipleship.[266] Afterward, he hosts a reception at his house for Jesus. Some of Matthew's fellow tax collectors and other persons of ill-repute are in attendance.[267] Pharisees and scholars who are present ask Jesus' disciples, "Why do you and your teacher eat with sinners?"[268]

Overhearing the question, Jesus answers, "Healthy people don't need a physician—sick people do. Those who think they're righteous refuse my help—those who know they're sinners accept it."[269]

Someone objects, "Disciples of John the Baptist and of the Pharisees frequently fast but yours eat and drink.[270] Why?"

Jesus asks, "Do the bridegroom's friends mourn while the bridegroom is with them? No. But when the bridegroom is taken away from them, they will fast."[271]

With illustrations Jesus explains why his followers are not observing this tradition: "No one tears cloth from a new garment and uses it to patch an old garment. Not only would the new cloth not match the old garment, but the new garment would be ruined! Furthermore, no one pours fresh wine into an old skin-bottle—the bottle will bust under pressure and the wine will spill.[272] Fresh wine belongs in an unused skin-bottle."

FEAST OR FAST?

The Pharisees and John's disciples observed fasts not prescribed by the Mosaic Law, perhaps hoping that their devotion would hasten the coming of the Kingdom. John the Baptist led an ascetic life, one imitated by his followers. (Matthew 11:18; Luke 1:15) Pharisees customarily fasted on the second and fifth days of the week. (Luke 18:12) According to some sources, the days they chose for fasting were the regular market days, when many people would be in town to observe their piety.

In the past, rightly motivated Israelites humbled themselves before God and showed repentance for sin by fasting. (1 Samuel 7:6; 2 Chronicles 20:3) Certain observances and occasions required fasting. (Leviticus 16:29; Zechariah 8:19) Nevertheless, Jesus did not come to patch up and prolong an old, worn-out system of worship that was ready to be discarded. The old covenant was no longer needed after fulfilling its purpose to lead Israel to the Messiah and his new covenant. (Galatians 3:13, 24-25; Colossians 2:14; Hebrews 9:15) Christianity will not conform to traditions of Judaism such as ritual fasting. (Matthew 6:16) It would be like putting a new patch on an old garment or new wine into a stiff, old wineskin.

Sabbath Day Miracle Creates Controversy
John 5:1-47

Jesus travels to Jerusalem in Judea for a religious festival.[273] Near the city wall's Sheep Gate[274] there is a large colonnaded pool called Bethzatha.[275] The many ill and infirm people who come to this pool believe that an angel will descend and disturb the water—the first one to step into the water will be healed.[276] At Bethzatha one Sabbath day,[277] Jesus sees a disabled man lying on a mat.[278] Sensing that the man has been there for some time, Jesus asks him, "Do you want to get well?"

"I need help getting into the pool," the man answers, "But whenever the water is stirred up, someone always pushes ahead of me."

Jesus commands, "Get on your feet, roll up your mat and walk!" Immediately made well, the man picks up his cot and starts walking.[279]

People[280] who see the man carrying his mat tell him, "It's against our Law for you to do that on the Sabbath."[281]

"But the one who healed me told me to roll up the mat and walk," answers the man. His accusers want to meet this supposed lawbreaker, but Jesus has disappeared into the crowd.[282]

Later, Jesus encounters the man in the Temple and tells him, "Now that you're in good health, sin no more, lest something worse happen to you."[283]

The man identifies Jesus for his accusers. As far as they are concerned, Jesus has disregarded the Sabbath by working a miracle. Jesus responds, "My Father continues to work, and I continue to work."[284] These people are ready to kill Jesus for calling God his Father, which they consider blasphemy.[285] To the charge of claiming to be God's equal, Jesus answers, "The Son can do nothing on his own; he can do only what he sees the Father doing. What the Father does, the Son does. The Father includes the Son in everything he does because he loves him. In fact, the Father will show the Son how to do even greater works than healing this man—works to fill you with wonder!"

Jesus provides an example of such wonderful works. "As the Father raises the dead, the Son enlivens anyone he wants to. The Father judges no one; he has entrusted judgment to the Son. Those who hear what I say and believe in the One who sent me have eternal life. Without being condemned they pass over from death to life.[286] I'm telling you the solemn truth. The time will come—actually, it is here—when the dead will hear a call from the Son, and those who listen will live. The Son possesses the gift of life, given to him by the Father, who also has life in himself."[287]

Yes, "dead" ones are listening to the Son and coming to life. "Furthermore," Jesus continues, "the dead and buried[288] will hear the Son's voice and come out. Resurrection will mean acquittal for the righteous but conviction for the unrighteous."[289]

Jesus reiterates that he can do nothing on his own.[290] "I judge as I hear from the Father," he says, "and my judgment is righteous because I strive to do his will, not my own. If I alone bear witness about myself, my testimony means nothing.[291] The Father who sent me has borne witness about me.[292] And these works that I am doing"—including the healing that he has just performed— "also testify that the Father sent me." Besides that, the Scriptures—the holy writings that his accusers claim to know so well—testify about Jesus. "If you believed what Moses wrote, you would believe in me. What Moses wrote, he wrote about me,"[293] Jesus concludes.

Jesus has spoken to his accusers so that they might "believe and be saved." But they "don't want to come to [him] for eternal life."

"The Son of Man Is Sovereign over the Sabbath"
Matthew 12:1-21; Mark 2:23-3:12; Luke 6:1-11

As Jesus travels with his disciples, they go through a grainfield.[294] Being hungry, the disciples pluck some grain, rub it in their hands and eat it.[295] But it is the Sabbath, and their actions do not go unobserved. Pharisees bring an accusation to Jesus: the disciples are harvesting and threshing on the day of rest.[296] Jesus refutes the accusation with examples from the Scriptures of so-called violations of the Sabbath law.

"Apparently, you haven't read what David did," Jesus begins, "when he and his men were hungry, how they entered God's tabernacle and ate the Showbread[297]—which only the priests are allowed by Law to eat. Furthermore, the Temple priests supposedly break the Sabbath law with impunity.[298] But we are speaking of more than just the Temple."[299]—1 Samuel 21:1-6.

Again, Jesus draws on the written Word to make his point: "If you had understood Scripture, which tells us that God prefers soft hearts to hard rules, you would not have been so quick to condemn the innocent. Man did not come into existence for the sake of the Sabbath—the Sabbath came into existence for the sake of Man.[300] And the Son of Man is sovereign over the Sabbath."[301]

On another Sabbath day, Jesus attends a synagogue where he meets a man whose right hand is paralyzed.[302] Pharisees and scholars are watching closely. They ask Jesus, "Does our Law allow healing on the Sabbath?"[303]

Knowing his accusers are trying to find a pretext for condemning him, Jesus sets the stage for a dramatic confrontation: first, he tells the man with the paralyzed hand to stand where the entire congregation can see him;[304] then, turning to the scholars and Pharisees, Jesus asks, "Are we allowed on the Sabbath to choose between doing good and doing evil, to choose between saving a life or allowing it to perish? If you have one sheep and that sheep falls into a pit on the Sabbath, who among you will not lift it out?[305] Well, a human being is much more valuable than a sheep!"

The religious leaders answer with silence.[306] Indignant, Jesus stares down his hard-hearted critics. Then he tells the man, "Hold out your hand," and as he does, his deformed hand is made whole.

The Pharisees fly into a senseless fury;[307] later, they consult with King Herod's supporters.[308] The two groups begin plotting to murder Jesus. Learning of his enemies' evil intentions, Jesus retreats with the disciples to the Sea of Galilee.[309] Great crowds flock to him from Galilee and Judea—from the northern coastal cities of Tyre and Sidon,[310] Perea in the east, and Jerusalem and Idumea[311] in the south. There are so many people that the disciples keep a small boat at the ready for Jesus so he can pull away from shore and keep the people from crowding him.[312] Those with serious diseases eagerly reach out to touch Jesus, and he cures them. Jesus fulfills the foretold role of God's Servant.—See "In His Name Nations Will Hope."

“IN HIS NAME NATIONS WILL HOPE”—Matthew 12:21.

To identify the Messiah for Jewish readers, Matthew’s gospel (12:17-21) quotes from Isaiah’s prophecy (42:1-4) and applies it to Jesus:

Here is my servant whom I chose—my beloved, whom I approved! I will put my spirit upon him, and he will proclaim justice to the nations. He will not strive nor shout, nor will his voice be heard in the streets. A bruised reed he will not break—a smoldering wick he will not extinguish—until he brings justice with victory. In his name nations will hope.

Twice God spoke from Heaven words of approval of his chosen servant, his anointed Son. (Matthew 3:17; 17:5; Mark 1:11; 9:7; Luke 3:22; 9:35; Acts 3:13; 2 Peter 1:17) Making evident God’s justice and showing that God’s spirit is upon him, Jesus relieved people of unjust burdens. (Luke 4:18) He carried a refreshing message to those who were like a bruised reed, broken down spiritually. (Matthew 11:28) Jesus would never extinguish the last spark of hope smoldering in humble and downtrodden people. He uplifted the meek with tenderness and love. However, he did not want people to learn about him through noisy advertising in the streets or through distorted second-hand reports. (Jesus denied to evil spirits that he expelled the privilege of testifying about him!—Mark 1:25.)

Based on the works and wisdom of Jesus Christ, people from all nations—not Israel only—place their hope in his name.—Acts 4:12.

Jesus Appoints His Apostles
Mark 3:13-19; Luke 6:12-16

After Jesus began his ministry, seven men—Andrew, Simon Peter, John, James, Philip, Nathanael (also called Bartholomew) and Matthew Levi—became his disciples. Now, from a larger following, he is ready to select twelve apostles.[313] Jesus spends a whole night in prayer on a mountain. Afterward, to his seven original disciples, Jesus adds five more: Simon the Zealot, Thomas,[314] James the Less, Thaddaeus (also known as Judas) and Judas Iscariot.

Judas Iscariot seems to be the only apostle from Judea.[315] The others, like Jesus, are from Galilee. Nathanael is from Cana. Philip, Peter and Andrew are originally from Bethsaida. Peter and Andrew in time move to Capernaum, where Matthew apparently lived. James and John also live in or close to Capernaum.[316]

A number of these men are Jesus' relatives. Brothers James and John are Jesus' first cousins, being sons of Mary's sister Salome. Jesus' adoptive father Joseph was the brother of Alphaeus (Clopas), making Alphaeus' son James and James' son Thaddaeus Jesus' kin by marriage.[317] Simon the Zealot may also have been a son of Alphaeus.[318]

It seems that most of the apostles did not play prominent roles in post-Pentecost Christianity. In Acts of Apostles, only Peter and John stand out. (They also authored seven of the New Testament's 26 books, including the Gospel of John; Matthew contributed another one of the gospels.) The other faithful apostles disappear from the biblical record after their attendance at Pentecost is noted.—Acts 1:13-2:1.

The suicide of Judas Iscariot and the execution of James the son of Zebedee are the only apostolic deaths recorded in the New Testament. (Matthew 27:5; Acts 1:18; 12:1-2) Tradition has it that, like James, the other apostles were martyred, except for his brother John, who died of old age.

The Sermon on the Mount[319]
Matthew 5:1–8:1; Luke 6:17-49

With his disciples and new apostles, Jesus comes down from the mountain and finds waiting for him a multitude of people—people from as far south as Jerusalem and from the northern coastal cities of Tyre and Sidon.[320] As they reach out to touch him, Jesus cures their illnesses and ministers to those troubled by evil spirits. Afterward, he finds a level place on the mountainside.[321] The crowd, including his disciples,[322] gathers around, and Jesus preaches a sermon on the mount.

Weals and woes. Jesus starts his sermon by describing people who are truly blessed, or happy.[323] "Those who are spiritually poor[324] are happy," he says, "because the kingdom of Heaven belongs to them."[325] Mourners, Jesus promises, "will be comforted."[326] Those who "weep now will laugh."[327] Humble ones "will inherit the earth."[328] Those who hunger for righteousness "will be filled."[329] Merciful ones "will be shown mercy."[330] "The pure in heart ... will see God."[331] "Peacemakers"[332] will be known as "God's children." To "those who are persecuted in the cause of righteousness ... the kingdom of Heaven belongs."[333] Indeed, a great reward in Heaven awaits those who are reproached and slandered on Jesus' account.[334]

After these Beatitudes follow four woes:[335] "Woe to you who are rich," says Jesus. "You have been paid in full.[336] Woe to you who are satisfied—you will go hungry. Woe to you who are carefree—you will mourn and weep. Woe to you who are well-spoken of by others—that's how their forefathers treated the false prophets."

Light and salt. Jesus' disciples "are the light of the world" and "the salt of the earth."[337] Salt is useless if it loses its strength,[338] and a lamp is useless unless it is set where it can shed light. (Compare Luke 14:34-35) "A lamp is set on a stand[339]—not under a basket—so it can give light to everyone in the room. Therefore," Jesus urges, "let your light shine in sight of others, enabling them to see your fine works and glorify your heavenly Father."[340]

Jot and tittle. To the religious leaders, Jesus is a lawbreaker deserving of death. Jesus declares, however, that he is here "to fulfill the law of Moses and the teachings of the prophets."[341] In fact, he says, "for as long as Heaven and Earth endure, not one word—not one letter[342]—will disappear from the Law until its purpose is fulfilled. Whoever, therefore, breaks the Commandments—even the least of them—and teaches others to do so will be least likely to enter the kingdom of Heaven. But whoever follows the Commandments and teaches them to others will be most likely to enter the kingdom of Heaven. However," Jesus tells his audience, "if your righteousness cannot surpass that of the scholars and the Pharisees, you'll never enter the kingdom of Heaven."[343]

Adultery and divorce. Jesus quotes God's commandment against adultery, then warns, "For someone who is married to look lustfully at someone they aren't married to is to commit adultery with them in the heart."[344] To prevent this, extreme measures may be necessary. "Gouge your right eye the moment you catch it in a lustful leer,"[345] Jesus says. "Better to live with one eye than to die with two."[346]—Exodus 20:14; Deuteronomy 5:18.

Jesus quotes the Law on divorce: "'Whoever divorces his wife must give her a certificate of forsaking'[347]—so you have heard.[348] I, however, tell you that a man and woman who divorce for a reason other than unfaithfulness[349] lay themselves open to a charge of adultery, and anyone whom they marry becomes guilty of adultery."[350]—Deuteronomy 24:1.

Brothers and enemies. Referring to the Sixth Commandment, Jesus continues: "'You must not murder,' but whoever commits a murder will answer to the courts[351]—so you have heard. I, however, tell you that whoever nurses anger[352] against a fellow believer[353] will also answer to the courts. In addition, whoever speaks to a fellow believer with contemptible words[354] will answer to the High Court;[355] whereas whoever calls someone morally worthless is in danger of eternal death."[356]—Exodus 20:13; Deuteronomy 5:17.

Unresolved wrath being such a serious matter, Jesus explains the lengths to which one should go to achieve peace: "When bringing your gift to the altar, if you remember that a fellow believer has a grievance against you, leave your gift at the altar and go make peace.[357] Then return to the altar and offer your gift."

Jesus also offers counsel on dealing with one's so-called enemies: "'Eye for eye and tooth for tooth'[358]—so you have heard. I, however, tell you: Don't resist a provocateur. If he slaps your right cheek, turn the other to him as well.[359] If he takes you to court and sues for your shirt, let him have it and your coat as well.[360] If he presses you into service for a mile, go with him for two miles."[361] In line with God's law to love one's neighbor[362] Jesus advises, "Keep loving your enemies, doing good to those who hate you, blessing those who curse you, praying for those who insult you."[363]

Jesus questions the virtue of doing good only to those from whom a good turn can be expected. "Even tax collectors love other tax collectors,"[364] he says. "If you greet only your fellow believers[365], what extraordinary thing are you doing? Even pagans do that."[366] On the contrary, if Jesus' listeners continue to love their enemies and to do what is good, their reward will be great; they "will be children of the Highest,[367] the one who is kind toward the ungrateful and wicked."

Jesus sums up this portion of his sermon, saying: "You must love completely, as your heavenly Father loves completely."[368]

Righteousness and hypocrisy. "Take care not to practice your righteousness in sight of others to be noticed by them,"[369] Jesus counsels. "When you give to charity[370] don't imitate hypocrites[371] who blow their own horns and accept the plaudits of others.[372] They have been paid in full[373]—and that's the truth. When you give to charity, your left hand mustn't know what your right hand is doing.[374] Charitable giving should be done privately. The One who sees all that takes place privately will openly reward you.

"When you pray," Jesus goes on, "don't be like hypocrites who choose where they pray—standing in synagogues and on busy street corners—to be seen by others.[375] Truth be told, that is the full of their reward. When you pray to your Father, do so privately, behind closed doors. The One who sees all that takes place privately will openly reward you. And don't repeat yourselves as pagans do in their prayers.[376] You must pray this way[377]..."

Jesus provides a model prayer of seven petitions; the first three recognize God's supremacy and his purposes: "Our Father in Heaven,[378] may your reputation be vindicated.[379] Let your Kingdom come;[380] your will be done on Earth as in Heaven."[381] Second come personal matters such as requests for daily sustenance[382] and for forgiveness of sins,[383] as well as requests not to be tempted beyond one's endurance and deliverance from the Tempter.[384]

Jesus concludes his criticism of hypocritical worship by discussing fasting.[385] "Don't imitate the dismal-looking hypocrites," he counsels, "who affect an appearance of denial so that others think they are fasting. Truthfully, that is their full reward. When you fast, do not make a show of your self-denial. The only one who should know you are fasting is your Father, the one who sees all that takes place privately. He will openly reward you."

Righteousness and rulership. Jesus illustrates the sincere worshiper's priority to seek first God's righteousness and rulership: "Let go of your anxiety over sustenance and clothing. Will anxiety add one day to your life? Look hard at the birds in the sky; they don't work for a living, but your heavenly Father feeds them. Are you not more valuable to him than birds? And when it comes to clothing, learn from how the wildflowers grow; they don't work for a living, but I tell you that not even Solomon in all his splendor was arrayed as one of these. If God so clothes the vegetation of the field that blooms today and withers in tomorrow's heat,[386] will he not surely clothe you, you of little faith?[387] So never worry about what you will eat or drink or what you will wear. These concerns dominate the thoughts of unbelievers. Your heavenly Father knows that you need all these things.[388] And they will be added to you if you always give priority to God's kingdom and his righteousness."[389]

Judging and forgiving. After counseling against hypocritical worship and discussing the priorities of sincere worship, Jesus admonishes his listeners against being judgmental. "If you don't want to be judged," he says, "stop judging. If you don't want to be condemned, stop condemning. If you want to be forgiven, be forgiving.[390] If you want to receive, give.[391] Should one blind person lead another blind person? Surely both will fall into a pit.[392] How, then, can you say to your fellow believer, 'Let me extract the sawdust from your eye,' when you can't see the plank in your own eye?[393] Hypocrite![394] First remove the plank from your own eye, and then you will see clearly how to extract the sawdust from someone else's eye."

Ask and receive. Returning to the subject of prayer, Jesus stresses persistence. "Continue asking,"[395] he says, "and it will be given to you." Emphasizing the heavenly Parent's readiness to give, Jesus continues, "If your child asks for bread, will you hand him a stone? If she asks for a fish, will you hand her a serpent?[396] Wicked as you are,[397] you know how to give what is good to your children. How much more so,[398] then, will your heavenly Father give what is good to those who ask."[399]

Gates and roads. Jesus urges his listeners to "enter through the narrow gate" and walk among the few finding the "cramped road leading to eternal life. The wide gate opens to a roomy road that ends in destruction,"[400] Jesus cautions, "and many are heading in that direction."

Doers and hearers. Jesus warns his listeners to watch out for false prophets, comparing them to ravenous wolves disguised in sheep's clothing.[401] "By their fruits,"[402] however, these pretenders can be recognized, as trees can be distinguished by their fruits. As Jesus says, "you don't get grapes from a thornbush." False prophets may call Jesus their "Lord" and even appear to perform miracles in his name, but he denounces these "lawbreakers."[403]

"Why, then," Jesus asks, "do you call me 'Lord'[404] when you don't do as I say? Whoever comes to me and hears my words and acts on them is like one who builds a house on a deep, solid foundation.[405] Such a well-built house will withstand a flood when it storms. On the other hand, whoever hears my words, but does nothing, is like one who builds a house without a foundation. When a storm comes and the floodwaters rise, that house will fall to ruin."[406]

With this pair of illustrations, Jesus concludes his sermon on the mount. He descends from the mountain, and large crowds follow him. The people are astounded at Jesus' way of teaching. His words have a ring of authority, not like the teachings of their religious leaders.[407]

Jesus reminded his listeners, "*You must not make a false vow; you must pay what you have promised to God.*" Israel's law allowed for the swearing of oaths or vows on certain serious occasions. (Numbers 30:2; Deuteronomy 23:21) In order to add weight to their word, people would swear by Heaven, by Earth, by Jerusalem, and even by the life of another person. This perversion of oath-taking led Jesus to recommend, *"A simple 'yes' or a simple 'no'—anything else is from the Evil one." (Matthew 5:33-37;* compare James 5:12) One who continually swears to what one says is not trustworthy and manifests the spirit of the original liar, Satan.—John 8:44.

"Stop storing up your treasures on Earth, where they are vulnerable to deterioration and theft. Instead, store up your treasures in Heaven." Material wealth is perishable and builds up no merit with God. But nothing or no one can take away a good standing with God or its reward of eternal life. *"Where your treasure is,"* Jesus said, *"there your heart's desire will be."—Matthew 6:19-21.*

"The body's lamp is the eye. If your eye is focused, your whole body will be bright." A figurative eye properly focused will enlighten its owner. (Ephesians 1:18) *"If, however, your eye is envious, your whole body will be dark." (Matthew 6:22-23)* As an unhealthy literal eye cannot see clearly, an envious "eye" cannot focus on what is truly important. To focus on material treasures instead of on the treasure of serving God is to pursue a selfish course

of life; one who does so could be drawn to things shady and dark.

"No one can serve two masters; one he will hate and the other love, or one he will stick to and the other despise. You cannot serve God and be enslaved to Riches." (Matthew 6:24) "Riches" is personified as a master, or a kind of false god. Money is not inherently evil. But "the love of money is the root of all evil." (1 Timothy 5:10, *King James Version)* A Christian cannot be enslaved to accumulating material possessions and at the same time give exclusive devotion to the True God.

"Do not feed what is sacred to dogs nor throw your pearls to pigs." (Matthew 7:6) God's law to Israel categorized dogs and pigs as unclean. (Leviticus 11:7, 27) Tradition forbade giving to dogs so-called holy flesh—meat of animal sacrifices. (Leviticus 22:14) And pigs certainly have no appreciation for the value of pearls. Similarly, people with "animal and unspiritual" dispositions cannot appreciate the treasure of God's Word.—Jude 19, *The Twentieth Century New Testament.*

"Treat others just as you want them to treat you." (Matthew 7:12; Luke 6:31) John Quincy Adams, sixth president of the United States, said of the Bible: "It is of all books in the world, that which contributes most to make men good, wise, and happy."[408] If everyone followed the Golden Rule and treated one another the way we want to be treated, would that not be wise? Would that not make us good and happy?

"A Faith So Great!"
Matthew 8:5-13; Luke 7:1-10

In Capernaum community leaders approach Jesus on behalf of a centurion.[409] The army officer's beloved servant is terminally ill.[410] The leaders assure Jesus that the Roman soldier is worthy of help. "He loves our country," they explain. "He built our synagogue himself."[411]

Jesus and the community leaders head for the officer's house. They are intercepted by messengers from the centurion. He feels unworthy to have Jesus in his home and is confident that his servant will be healed if Jesus just gives the word.[412]

"With no one in Israel have I found a faith so great!"[413] Jesus comments. "For a fact, I tell you that many will come from east and west and dine with Abraham, Isaac and Jacob in the kingdom of Heaven.[414] Meanwhile, the Kingdom's own children will be thrown into the darkness outside where they will weep and grind their teeth."[415]

On returning to the centurion's house, his messengers discover that the servant who was sick is now in good health. What the officer believed could happen has happened!

Jesus Brings a Boy Back to Life
Luke 7:11-18

Jesus leaves Capernaum, his disciples and a throng of followers traveling with him. On the outskirts of Nain[416] they encounter a funeral procession.[417] The body of a young man is being borne out of the city for burial. The young man's mother is a widow, and her only child is dead.[418] Moved with compassion for the woman, Jesus tells her that she can stop crying. He approaches and touches the bier on which the body rests.[419] The pallbearers stop in their tracks. Jesus commands the young man, "Rise!" The dead man sits up and starts to speak! Jesus has returned a son to his mother.

Awestruck, the people glorify God. "He has favored us by raising up a great prophet among us," they say.[420] News of this miracle reaches the disciples of John the Baptist, who carry it to their master.[421]

"Come to Me"
Matthew 11:2-30; Luke 7:19-35

From jail John the Baptist dispatches two of his disciples to ask Jesus a question: "Are you the Messiah, or should we expect another?"[422]

Jesus responds with miraculous demonstrations of his credentials, curing sick and diseased people, expelling demons from the possessed, and giving sight to the sightless. (See Isaiah 26:19; 29:18-19; 35:5-6; 61:1) "Go," he tells John's disciples, "and report to your master what you have witnessed."

After John's disciples leave, Jesus tells bystanders that John is "far more than a prophet"; he is the foretold "Elijah" and the Messenger.[423] "Truthfully, there is not a mother's son greater than John the Baptist," says Jesus. "That being said, the one who is least important in Heaven's kingdom is more important than John."[424]

John has lived a simple life, fasting and abstaining, and people call him demonized. Jesus, in contrast, eats and drinks in moderation, but is accused of excesses.[425] "The adults of this generation," Jesus declares, "are like children complaining to their playmates: 'You didn't dance when we played the flute for you; you didn't mourn when we sang a dirge.'[426] All the same, wisdom is known by her children."[427]

Jesus upbraids the Galilean cities that see many of his miraculous works:[428] "Woe to Chorazin! Woe to Bethsaida! If the miracles that you witness had been seen in Tyre and Sidon, they would have repented in sackcloth and ashes long ago.[429] That's why Judgment Day will be more endurable for them than for you.[430] Now, Capernaum: will you exalt yourself to Heaven? Down to Hades you will go![431] If Sodom had seen the miracles that you witness, it would exist today. That's why Judgment Day will be more endurable for Sodom than for you."[432]

Jesus praises his Father, who conceals precious spiritual truths from wise and educated people but reveals them to child-like, teachable ones.[433] He invites, "Come to me, all you who are toiling and over-burdened, and I will relieve you. Shoulder my yoke and learn from me, for I am humble[434] and lowly in heart,[435] and you will be refreshed. My yoke fits easily, and the load is light."[436]

"Your Faith Has Saved You"
Luke 7:36-50

A Pharisee named Simon invites Jesus to his house for a meal. Customarily, guests receive a welcoming kiss from their host,[437] who provides water for the guest to wash their feet.[438] Hosts also pour oil on the heads of their guests. When he arrives at Simon's home, Jesus receives no such cordial attention.

During the meal, an uninvited woman quietly enters the room.[439] Carrying an alabaster jar of perfumed oil,[440] she approaches Jesus and kneels. Tears fall from her eyes onto his feet; she wipes them with her hair, tenderly kisses and pours oil on them. This woman, however, has an unsavory reputation. Simon the Pharisee says to himself, "If Jesus were really a prophet, he would know that he's being touched by a sinner."[441]

Suddenly, Jesus announces, "Simon, I have something to say to you."

Simon replies, "Proceed, Teacher."

"Two men were in debt to a certain creditor;[442] one man owed what amounted to 500 days' wages,[443] the other 50 days' wages. They could not pay him back, so he forgave both debts free and clear. Now which man will love him more?"

"I suppose," Simon answers, "the one who had more debt to forgive."

Jesus agrees. Then turning to the woman, he says to Simon, "When I entered your home, you gave me no water to wash my feet; this woman washed my feet with her tears and wiped them with her hair. You gave me no kiss; she hasn't stopped tenderly kissing my feet. You did not anoint my head with oil; she poured perfume on my feet. Therefore, because she showed so much love, her sins—her many sins—have been forgiven. On the other hand, one who has little to forgive loves little in return."[444]

Ignoring the whispers of the other guests, Jesus tells the woman, "Your faith has saved you. Go in peace."

Jesus' True Family
Matthew 12:22-50; Mark 3:20-35; Luke 8:1-3, 19-21

Jesus begins another tour of Galilee. Traveling with him are the 12 apostles, as well as certain women whom he has cured of sickness and demonic possession. Among them are Mary Magdalene,[445] Susanna and Joanna,[446] whose husband is an officer of King Herod Antipas. These women provide for the party from their own resources.[447]

As the pace of Jesus' ministry intensifies, so does the controversy surrounding him. His own family thinks he has lost his senses; Mary and her other sons set out to take charge of him.[448]

Enclosing the house where Jesus stays is a crowd so large that he and his disciples cannot even eat in peace. A demon-possessed man, who is blind and mute, is brought to Jesus. When Jesus liberates him from control of the demon and restores his abilities to speak and see, the crowd is astonished. "Could this be the Son of David?"[449] the people consider.

In the crowd are Pharisees and scholars from Jerusalem.[450] They are telling people that the source of Jesus' power to expel demons is Beelzebub.[451] To this charge Jesus answers: "A house divided cannot stand.[452] If Satan expels Satan, he is divided. And how will his house stand? Moreover," Jesus continues, "if I am empowered by Beelzebub, what about your followers[453]? They too expel demons, so they will condemn you for what you have said. But if I expel demons by the power of God's spirit, God's kingdom has overtaken you[454]."

The Pharisees and scholars accuse Jesus of being in league with the Devil. Jesus warns his opposers, "Whoever blasphemes God's spirit is guilty of eternal sin and will not be forgiven—not now, not ever![455] Trees are known by their fruit: good trees produce good fruit; rotten trees produce rotten fruit. Brood of vipers,[456] how can you, rotten as you are, say anything good? What fills the heart rises to the lips. For every slander that people speak they will be held accountable on Judgment Day. By your own words you will be either acquitted or condemned."[457]

The Pharisees and scholars demand to see a sign from Jesus, even after all the miracles he has performed. "A wicked, unfaithful[458] generation looks for a sign," Jesus retorts. "But the only sign it will see is the Sign of Jonah the Prophet: Jonah was in the stomach of a big fish[459] for three days and three nights; the Son of Man will be in the heart of the earth for three days and three nights."[460] Jesus compares his contemporaries to a person from whom a wicked spirit comes out. Because the human host does not fill the void with good things, the spirit returns with seven even more wicked spirits, and they possess the person.[461]

While Jesus is speaking, Mary and her other sons arrive and stand at the edge of the crowd. Word of their presence travels to some of those sitting near Jesus, who tell him, "Your mother and brothers are here to see you."

Gesturing to his followers, Jesus says, "My mother and brothers are these ones who hear God's word and act."[462]

The Kingdom Illustrated
Matthew 13:1-53; Mark 4:1-34; Luke 8:4-18

That same day, as Jesus sits by the Sea of Galilee, crowds gather. Jesus boards a boat, pulls out from shore and teaches about God's kingdom with parables.[463] "As a sower was sowing," Jesus begins, "some seeds fell along the path—they were walked on and eventually eaten by birds.[464] Other seeds fell on bedrock[465]—they sprouted but dried up for lack of moisture and soil. And other seeds fell among weeds,[466] which came up and choked them. Still others fell on rich soil and yielded a crop a hundred times greater than what was sown."[467]

In another parable, Jesus again compares the Kingdom to someone who sows seed. In this story, however, a rival secretly sows weeds among the wheat.[468] The sower's servants ask if they should pull up the weeds. "No," the sower replies. "I'm afraid you might uproot the wheat with the weeds.[469] Let both grow together until harvest time, when I will tell the reapers,[470] 'First collect the weeds and bind them in bundles to burn them; then gather the wheat into my storehouse.'"[471]

Jesus dismisses the crowds and returns to the house where he is staying. His disciples ask, "Why do you use parables to teach people?"[472]

"Parables are for those who have not received understanding of the Kingdom's hidden truths,"[473] Jesus answers. "You, however, have received. To those who have received, more will be given, and they will flourish. From those who have not received, what they think they have will be taken.[474] That's why I speak to them through parables. They have eyes but cannot see. They have ears but cannot hear or understand. Happily, however, your eyes see, and your ears hear.[475] Many prophets and righteous ones longed to see and to hear what you are seeing and hearing but did not."—Hebrews 1:1-2; 1 Peter 1:10-12.

Because his disciples desire to understand hidden truths of the Kingdom, Jesus explains his parable about the seeds in different kinds of soil. "The seed represents God's message," Jesus says. "Where anyone hears the Kingdom message but does not understand it, the Devil comes and snatches away what has been sown in the hearer's heart—this is what happens to the 'seeds' along the road.[476] The 'seeds' fallen on rocky ground represent one who hears and immediately accepts the message joyfully. However, the message doesn't take root because, in a time of trial on account of the message, the hearer loses faith.[477] The 'seeds' fallen among the thorns represent one who hears the message, but growth is choked by life's anxieties and the trap of wealth.[478] Finally, the 'seeds' sown upon the rich soil represent one who hears and understands the message from the heart, yielding fruit with endurance."[479]

Jesus adds, "Those with ears to hear, listen and pay attention. With the measure that you are measuring out, you will have it measured out to you; yes, more will be given to you."

The disciples want to learn more. "Explain to us," they ask Jesus, "the parable about the weeds in the field."[480]

Jesus responds, "The sower of the fine seed represents the Son of Man; the field represents the world of humankind. The fine seed represents the children of the Kingdom, but the weeds represent the children of the Evil One, and the rival who sowed them represents the Devil himself. The harvest means an end of an age,[481] and the reapers represent angels. Therefore, just as the weeds are uprooted and burned up, so will it be at the end of the age. The Son of Man will send his angels to uproot from the Kingdom all lawbreakers and stumbling stones. They will be thrown into a furnace, where they will weep and grind their teeth. Then, at last, the righteous ones will shine like the sun in their Father's kingdom."—Daniel 12:3.

Finally, Jesus asks his disciples, "Do you understand everything?"

"Yes," they answer.

"That being so," says Jesus, "every teacher who is instructed about the kingdom of Heaven is like a householder who brings out of his store both new treasures and old."[482]

"... someone who casts seed on the ground, then sleeps and wakes night and day. The seeds sprout and grow—but how? On its own the ground bears fruit gradually, first the stalk, then the head, finally the full head of grain. When the crop is ready, the farmer thrusts in the sickle, because it's harvest time."[483]—Mark 4:26-29.

This parable is unique to the Gospel of Mark; it presents a complete picture of the coming of God's kingdom: (1) sowing; (2) growth; (3) harvest. As surely as there was a sowing of the seed, there must be a harvesting. What we sow with in relation to God's kingdom leads to what we will harvest or reap. (Galatians 6:7-8) This parable also teaches a lesson in patience, both with fellow believers and with ourselves. Like the growth of seeds, spiritual growth takes place gradually and in stages; it cannot be forced or speeded up.—1 Corinthians 3:7; Hebrews 6:1; James 5:7-8.

... a mustard grain, a tiny seed that grows into a tall plant.—Matthew 13:31-32; Mark 4:30-32.

"The kingdom, like the mustard seed ..., is unpretentious in its beginnings but destined for enormous growth." (The Jerusalem Bible, Matthew chapter 13 note g; Daniel 4:12, 21; Ezekiel 17:23; 31:6; see "A Mustard Seed, A Mountain and Faith.") Black mustard is commonly cultivated in Israel. From a small seed—measuring one millimeter (0.039-0.063 in) and weighing a single milligram (0.000035 oz)—it grows into a treelike plant standing 4 and-a-half meters (15 ft) tall.

... yeast in a bushel of flour, which causes the mass to rise.—Matthew 13:33.

Yeast refers to a small piece of fermented dough held over from a previous kneading and mixed into a new batch of dough to make it rise. Jesus used yeast "as a positive symbol of the permeating effect of the gospel."—The NIV Topical Study Bible, page 113.

"... a treasure, hidden in the field, that someone found and hid again—someone who joyfully sells their possessions and buys that field."—Matthew 13:44.

The value of the Kingdom far outweighs any cost for possessing it. The sacrifices made by one who finds hidden treasure can be compared to the sacrifices made to satisfy one's spiritual need.—Matthew 5:3; 19:21.

"... a merchant seeking choice pearls. Upon finding one pearl of exceptional value, the merchant promptly sold everything and bought it."—Matthew 13:45-46.

In Bible times, fine pearls were harvested from the Red Sea, the Persian Gulf and the Indian Ocean. This explains why the merchant had to travel and expend effort to seek such a pearl. The treasure in the previous illustration, by contrast, was found by chance. No matter how a person learns Kingdom truths, their value is beyond estimation.

... a dragnet that gathers up fish of every kind. When the fish are separated, the keepers are put in containers, but the unsuitable ones are thrown away.[484]—Matthew 13:47-48.

Dragnets in Jesus' day were likely made from the fibers of the flax plant. A dragnet might have been as long as 300 meters (1,000 ft) with weights attached to the bottom edge and floats attached to the top. Fishermen used a boat to drop the dragnet into the water. Sometimes they would take the long ropes attached to the ends of the net ashore, where several men on each rope gradually pulled the net onto the beach. The net gathered everything in its path. (See "Fish and Fishing in the Sea of Galilee.") Jesus was doing a type of spiritual fishing when he called his first disciples. (Mark 1:17) However, his dragnet illustration applies "in the end of the age," when Christ's followers catch symbolic fish of every kind, and "the angels separate the righteous from the wicked."—Matthew 13:49.

Power Over Forces Natural and Unnatural
Matthew 8:18, 23-34; Mark 4:35-5:20; Luke 8:22-39

At the end of a long day, Jesus and his apostles set sail on the Sea of Galilee. In the stern of the boat, Jesus lays his head on a pillow and falls asleep.[485] Without warning, a gale of wind breaks loose over the lake.[486] Waves swamp the boat. Jesus, however, continues sleeping. The seamen rouse him with their cries: "Save us, Lord! We're about to die! Don't you care?"

Jesus opens his eyes and looks at the wind and the sea. "Quiet!" he commands. "Be still!" The wind abates; calm sets in. "Why were you afraid," he asks the apostles, "you of little faith?"

An unusual fear grips the apostles. "Who really is this man?" they say to one another. "Even the wind and the waves obey him!"

They come ashore in the region of the Gadarenes (or "Gerasenes").[487] Jesus gets out of the boat and immediately encounters two demon-possessed men.[488] They are so violent that no one comes near this place. One of the men is naked, except for the broken chains and fetters on his hands and feet. From a nearby cemetery[489] he is often heard screaming as he slashes his skin with sharp stones. Now this man runs up to Jesus and falls at his feet. Jesus orders the "foul spirit" to "come out of him."

The demons controlling the man strangle screams from his mouth: "Son of God, what do you want with us? Are you here to torment us before our time comes?"[490] This "legion"[491] of devils begs Jesus not to banish them to the Abyss. "If you expel us," the demons say, "send us into the swine."

A large herd of swine is grazing nearby. With Jesus' permission the demons enter the animals and, as the herdsmen helplessly watch, stampede all 2,000 of them over a cliff into the water below.—See "Demonic Possession."

The swine herders run away and tell anyone who will listen what they have just witnessed. Curiosity seekers arrive on scene and observe that one of the madmen Jesus healed is now clothed and composed, sitting at the Master's feet. Not understanding what this may mean for them, the townsfolk urge Jesus to leave.[492] As Jesus boards his boat, the former demoniac begs to come along. Jesus tells him to go home and tell others about the compassion shown to him.[493] Throughout the Decapolis this new disciple publicizes what Jesus did for him, amazing all who hear his story.

It seems that spirit creatures derive sadistic pleasure from inhabiting fleshly bodies. In Noah's time, rebellious angels allied themselves with Satan and materialized in human form to cohabit with women. The Flood forced them to return to spirit form for their own preservation. (Genesis 6:1-4, 17) Not thereafter having the power to materialize fleshly bodies for their use, it seems that these fallen angels did the nearest thing to it that was in their power, and that was to possess human bodies, which they could drive to the satisfying of their unnatural desires. This was a form of perversion, just as some degenerate persons sink to bestiality for sexual gratification. When the demons could not remain in the two men, they asked Jesus' permission to enter the swine to satisfy their lusts.

Jesus allowed the demons to possess the swine (but did not command them to do so). For them to enter the swine would demonstrate for observers Jesus' power over the demons and demonic power over fleshly creatures. Demonic possession is not superstition but a real threat to humankind; it is to be taken seriously, as is Jesus' power over evil spirits.

The Power of Faith

Matthew 9:18-34; Mark 5:21-43; Luke 8:40-56

News of Jesus' return from the Decapolis brings many people to the Sea of Galilee. Present is a director of the local synagogue, a man named Jairus.[494] He falls at Jesus' feet and begs, "My only child is dying. Please come and lay your hands on her to cure her. Save her life, please!"

A crushing-size crowd moves with Jesus on his way to Jairus' house; among the multitude is a woman who has heard about Jesus. She has suffered from a menstrual hemorrhage for many years. Despite spending all her money on various treatments recommended by different physicians,[495] her condition has deteriorated. She inconspicuously makes her way through the crowd, saying to herself, "I'll be healed if I touch just his clothes[496]." She does so, and immediately senses that her bleeding has stopped.

Jesus, too, senses something—a draw on his power to heal. "Who touched me?"[497] he asks. Trembling with fear, the woman falls before Jesus and confesses. Jesus comforts her: "Daughter,[498] your faith has healed you.[499] Go in peace; this malady[500] will never trouble you again."[501]

Now some men arrive from Jairus' home and tell him, "There's no need to bother the Teacher anymore—your daughter is dead."

Jesus overhears the report. "Don't be afraid," he tells Jairus. "Hold on to your faith!"

Jesus, along with Peter, James and John, accompanies Jairus back to his home; there, minstrels are playing death dirges; mourners are weeping, wailing and beating themselves in grief. Jesus tells them all to leave because the girl is not dead, just sleeping.[502] The people laugh scornfully. Jesus sends everyone outside[503] except for his three apostles and the girl's parents;[504] these five and Jesus go to where the girl lies. Clasping her hand, Jesus tells her, "Wake up, little one!"[505] The girl rises and begins walking! Jairus and his wife are ecstatic and unable to keep what Jesus has done to themselves despite his orders to not make it known.[506]

As Jesus leaves Jairus' home, two blind men follow him. "Son of David!"[507] they shout. "Have mercy on us." Jesus seems to ignore their cries.

After the two men make their way into a house where Jesus is staying, he asks them, "Do you have faith that I can help you?"

"Yes, Lord!" they answer confidently.

Jesus touches their eyes and says, "Receive what your faith expects." Suddenly they can see! Jesus directs the men to not publicize what he did, but they will talk about him far and wide.

As these two men are leaving, people bring to Jesus a man who cannot speak because he is demon-possessed. Jesus expels the demon, and instantly the man begins to talk. The crowds marvel at this. "Nothing like it was ever seen in Israel!" they proclaim.

Also present are Pharisees, repeating their charge as to the source of Jesus' power: "He expels the demons with help from their ruler."[508]

A Prophet without Honor
Matthew 13:54-58; Mark 6:1-6

Accompanied by the disciples, Jesus heads back to his hometown, Nazareth.[509] On the Sabbath, Jesus returns to the synagogue to teach.[510] His fellow Nazarenes are astounded. "Where did the carpenter's boy get such wisdom?"[511] they wonder. "His mother, brothers[512] and sisters are just like us.[513] Why would he of all people be empowered to perform miracles?"[514]

Jesus matter-of-factly observes, "In his hometown, among his relatives, and in his own house are the only places where a prophet is dishonored." Amazed at the lack of faith he has encountered, Jesus performs no miracles in Nazareth, except to lay his hands on a few sick ones and cure them.[515]

The Master Sends Workers into His Harvest
Matthew 9:35–11:1; Mark 6:7-13; Luke 9:1-6

Jesus embarks on another tour of Galilee—teaching, preaching and healing wherever he goes. He takes pity on people who are spiritually neglected, like sheep without a shepherd.[516] "The harvest is great, the workers are few," Jesus tells his disciples. He divides the 12 apostles into pairs, making six teams of spiritual harvest workers. Their message will be: "The kingdom of Heaven is near."[517]

Jesus empowers his apostles to cure the sick and even raise the dead.[518] Because they are going to fellow Jews—Israel's "lost sheep"—material preparations will not be necessary: no change of clothes, no traveling money, no sustenance provisions.[519] "The worker deserves his food," says Jesus. Wherever the disciples enter a home, there they should stay.[520] "When you enter the house, greet the household with wishes for peace," Jesus instructs. "If the household is undeserving, your peace will return to you.[521] When you leave a house or city that did not welcome you or hear you, shake the dust from your feet, showing that you abandon them to their fate.[522] Judgment Day will be more endurable for Sodom and Gomorrah than for that city[523]—and that's the truth!"

Jesus is sending out his apostles "as sheep among wolves." He warns them, "Be cautious as serpents, yet innocent as doves.[524] Be on your guard! You'll be dragged into courts and scourged in synagogues.[525] Because of me you'll be hated by all people. But endure to the end[526] and you will be saved."

Jesus' enemies accuse him of being in league with the Devil and his followers can expect no better treatment.[527] (Matthew 12:24; Mark 3:22; Luke 11:15) The twelve evangelizers will therefore need to be discreet, yet courageous. "When they persecute you in one town, escape to the next," Jesus says. "Proclaim publicly what I tell you privately; from the housetops declare what I whispered in your ears![528] Never fear those who can kill the body but are powerless to kill the soul! Far better to fear the One who has the power to destroy body and soul[529] in the fires of annihilation[530]."

The disciples' message has potential to divide households, some members accepting it and others not. "Siblings will betray siblings, parents will betray children and children will betray parents to be put to death," Jesus foresees. "Family members could be your worst enemies." (See Micah 7:6) Jesus' followers must be willing to make sacrifices for him. "If you favor father or mother over me," he tells them, "you don't deserve me. If you favor your own child over me, you don't deserve me. If you are unwilling to die for me, you don't deserve me.[531] If your first concern is for yourself, you'll never find yourself. Forget about yourself and look to me, and you'll find both yourself and me."

However, some people will receive the disciples favorably, and in doing so, receive Jesus himself. "Whoever receives God's messenger will also receive that messenger's reward," says Jesus, "a reward that lasts forever."[532]

Equipped with Jesus' instructions, warnings and encouragement, the apostles go from village to village. In addition to declaring the gospel, they expel demons and perform cures. Jesus, meanwhile, teaches and preaches in the towns around Capernaum.

"Give Me the Head of John the Baptist"
Matthew 14:1-12; Mark 6:14-29; Luke 9:7-9

"It's John the Baptist! The man I beheaded has risen from the dead!" So, exclaims "King" Herod Antipas upon hearing reports of Jesus' miracles. The events leading up to the execution of John explain Herod's guilty fear.

Herod arranges a large celebration in his own honor.[533] The *crème de la crème* of Galilee attend, including highly placed officials and military commanders. Salome, daughter of Herod's wife Herodias,[534] dances for the guests. Her performance enthralls the men, especially her stepfather. "Whatever you want," Herod swears to Salome, "ask me for—I'll give it to you—as much as half my kingdom!"[535]

Before answering, Salome consults with her mother. Herodias, who nurses a grudge against John the Baptist, instructs Salome to demand John's life.

Immediately, Salome returns to Herod. "Give me the head of John the Baptist on a platter right now!" she says.

The thought of executing a holy man distresses Herod. Up till now the king has protected John from Herodias' lust for revenge. Nevertheless, bound by his public promise to Salome,[536] Herod dispatches an executioner to the prison.[537] The man returns with John's head on a platter. He gives the grisly trophy to Salome, and she delivers it to her mother.

When John's disciples hear what has happened to their master, they claim his body and bury it. Then they deliver the tragic news to Jesus.

BIOGRAPHICAL SKETCH: HEROD ANTIPAS

On his deathbed, Herod the Great made a new will, dividing his realm between three of his sons: half to Archelaus and half to Philip and Antipas. The domain of Antipas consisted of Galilee and Perea, where Jesus conducted much of his ministry. Although Antipas was popularly called King Herod, his position was more like that of a governor. (Mark 6:14) He certainly was not a king in the sense that his father had been.—Matthew 14:1, 9; Mark 6:22, 25-27; Luke 9:7.

Antipas went to Rome in hopes of gaining more honor and territory; and not only once, but time and again. On one such mission, Antipas stayed with one of his half-brothers, Herod Philip, not to be confused with the brother and tetrarch of the same name. (Luke 3:1) This Philip had been disinherited by Herod the Great and was married to Herodias, daughter of Aristobulus, another son of Herod the Great.[538] This ambitious woman so successfully played upon Antipas' emotions that he took her with him when he returned to Galilee. With a new "queen," Antipas divorced his wife—daughter of the Arabian King Aretas IV—who returned to her father. (2 Corinthians 11:32) Insulted, Aretas invaded Antipas' dominion. Rome's intervention saved Antipas from being overthrown.

A builder like his father, but on a far smaller scale, Antipas built a city on the Sea of Tiberias (or Galilee) and named it Tiberias, after the emperor. (John 6:1, 23) Another city, Julias, he named for Augustus' wife, Julia (more commonly called Livia). He also constructed forts, palaces and theaters.

As the years went by Antipas wearied in his unsuccessful efforts to gain more territory. Herodias, on the other hand, was as ambitious as ever. When her brother Agrippa was made king of Philip's domain by Gaius Caesar (Caligula), Herodias encouraged Antipas to request a kingship from the emperor. Unfortunately, reports insinuating that Antipas was plotting sedition—reports that originated with Agrippa—reached Caesar at the same time that Antipas and Herodias arrived in Rome. Unable to refute the charges, Antipas was banished to Gaul. As Agrippa's sister Herodias could have escaped punishment. Nevertheless, she chose to be exiled with her husband. Antipas' domain and wealth, as well as Herodias' estate, were given to Agrippa.

Five Loaves of Bread and Two Fish Feed Thousands[539]

Matthew 14:13-33; Mark 6:30-52; Luke 9:10-17; John 6:1-21

The apostles return to Jesus, relating their experiences of evangelizing and healing throughout Galilee. In search of privacy, the 13 men board their boat and set sail on the Sea of Galilee.[540] However, many people see them leave, and others learn about it. As Jesus and the apostles come ashore at Bethsaida, a huge crowd waits for him.[541] Taking pity on the people, Jesus gets out of the boat and cures anyone who needs healing. He also teaches them about God's kingdom.

As this long day grows longer, the apostles suggest to Jesus that he dismiss the crowd. Instead, Jesus tells them to give the people something to eat.[542] There are about 5,000 men, not counting women and children.[543] The apostle Andrew introduces a little boy who has five barley loaves and two small fish.[544] Jesus has his apostles instruct the people to recline on the springtime grass in rows of 50 and of 100. He takes the five loaves and two fish, looks up to Heaven and says a blessing. Then he breaks the loaves and divides up the fish.[545] Jesus gives these to his apostles to distribute to the people. All eat to satisfaction. Then Jesus tells his apostles to gather the leftovers. The uneaten bread (aside from the fish) fills 12 baskets.[546]

Concluding that he is the foretold Prophet, some people want to make Jesus their king.[547] (Deuteronomy 18:15, 18) Jesus, however, dismisses the crowd and instructs his apostles to get back in their boat and set sail. Jesus withdraws to the mountains to pray alone that night.

Sometime before dawn,[548] Jesus observes the boat from a distance, three or four miles offshore on the lake.[549] A strong wind is whipping up the waves as the apostles struggle to row. Jesus descends from the mountain and walks on the water toward the boat.[550] The apostles think they are seeing things when they observe Jesus passing by.[551] Jesus identifies himself and tells them not to fear.

Peter calls, "Lord, if it is you, command me to cross the water to you."

"Come!" Jesus answers.

Peter gets out of the boat and—buoyed by the waves—walks toward Jesus. But when Peter sees the strength of the storm fear overtakes him, and he starts to sink. “Lord, save me!” he cries.

Stretching out his hand, Jesus catches hold of Peter and asks, “Why did you give in to doubt, you of little faith?”

Peter and Jesus get into the boat, and the wind abates. The others are amazed, their heads as hard as the bread Jesus earlier broke. Bowing down to Jesus, they declare, “You truly are the Son of God!”

"WHY DID YOU GIVE IN TO DOUBT?"—Matthew 14:31.

In response to Peter's faith in him, Jesus was keeping Peter above the waves. But Peter got distracted and became afraid. Although apparently a good swimmer, he began to sink. (John 21:7-8) Years later, the disciple James compared "one who doubts" to "a wave of the sea, driven and tossed by the wind." (James 1:6, *New Heart English Bible)* Doubt can be a powerful, destructive force (Jude 22-23); yielding to it could erode our faith and cause us to sink spiritually. Dwelling on what scares us, what discourages us, what distracts us from Jesus will feed our doubts. Focusing on Jesus will keep corrosive doubts at bay.

The Bread of Life

Matthew 14:34-36; Mark 6:53-56; John 6:21-71

At Gennesaret Jesus and the apostles drop anchor and go ashore.[552] People there recognize Jesus and, with others from the surrounding country, bring their ailing ones to him. Touching just the fringe of Jesus' robe, the sick are made completely well.

Eventually, people whom Jesus miraculously fed the day before arriving by boat.[553] Finding Jesus, they ask, "Teacher, when did you get here?"

Jesus rebukes them: "You're looking for me because you hope to eat again. That's the truth, isn't it? Work for food that will nourish you forever,"[554] he admonishes, "not for food that perishes."

"What is the work that God wants us to do?" the people wonder.

"The work that God asks of you," Jesus answers, "is to demonstrate faith in me, the one whom he sent."[555]

"So what work are you doing?" they ask. "What sign will you show us? Moses gave our forefathers manna—the bread from Heaven—for food in the desert."[556]—Exodus 16:4-5; Nehemiah 9:15; Psalm 78:24-25.

"Truth is," Jesus corrects, "what Moses gave was not the true bread from Heaven. My Father now gives you the Bread of God—the one who comes from Heaven and gives eternal nourishment to the world."[557]

"Sir, give us this bread forever!" the people plead.

Jesus explains, "I am the Bread of life. Whoever comes to me will not hunger; whoever demonstrates faith in me will never thirst. From Heaven I have come to do, not my own desire, but the desire of the One who sent me. And he desires that I should lose none out of all those whom he has given me, but that I should resurrect them on Judgment Day.[558] My Father desires that everyone who recognizes the Son and demonstrates faith in him should have eternal life."

The people ask one another, "How can he say he has come from Heaven? This is Jesus, son of the carpenter Joseph. We know his mother…"

"Stop whispering to each other," Jesus interrupts. "The Father sent me, and only those whom he attracts can come to me."[559] Jesus quotes the prophet: "All your children shall be taught of JEHOVAH."[560] He continues, "Everyone who has listened to and learned from the Father comes to me. I tell you the solemn truth: whoever demonstrates faith in me possesses eternal life.[561] Yes, the forefathers ate manna in the desert—and died. I am the Bread of life—the living bread that came down from Heaven. If anyone eats this bread, he will live forever; and the bread that I will give for the life of the world is my own flesh".

Jesus' words set off a fierce wrangling among the people. "How can this man give us his flesh to eat?" they wonder.

"Hear the solemn truth," Jesus answers. "If you don't eat the flesh of the Son of Man and drink his blood, you have no life in you at all. My flesh and my blood are genuine food and drink. Therefore, whoever consumes my flesh, and my blood possesses eternal life,[562] and we are united. I draw life from the Father who sent me, and whoever feeds on me draws life from me, the true Bread from Heaven. Anyone who eats this bread—unlike the forefathers who ate the manna but died—will live forever."

The thought of eating Jesus' flesh and drinking his blood is more than some believers can stomach. "Are you offended?"[563] Jesus asks. "It means your lives to believe what I tell you; yet some of you don't believe."

Many followers stop walking with Jesus.[564] He asks his apostles, "Do you want to leave, too?"

Answering for all, Peter speaks up: "Leave and go where, Lord? You have sayings of eternal life. We believe in you. You are the Holy One of God!"

Jesus observes, "I chose the twelve of you, did I not? Yet one of you is a devil[565]." That "devil" is the apostle who will betray him, Judas Iscariot.

Blind Leaders of the Blind
Matthew 15:1-20; Mark 7:1-23

Jesus is a wanted man in Judea; for a time, he restricts his activities to Galilee. (John 7:1) Here he is approached by scholars and Pharisees from Jerusalem. "Why do your disciples ignore the elders' teaching and not wash their hands before eating?"[566] they ask.

Jesus' counter-questions, "Why do you ignore God's commandment for the sake of your teaching?"[567] To these hypocrites Jesus applies a prophetic description: "And LORD JEHOVAH said: '... this people approaches me with its mouth and by its lips it honors me, and its heart is far from me, and their worship of me was by the commandment and in the teaching of man.'"—Isaiah 29:13, *Peshitta Holy Bible* by Glenn David Bauscher.

"For example," Jesus continues, "God commands us to honor our parents. But according to you, we don't have to honor our parents if we tell them, 'I am making a Temple offering of all the support you might have received from me.'[568] And so, your teaching invalidates God's commandment."—Exodus 20:12; Deuteronomy 5:16.

To the crowd that has gathered Jesus calls, "Listen and understand: What comes out of your mouth—not what you put into your mouth—defiles you."

Later, the apostles tell Jesus that he offended the Pharisees. He responds, "Never mind those blind leaders of the blind. When the blind lead the blind, all fall into a ditch."

Peter asks for clarification about what defiles a person. Jesus answers, "Whatever goes into the mouth passes through the stomach and out of the body. But whatever comes out of the mouth originates in the heart."[569] Jesus specifically mentions wicked thoughts, murder, fornication, theft, lies, blasphemy, shameless conduct, pride and jealousy.[570] "These things defile a person," he says, "not eating with unwashed hands."[571]

"Your Faith Is Amazing!"
Matthew 15:21-28; Mark 7:24-30

With his apostles Jesus travels to the regions of Tyre and Sidon in Phoenicia.[572] He locates a house for them to stay in, hoping to remain unrecognized. Even in a foreign land, however, he cannot escape notice. A woman finds Jesus and begs, "Lord, my daughter is possessed by a cruel demon. Have mercy on me, Son of David!"[573]

But Jesus refuses. "I was sent to the straying sheep of Israel, not to anyone else,"[574] he explains. The apostles urge Jesus to send the crying woman away. She falls at Jesus' feet, pleading for his help. Jesus responds, "First I should feed my own family. It wouldn't be right to take food from the children and give it to pets[575]."

The woman observes, "Yes, Lord, but the pets under the table eat the crumbs spilled by the children."[576]

"Your faith is amazing!" Jesus exclaims, assuring her, "The demon has left your daughter." When the woman returns home, she finds her daughter resting in bed and completely well.

Loaves and Leaven
Matthew 15:29–16:12; Mark 7:31-8:21

From Tyre, Jesus and his apostles travel through Sidon to the Sea of Galilee and end up in the Decapolis district.[577] On a mountain, crowds flock to Jesus to hear him and to be healed;[578] among them is a deaf man with speech difficulty.[579] Jesus leads him away from everyone.[580] When they are alone, Jesus puts his fingers into the man's ears; then spits and with his saliva moistens the man's tongue.[581] Looking toward Heaven, Jesus sighs deeply and says, "Open!"[582] At that, the man's hearing is restored, and he can speak plainly. Jesus does not want this miracle publicized, but his wishes are ignored.[583] People are astounded at Jesus' powers, and they glorify "the God of Israel."[584]

Three days later, the provisions are depleted and there is nothing left to eat. Jesus pities the people, telling his apostles, "Some of them live far away and if I send them home hungry, they will have no strength for the journey."

The apostles wonder, "Where will we get enough food out here for so many people?" and inform Jesus that they have just seven loaves of bread "and a few small fish."

Jesus has the people sit on the ground. He offers thanks for the loaves, breaks them and gives them to his apostles. As the apostles serve the people, Jesus says a blessing over the fish; these, too, he gives to his apostles to share with the crowd. More than four thousand people eat to satisfaction.[585] The leftovers collected fill seven large provision baskets.

After Jesus dismisses the crowds, he and the apostles board a boat and cross the Sea of Galilee to Magadan (also called Dalmanutha).[586] Here, Pharisees and Sadducees try to test Jesus with a demand for a miracle. Jesus heaves a heavy sigh[587] and says, "A wicked and unfaithful generation keeps seeking a sign; it will receive no sign except the Sign of Jonah."[588]

Jesus and his apostles get back in their boat and sail toward the opposite shore. Enroute, the apostles discover that they are low on foodstuffs, having just one loaf of bread. Jesus suddenly breaks in with a warning: "Open your eyes and watch out for the leaven of the Pharisees and the Sadducees."[589] The apostles think Jesus refers to their not bringing sufficient bread.[590] "We are not talking about loaves of bread," Jesus corrects. "Do you not yet see the point? Remember how many baskets of scraps you collected when five thousand men were fed with five loaves, and how many large baskets of scraps you collected when four thousand men were fed with seven loaves?[591] How is it you don't understand that I'm not talking about bread?[592] I said, "Watch out for the leaven of the Pharisees and the Sadducees." Finally, the apostles grasp that Jesus is not talking about baker's yeast; he is warning them about the teachings of the Pharisees and the Sadducees.[593]

A Confession Made, A Foundation Laid
Matthew 16:13-23; Mark 8:22-33; Luke 9:18-22

Jesus and his apostles arrive by boat at Bethsaida. People bring a blind man to him and beg Jesus to heal him. Taking the man by the hand, Jesus leads him outside the village. He moistens the man's eyes with saliva and lays his hands on him. "Do you see anything?" Jesus asks.

The man opens his eyes and says, "I see what looks like trees walking about—People!" Jesus lays his hands on the man's eyes, then tells him to open them again. His vision gradually comes into focus until he can see clearly.[594] Jesus sends the man home with instructions to stay out of the village.[595]

During a trip to Caesarea Philippi,[596] the apostles find Jesus alone praying. Just then he asks, "What are people saying about me?"

They reply, "Some believe you're John the Baptist, others think Elijah; still others say that one of the ancient prophets, like Jeremiah, has returned."[597]

Jesus puts the question to them: "And who do you say I am?"

Peter speaks up, "You are the Messiah[598], Son of the living God."[599]

Jesus announces, "Simon, son of Jonah, you are blessed because my Father in Heaven—not any human[600]—revealed this to you. I will build my congregation[601] on this rock, Peter,[602] and the power of Death[603] will not overcome it.[604] Furthermore, I will give you the keys to the kingdom of Heaven. What is locked in Heaven you will lock on Earth; what is unlocked in Heaven you will unlock on Earth."[605]

Jesus charges the disciples to reveal to no one his identity as the Messiah.[606] He foretells that he will suffer at the hands of Jerusalem's community and religious leaders, be killed and, three days later, be raised from the dead.[607]

Peter takes Jesus aside and chides him: "God forbid this should happen to you!"

Jesus turns his back and answers, "Get away from me, you satan![608] You're seeing the human viewpoint, not God's viewpoint. You're a stumbling-stone to me!"[609]

Transfiguration: "The Son of Man Coming in His Kingdom"

Matthew 16:24–17:13; Mark 8:34-9:13; Luke 9:23-37

Followers of Jesus must be willing to give up their desires and even their lives. To the apostles and others Jesus says,[610] "Those who want to save their lives will lose eternal life. But those who sacrifice their lives for me and for the gospel will gain eternal life. What value is there in winning the world but losing eternal life?[611] The Son of Man, when he comes with the angels in his Father's glory,[612] will be ashamed of everyone who is ashamed of me and my teachings. Everyone will then be repaid according to their own works.[613] Truthfully, however, certain ones standing here will not die before they see the Son of Man coming in his kingdom."[614]

About a week later, Jesus takes Peter, James and John up to a lofty mountain.[615] As Jesus prays, his appearance changes—his face shines as the sun;[616] his clothes glisten, looking whiter than fresh snow. Then two figures—Moses and Elijah[617]—appear and talk with Jesus about his "departure."[618] Peter, not realizing what he is saying, suggests, "Teacher, let's put up three tents[619]—one for you, one for Moses and one for Elijah."

While Peter is speaking, a bright cloud envelops them[620] and a voice announces, "This is my beloved Son, with whom I am well-pleased.[621] Listen to him."[622] Hearing the voice of God, the apostles fall on their faces in fear. Jesus draws near and touches them, telling them to get up. They do and see no one except Jesus.

The next day, when they are coming down the mountain,[623] Jesus enjoins the three men, "Tell no one what you saw[624] until the Son of Man is raised from the dead."[625]

The appearance of Elijah raises a question. "Why," the apostles ask, "do the scholars say that Elijah must come before the Messiah appears?"[626]

Jesus replies, “They didn’t even recognize ‘Elijah’ when he came. And as sure as they mistreated him, they will mistreat the Son of Man.” The disciples understand Jesus to be speaking about John the Baptist.[627]

Mountain-Moving Faith
Matthew 17:14-21; Mark 9:14-29; Luke 9:37-43

An excited concourse of people, surprised to see Jesus, welcome him and his three apostles. A party of scholars is criticizing the disciples because they have failed to heal a demon-possessed boy.[628] When Jesus inquires about the dispute, a man in the crowd kneels before him and explains, “Teacher, I beg you to help my son, my only child. An evil spirit seizes him—suddenly he cries out and starts shaking. He foams at the mouth, grinds his teeth and goes stiff. By the time it finally leaves, my boy is beaten and bruised. I pleaded with your disciples to expel the spirit, but they couldn’t.”

“Ah, faithless and misguided ones,”[629] Jesus sighs, “how long must I put up with you?” Jesus tells the father that he will see his son. As the boy approaches Jesus, the demon throws him into a violent convulsion.[630] He writhes on the ground, foaming at the mouth.

“This has been happening to him since childhood,” the father tells Jesus. “The spirit has tried to drown him and throw him into a fire to kill him. Can you do anything? Have mercy and help us if you can.”

“If I can? Anything can be done,” Jesus assures him, “if you have faith.”

“I do have faith!” the father cries. “Help the little faith I have.”[631]

With the crowd looking on, Jesus rebukes the demon: “You mute and deaf spirit,[632] I order you to get out of him and stay out!”

In departing, the demon causes the boy to scream and convulse. Suddenly, the boy is quiet and stops moving. “He’s dead!” some observers say. But Jesus takes his hand and brings him to his feet—he is alive and well! The people marvel at the mighty power of God.

Later, in private, the disciples ask Jesus, "Why couldn't we drive out the demon?"

"Because your faith was weak,"[633] answers Jesus, explaining, "That kind of demon can come out only by prayer." Jesus concludes, "With faith the size of a mustard seed you can tell a mountain to move, and it will move. You can do anything—and that's the truth!"

The mustard seed was used in ancient Hebrew writings as a figure of speech for the very smallest measure of size. (It was evidently the tiniest of seeds gathered and sown by Galilean farmers in Jesus' time, although there are smaller seeds known today.) Using it Jesus emphasized what little faith the disciples had manifested in their effort to heal the possessed boy. Previously they had cast out demons and healed the sick. (Matthew 10:1; Mark 6:7; Luke 9:1-2, 6; 10:17) The power was there but this time they failed to appropriate it. They had a little faith, but it needed to grow. (Matthew 6:30; 8:26; 14:31) Just as the mustard seed, when watered and cultivated, would grow into a tree, so a little faith, when nourished, would grow strong enough to move a mountain. (Matthew 13:32) Jesus could have been speaking of Mount Hermon, site of the Transfiguration. "Mountain," however, may also refer to imposing obstacles to strengthening faith, something as insurmountable and immovable as a literal mountain. (Isaiah 40:4; Zechariah 4:7) Without faith a molehill looks like a mountain, but strong faith shrinks mountains to molehills.

The Greatness of Humility
Matthew 17:22–18:5; Mark 9:30-37; Luke 9:43-48

Leaving Caesarea Philippi, Jesus and his apostles travel alone toward Capernaum.[634] Enroute he tells them, "The Son of Man is going to be betrayed into the hands of killers, but he will be raised up three days later." Saddened and dismayed, the apostles cannot bring themselves to ask Jesus what he means.

In Capernaum, tax collectors for the Temple approach Peter and ask, "Does your teacher pay the Temple tax[635], or not?" Peter hastily replies in the affirmative.[636]

Jesus, aware of what has occurred, later questions Peter: "From whom do kings receive dues or taxes—from their children or from their subjects?"

Peter answers, "From their subjects."

"Then the children are tax-exempt,"[637] Jesus observes. "But we don't want to offend anyone. Now go to the sea, and the first fish you hook will have in its mouth a silver coin[638]—give that to the collectors for both of us."

Later, Jesus asks his apostles, "What were you arguing about on the way here?"

At first the men make no reply. But finally, they present to Jesus a question they have been debating: "Who is the greatest in the kingdom of Heaven?"[639]

Jesus calls a boy and stands him in their midst.[640] With his arms around the tyke, Jesus answers the apostles, "Truthfully, if you don't change your ways and become like little children, you won't even get into the Kingdom. Whoever makes himself as small as this child is the greatest in the kingdom of Heaven;[641] and whoever receives a child like this in my name receives me, too." Jesus concludes, "The lowliest of you all is the greatest."

"Woe to the World for Its Stumbling-stones!"
Matthew 18:6-14; Mark 9:38-48; Luke 9:49-50

John reports to Jesus that he and the other apostles saw someone expelling demons in Jesus' name. "We tried to stop him," says John, "since he is not one of us."

"Whoever is not our enemy is our ally," Jesus responds. "You shouldn't have tried to stop him. Will anyone who performs a miracle in my name say anything against me?[642] Woe to whoever puts a stumbling-stone before[643] one of these humble believers[644]—better for that one to jump into the sea wearing a millstone necklace[645]! Do not despise one of these humble believers, for their angels in Heaven have unfettered access to[646] my Father."

Jesus illustrates every believer's value to God: "If a shepherd has 100 sheep and one of them strays, will he not leave the 99 to search for the one? And if he finds it, he rejoices more over it than over the 99 that have not strayed. And so, our heavenly Father does not want to lose even one of these humble believers."[647]

Jesus says that his followers should get rid of anything that causes them to stumble into sin, even a "hand," a "foot" or an "eye."[648] It is better to be without a cherished thing and live forever than to hold on to it and be destroyed. "Woe to the world," says Jesus, "for its stumbling-stones!"

Peace and Forgiveness
Matthew 18:15-35; Mark 9:49-50

On how to "keep peace with one another"[649] Jesus advises his followers, "If a fellow believer[650] wrongs you, privately discuss the problem together. If you are heard, you have won back a believer. But if you are not heard, bring with you one or two witnesses—their testimony may be needed as evidence.[651] If that does not settle the matter, take it to the congregation.[652] Anyone who pays no heed to what the community of believers has to say should be viewed as an unbeliever[653]." What is thus "bound" on Earth will already have been "bound" in Heaven.[654]—Deuteronomy 19:15.

Peter asks, "Lord, how many times must I forgive my fellow believer? Seven?"[655]

Jesus corrects, "More like seven times seventy!"[656] He then relates a story about an unforgiving slave who fails to imitate his merciful master.

"A king decided to settle accounts with his servants," Jesus begins. "A debtor who owed the king a huge amount[657] appeared before him. Since the servant could not repay, the king ordered him to be sold—along with his wife, his children and his property—as settlement. The debtor sank to his knees, pleading, 'Be patient with me, my lord, and I will pay you back.' Mercifully, the king canceled the debt and let him go. Later, that debtor found one of his fellow servants who owed him a comparably small amount.[658] He grabbed him by the throat, demanding, 'Pay back what you borrowed!' On bended knee the man begged, 'Be patient with me, and I will repay you.' But he refused. Instead, he had the man put in prison until he satisfied the debt. The other servants were horrified by this and reported the whole affair to their master. The king called the unmerciful servant into his presence. 'I pitied you,' said the king, 'and forgave your entire debt because you begged me to.[659] And you have no pity for your fellow servant?' Then his master handed the servant over to the jailers until he paid back the whole debt.[660]

"And that's how my heavenly Father will deal with you," Jesus concludes, "if you don't whole-heartedly forgive your fellow believer."[661]

Who Is Fit for God's Kingdom?
Matthew 8:19-22; Luke 9:51-62; John 7:1-10

Soon the Festival of Tabernacles will be celebrated.[662]` The fulfillment of Jesus' destiny also draws near. He is determined to go to Jerusalem, despite the danger to his life. Jesus' half-brothers, who do not believe that their sibling is the Messiah, encourage him to go to the festival. "Then and there show the world you are who you claim to be," they urge him.[663]

Jesus replies, "Now is not the time.[664] Remember, the world has no reason to hate you; it hates me because my testimony exposes its wicked works. So, you go on to the festival; I'm not going yet."

Sometime after his brothers leave for Jerusalem, Jesus and the apostles depart in secret, through Samaria.[665] He sends messengers ahead to prepare their accommodations. The Samaritans refuse hospitality to these Israelites on pilgrimage to Jerusalem. James and John (the so-called Sons of Thunder; Mark 3:17) angrily ask, "Lord, shall we call down fire from Heaven and annihilate them?" Jesus rebukes the brothers for even suggesting such a thing.[666]

On the road, Jesus meets people who want to follow him but appear unprepared for the demands of discipleship. A scholar approaches Jesus, saying he is willing to follow the Teacher wherever he goes.[667] Jesus advises caution: "Foxes have dens and birds have nests,[668] but the Son of Man has no home of his own."[669]

When Jesus invites a different man to follow him, the man begs off. "When my father dies, allow me to bury him first," he requests.

"Let the dead bury their dead,"[670] answers Jesus. "You go and announce, far and wide, God's kingdom."

Another procrastinator tells Jesus, "I will follow you, Lord, but first let me say good-bye to my family."

Jesus answers, "Once the hand is put to the plow, no one who looks back is fit for God's kingdom."[671]

Jesus Shares His Divine Education
John 7:11-31

"Where is that man?" wonder those who are looking for Jesus in Jerusalem at the Festival of Tabernacles. Although some accuse Jesus of misleading the masses, others believe he is a good man. No one, though, speaks out in his defense for fear of how Judea's leaders will react.

Partway through the festival, Jesus arrives at the Temple and begins teaching. Learned ones are astonished. "How can an uneducated[672] man know the Scriptures so well?" they wonder.

Jesus explains, "The education that I share is not my own; it belongs to the One who sent me.[673] Anyone who wants to do his desire will know whether the education is from God or originates with me. Pretenders praise themselves and seek honor from others. I have no such motives. I seek only the honor of the One who sent me to speak truth on his behalf. Moses gave you the Law, did he not? And yet not one of you obeys the Law." Suddenly, Jesus asks, "Why do you want to kill me?"[674]

"You're possessed!" his learned listeners respond. "Who wants to kill you?"

"A boy can be circumcised on a sabbath so that Moses' law may not be broken," says Jesus. "So why are you angry with me because I healed a man on a sabbath?"[675]

Certain residents of Jerusalem wonder, "Is this the public speaker that the authorities want to kill, this man for whom they have no answer? Have they decided that he is the Messiah after all? When Messiah comes, no one will know where he's from. But we know where this man is from."[676]

"Do you really know me and where I'm from?" Jesus asks in a raised voice. "Well, know this: I have not come of my own accord; the True One sent me—the one you don't know. I know him because he sent me as his representative."

Because it is not yet time for Jesus to die, an attempt to lay hold of him fails. Still, many people put faith in Jesus. "When the Messiah comes, he surely won't perform more miracles than this man!" they insist.

"No One Ever Spoke Like He Speaks"
John 7:32-52

The discussion of Jesus' origin and education eventually comes to the Pharisees' attention; they and the chief priests dispatch officers to arrest Jesus.[677] Meanwhile, he continues speaking in the Temple. "I will be with you a little longer before I return to the One who sent me," Jesus says. "You will look for me, but you will not find me, because where I will be you cannot come."[678]

His listeners do not understand. "Where does this man intend to go," they wonder, "so that we will not find him? Surely, he doesn't mean to go to where our people are scattered among the Greeks and teach the Greeks!"[679]

On the seventh and final day of the festival, Jesus stands up in the Temple and proclaims, "If you are thirsty, come to me and drink.[680] Put faith in me, and from deep within you living water will stream."[681]

Although it is not yet the time for anyone to fully comprehend Jesus' words,[682] some among his listeners recognize him as the Messiah and the Prophet. (Deuteronomy 18:15, 18) Others, however, argue that the Messiah will be a descendant of David from Bethlehem, not from Galilee.[683]—2 Samuel 7:12; Psalm 89:3-4; Micah 5:2.

Some people want Jesus arrested but no one lays a hand on him. When the Temple police return to the priests and Pharisees without Jesus, the religious leaders ask, "Why didn't you bring him in?"

"No one ever spoke like he speaks,"[684] the officers reply.

"Have you been misled too?" the religionists sneer. "Have any rulers or Pharisees put faith in him? No! Only this damned rabble[685] that doesn't know the Law."

Nicodemus, a member of the Sanhedrin who believes in Jesus, speaks up. "The Law does not judge a man before hearing from him and learning about him," he says.

The others retort, "What are you, a Galilean?[686] No scripture says that a prophet will be raised up out of Galilee."[687]

"CAST THE FIRST STONE."—JOHN 8:7.[688]

Early the next morning Jesus returns to the Temple. A crowd quickly gathers, and Jesus sits down to teach them. As he speaks, scholars and Pharisees bring forward a woman whom they have caught in the act of adultery. They stand her in front of everyone and tell Jesus what she has done. "The law of Moses says to stone her," they remind Jesus. "What do you say?"—Deuteronomy 22:22-24.[689]

Without uttering a word, Jesus leans forward and draws in the dust with his finger. The religious leaders demand an answer. Looking up Jesus says, "Let the one who has never sinned cast the first stone." He resumes drawing in the dust.

One by one the woman's accusers slip away. Finally, only the woman and Jesus remain in the middle of the crowd. Looking up again Jesus asks the woman, "Where did they go? Didn't even one of them condemn you?"

"No, sir," she answers.

"Neither do I. Be on your way and sin no more."

"The Truth Will Set You Free"
John 8:12-59

Jesus continues teaching at the Temple.[690] "I am the light of the world,"[691] he announces. "Whoever follows me will possess the light of life and never walk in the darkness of death."

The Pharisees object: "Here you are, appearing as your own witness. Your testimony is invalid."

Jesus acknowledges that the Law states, "The testimony of two men is true,"[692] and continues, "I testify about myself, and so does the Father who sent me."

"And where is your father?" the Pharisees ask.

"If you knew who I am, you would also know who my Father is," Jesus answers. "I am going away. You will look for me but not be able to follow me, and you will die in your sin."

The Pharisees wonder if he intends to 'go away' by means of suicide. "I came from the realms above," Jesus explains. "This world is your home, not mine. And you will die in your sin because you do not believe that I am who I am."[693]

"Well, who are you?" they ask.

"Once you have lifted up the Son of Man,"[694] Jesus replies, "you will know who I am and that I do nothing on my own authority—I speak only what the Father taught me. And the One who sent me is with me because I always do what pleases him."

To the people who claim to believe in him, Jesus says, "My true disciples continue in my teaching. You will learn the truth, and the truth will set you free."[695]

But some protest, "We are Abraham's descendants and have never been anyone's slaves.[696] How can you tell us that we will be set free?"

Jesus points out, "Anyone who continues to sin is, in fact, sin's slave. A slave, moreover, has no permanent place in the master's house; the son, on the other hand, remains forever. If the Son sets you free, then you will be truly free."[697]

Jesus acknowledges Abraham as the forefather of the Israelites. "But," he says, "you want to kill me because there's no room in your hearts for my message. As I speak what I learned from my Father, so you act as you were taught by your father."

"Abraham is our father," insist the Pharisees.

Jesus replies, "If you are Abraham's children, do Abraham's deeds.[698] You're trying to kill me, a man who told you the truth he heard from God. Abraham wouldn't do this. You're doing your father's deeds."

"We are not bastards!"[699] they protest. "God is our one and only Father."

Jesus answers, "If God were your Father, you would love me, for I came here from God. Your father is the Devil,[700] the father of all liars and a murderer from the start.[701] I, on the other hand, tell you the truth but you don't believe me. A child of God listens to what God says. You are not God's children—that's why you don't want to hear the truth."

The Pharisees insult Jesus, calling him a demonized Samaritan.[702] "I am not possessed," Jesus responds. "I honor my Father, but you dishonor me." Then he promises: "Whoever observes my teaching will never know what it means to die."[703]

"Now we know you're possessed!" the Pharisees gloat. "Are you better than Father Abraham? He died. The prophets died. Who do you think you are?"

"Abraham delighted at the thought of seeing my day," Jesus tells them, "and he did see it and rejoiced."[704]

The Pharisees scoff, "You are not yet fifty years old, and you expect us to believe that Abraham saw you?"

"Truthfully," Jesus answers, "I existed before Abraham was even born."[705]

The Pharisees pick up stones to throw at Jesus, but he escapes unharmed.[706]

"To Make the Sightless See, to Make the Sighted Blind"
John 9:1-41

One Sabbath Day, Jesus and his disciples encounter a beggar who has been blind from birth.[707] The disciples ask Jesus, "Teacher, for whose sin was this man born blind—his own or his parents'?"

"Neither!"[708] answers Jesus. "This is an opportunity for a man to benefit from the work of God. His works I must perform while it is daytime. Soon it will be nighttime when no one can work.[709] But for as long as I am in the world, I am its light."

Jesus spits on the ground and with the saliva makes a paste.[710] He dabs a little mud on the man's eyes and sends him to wash in a pool called Siloam.[711] The man goes away blind and comes back sighted![712] His neighbors and others are amazed and ask him what happened. He replies, "The man called Jesus made clay, smeared it on my eyes and told me to wash in the pool. I did as he said and now, I can see!"

The people would like to meet this miracle-worker, but the beggar does not know where Jesus has gone. They take him to the Pharisees, who want to hear how he gained sight.[713] The man retells his experience with Jesus, and the opinion of the Pharisees is divided. "This Jesus is not a man of God," some claim, "because he doesn't observe the Sabbath."[714] Others wonder how a lawbreaker could perform such a miracle.

The Pharisees ask the beggar what he thinks about Jesus. He answers, "The man is a prophet."

Unconvinced, the Pharisees decide to interrogate the beggar's mother and father. The parents appear before the Pharisees, knowing that anyone who acknowledges Jesus as the Messiah faces excommunication.[715] Under questioning they respond, "Yes, this is our son who was born blind. But we do not know who opened his eyes or how. Ask him. He is of age and can speak for himself."[716]

The Pharisees demand the truth, telling the beggar, "This Jesus is a sinner, and we know it!"

"I don't know if he's a sinner," says the beggar. "I only know that I was blind but can see now."

The Pharisees continue, "How did he do it? What did he do?"

The man replies, "I told you already. Weren't you listening? Why do you want to hear it again? Because you want to become his disciples, too?"

"You may be that man's disciple," the Pharisees charge, "but we are Moses' disciples. We know that God spoke to Moses, but we don't know who sent this Jesus here."

"You don't know who sent him here," the beggar wonders, "this man who opened my eyes? Remarkable! We know that God doesn't listen to sinners. God listens to those who fear him and do his will. We also know that no one has ever given sight to one born blind. Could this man do such a thing if he were not sent here by God?"[717]

The Pharisees revile the beggar: "You sinner![718] You dare try to teach us?" Then they throw him out.[719]

When Jesus hears what happened, he finds the beggar and asks, "Do you believe in the Son of Man?"

The beggar responds, "Tell me who he is, sir, so that I may show my faith in him."

"You have met him," says Jesus. "In fact, he is talking with you now."

The man replies, "Lord, I believe," and kneels before Jesus.[720]

"It is for judgment that I have come into this world," Jesus states, "to make the sightless see, to make the sighted blind."[721]

Some Pharisees who happen to be on the scene ask defensively,[722] "So now we are blind?"

"If you were blind," Jesus answers, "you would be guilty of no sin. But you are in fact guilty because you claim that you can see."[723]

The Good Shepherd
John 10:1-21

Illustrating the Pharisees' unfitness to feed God's flock,[724] Jesus allegorically draws on sheep and sheepfolds.[725] "I tell you the solemn truth," he begins, "only a thief or a robber would enter a sheepfold by any way except the door.[726] The shepherd of the sheep enters through the door—to him the doorkeeper opens;[727] to his voice the sheep listen. As he calls them by name and leads them out, they follow him because they recognize his voice.[728] A stranger they would never follow—in fact, they would run from him—because they don't recognize his voice."[729] The willfully blind Pharisees fail to see themselves in the illustration.

"I am the door for the sheep," Jesus continues. "Those who came before me were thieves and robbers;[730] the sheep did not obey them. Whoever enters through me—the door[731]—will be saved; he will go in and out and find pasturage. The thief comes only to steal, slay and destroy. I have come that they may have life—and have it abundantly! I am the good shepherd, who lays down his life for the sheep.[732] But the hired hand abandons the sheep and runs when he sees the wolf coming—and the wolf snatches them and scatters them.[733] He is a hired hand, not a shepherd—he doesn't care for the sheep and the sheep do not belong to him.[734] I, the good shepherd, know my sheep and my sheep know me, just as the Father knows me and I know the Father. He loves me because I surrender my life, so that I may receive it again. No one takes my life away from me; I surrender it voluntarily. I have authority to surrender it, and I have authority to receive it again.[735] This commandment I received from my Father."

The Pharisees' opinion about Jesus remains divided. (John 9:16) Many of them call Jesus demonized; others answer that "a demon cannot open blind people's eyes."

Coming Soon: God's Kingdom
Luke 10:1-24

After the journey to Jerusalem, Jesus dispatches a large number of disciples to places where he might follow. As he did when preparing his 12 apostles to preach in Galilee the previous year, Jesus provides instructions for these evangelizers.[736]

"Do not carry a purse or a traveler's bag or an extra pair of footwear,"[737] says Jesus, "and do not stop to greet anyone you may encounter on the road.[738] When you enter a home, first pronounce a blessing of peace. If a child of peace is there, your peace will rest there—if not, it will return to you.[739] The worker is worth his wage so stay at that house and accept their hospitality. Do not move from home to home.[740] Also, when you enter a city where they receive you, eat what is set before you, heal the sick there, and tell them, 'God's kingdom is upon you.'

"When you enter a city where they do not receive you," Jesus continues, "go into its main streets and say, 'The dust of your city that sticks to our feet we wipe off to your shame.[741] But know this: God's kingdom is near.' Judgment Day will be more bearable for Sodom than for that city."

Jesus dismisses his disciples with a reminder: "Whoever listens to you listens to me; whoever rejects you rejects me. And whoever rejects me rejects the One who sent me."—See Matthew 10:40.

After their mission, the evangelizers return to Jesus. "By the use of your name, Lord," they tell him, "even the demons yield to us!"[742]

Jesus encourages them to rejoice, not because wicked spirits submit to them, but because their "names have been recorded in Heaven."[743] He announces, "Already I can see Satan falling like lightning from the sky![744] See, I have given you authority over the Enemy's every power, to trample underfoot 'serpents' and 'scorpions'[745]—absolutely nothing will harm you."

Jesus praises the Father for using his humble servants in such a mighty way.[746] The disciples truly are blessed to see and hear things the like of which God's servants of old could only wish to have witnessed and heard!—1 Peter 1:10-12.

The Good Samaritan
Luke 10:25-37

A lawyer puts to Jesus a testing question:[747] "What must I do to inherit eternal life?"[748]

Jesus responds, "What do you understand the Law to teach?"

The man quotes from the Torah:[749] "Love JEHOVAH your God with all your heart, and with all your soul,[750] and with all your might";[751] and "love your neighbor as you love yourself."[752]—Deuteronomy 6:5, *New Heart English Bible:* Jehovah Edition; Leviticus 19:18, *The Voice Bible.*

Jesus commends the man: "Correct. Do just so and endless life will be yours."—See Leviticus 18:5.

Seeking to justify himself, the man asks, "Just who is my neighbor?" Jesus takes up the question by telling a short story.

"A man traveled from Jerusalem to Jericho,"[753] Jesus begins. "He encountered robbers, who took everything he had, beat him and left him for dead. Now it just so happened that a priest was going down the same road. When he saw the injured man, he crossed to the other side of the road and continued on his way. Likewise, a Levite came by that spot and saw the man; he, too, crossed to the other side of the road and kept going.[754]

"A Samaritan, who was on a journey, came to where the injured man lay. The sight of him moved the Samaritan to help him, bandaging his wounds and treating them with oil and wine.[755] Then he placed the man on his donkey, took him to an inn,[756] and cared for him. The next day, he gave two days' worth of wages[757] to the innkeeper, saying, 'Take care of the man, and when I return, I will reimburse you for any additional costs.'"

Now Jesus asks the lawyer, “Which of these three men was a neighbor to the victim of the robbers?”

“The one who showed him kindness,”[758] the lawyer replies.

“Go,” Jesus urges, “and do the same.”

Israelites would view themselves as righteous for treating their own countrymen kindly. However, they gave themselves permission to treat foreigners unkindly because a Gentile was not a true neighbor. In asking "Who is my neighbor?" the lawyer sought to limit his responsibility to love by suggesting that some people were not his neighbor. Had Jesus simply told him that foreigners also were his neighbors, the lawyer and other Israelites listening would likely not have accepted that. However, from a simple story with details that the listeners can identify with, the answer to the question becomes obvious: a true neighbor is someone who shows mercy. Jesus, in essence, was saying, 'Don't think about who they are; think about who you are. Ask not "Who is my neighbor?" but "Whose neighbor am I?"'

Priorities
Luke 10:38–42

Coming to the village of Bethany,[759] Jesus pays a call on sisters Martha and Mary.[760] Martha sets to work preparing an elaborate meal.[761] Mary, meanwhile, sits at Jesus' feet and listens to him teach.[762] In time, Martha complains to Jesus: "Lord, don't you care that my sister is letting me do all the work? Tell her I need help."

Jesus counsels, "Martha, Martha,[763] you let unimportant details distract you. Just one thing—the most important thing—is necessary. That's what Mary chose, and I will not take it away from her."[764]

Persistence
Luke 11:1-13

One of his disciples, after hearing Jesus pray, asks, "Will you teach us how to pray, Lord?"[765]

Jesus responds with an abbreviation of the model prayer from his Sermon on the Mount:[766]"Father,[767] may your name be sanctified. Let your reign begin.[768] Give us bread daily according to our needs. Forgive our sins, as we forgive our debtors[769]; and lead us away from temptation."

Illustrating the importance of persisting in prayer, Jesus continues: "It is midnight, and you go to your neighbor and say, 'My friend who is on a journey just dropped in. Lend me three loaves—I'm out of bread.' From inside his house your neighbor replies, 'Stop bothering me. The door is locked, and my children are in bed with me.[770] I can't get up and give you bread.' Eventually, however, your neighbor will get up and give you as much bread as you need—not because he is a good neighbor but because of your persistence."

Jesus concludes, "Keep asking, and you will receive; keep seeking, and you will find; keep knocking, and the door will be opened. Everyone asking receives, everyone seeking finds, and to everyone knocking, the door will be opened."

“KEEP ASKING, AND YOU WILL RECEIVE.”—Luke 11:9.

As reflected in Jesus’ illustration, hospitality was a duty and an honor in Middle Eastern culture. Even though the traveler arrived unexpectedly and late (suggesting the uncertainties of travel at that time), the host felt compelled to feed him, even if that meant disturbing his neighbor to borrow bread. The persistent host does not feel ashamed or hold back from asking his friend for what he needs; in praying to God, we should be just as persistent.

God does not fulfill all our wants, but he gives us the good that we need. If an imperfect human parent gives to his or her children what is good for them, how much more so will our heavenly Parent give us the good things we pray for!—Luke 11:13; Matthew 7:11.

"Hear God's Word and Keep It"
Luke 11:14-36

When Jesus drives out of a man a demon that prevents him from speaking, onlookers are amazed. Skeptics, however, are ready with a standard accusation: "This man expels demons by the power of their ruler."[771] Others try to test Jesus with a demand for a sign from Heaven.[772]

"If I expel the demons by the power of their ruler," Jesus responds, "by whose power do your exorcists[773] expel them?" Illustrating that he expels demons by the power of God,[774] Jesus says, "When a strong, well-armed man guards his house, his possessions are safe. But when a stronger man attacks and overpowers him, he takes away the strong man's trusted weapons and divides the spoils.[775]

"Whoever is not with me is against me," Jesus declares, "and whoever does not help me gather is actually scattering."[776]

One of Jesus' female listeners is moved to exclaim, "The woman who birthed you and nursed you is blessed indeed!"[777]

"The ones who are blessed," Jesus corrects, "are those who hear God's word and keep it."

Regarding the demand for a sign, no miraculous proof will be given to this "evil generation" but "the sign of Jonah. As Jonah was a sign to the Ninevites," says Jesus, "the Son of Man will be a sign to this generation. On Judgment Day, when this generation is on trial, the Ninevites will rise and condemn it because they repented at what Jonah preached. Now one greater than Jonah is here."[778]

Jesus has words of warning for his dark-minded critics. "No one lights a lamp and then hides it under a basket," he says. "A lamp belongs on a lampstand so that those in the room may see. Your body has a lamp, the eye.[779] When your eye is clear, your body is full of light; but when it is defective, your body is darkened.[780] Beware, then, that the 'light' in you is not really darkness."

Woe to the Hypocrites!
Luke 11:37-54

A Pharisee invites Jesus to dine with him and he accepts.[781] After taking his place at the table, however, Jesus does not ritualistically wash.[782] Noticing his host's surprise, Jesus remarks, "You Pharisees scrupulously clean the outside of the cup and dish, but inside you there is nothing but greed and wickedness. Fools![783] Did not the One who made the outside make the inside, too? To be completely clean, give as charity the qualities of the heart[784].

"Woe to you Pharisees!" Jesus continues. "You tithe your mint and rue and every other herb but disregard God's love and justice.[785] You should have practiced the latter without leaving the former undone. Woe to you for loving the best seats[786] in the synagogues and the greetings in public[787]. You're like unmarked graves that people walk on without realizing what corruption is underneath their feet.[788] Woe to you!"

One of the legal scholars who are present complains, "Teacher, you have insulted us, too, in what you just said."[789]

"And woe to you lawyers!" Jesus responds. "You crush people under unbearable burdens without lifting a finger to help them.[790] Woe to you for building memorial tombs for the prophets killed by your own forefathers.[791] This generation will be charged with spilling all the prophets' blood![792] Woe to you for taking away the key to knowledge. You did not enter the Kingdom, and you hinder those who are on their way in."[793]

As Jesus departs, his critics assail him with questions. They want to provoke Jesus into saying something for which they can have him arrested.

Treasures New and Old from the Teacher's Storehouse
Luke 12:1-13:9

In the meantime, an immense crowd has gathered to hear Jesus. The Teacher alternates between addressing the people in general and his disciples specifically.[794]

"First and foremost," Jesus exhorts his followers, "watch out for the leaven—the hypocrisy—of the Pharisees."[795] Such self-deception will be exposed, so there is no need to fear other humans; rather, Jesus' followers must fear God, who holds their lives in his hands. (Romans 2:16; 1 Corinthians 4:5; 1 Timothy 5:24-25; Hebrews 4:13) Illustrating the heavenly Father's care for his followers, Jesus tells them, "Five small birds cost two coins[796] yet God remembers each one. Even the number of hairs on your heads he knows.[797] So do not fear—you are worth more than many birds." Jesus' followers have no reason to fear identifying themselves publicly as such. "Whoever acknowledges the Son of Man," says Jesus, "the Son of Man will acknowledge to God's angels." If they are brought before religious inquisitions or governmental authorities, the disciples will not have to worry about what to say in their defense because God's spirit will give them the right words at the right time.

A man in the crowd interrupts: "Teacher, tell my brother to share his inheritance with me."

Jesus asks the man, "Who appointed me judge or arbitrator between you two?"[798] He warns the brothers to "guard against greed[799] because an abundance of possessions does not give life." Jesus illustrates his point with a parable.

"A rich man's land yielded abundantly," Jesus begins, "and he thought to himself, 'What now? I don't have room for this harvest. I know! I'll tear down my storehouses and build bigger ones—big enough to gather all my grain. Then, with many goods laid up for many years, I will take it easy—eat, drink and be merry.' But God said to him, 'Fool![800] Tonight, you will pay for your arrogance with your life! Then who will have the goods you stored up?' And so it goes for people who amass wealth for themselves but are poor in God's eyes."[801]

Turning his attention back to the disciples, Jesus counsels, "Don't be anxious about sustenance and covering[802]—there are more important things than food and clothing. Consider the ravens: they neither sow nor reap, they have neither storehouse nor barn, but God feeds them.[803] You are much more valuable than birds! Can anxiety add a single hour to your life?[804] If it can't, why be anxious about anything? Consider how the wildflowers grow: they neither work nor weave; yet, even Solomon in all his splendor was not attired as one of these. That's how God dresses the grass—grass that's in the field today and fueling the oven tomorrow. How much more ready will he be to dress you of little faith![805] So stop worrying about what you will eat or wear—about such things there's no need to feel unsettled.[806] The nations of the world worry about these things. Your Father knows that you need them, and he will supply them to you as you continually seek his kingdom."[807]

Jesus assures his disciples, "Your Father delights to give you the Kingdom." He admonishes them to sell their belongings and give to the poor.[808] Inexhaustible treasure awaits in Heaven, "where no thief gets near, which no moth consumes. For where your treasure is," says Jesus, "your heart is, too."

Furthermore, the disciples need to "be dressed and ready like servants waiting for their master to return from his wedding,[809] so when he comes and knocks, they may immediately open the door. Those slaves are happy," says Jesus, "because the master finds them on alert. The master himself will dress for service and will serve them at his table."[810] Jesus brings himself into the illustration: "The Son of Man is coming at a time that you don't expect him. Be alert!"[811]

Peter asks, "Are you telling this illustration to everyone, Lord, or just to us?"[812]

Jesus explains that his illustration is for "the trustworthy and wise servant,[813] the one whom his master will charge with giving timely sustenance to his domestics.[814] If the master comes and finds him faithful to his duty," says Jesus, "that happy servant will be appointed over everything the master has.[815]

"However," Jesus warns, "if that servant ever thinks to himself, 'My master is late,' and gets drunk and mistreats the other servants, the master will come unexpectedly, severely punish that slave, and condemn him with the untrustworthy ones." Much will be demanded of the one to whom much was entrusted.

The "fire" of divine judgment will soon begin to burn.[816] Jesus expands his warning to include "hypocrites" who fail to understand "signs of the times." Some people in the crowd bring up certain Galileans who were killed by Judea's governor Pontius Pilate.[817] Jesus responds, "You too will die unless you repent." He frames another tragedy as a warning: "Those 18 people killed when the tower in Siloam collapsed on them[818]—do you think that they were worse sinners than everyone else in Jerusalem?[819] Well, they weren't. But unless you repent, you too will die."

Jesus concludes this discussion with another parabolic warning: "A man plants a fig tree in his vineyard. For three years he looks for fruit but finds none.[820] Finally, he says to his vinedresser, 'Cut it down! Why should it waste the ground any longer?'[821] The vinedresser replies, 'Master, let the tree stand for one more year. If I dig around it and fertilize it, perhaps the tree will bear fruit. But if it doesn't, it will be cut down.'"[822]

Disabled by the Devil
Luke 13:10-22

One Sabbath day, Jesus is teaching in a synagogue. He sees a woman crippled for many years by disability—she is bent forward, unable to stand straight.[823] As he lays his hands on her, he says, "You are released from your infirmity." Instantly, she stands straight and praises God!

This upsets the director of the synagogue, who scolds the congregation. "There are six working days—come and be healed on one of them," he says, "not on the Sabbath."[824]—Exodus 20:9-10; Deuteronomy 5:13-14.

Jesus responds, "Hypocrites! Each one of you unties your bull or donkey from the stall and leads it to drink on the Sabbath. Was it wrong for this daughter of Abraham tied up by Satan for eighteen years to be released on the Sabbath?"

Jesus' opposers feel shame but the crowds celebrate everything they see him do. Answering their joy, Jesus directs them to God's kingdom, comparing it to a mustard seed that grows into a tree, and to leaven mixed into batches of flour which causes the dough to rise.[825]

Jesus continues teaching as he travels through cities and villages enroute to Jerusalem.

"The Father and I Are One"
John 10:22-42

Jesus has come to Jerusalem for the Festival of Dedication.[826] As he walks in the Temple in Solomon's Colonnade,[827] his persistent critics surround him and demand, "If you are the Messiah, say, 'I am the Messiah.' You've kept us in suspense long enough!"

"The deeds that I am doing in my Father's name speak for me," Jesus responds. "You don't accept my credentials because you're not my sheep. My sheep obey my voice and follow me. I know them and give them eternal life—they will never be destroyed. No one will snatch them out of my hand because they were given to me by my Father, who is greater than all, and no one can snatch them out of his hand. You see, the Father and I are one."[828]

Jesus' words so anger his critics that they pick up stones to throw at him. "For which of my good deeds are you going to stone me?" Jesus wants to know.

They reply, "We are not stoning you for anything you did, but for what you just said. You make yourself out to be God[829], you blasphemer!"

Jesus answers, "Certain men whom God speaks to in the Scriptures[830] are called 'gods.'[831] Yet you accuse the Son of God, whom the Father sanctified and sent into the world, of blasphemy? If I'm not doing my Father's work, don't be convinced. But if I am, let the deeds convince you where I cannot. You may see clearly and be certain that the Father and I are in union with one another."—Psalm 82:6.

They attempt to capture Jesus, but he escapes,[832] leaving Jerusalem and crossing the Jordan River to Bethany, where John the Baptist began his ministry years earlier. (John 1:28) Crowds come to Jesus, declaring, "John did not perform a single sign, but everything he said about this man is true." Thus, many people put faith in Jesus.

Jerusalem, "Your House Is Abandoned to You!"
Luke 13:23–35

As Jesus continues his teaching travels, a man approaches him and asks, "Is it just a few, Lord, who will be saved?"[833]

Jesus shifts the issue from how many will be saved to what must be done "to enter through the narrow door" into salvation. "Strain every nerve,"[834] he says, "because many will try to enter but fail.[835] After the head of the house locks the door, many will stand outside knocking and pleading, 'Sir, open the door! We ate and drank with you. You taught in the streets of our town.' But he will answer, 'I don't know you.[836] Get out of here, all of you—you and your wicked ways!' From outside—amidst all the weeping and teeth-grinding[837]—you will see Abraham, Isaac, Jacob and all the prophets in God's kingdom. With them, people will come from everywhere to dine[838] in the Kingdom. The last will be first, the first will be last."[839]

Pharisees approach Jesus and warn him that Herod Antipas means to take his life.[840] Jesus responds, "You can tell the old fox that I will continue driving out demons and healing people until I am finished."

Jesus will return to Jerusalem because, as he says, "it is unacceptable for a prophet to meet his death anywhere but Jerusalem."[841] The city will not see him again, however, until the day when she blesses the one "coming in the name of Jehovah."—Psalm 118:26, Young's *Literal Translation*.

Happy to Dine in God's Kingdom
Luke 14:1-24

A prominent Pharisee invites Jesus to his house for a Sabbath meal.[842] The other guests watch closely to see what Jesus might do about a man present who suffers from edema.[843] Jesus questions the Pharisees and the Law experts: "Is it legal to heal on the Sabbath or not?" The experts make no reply. Jesus heals the man and sends him on his way. "Who of you," Jesus asks, "if your child or animal falls into a pit on the Sabbath, will not immediately rescue it?" Again, nobody answers.

Jesus observes the other guests choosing exalted stations in the dining room. "Don't take the most prominent place when you're invited to a reception," he counsels. "If someone more important has also been invited, the host will come to you and say, 'Let this guest have your place.' Then you will have to sit embarrassed at the lowest place. When you receive an invitation, go to that lowest place. Your host will come and say to you, 'Friend, take the most prominent place.' Then you will be honored before the other guests. Those who exalt themselves will be humbled, and those who humble themselves will be exalted."[844]

Jesus gives his host a lesson in spiritual etiquette. "When you hold a banquet, don't invite your friends or family, or even your rich neighbors—the ones who will repay your hospitality. Instead," Jesus advises, "invite the poor, the crippled, the lame, the blind—the ones who can't repay you. You'll be happy now and later be rewarded in the resurrection of the righteous ones."[845]

A fellow guest concurs, "Happy is the one who dines in God's kingdom!" But that prospect is not prized by all, as Jesus illustrates with a story.

"A man invited many people to a banquet," Jesus begins. "When he sent out his servant to announce that everything was ready, all the guests began to beg off. One said to the servant, 'Please excuse me. I bought a field and must go out to see it.' Another said, 'Have me excused because I bought five teams of cattle and am going to examine them.' Still another said, 'I can't come because I just got married.'[846] The servant reported all this to his master. The master, his anger stirred, said to the servant, 'Quickly go to the city's main streets and alleys, and bring in here the poor, the crippled, the lame and the blind .'[847] After the master's orders had been carried out, his servant reported, 'There's room for more.' The master said, 'Go out to the highways and byways and compel people to come in, so that my house may be filled. Not one of those who were first invited will taste my banquet!'"[848]

The Cost of Discipleship
Luke 14:25-35

A crowd of people follows Jesus. He explains to them what it means to follow him to the full. "Anyone who comes to me," he says, "but does not love less[849] parents, spouse, children, siblings—even life itself—cannot be my disciple; nor can anyone who is not prepared to follow in my steps to their own death." He adds, "If you can't bear the cost of parting with your possessions, you can't be my disciple."[850] He illustrates what it means to count the cost of discipleship.

"If you intend to erect a tower," says Jesus, "first you figure out the expense to see if you can afford to build.[851] Otherwise, you might lay its foundation but not be able to complete it, and onlookers will ridicule you for not finishing what you started. A king, before marching out to war against another king, first considers if his 10,000 troops can stand up to his enemy's 20,000. He might decide instead to send an ambassador to sue for peace."[852]

Discipleship without sacrifice is meaningless,[853] as salt without flavor is useless. Tasteless salt "is good neither for soil nor for manure,"[854] Jesus observes. "People throw it out."

Lost and Found
Luke 15:1-32

Pharisees and scholars notice that social outcasts, such as tax collectors, are drawn to Jesus. "This man welcomes sinners and even eats with them,"[855] the religious leaders grumble. With three parables Jesus illustrates that a sinner's repentance is a cause for joy, starting with a question about a lost ***sheep.***

"Who among you with a hundred sheep will not leave 99 behind to search for the one that gets lost?" Jesus asks. "When a shepherd finds a lost sheep, he puts it on his shoulders and carries it home, rejoicing.[856] Then he calls his friends and neighbors together and invites them to rejoice with him. Likewise, there is more joy in Heaven over one sinner who is recovered[857] than over 99 righteous ones who never strayed."[858]

Jesus' second illustration concerns a lost ***coin:*** *"*What woman with ten silver coins does not light a lamp[859] and scour[860] the house, searching diligently until she finds the one coin she lost?[861] When she finds it, she calls her friends and neighbors together and invites them to rejoice with her. There is similar rejoicing among God's angels when one sinner is recovered."

Finally, Jesus relates a parable about a lost ***son:*** "A man had two sons. The younger one said to his father, 'Give me now my share of your estate.' The man divided his belongings between the brothers.[862] A few days later, the younger son moved to a distant country where he squandered his inheritance with prodigal living[863]. He was already destitute and facing starvation when a severe famine struck that country. He even accepted work herding pigs for one of the local landowners. He was almost reduced to eating the carob pods that he fed to the pigs.[864] 'I'm starving,' he said to himself, 'while my father's hired hands have more than enough to eat!'

"In the son's calamity and despair, he came to his senses and decided to go home. The father saw his son approaching from a distance and took pity on him. He ran to embrace his son and covered him with kisses.[865]

Then the son said, 'Father, I have sinned against Heaven and against you. I am no longer worthy of being called your son. Please take me on as a hired hand.'[866]

"As if he had not heard what his son said, the father ordered his servants to clothe the boy with his best robe and to put a ring on his hand and sandals on his feet.[867] 'Slaughter the fattened calf,'[868] the father commanded. 'Let's eat and celebrate! My "dead" son has come to life—he was lost and has been found.'

"As the elder son returned from the field and got near the house, he heard music and dancing. He asked one of the servants what was happening. 'Your brother has come home,' said the servant, 'and your father slaughtered the fattened calf because he got him back alive and well.'

"Furious, the elder son refused to attend the celebration. His father pleaded with him to join them. The son answered, 'I have slaved for you, Father, and done everything you told me to for all these years, yet you never threw a party for me and my friends. But when the son who squandered your money on prostitutes came home, you made a banquet in his honor!'"

Jesus ends the story with the father's appeal to his older son: "You have always been with me, and everything I have is yours.[869] But we just had to celebrate and rejoice. Your brother was dead and has come to life—he was lost and has been found."

While all three illustrations in Luke chapter 15 are about loss and recovery, the parable of the prodigal is also concerned with restoration. The son is lost because he chooses to be lost; this loss is not due to following natural inclinations (as in the case of a sheep who strays) or to carelessness (as with someone who loses a coin). In this parable, Jesus highlights the intimate relationship between a father and his sons, portraying the deep compassion and love that the heavenly Father has for his earthly children, both those who remain with him and those who return to him.

In contrast to Christ and his "Gospel to the lost," Israel's religious leaders "had nothing to say to sinners. They called upon them to 'do penitence,' and then Divine Mercy, or rather Justice, would have its reward for the penitent. Christ's Gospel ... told them of forgiveness, of what the Saviour was doing, and the Father purposed and felt for them; and that, not in the future and as reward of their penitence, but now in the immediate present. ... He not only received them when they sought Him, but He sought them, so as to bring them to Him; not, indeed, that they might remain 'sinners,' but that, by seeking and finding them, they might be restored to the Kingdom, and there might be joy in heaven over them."—*The Life and Times of Jesus the Messiah*, page 650.

In the spirit of the older son, the scholars and the Pharisees were critical of the mercy and attention accorded repentant sinners. Their criticism of Jesus for welcoming sinners prompted this parable. Also, the religious leaders took pride in their obedience to tradition, as the older son was proud for never having disobeyed his father. Obedience is important. (1 Samuel 15:22) But sacrifice without mercy is valueless.—Hosea 6:6; Matthew 9:13.

Friends and Riches

Luke 16:1-12

Jesus tells his disciples a story about an estate manager who is accused of mishandling his wealthy master's assets. On the verge of despair, the manager hatches a shrewd plan. He summons his master's debtors, asking them how much they owe. One person's debt he cuts in half; another's he reduces twenty percent.[870] For his business acumen, the steward receives commendation from his master. Now when the steward loses his job, "my friends will welcome me into their homes," he says to himself.

"The children of this world are shrewder than children of the light," observes Jesus, counseling his disciples, "Win friends for yourselves with worldly wealth. Money will lose its value, but you'll have a home with your friends forever."[871]

Trust in minor matters must be earned before trust in important matters is received. Jesus asks his disciples, "If you can't be trusted with worldly wealth, who will entrust you with righteous riches? If you can't be trusted with another's belongings, who will give you something for yourselves?"[872]

Rich Man, Poor Man

Luke 16:13-31

"No servant can slave for two masters," says Jesus. "He will hate[873] one and love the other or stick with one and scorn the other. You can't slave for God and for Gold[874]."

Pharisees scoff and sneer at Jesus' remarks on riches. Jesus responds, "You declare yourselves righteous before men, but God knows your hearts. What is exalted to men is disgusting to God." To these avaricious religious leaders, Jesus relates an illustration.[875]

"There was a rich man,"[876] Jesus begins, "decked in purple[877] and fine linen, who feasted sumptuously day after day. At the rich man's gate sat poor Lazarus, a beggar.[878] He was covered with sores that dogs would lick,[879] and he hungered for scraps from the rich man's table. Well, this beggar died, and angels carried him into Abraham's presence. The rich man also died and was buried. From among the dead[880] he looked up and saw Abraham far away with Lazarus in his arms[881]."

"Father Abraham," the rich man invoked, "have mercy on me! Send Lazarus to me with a drink of water—I'm burning up here!"[882]

Said "Father Abraham" to the rich man, "Remember, my son, that you had good things in your lifetime, while Lazarus suffered the bad. Now he is comforted here, and you are the one in agony."[883]

The rich man begs Abraham to send Lazarus to the house of the rich man's father. "Warn my five brothers about this place!" he pleads.

"They have the warnings of Moses and the Prophets," answers Abraham. "If your brothers aren't moved to repent by Moses and the Prophets, they won't be persuaded by someone risen from the dead."[884]

THE UNRIGHTEOUS STEWARD & THE UNRIGHTEOUS POSSESSOR

The parable of the unrighteous steward was addressed to those "'publicans and sinners' whom Jesus had received, to the great displeasure of the Pharisees (Luke 15:1, 2). Them He would teach concerning the Mammon of the unrighteousness. And, when the Pharisees sneered at this teaching, He would turn it against them, and show that, beneath the self-justification (Luke 16:15), which made them forget that now the Kingdom of God was opened to all (ver. 16), and imagine that they were the sole vindicators of a Law (ver. 17) which in their everyday practice they notoriously broke (ver. 18), there lay as deep sin and as great alienation from God as that of the sinners whom they despised."

In both parables "the subject is Unrighteousness. In the first, ... it is the Unrighteous Steward, making unrighteous use of what had been committed to his administration by his Master; in the second Parable, ... it is the Unrighteous Possessor, who uses only for himself and for time what he has, while he leaves Lazarus, who, in his view, is wretched and sore-covered, to starve or perish, unheeded, at his very door. ... [T]he first Parable points [out] a lesson, while the second furnishes a warning. In the first Parable we are told what the sinner when converted should learn from his previous life of sin; in the second, what the self-deceiving, proud Pharisee should learn as regarded the life which to him seemed so fair but was in reality so empty of God and of love."

By outward righteousness and pretenses, the Pharisees "sought to appear just before men, but God knew their hearts; and that which was exalted among men, their Pharisaic standing and standing aloof, was abomination before Him (ver. 15). These two points form the main subject of the [second] Parable. Its first, object was to show the great difference between the 'before men' and the 'before God;' between Dives as he appears to men in this world, and as he is before God and will be in the next world. Again, the second main object of the Parable was to illustrate that their Pharisaic standing and standing aloof—the bearing of Dives in reference to a Lazarus—which was the glory of Pharisaism before men, was an abomination before God. Yet a third object of the Parable was in reference to their covetousness, the selfish use which they made of their possessions—their Mammon. But a selfish [use] was an unrighteous use; and, as such, would meet with sorer retribution than in the case of an unfaithful steward."—*The Life and Times of Jesus the Messiah*, pages 658, 659, 666-67.

"Increase Our Faith"
Luke 17:1-10

Turning his attention to the apostles, Jesus warns, "Occasions for falling into sin[885] will inevitably come. But woe to the one through whom they come! Better for that one to be thrown into the sea with a millstone[886] hung from the neck than to stumble[887] one of the humble ones.[888] Watch yourselves! If another believer sins, rebuke that one; if there is repentance, forgive. Even if your fellow believer[889] sins against you seven times in one day, you must forgive if that one repents seven times."[890]

The apostles ask Jesus to increase their faith. In response he asks, "Who among you will say to his servant when he finishes his work, 'Come at once and sit down at the table'? Wouldn't you tell him to fix your meal and serve it; and after you've finished, he can eat and drink? Does the master thank the servant for doing what he is assigned to do? When you have done everything assigned to you, say, 'We are humble servants who have only done our duty.'"[891]

Instead of miraculously increasing his apostles' faith, Jesus assures them, "With faith as little as a mustard seed[892] you can say to the black mulberry tree,[893] 'Uproot yourself and plant yourself in the sea!' and it will obey you."[894]

"I Am the Resurrection and the Life"
John 11:1-54

From Bethany[895] in Judea Jesus receives a message: Lazarus, brother of Mary and Martha, is sick. "His illness will not end in death," Jesus declares, "but with glory for God through the Son."[896]

Two days later, Jesus suggests to his apostles returning to Judea. They protest, "Teacher, some Judeans just tried to stone you, and you want to go back?"[897]

In response Jesus asks, "Are there not twelve hours of daylight? No one stumbles when walking in daylight, only when walking at night."[898] Then Jesus announces, "Our friend Lazarus has fallen asleep, but I'm going to wake him up."[899]

The apostles assume that Jesus means Lazarus is resting. "If he's sleeping," they say, "he'll recover."

Jesus tells them plainly, "Lazarus has died. For your sake and for the good of your faith, I'm glad I wasn't there.[900] But now we go to him."

At the risk of their lives, the apostles accompany Jesus on this mission of mercy. By the time they reach the outskirts of Bethany, Lazarus has been dead and buried for four days.[901] His sisters Mary and Martha are mourning; friends and relatives have come from Jerusalem to their home to console them. Then someone tells Martha that Jesus is approaching, and she hurries to meet him.

"Lord," Martha says to Jesus, "if you had been here, my brother wouldn't have died. Yet even now I know that God hears you still."[902]

Jesus assures Martha, "Your brother will rise."

Martha expresses with conviction, "I know he will, in the resurrection on Judgment Day."[903]

"I am the resurrection and the life,"[904] Jesus declares. "The one who demonstrates faith in me, and dies will live again; thereafter, no one living who demonstrated faith in me will die.[905] Do you believe this?"

Martha affirms, "Yes, Lord, I believe that you are the Messiah, the Son of God—the one the world is waiting for!"

Martha hurries home and tells Mary in private that Jesus has arrived and wants to see her. Mary leaves; others, who assume she is going to Lazarus' tomb, follow.[906] When Mary finds Jesus, she crumbles at his feet and weeps. The people who followed her are crying, too. Distressed, Jesus groans and gives way to tears.[907] Onlookers are touched by Jesus' affection for Lazarus. But "if Jesus could open a blind man's eyes," some ask, "could he not save Lazarus from dying?"[908]—John 9:6-7.

Accompanied by Martha and Mary and a crowd of mourners, Jesus comes to the burial chamber of Lazarus—a cave with a stone covering the entrance. Jesus directs that the stone be rolled away but Martha objects: "It's been four days, Lord, and there must be a smell by now."[909]

Jesus reminds her, "Believe, and you will see God's glory."

The stone is removed. Jesus looks heavenward and prays, "Father, thank you for hearing me. Yes, you always hear me; but I speak for the crowd's benefit, that they may believe that you sent me." Then in a loud voice, Jesus cries, "Lazarus, come out!" Swathed in cloth wrappings, Lazarus emerges from his burial chamber. "Remove the grave clothes and let him go,"[910] Jesus orders.

Many eyewitnesses of this miracle put faith in Jesus; others tell the religious leaders what Jesus has done. The Sanhedrin—Israel's supreme court— is called into session. Some Pharisees lament, "Why don't we stop this man who performs so many miracles? Soon everyone will follow him, and the Romans will come and destroy our holy Place and our nation."[911]

High Priest Caiaphas speaks up. "You men know nothing," he berates. "It's better for one man to die for the people than for the whole nation to be destroyed." Thus, Caiaphas unwittingly foretells that Jesus will die for Israel and so unite all of God's scattered children.[912]

From that day forward, the Sanhedrin schemes to assassinate Jesus.[913] With his disciples, Jesus travels to the city of Ephraim,[914] away from his enemies.

THE SANHEDRIN—THEOCRACY'S HIGH COURT

The New Testament word for Sanhedrin was a general term for an assembly or a meeting; it commonly referred to a religious judicial body, or court. In Jesus' day, the Sanhedrin had 71 members—the high priest and 70 of Israel's principal men belonging to the sects of the Pharisees and the Sadducees.—Mark 15:1; Acts 4:5-6; 23:6. See "Who Were the Pharisees and the Sadducees?"

Tradition traces the Sanhedrin's origin to Moses' 70 assistants.[915] (Numbers 11:16-17) As a matter of history, however, it was not until the Persian domination of Israel that something resembling the Sanhedrin of Jesus' time came into existence. Exiles who returned to Judah from Babylon in the sixth century before Christ had a national organization—princes, elders, nobles, deputy rulers—the beginning of a future Sanhedrin.—Ezra 10:8; Nehemiah 5:7.

In accounts of Seleucid domination of Judea, which began in 198 B.C., is found the first reference to a senate of the Jews. This assembly, albeit having limited powers, gave the Judeans a semblance of self-government. The Maccabees shook off Seleucid rule and established the Hasmonaean dynasty. Meanwhile, the scholars and the Pharisees—leaders of the masses who backed the revolt—gained power in state administration at the expense of the priestly class. The Sanhedrin as depicted in the New Testament had begun to take shape.

By the first century, Rome possessed Judea. Apart from appointing and deposing the high priest—who was president of the Sanhedrin—and levying taxes, the Romans intervened in Judea's affairs only when their own sovereignty and interests were at stake.[916] Rome's policy of granting subject peoples considerable self-determination allowed Judeans a measure of freedom. The Sanhedrin thus ran most internal Judean affairs. To justify its privileges,[917] the Sanhedrin had to keep the peace and support Roman rule. If, however, political offenses were suspected, Rome took action.[918]

The court particularly concerned itself with matters involving Jerusalem and its Temple.[919] Strictly speaking, the Sanhedrin's civil jurisdiction encompassed Judea only. But since the Sanhedrin was considered the supreme interpreter of Israel's law, it exerted moral authority in Jewish communities everywhere.[920] Israelites highly esteemed the Sanhedrin, and judges in lower courts were bound, on pain of death, to accept its rulings.

The Sanhedrin was made up of priestly nobles—mainly Sadducees—lay aristocrats and learned men of the Pharisees. The priestly aristocracy, supported by distinguished laymen, dominated the court. Whereas the Sadducees were conservative, the Pharisees were liberal and were chiefly commoners who had great influence with the people. According to the historian Josephus, the Pharisees' demands were reluctantly met by the Sadducees.[921]

Considering the aristocratic nature of the Sanhedrin, membership was probably permanent with vacancies filled through appointments made by existing members.

Since the high court supervised the judiciary of the whole country, it seems logical that men who had distinguished themselves in lower courts would be elevated to a seat in the Sanhedrin. New members had to be men who could produce genealogical records proving the purity of their family tree.

Except on Sabbaths and holy days, the Sanhedrin sat in its decision chamber daily from the morning sacrifice to the evening offering. Trials were held only in the daytime. Since capital sentences were not pronounced until the day following the trial, such cases were not held on the eve of a Sabbath or of a festival. Witnesses were severely admonished regarding the seriousness of spilling innocent blood. Judges of capital cases endeavored to save the defendant during unhurried sessions.[922]

At least a few court members—including Nicodemus, Gamaliel and Joseph of Arimathea—seem to have been principled men. (Matthew 27:57-60; Mark 15:43-46; Luke 23:50-53; John 3:1-2; 7:50-51; 19:38-42; Acts 5:34-39) A rich ruler who Jesus invited to become a follower may have been a member of the Sanhedrin. (Luke 18:18-23) As a body, however, the court was characterized by dishonesty, jealousy, corruption and lust for power. (John 11:47-48; Acts 5:17) In A.D. 70 Rome destroyed Jerusalem and its Temple, bringing an end to the Jewish system of things and eventually to the Sanhedrin itself.

"Where Are the Other Nine?"
Luke 17:11-19

With his disciples, Jesus travels through Samaria and into Galilee.[923] Upon entering one village, he encounters ten people with leprosy.[924] From a distance they cry, "Jesus! Master, have mercy on us!"

Jesus directs them: "Go and present yourselves to the priests."[925] Enroute the lepers begin to see and feel change taking place—they have been restored to health! Nine continue on their way; one, a Samaritan, returns to Jesus. With the man at his feet giving thanks, Jesus wonders aloud, "All ten were healed, were they not? So where are the other nine? It seems this foreigner is the only one who returned to glorify God."

Jesus tells the Samaritan, "Get up and be on your way; your faith has made you whole."[926]

When Will God's Kingdom Come?
Luke 17:20-37

Pharisees ask Jesus when the Kingdom is coming, which they expect will be "with outward show[927]." However, Jesus says, "God's kingdom is in your midst[928]." He warns his disciples: "The time will come when you desire—and desire in vain—to see one of the days of the Son of Man.[929] People will tell you, 'There it is!' or, 'Here it is!' Don't believe them. In his day the Son of Man will be as evident as lightning flashing from one horizon to another."[930]

Jesus compares "the days of the Son of Man" to "the days of Noah"[931] and "the days of Lot." People were obliviously living their lives "until the day Noah entered the ark[932] and the Flood destroyed them all," recounts Jesus. "Likewise, on the day that Lot left Sodom, fire and sulfur rained from the sky and destroyed the Sodomites. It will be the same when the Son of Man is revealed."—Genesis 7:23; 19:24-25.

"On that day," Jesus continues, "a person on the roof whose belongings are inside should not retrieve them.[933] Likewise, a person in the field should not return home for anything. Remember what happened to Lot's wife.[934] Those who try to save their lives will lose them; those prepared to lose their lives will save them.[935] That night two people will be sleeping in a bed; one will be taken along but the other will be abandoned. There will be two people working at the same station; one will be taken along but the other will be abandoned."[936]—Genesis 19:26.

The disciples interpose, "Taken where, Lord?"

"Where the carcass is," answers Jesus, "the eagles will gather."[937]

An Unrighteous Judge, A Self-Righteous Pharisee
Luke 18:1-14

After discussing the tests his disciples will face "when the Son of Man arrives," Jesus illustrates for them the need to persist in prayer.[938]

"In a certain city," he begins, "there was a judge and a widow who approached him repeatedly. 'Give me justice against my adversary-at-law,' she would appeal. At first, he was unwilling to help her, but eventually changed his mind. 'Although I do not fear God or respect anyone,'[939] said the judge, 'I will see that justice is done for this widow; if I don't, she'll keep making trouble and wear me out with her appeal.'"

Directing attention to the words of "the unrighteous judge," Jesus says, "God, patient as he is, will certainly see that justice is done—and done speedily—for his chosen ones who appeal to him day and night.[940] Nevertheless, when the Son of Man arrives, will he find such faith on Earth?"[941]

To those who are self-righteousness and condescending,[942] Jesus teaches a parabolic lesson in humility. "Two men—a Pharisee and a tax collector—went to the Temple,"[943] Jesus relates. "The Pharisee stood and prayed, 'God, I thank you that I am not like other people—extortionists, the unrighteous, adulterers—or even like this tax collector. I fast twice a week.[944] I tithe everything.'[945] Standing at a distance, the tax collector wouldn't even look up but kept beating his chest, saying, 'O God, have mercy on me, sinner of all sinners[946].'"

Jesus concludes, "When these two men went home, only one of them did so with God's approval. Thus, the exalted will be humiliated, but the humble will be exalted."[947]

'Let the Children Come to Me'
Matthew 19:1-15; Mark 10:1-16; Luke 18:15-17

From Galilee, Jesus and his apostles cross the Jordan River and arrive at the frontiers of Judea.[948] People flock to hear Jesus and to be healed. In the crowd are Pharisees who attempt to trap Jesus with a question: "Is it legal for a man to divorce his wife for any reason he wants?"[949]

Jesus responds, "What was Moses' ruling on that?"

"Moses made provision for a man to divorce his wife by giving her a certificate of dismissal,"[950] the Pharisees answer.

"Out of regard for human obstinance," Jesus tells them, "Moses made that concession.[951] In the beginning, however, the Creator of man and woman said, 'Man will leave his parents' home to join with his wife, making the two of them one flesh.' Therefore, let no one separate what God has united."[952] (Genesis 2:24) Jesus adds, "Except in cases of unfaithfulness[953], a divorced man or woman who remarries commits adultery.[954] And those whom they marry are also guilty of adultery."[955]

The apostles are moved to say, "If that's the case, it's better not to marry at all."

Not everyone, however, can remain unmarried. Jesus explains that some men are born eunuchs, some are made eunuchs. Others, however, live as if they were eunuchs, doing so "for the kingdom of Heaven,"[956] and Jesus encourages those who can, to make such use of their singleness.

People begin to bring their children to Jesus for his blessing, only to be stopped by the apostles. Jesus indignantly orders the men not to interfere. "Let the little ones come to me because God's kingdom belongs to the child-like," says Jesus, reminding his followers that "only those who welcome the Kingdom with a child's disposition will enter it." Jesus folds the young ones in his arms and blesses them.[957]

The First and the Last
Matthew 19:16-20:16; Mark 10:17-31; Luke 18:18-30

A prominent and wealthy young man approaches Jesus.[958] On his knees the man asks, "Teacher, what good must I do to inherit eternal life?" If the man wants to live forever, Jesus says he must observe God's commandments. Jesus cites five of the Ten Commandments—concerning murder, adultery, stealing, bearing false witness, honoring one's parents—and then adds another commandment: to love one's neighbor as oneself.[959]—Exodus 20:12-16; Leviticus 19:18; Deuteronomy 5:16-20.

"For my whole life I have kept every one of these commandments," the man answers. "What more can I do?"

Jesus' heart goes out to this man. "For all you have," Jesus tells him, "you lack one thing: treasure in Heaven. Sell your possessions and donate the proceeds to the poor,[960] then come and follow me."[961] The man's heart sinks. As he walks away Jesus observes, "It is easier for a camel[962] to go through a needle's eye than for a wealthy person to enter God's kingdom."[963]

Astounded, the apostles ask, "Who possibly can be saved?"[964]

Jesus looks straight at them and answers, "With God anything is possible."

Unlike the rich young man, the apostles have left everything to follow Jesus. (Matthew 4:20, 22) "So what will be our inheritance?" Peter asks.

"When the world is born anew,"[965] answers Jesus, "and the Son of Man sits down on his glorious throne, you my followers will sit on thrones of your own, ruling over[966] the 12 tribes of Israel. Everyone who has left behind homes, property, even families for me[967]—for the gospel and for the Kingdom—will inherit a hundred times as much—though not without persecution—and have eternal life in the age to come."[968]

Jesus adds, "Many among the first will be last, and the last will be first."[969] Underscoring this statement, Jesus propounds a parable comparing "the kingdom of Heaven" to the owner of a vineyard.

"The landowner went out at daybreak to hire laborers," Jesus begins. "He agreed to pay the men the regular daily wage of a silver coin[970] and sent them to work in his vineyard. Three hours later he went out again and saw some men standing idly in the marketplace.[971] 'Work in my vineyard,' he told them, 'and I will pay you what is fair.'[972] So they went. At midday and again three hours later the employer returned to the marketplace and made similar arrangements. About an hour before sunset, he was back at the marketplace where he saw men standing around. 'Why are you wasting the whole day here doing nothing?' he asked them. 'No one hired us,' they answered. 'Then go and join the other workers in my vineyard,' he told them."

Jesus describes what happened at the close of the workday: "When evening fell, the landowner told his foreman, 'Pay the workers their wages, starting with those who were hired last.' The men who had worked for one hour were paid one silver coin each. The first men to be hired anticipated receiving more; but they too were given one silver coin each. As they took their money, they grumbled against their employer.[973] 'We put in a whole day's work in the hot sun,' they carped to him, 'yet you paid these men who worked for an hour the same as you paid us!' The employer answered the complainers, 'I have not cheated you. You agreed to do a day's work for one silver coin. Now take your money and go. I choose to pay everyone the same, regardless of how long they worked. Don't I have the right to do as I wish with what is mine? Or are you jealous because I am generous?'

"So," Jesus concludes, "the last will be first, and the first will be last."

“INTO THE VINEYARD”—Matthew 20:4.

The Old Testament depicts Israel’s God as the owner of a vineyard, which represents his chosen nation. (Psalm 80:8-9; Isaiah 5:3-4) In Jesus’ illustration, Israelites are likened to contract workers in the vineyard. (Matthew 20:2; compare Romans 3:1-2; 9:4; Ephesians 2:12) The workers without a contract represent Gentiles. The Owner of the vineyard sent Jesus to call these people to work for God as Christ’s disciples. The Israelites viewed these 11th-hour vineyard workers as “last.” (Compare Luke 13:25-30) But it is the unbelieving Israelites who became “last” when their nation was replaced with one producing fruit befitting the Kingdom. Gentile Christians would henceforth be “first.”—Matthew 19:30; 20:16; 21:43; 23:38; Galatians 6:16.

To all who work in his vineyard, God will give all that he has agreed to and more than he has stipulated.

Whoever Wants to Be Great Must Serve

Matthew 20:17-28; Mark 10:32-45; Luke 18:31-34

Enroute to Jerusalem, Jesus confides in his apostles that everything foretold by God's prophets concerning the Messiah is about to be fulfilled. "The Son of Man will be betrayed into the hands of the religious leaders and scholars, who will condemn him to death," warns Jesus. "They will deliver him to foreigners, who will treat him terribly—mocking him, spitting on him,[974] whipping[975] him —ultimately killing him. Three days later, however, he will rise."[976] But the apostles do not understand.[977]

Others are traveling in Jesus' party, among them his aunt Salome, mother of the apostles James and John. (Matthew 27:55-56; Mark 15:40; John 19:25) On their behalf she approaches Jesus, bows before him and requests, "Give my two sons here positions in your kingdom—one sitting at your right hand and one at your left."[978]

To James and John Jesus says, "You don't know what you're asking for. Can you drink from my cup? Can you undergo my baptism?"[979]

"We can!" the brothers assert.

"You will drink from my cup and undergo my baptism,"[980] Jesus affirms. "However, the positions you ask for are not mine to give—that is my Father's prerogative."[981]

On learning about James and John's request, the other apostles are indignant. Jesus calls the twelve together and counsels, "Rulers dominate their nations and the powerful tyrannize over them. Among you, though, whoever wants to be great must be a servant[982], and whoever wants to be first must be a slave; just as the Son of Man came to serve—not to be served—and to surrender his life as the redemption price[983] for many."[984]

"To Seek and to Save the Lost"
Matthew 20:29-34; Mark 10:46-52; Luke 18:35–19:10

In the city of Jericho[985] two blind beggars—one of whom is named Bartimaeus—hear the tramp of many feet and the sound of many voices. "Jesus the Nazarene"[986] and those traveling with him are passing through. The sightless men shout, "Lord! Son of David,[987] take pity on us!" People try to scold them to silence, causing the beggars to cry even louder.

Jesus' attention is aroused, and he asks the two men, "What do you want from me?"

"Lord, we want our sight!" they plead.

Jesus touches their eyes and says with compassion, "Receive your sight. Your faith has saved you."[988] Immediately, the two men can see, and they join Jesus' train of followers.[989] Witnesses to this miracle praise God.

As Jesus walks through Jericho, a crowd surrounds him. Head tax collector Zacchaeus,[990] a short man, scales a sycamore tree so he can see Jesus.[991] Noticing Zacchaeus in the tree, Jesus tells him, "Come down quickly, and I will be your guest today." Zacchaeus climbs down and hurries home to prepare for his visitor.

As Jesus enters Zacchaeus' house, murmurs of disapproval run through the crowd. "He is accepting hospitality from a sinner!"[992] people complain.

However, Zacchaeus vows to Jesus, "I am giving half of my belongings to charity, and I will repay four times[993] whatever I took from anyone I falsely accused[994]."

Jesus announces, "Today salvation has come to the house of Zacchaeus, child of Abraham. The Son of Man has come to seek and to save the lost."

Serving to Increase the Master's Wealth
Luke 19:11-28

Jesus is nearing Jerusalem, and some people believe that Messiah's kingdom reign will soon commence.[995] In response, Jesus propounds a parable about a nobleman who journeyed to a distant land for his coronation as king.[996] Before departing the man summoned ten servants and gave each a piece of silver money,[997] telling them to take care of business in his absence. Jesus says that the nobleman's own countrymen hated him and did not want him for their king. Nevertheless, the nobleman secured his royal authority and returned, whereupon he summoned his servants. "He wanted to know how much more money they had after putting it to use," Jesus relates. "The first servant presented himself and said, 'Sir, the piece of money you gave me to invest has made ten more pieces of money.'

"'You're a good servant,' the king commended. 'Because you have proven trustworthy with one piece of money, I am putting you in charge of ten cities.' The second servant came and said, 'Sir, the piece of money you gave me to invest has made five more pieces of money.' The king said to him, 'You will be in charge of five cities.'"

Jesus continues, "Another servant came, saying, 'Sir, here is your money. I hid it in a handkerchief because I was afraid of you. You are a difficult man who withdraws what he has not deposited and gathers where he has not planted.' The king said to him, 'Your own words condemn you, useless servant. If I am such a difficult man—who picks up what he has not put down and gathers where he has not planted—why didn't you put my money in the bank? I could have at least collected interest when I returned.' Then he told his attendants to give the worthless servant's piece of money to the one with ten pieces of money."

Jesus concludes, "To the one who has much, more will be given. From the one who has little, even that will be taken away."[998] He adds that the nobleman's enemies, who did not want him as their king, were executed.

Jesus resumes his journey to Jerusalem.

Jesus is the nobleman who travels to a distant land—to Heaven—where his Father will give him royal power. His disciples are like the ten servants, using their assets to produce more disciples. Jesus will recognize and bless their loyal efforts. (Matthew 28:19-20) Not all of Jesus' followers have the same circumstances or opportunities to increase the wealth of their master's kingdom. But a "servant" who fails to work will experience loss and will not find a place in that Kingdom. (Matthew 13:12; Mark 4:25; Luke 8:18) Those who oppose Jesus (some even want to kill him) and persecute his disciples make it clear that they do not want Jesus as their king.—John 19:15; Acts 5:40.[999]

Jesus Anointed for Burial

Matthew 26:6-13; Mark 14:3-9; John 11:55–12:11

Many celebrants have arrived in Jerusalem for Passover, having come early to cleanse themselves ceremonially.[1000] Some of these early arrivals gather at the Temple and speculate on whether Jesus will attend the festival. The religious leaders want to arrest Jesus and execute him. In fact, they have ordered that anyone who knows of Jesus' whereabouts must report to them.[1001]

Six days before Passover Jesus is in Bethany.[1002] Lazarus, Martha and Mary spread an evening meal for Jesus and his apostles at the home of one known as "Simon the leper."[1003] While Martha serves the guests, Mary is particularly attentive to Jesus. She breaks open an alabaster case containing about a pound of perfumed oil, pure nard.[1004] Mary pours this precious oil on Jesus' head and feet,[1005] then wipes his feet with her hair. The fragrance fills the house.[1006]

This perceived waste annoys the apostles, in particular Judas Iscariot. "That oil is worth a year's wages[1007]!" he protests. "Why didn't we sell it and give the money to poor people?" But charity is not what concerns this hypocrite—he has been stealing from the apostles' money box.

"You will always have opportunities to help the poor," Jesus tells the apostles. "But you will not always have me.[1008] Don't embarrass Mary. Putting oil on my body was her way of anointing me for burial.[1009] What she did for me was beautiful![1010] Indeed, wherever in the world the gospel is preached, this act will be recounted in her memory."[1011]

Word of Jesus' presence in Bethany brings a large crowd to Simon's house. People want to see, not only Jesus, but also Lazarus, whom he had raised from the dead. Based on that miracle, many are putting faith in Jesus. Now the chief priests conspire to kill Lazarus as well.[1012]

The King Comes to Zion[1013]

Matthew 21:1-11, 14-17; Mark 11:1-11; Luke 19:29-44; John 12:12-19

The next day, Jesus and his apostles leave Bethany and head to Jerusalem for the Passover celebration. As they approach Bethphage,[1014] Jesus tells two of his apostles to go into the village, where they will find a donkey hitched and her colt. "Untie them and bring them to me," Jesus commands.

In Bethphage the apostles take the colt and its mother, prompting the animals' owners to ask what they are doing. The apostles explain that the animals are for the Lord, so there is no further objection.[1015] They bring the beasts to Jesus, saddling them using their cloaks. Jesus mounts the colt and rides toward Jerusalem.[1016] Crowds of people[1017] carpet the road with their cloaks and palm branches, shouting praises to "the one coming in the name of Jehovah."[1018]

Pharisees in the crowd tell Jesus to restrain his followers. He replies, "If these remained silent, the stones would burst into cheers."[1019]

The sight of Jerusalem causes Jesus to break down crying, for the city does not discern her day of reckoning.[1020] Sharing what he foresees for the holy city, Jesus warns, "Your enemies will throw up ramparts around you, encircle and besiege you from all sides.[1021] They will level you to the ground—leaving not one stone upon another—and your children within your walls."

The city is shaking with excitement when Jesus enters. He goes to the Temple to teach; also, he heals blind and lame ones.[1022] Youngsters[1023] cry out, "Please save[1024] the Son of David!"

The infuriated religious leaders ask Jesus, "Do you hear what these children are saying?"

Jesus responds by quoting scripture: "From the lips of children and infants you have established praise."—Psalm 8:2, *New Heart English Bible.*

"What can we do?" the Pharisees lament. "It seems the whole world is following him now!"

Faith and the Fig Tree
Matthew 21:12-13, 18-22; Mark 11:12-25; Luke 19:45-48; John 12:20-50

The following morning, Jesus and his apostles are heading to Jerusalem. Seeing a fig tree that seems to have sprouted early,[1025] Jesus decides to satisfy his hunger.[1026] But the tree's appearance is deceptive; it has leaves but no fruit. Jesus curses the tree: "No one will eat from you again." Immediately the tree starts to wither.[1027]

Jesus and the apostles reach Jerusalem. Upon entering the Temple,[1028] Jesus evicts the merchants and their customers, not even allowing anyone to carry a utensil through the courtyard.[1029] He condemns the conversion of "a house of prayer"[1030] into "a den of thieves."[1031] Word of what Jesus has done reaches the chief priests, scholars and other community leaders, and it steels their resolve to destroy him. However, they do not know how to have Jesus killed, because people are always around listening to him.

Certain foreigners who have come to worship at the festival approach Philip and ask to meet Jesus.[1032] Phillip and his brother Andrew take the request to the Lord. In answer Jesus announces, "The time has come for the Son of Man to be glorified.[1033] A single kernel of wheat that falls to the ground and dies produces much grain. Love your life and lose it; hate your life and keep it forever."[1034] Troubled as he is that his "time has arrived," Jesus refuses to ask the Father to spare him "from what is coming." Instead, he prays, "Father, glorify your name."

A voice from above responds, "I have glorified my name, and I will glorify it again."[1035] Some people think that they have heard thunder; others believe an angel has spoken.

"This voice was heard," says Jesus, "for your sake, not mine." Referring to his impending death, Jesus declares, "Once I am lifted up from the earth, I will draw everyone to me."[1036]

Some in the crowd respond, "According to Scripture, the Messiah remains forever. How can you say that the Son of Man must be lifted up? Who is he?"—See Psalm 45:6; 110:4; Isaiah 9:7; Daniel 7:14.

Jesus urges the people, "I have come as a light into the world. No one who puts faith in me remains in darkness. While you have the Light, demonstrate faith in the Light, so that you may become his children.[1037] Whoever puts faith in me also puts faith in the One who sent me. If anyone hears my sayings but does not keep them, it is not I who judges; I am here to save the world, not to judge it. Whoever disregards me and does not receive my sayings will ultimately be judged by my words[1038]—words given to me by the Father, the one who sent me. I know that his commandment means eternal life, and so I speak, not of my own accord, but what the Father told me."

On their way to Jerusalem the following morning,[1039] Jesus and his apostles come to the cursed fig tree. Peter exclaims, "Look, Teacher! The fig tree that you cursed has withered."

Jesus responds, "If you have faith without doubts, you can do what I did to the fig tree. Even if you say to this mountain,[1040] 'Move and throw yourself into the sea,' it will happen. Have faith that everything you pray for you have received, and you will have it."

Jesus Debates the Hypocrites—Round One
Matthew 21:23-22:22; Mark 11:27-12:17; Luke 20:1-26

A question of authority. When Jesus arrives at the Temple, there to challenge him are chief priests, scholars and community leaders.[1041] They demand of Jesus, "By whose authority do you do what you do?"[1042]

Jesus replies, "I will reveal the source of my authority if you answer one question: Did John's authority to baptize come from Heaven or from humans?"

Jesus' critics debate: "If we say, 'From Heaven,' he will ask, 'Why didn't you believe him?' But if we say, 'From humans,' the people will stone us because they respected John as a prophet." Unable to come up with an appropriate answer, Jesus' opponents reply, "We cannot say."

Jesus responds, "Then I cannot say who gives me authority to do what I do."[1043]

Jesus proceeds with a story about a vineyard owner who had two sons: "To the first son he said, 'Go work today in the vineyard.' This one answered, 'I will,' but did not go to work. Approaching the second son, the father said the same. This one replied, 'I will not work,' but regretted it afterward and went into the vineyard. Now," Jesus asks, "who did his father's will?"

"The second son," his critics answer.

"Tax collectors and prostitutes are entering God's kingdom ahead of you,"[1044] he responds. "And that's the truth! John the Baptist came to you on a righteous mission. You didn't believe John, but the tax collectors and the prostitutes did. And even when you saw this, you felt no regret for not believing him."

"God will take his kingdom from you…" "Hear another parable," Jesus announces. "A man planted a vineyard, fenced it in, dug a vat for the winepress,[1045] erected a watchtower.[1046] Then he leased his vineyard to tenants and traveled abroad. When the grapes were getting ripe, the owner sent his servants to the tenants to collect his share of the crop.[1047] But the tenants captured the servants—one they cruelly beat, one they pelted with stones, one they killed. Lastly, the owner sent his beloved son, reasoning, 'They will respect my son.' But when the tenants saw him, they said to each other, 'This is the heir. Let's do away with him and make his inheritance ours.'[1048] They pounced on the son, killed him and threw his body outside the vineyard. And now," Jesus asks, "what will the owner of the vineyard do?"

His opponents answer, "He will bring those wretches to a wretched end and lease the vineyard to other tenants, who will pay him the fruits he is due."

Applying the lesson of his parable,[1049] Jesus says, "God will take his kingdom from you and give it to a nation that will pay him the fruits he expects."[1050] Jesus' opponents reject the Son of God[1051]—the "cornerstone"[1052] of that new nation—and know that his parable illustrates their rejection. They want to have him arrested but fear the crowds, who esteem Jesus as a prophet.—Psalm 118:22; Isaiah 8:14-15.

Many invited, few chosen. Jesus relates a third parable, comparing "the kingdom of Heaven" to a king who made a wedding for his son. "He sent his servants to summon guests to the marriage banquet," Jesus begins, "but those invited refused to come. The king sent other servants to the invitees, some of whom simply declined and went about their business. But the rest captured his servants and killed them. Enraged, the king sent his armies and destroyed those murderers and their city.[1053] Then he said to his servants, 'The banquet is ready, but those invited were unworthy. Take to the roads leading out of the city—invite anyone you find.'[1054] Many people—good and bad—are found and brought inside the wedding hall.[1055] When the king inspected his guests, he saw a man not dressed for a wedding. 'How did you get in here dressed so inappropriately?'[1056] the king asked him. The man didn't know what to say. Then the king told his attendants, 'Bind this man hand and foot and throw him outside; there in the darkness he will weep and grind his teeth.'

"Many are invited," Jesus concludes, "but few are chosen."[1057]

Caesar's Things, God's Things. Jesus' critics reconsider their strategy to have him arrested. Conspiring with the Herodians,[1058] the Pharisees bribe some men to approach Jesus with flattery and a sensitive question. "Teacher," these say, "we know you teach God's truth—no matter what people say about you—so we want to know what you think: Is it right for us to pay head tax to Caesar or not?"[1059]

Jesus sees through this duplicity. "Hypocrites," he responds, "why are you testing me? Let's see the tax coin." They produce such a coin, whereupon he asks, "Whose likeness is this?"[1060]

"Caesar's," they reply.

"Then pay to Caesar what belongs to Caesar," Jesus directs. "But give to God what belongs to God."[1061] The plot to snare Jesus in his speech before the people fails.

Jesus Debates the Hypocrites—Round Two
Matthew 22:23-46; Mark 12:18-37; Luke 20:27-44

One bride for seven brothers. As the Pharisees and Herodians retreat, Sadducees take up the attack on Jesus with a hypothetical question involving the resurrection of the dead,[1062] which the Sadducees do not believe in. They remind Jesus that if a man dies leaving behind a wife but no children, the Mosaic Law requires his brother to marry the widow and give his brother descendants.[1063]—Deuteronomy 25:5-6.

"Now let's say there were seven brothers," the Sadducees begin. "The oldest brother took a wife but left no descendants when he died. The second-born brother married the widow but died without descendants, and so did the third-born. In the end, all seven brothers married the widow and died without descendants; then she died, too. In the resurrection, to which of her seven husbands will she be married?"[1064]

Jesus tells the Sadducees, "You don't understand what God said or how he works,"[1065] and explains, "Marriage is for the children of this age, not for the worthy ones who are resurrected from the dead in the coming age. Children of the resurrection—God's children—will be like angels,[1066] and never die again."

For proof that the dead will live again, Jesus refers to "the book of Moses,"[1067] where Jehovah declares himself to be "the God of Abraham, the God of Isaac, and the God of Jacob." (Exodus 3:6) Jesus explains, "The living God is God of the living, not of the dead—to him they live still."[1068] Jesus' listeners, including some of his critics, are astounded.[1069]

Love God, love your neighbor. Jesus has silenced both the Pharisees and the Sadducees; now a coalition of these opposers comes to test him further. Representing them, a legal scholar asks, "Teacher, what is the Law's most important commandment?"[1070]

In answer Jesus again cites Scripture: "Hear, Israel: JEHOVAH is our God, JEHOVAH is one . And you shall love JEHOVAH your God[1071] with all your heart,[1072] and with all your soul, and with all your might[1073]." To this Jesus adds the commandment of second greatest importance: "love your neighbor as yourself." He explains, "These two commandments to love are the thrust of Moses' law and the prophets' teachings."—Deuteronomy 6:4-5; Leviticus 19:18, *New Heart English Bible:* Jehovah Edition.

The scholar admits, "That is a fine, true answer, Teacher. There is one God—no other besides him; and to love him and one's neighbor means more than all the whole burnt offerings and sacrifices."[1074]

Jesus responds, "You are closer than you realize to God's kingdom."

The Messiah—David's "son" and "Lord." The religious leaders lack the courage to question Jesus further, so he turns the tables on them, asking, "How can the scholars say that the Messiah is David's son?" Jesus quotes "the statement of Jehovah to [David's] Lord: 'Sit at My right hand,[1075] until I place Your enemies as Your footstool[1076].'" (Psalm 110:1, *A Literal Translation of the Bible)* Jesus asks, "If Messiah is David's Lord, how can he be his son?"[1077] No one dares to question Jesus now.

Woe to the "Blind Guides"!
Matthew 23:1-39; Mark 12:38-44; Luke 20:45-21:4

The debate between Jesus and his critics at the Temple is overheard by the disciples and others. To these Jesus now gives words of warning about his religious enemies.

The scholars[1078] and the Pharisees presume to be substitute teachers for Moses. "Do as they say," counsels Jesus, "but not as they do.[1079] They burden you with rules that they themselves won't follow. Everything they do is for show, like wearing robes with longer tassels and extra-large phylacteries as if they were lucky charms.[1080] They enjoy their places of honor at meals and in the synagogues[1081] and relish being hailed in public with greetings of 'Rabbi!'[1082] But among you my followers there are no rabbis, for you have one Teacher, and all of you are students[1083]. Moreover, don't call anyone on Earth 'Father,'[1084] for you have one Father in Heaven; neither be called masters, for you have one Master, the Messiah.[1085] The only superior among you is the one who serves the others. The exalted will be humbled, and the humble will be exalted."

Denouncing them as "blind guides," Jesus curses the scholars and the Pharisees: "Woe to you, hypocrites, for shutting the door to the kingdom of Heaven in others' faces; since you can't get in, you allow no one to go in. You scour land and sea to make a one convert,[1086] who becomes twice as ripe for destruction as you are.

"You say, 'It counts for nothing when someone swears by the Temple or by the altar; but if someone swears by the gold of the Temple or by the gift on the altar, he is bound by his oath.'[1087] Blind fools, which is greater—the gold or the Temple that sanctifies the gold? The gift or the altar that sanctifies the gift?

"You tithe every little herb but give no thought to God's love and justice,[1088] straining out gnats but swallowing camels![1089] You clean the outside of your cup and bowl which brim with robbery and self-indulgence. Clean the inside first and the outside will be clean as well. You resemble whitewashed graves:[1090] beautiful outside, dead inside. On the outside you appear righteous; on the inside there is nothing but hypocrisy and lawlessness.[1091]

"You build memorials to the prophets and decorate the tombs of the righteous, boasting, 'If we had lived in the days of our forefathers, we wouldn't have shared with them in killing the prophets.' And so, you identify yourselves as children of the prophets' killers. What your forefathers started you will finish."[1092]

Jesus condemns this "brood of vipers" to destruction.[1093] "Because of what you are," he continues, "when I send to you prophets, counselors and teachers, some you will execute, some you will scourge in your synagogues, others you will hunt down from one city to another. You will thus bring guilt upon yourselves for the murders of all the martyrs from Abel to Zechariah.[1094] For all that bloodshed your generation will be held responsible[1095]—and that's the truth!"

Jesus mourns for Jerusalem, "killer of the prophets and stoner of the messengers sent to her." In a lament of mingled anguish, love and warning, he cries, "How I wanted to gather your children to me as a mother bird gathers her chicks under her wings![1096] But you didn't want it. See, your House is abandoned to you!"[1097] This is the last day that Jerusalem will see Jesus until she praises "the One coming in the name of Jehovah."[1098]—Psalm 118:26, *New World Translation of the Holy Scriptures—with References.*

THE WIDOW'S MITE

After muzzling his critics, Jesus moved to a part of the Temple where he observed people depositing money into treasury chests. According to rabbinic sources, the Temple contained 13 treasury chests, called shofar chests. In Hebrew they were called trumpets, because they had a small opening at the top in the shape of the bell of a trumpet. Each of these trumpets bore an inscription indicating for what purpose the contributions were to be used.[1099] Jesus saw rich people dropping in many coins they would never miss. Then a destitute widow contributed two small coins[1100] of little value. A widow was not required to pay the head tax, and this woman of limited means was probably not able to meet the minimum requirements for the burnt offerings or the wood or incense offerings. Jesus brought her sacrifice to his apostles' attention, telling them that the "poor widow gave more than all the others who contributed from their wealth; she contributed from her want, giving all she had."—Mark 12:41-44; Luke 21:1-4.

The rich leaders evidenced no faith and stole from others, even from God. (Matthew 21:13; Mark 11:17; 12:40; Luke 19:46; 20:47; John 2:16) The poor widow evidenced great faith and gave out of her extreme poverty everything she had. Her two small coins might not have made much noise when she deposited them, but the size of a contribution does not necessarily give a true picture of the giver's generosity. Both the widow and her contribution were valuable to God.—2 Corinthians 9:7.

A Sign of Things to Come

Matthew 24:1-51; Mark 13:1-37; Luke 21:5-38

For the final time, Jesus leaves the Temple; its buildings are adorned with fine stones and dedicated gifts.

"What splendid architecture!"[1101] one of the apostles exclaims.

"As for these buildings that you admire," says Jesus, "a day is coming when not a single stone will remain—everything will be destroyed."[1102]

"By what sign ...?" Later, Jesus and four apostles—Peter, Andrew, James and John—are sitting on the Mount of Olives[1103] with the Temple in view.[1104] The apostles ask Jesus, "By what sign will we know when these things are about to occur?"[1105]

"Beware that no one misleads you," Jesus cautions. "Impostors claiming to be the Messiah will claim that the end is near. Don't be deceived into following them.[1106] You will hear the noise of battles nearby and news of battles far away.[1107] Don't be alarmed—these things must happen. But they are just the beginning of pangs of distress."[1108] Those "pangs" will also include great earthquakes,[1109] widespread famine and pestilence.[1110] In addition to distress on Earth, "there will be fearful sights from Heaven," Jesus adds.

Meanwhile, as Jesus' followers proclaim the Kingdom gospel everywhere,[1111] persecution will come upon them from all corners. Christians will be compelled to appear in courts and give testimony before powerful people. "When you are arrested and taken into custody," Jesus tells the apostles, "don't worry about what to say. At the right time, God's spirit will speak for you."[1112] Jesus promises to give his followers words of wisdom that no opposer will be able to resist or refute. "You will be betrayed by friends and family," he warns, "some of whom will even send you to your death. But not so much as one hair on your head will perish.[1113] Endurance[1114] will save your life[1115]." Because they bear his name, Jesus' followers "will be hated by all nations.[1116] Then, too, many will lose faith[1117] and will betray and hate one another." Lawlessness will increase, and the love of many people will chill.[1118] "But those who persevere,"[1119] Jesus says, "will be saved."

Great Tribulation. "When you see Jerusalem encircled by armies," Jesus warns, "take refuge in the mountains—her desolation is near![1120] The one who comes down from the roof must not collect goods from inside the house, and the one in the field must not return to pick up a coat. Pray that you won't have to flee in the winter or on the Sabbath.[1121] Jerusalem will be trampled upon by foreigners[1122] until their day of dominion over her comes to its end. Those will be days for meting out justice in fulfillment of all that was foretold. Unless God limits this calamitous time, no one will survive. But because he loves his chosen ones, he will shorten those days."[1123]—Isaiah 61:1-2; Daniel 12:1.

The Sign of the Son of Man. Jesus sees fear-inspiring events in the future—signs in the sky,[1124] anguish on Earth. Fear and foreboding will stop human hearts.[1125] Then a special "sign" will manifest.[1126] Says Jesus, "all the world will mourn[1127] when the Son of Man comes on the clouds[1128] of Heaven in overwhelming power and glory.[1129] With a great trumpet blast, he will send his angels to gather his chosen ones from all directions,[1130] from one horizon to another." As these things start to occur, the chosen ones will know their deliverance is near, just as the nearness of summer is portended by trees in the bud.[1131]—Daniel 7:13-14.

"That Day and Hour." Jesus compares "the presence[1132] of the Son of Man" to "the days of Noah.[1133] In those days before the Flood," he says, "people ate and drank, got married, and took no notice until Noah boarded the ark; then the Flood swept them all away. And so, the presence of the Son of man will be. At that time, two hands will be in the field; one will be taken along and the other abandoned. Two workers will be grinding at the mill;[1134] one will be taken along and the other abandoned.[1135] So stay alert! You don't know on what day your Lord is coming." That day, says Jesus, "will visit everyone the whole world over.[1136] Keep awake, then, praying constantly to succeed in escaping all these impending troubles, and in standing before the Son of Man."[1137]

Since "nobody knows that day and hour,"[1138] Jesus illustrates the need for spiritual attentiveness, saying, "It is like a man traveling abroad who left his servants in charge of the house—each one with his own work to do—and ordered the watchman to be on guard.[1139] Since you don't know when the master of the house is returning," Jesus admonishes, "keep watching. He comes suddenly—in the evening, at night, before dawn[1140] or in the morning—so don't let him catch you sleeping."

"Not expecting the arrival of the Lord in the night-time (which is the most unlikely for His Coming), we might go to sleep, and the Enemy, taking advantage of it, [might] rob us of our peculiar treasure (Matt. 24:43, 44). Thus, the Church, not expecting her Lord, might become as poor as the world. This would be [her] loss. But there might be even worse. According to the Master's appointment each one had, during Christ's absence, his work for Him, and the reward of grace, or else the punishment of neglect, were in assured prospect. The faithful steward, to whom the Master had entrusted the care of His household, to supply His servants with what was needful for their support and work, would, if found faithful, be rewarded by advancement to far larger and more responsible work. On the other hand, belief in the delay of the Lord's Return would lead to neglect of the Master's work, to unfaithfulness, tyranny, self-indulgence and sin (ver. 45, end). And when the Lord suddenly came, as certainly He would come, there would be not only loss, but damage, hurt, and the punishment awarded to the hypocrites. Hence, let the Church be ever on her watch (ver. 42), let her ever be in readiness! (ver. 44)."—*The Life and Times of Jesus the Messiah,* page 786. See also Luke 12:35-48.

Matthew 24:45 describes the servant as faithful and wise. In Matthew chapter 25 "the parable of the ten virgins explains the need for wisdom (vv. 1-13); the following parable of the talents (vv. 14-29) shows the need for faithfulness."—Matthew 25:2 footnote, *The Nelson Study Bible*.

The Bridesmaids
Matthew 25:1-13

Following a "sign" of future events that commands spiritual vigilance,[1141] Jesus tells a story about ten bridesmaids[1142]—five of whom are "foolish," five of whom are "wise[1143]." (Matthew 24:3) All ten bridesmaids went out to meet the bridegroom. Along with their lamps, the wise ones took flasks of oil.[1144] But the wedding procession was late, and the bridesmaids fell asleep. In the middle of the night someone announced, "Here comes the bridegroom! Go out to meet him."

The bridesmaids woke up and "put their lamps in order."[1145] However, the lamps of the foolish bridesmaids were burning low, so they said to their wise counterparts, "Give us some of your oil."

The wise bridesmaids answered, "There won't be enough for all of us. Go to those who sell oil and buy your own."

While the foolish bridesmaids were trying to find oil, the bridegroom arrived. The wise bridesmaids went in with him and shut the door. Later, the rest of the bridesmaids arrived and called, "Sir, please let us in!"

The bridegroom answered, "Truthfully, I don't know you."[1146]

In conclusion Jesus reiterates, "Keep watching because you know neither the day nor the hour."

"HERE COMES THE BRIDEGROOM!"—Matthew 25:6.

In Bible times, an important feature of the marriage ceremony was the solemn procession to bring the bride home. The bridegroom, in his best attire and escorted by friends, would leave his house in the evening for the home of the bride's parents. From there, accompanied by musicians and singers, the couple made their way toward the home of the bridegroom or his father. (Matthew 1:20) People along the route would take great interest in the procession. (Isaiah 62:5; Jeremiah 7:34; 16:9) Young women carrying torches or lamps on poles were among those joining the procession.[1147] As there was no haste, the procession might be delayed, which might require refilling the lamps carried in the procession with oil. After the bridegroom and his entourage entered the house and closed the door, it was too late for tardy guests to enter.

Per Jesus' parable, the bridegroom refers to Christ himself. (Compare Luke 5:34-35) The bridesmaids are his "little flock" of followers whom he admonished, "Be dressed and ready and have your lamps burning." (Luke 12:32, 35) Does this mean that half of those who inherit the Kingdom are foolish and the other half are wise? No. Jesus is illustrating the need for Christians to be like the five wise bridesmaids, prepared and vigilant, because the Bridegroom is coming to reward those who "keep on the watch" during his "presence."—Matthew 24:3; 25:13.

The Talents
Matthew 25:14-30

Continuing his answer to the apostles' questions (Matthew 24:3; Mark 13:4; Luke 21:7), Jesus tells the story of "a man preparing to travel abroad." Before departing, the man committed to his servants valuable belongings. He gave five talents to one servant, two talents to another servant and one talent to still another—"to each according to his own ability," as Jesus says.[1148] Immediately after their master leaves, the servant who received five talents did business with them and gained five more. The servant who received two talents similarly earned a profit of two talents. But the third servant dug a hole in the ground and buried his one talent.[1149]

"After a long time," the master returned to settle accounts with his servants. For the first two servants, their master had the same commendation: "Well done, good and faithful servant! Because you faithfully handled a small amount, I will give you big responsibilities. Come and share your master's joy."[1150]

The servant who received one talent returned it to his master, telling him, "I know you to be a hard man, reaping where you don't sow and gathering where you don't thresh. I was afraid so I hid your talent in the ground."[1151]

To this "wicked and lazy servant," the master said, "You should have deposited my money in the bank where it would have earned interest for me."[1152] His talent was taken away and given to one of the servants who applied himself diligently. "The good-for-nothing servant" was thrown out. The master set forth his standard: "Those who use well what they are given will receive more and have an abundance. Those who waste what little they have will lose everything."[1153]

"COME AND SHARE YOUR MASTER'S JOY."— Matthew 25:22, 24.

"The Parable of the Talents—their use and misuse (Matt. 25:14-30)—follows closely on the admonition to watch, in view of the sudden and certain Return of Christ, and the reward or punishment which will then be meted out. Only that, whereas in the Parable of the Ten Virgins the reference was to the personal state, in that of 'the Talents' it is to the personal work of the Disciples. In the former instance, they are portrayed as the bridal maidens who are to welcome His Return; in the latter, as the servants who are to give an account of their stewardship."—*The Life and Times of Jesus the Messiah*, page 791.

In an earlier, similar illustration, Jesus likened himself to a man who traveled abroad. (Luke 19:12) Jesus is also the traveler in this illustration. After three years-plus of ministry, Jesus is going away, confident that his servants will carry on his work. (Matthew 10:7; Luke 10:1, 8-9; compare John 4:38; 14:12) What Jesus is entrusting to them is of great value, and he expects them to be diligent in using this privilege. "Every good and faithful servant of Christ must, whatever his circumstances, personally and directly use such talent as he may have to make gain for Christ."—*The Life and Times of Jesus the Messiah*, page 794.

The Sheep and the Goats
Matthew 25:31-46

To the apostles' questions about future events, Jesus ends his answer with a parable about the last judgment. (Matthew 24:3; Mark 13:4; Luke 21:7) "When the Son of Man comes in his glory escorted by the angels,"[1154] Jesus tells them, "he will sit down on his royal throne, and all humankind[1155] will assemble before him. Then, as a shepherd separates sheep from goats,[1156] he will separate people from one another, putting the 'sheep' on his right hand and the 'goats' on his left.[1157] Then this king will say to those on his right, 'Come, my Father's blessed ones, inherit the Kingdom reserved for you since the founding of the world.'"[1158]

The King explains to the sheep-like ones why they receive his favor: "When I was hungry and thirsty, you gave me food and drink. I was a stranger and you welcomed me; naked[1159] and you clothed me. When I fell sick, you cared for me. When I was in prison, you visited me." When the "sheep" ask in what way they rendered these services to the King,[1160] he answers, "In every way you ministered to the least important of my brothers and sisters[1161], you ministered to me."

To the so-called goats, the King says, "Away from me, cursed ones,[1162] into the unquenchable fire reserved for the Devil and his demons. When I was hungry and thirsty you gave me nothing to eat or drink. I was a stranger, but you didn't welcome me; naked, but you didn't clothe me; sick and in prison, but you didn't care." Unlike the "sheep," the "goats" did nothing for Jesus' brothers and sisters—and by extension for Jesus himself.[1163] Therefore, "these will depart into eternal destruction[1164], but the righteous ones into eternal life."

Israelites celebrated the first Passover on the eve of their exodus from Egypt. That night, God "passed over the houses of the Israelites in Egypt when he plagued the Egyptians." (Exodus 12:27, *New World Translation)* Passover, on the fourteenth day of the month of Nisan, was immediately followed by the Festival of Unleavened Bread, Nisan 15-21. (Leviticus 23:5-6; Numbers 28:16-17) In Jesus' time, all eight days were treated as one celebration. (Mark 14:1; Luke 22:1) During the daytime of Nisan 13,[1165] his apostles prepared for Jesus' last Passover, which was celebrated after sundown (when the new day begins) on Nisan 14. (Mark 14:16-17) Essential items at the Passover meal were roast lamb (no bones in the animal were to be broken), unleavened bread and bitter greens (lettuce, chicory, pepperwort, endive or dandelion).[1166] (Exodus 12:5, 8; Numbers 9:11) There were at least four cups of wine passed among the Passover participants. The Old Testament says nothing about this custom, but Jesus accepted it; he drank wine with his apostles after saying a blessing.—Luke 22:17; 1 Corinthians 10:16.

Thirty Pieces of Silver

Matthew 26:1-5, 14-19; Mark 14:1-2, 10-17; Luke 22:1-13; John 13:1

The Passover festival begins in two days. In the courtyard of High Priest Caiaphas, Jesus' civic and religious enemies craftily conspire to do away with him.[1167] They and the Temple police[1168] receive a visitor—Judas Iscariot. "What will you give me if I hand Jesus over to you?" Judas asks them. A deal is struck to pay Judas in silver—exactly 30 pieces.[1169]

At the onset of the Festival of Unleavened Bread, Jesus dispatches Peter and John from Bethany to prepare their Passover celebration. "In Jerusalem you will meet a man carrying a water jug,"[1170] Jesus tells them. "He will lead you to a house. Speak to the owner,[1171] and he will show you a large, furnished second-story room—make things ready for us there."[1172]

In Jerusalem, Peter and John find everything just as Jesus had said. They see to it that arrangements for the meal are in place.[1173] Jesus and the ten other apostles arrive that evening and find everything ready. Knowing the time has come for him to leave this world, Jesus earnestly desires to share this final meal with the men he loves so much.

The Last Supper

Matthew 26:20-25; Mark 14:18-21; Luke 22:14-18, 21-23; John 13:2-30

"I have wanted so much to share this Passover meal with you before I suffer,"[1174] Jesus confides to his apostles. "I will not eat another one until its meaning is fulfilled by God's kingdom."[1175] Accepting a cup of wine,[1176] he gives thanks and then tells the apostles to pass it among themselves. "From now on," Jesus vows, "I will not drink from the fruit of the vine until God's kingdom comes."[1177]

At some point during the dinner, Jesus gets up, removes his robe, and wraps a towel around his waist. Then he pours water into a basin, intending to wash his apostles' feet.[1178] Peter initially refuses this service, but Jesus tells him, "You can have no part with me[1179] unless I wash you."

"Lord, wash my feet—and hands and face, too!" Peter excitedly responds.

"Whoever has bathed doesn't need to have more than the feet washed,"[1180] Jesus answers, stressing holiness and not hygiene. "You men are clean, but not every one of you."[1181] Jesus knows that the Devil has sown his seed in the heart of Judas Iscariot.

After washing the feet of all 12 apostles, Jesus puts on his robe and reclines at the table. "Do you understand what I have done?" he asks. "You correctly address me as 'Teacher' and 'Lord,'—that's who I am. And if I, Lord and Teacher, washed your feet, you are obligated to wash one another's feet. That is your example to imitate.[1182] Certainly, a slave is not greater than the master; one who is sent is not greater than the sender. Now that you know these things, do them and be blessed."

Jesus quotes King David's prophetic words: "Even a friend of mine whom I trusted, who ate my bread, has turned against me."[1183] In great anguish Jesus explains, "One of you breaking bread with me will turn against me."

The apostles look at one another, and each asks, "Can you mean me, Lord?"[1184]

At Peter's urging, John,[1185] who is reclining close to Jesus,[1186] leans in to ask, "Who is it, Lord?"

"My betrayer is with me at the table,"[1187] Jesus reiterates. "The Son of Man is going the way foretold for him in the Scriptures.[1188] But woe to that man who betrays him! It would have been better for him if he had never been born."

Judas Iscariot asks, "It is not I, is it, Teacher?"

"Isn't it?"[1189] Jesus answers. He dips a morsel of bread in a dish on the table and gives it to Judas.[1190] At this point, Satan possesses Judas.[1191] "Get it over with," Jesus says. The other apostles imagine that Judas, who is holding their money,[1192] is being told to make a purchase for the festival or to donate to the poor. Judas exits.[1193]

"Do This to Remember Me"
Matthew 26:26-29; Mark 14:22-25; Luke 22:19-20

Jesus now takes some bread and, after giving thanks, breaks it and gives it to his apostles.[1194] "Eat this bread; it means[1195] my body, given for your sake," he explains. "Do this to remember me." The bread is shared amongst the apostles. Then Jesus prays over a cup of wine and gives it to them.[1196] "You must all drink from it," he says. "This cup means the new covenant written in[1197] my blood." Jesus' blood will be "poured out to set many free from their sins."[1198] He repeats, "Do this to remember me."[1199]—1 Corinthians 11:25.

"Before a Rooster Crows..."
Matthew 26:31-35; Mark 14:27-31; Luke 22:24-38; John 13:31-38

Once again, the apostles fall to wrangling over who among them is the most important.[1200] Jesus reasons with them: "In the world, kings lord it over their subjects, and those who wield authority are called Benefactors.[1201] Not so with you; with you, the senior must take the junior role, and the leader must act the servant's part. Isn't the diner more important than the server?" Reminding the apostles of his own example, Jesus says, "I am the one who plays the servant's part among you."[1202]

Despite their imperfections, the apostles have stuck with Jesus through many challenges. "I give to you the royal authority that my Father has given to me,"[1203] Jesus tells them. "In my kingdom, you will dine at my table[1204] and sit on thrones ruling over[1205] the 12 tribes of Israel."

Addressing the apostles as his "beloved children,"[1206] Jesus tells them, "I'll be with you for just a little longer. Afterward, you'll look for me but—as I said before—where I'm going you cannot follow." (John 7:33-34) Jesus gives his apostles "a new commandment: love one another just as I have loved you.[1207] Everyone will recognize you as my disciples by your love for one another."

Peter asks Jesus where he is going. Jesus answers, "Where I'm going, you'll follow later but not now." Peter wants to know why he cannot follow Jesus now.

"Simon! Simon, take heed! Satan has demanded to have you all to sift as wheat."[1208] Jesus tells the apostles that every one of them will desert him and scatter, in fulfillment of prophecy. (Zechariah 13:7) "But after I have been raised up," he promises, "I will meet you in Galilee."[1209]

Peter protests, "Everyone else might desert you but I won't!"

Jesus tells Peter that he has prayed for him,[1210] that his faith may not fail.[1211] "Once you have recovered,"[1212] says Jesus, "support your brothers." Peter assures Jesus that he will follow him anywhere, even if doing so leads to prison or death. Jesus responds, "On this very night, you will disown me three times before a rooster crows twice."[1213]

Jesus cautions the apostles that events foretold of him are being fulfilled.[1214] "And so," he directs, "let the one who has a money bag carry it, likewise a food pouch, and let the one who has no sword sell his coat and buy one."[1215] The apostles produce two swords. "That will do,"[1216] Jesus responds.

"Set Your Troubled Hearts at Ease"
John 14:1-31

Encouraging them to have faith in him and in God, Jesus gives the apostles reason not to be troubled over his imminent departure. "There are many rooms in my Father's house,"[1217] he tells them. "If I leave to prepare a place for you, I will return and take you home with me, so that you may be where I am. And you know the way to where I'm going."[1218]

Thomas asks, "Lord, we don't know where you're going. How can we know the way?"

"I am the way—and the truth and the life,"[1219] Jesus answers. "No one comes to the Father except through me. If you have learned to know me, you'll know my Father, too. And from now on you know him—you have seen him."[1220]

Philip requests, "Lord, show us the Father—that will satisfy us."

"Seeing me is like seeing the Father himself!"[1221] Jesus replies. "How can you ask me to show you the Father? Believe me, the Father is part of me, and I am part of him; if for no other reason, believe because of the works you see me do.[1222] Whoever demonstrates faith in me will do not only the works that I do, but even greater works.[1223]

"Because I am going to the Father," Jesus continues, "I will ask him for another helper[1224] to be with you forever, and he will give you the Spirit of Truth, which the world cannot accept. Moreover, anything you ask in my name,[1225] I will do it. I am not leaving you bereaved[1226], because I will return to you.[1227] Shortly, the world will see me no more, but you will see me;[1228] because I live, you will live."—See 1 Corinthians 2:13-14.

Thaddaeus interrupts, "Lord, you intend to show yourself clearly to us but not to the whole world?[1229] Why?" Jesus describes those to whom he will reveal himself, and why:

"Those who love me will observe my word and be loved by my Father—with them we will be[1230]. The word that you are hearing isn't mine—it belongs to the Father who sent me. What I have spoken to you while with you the Helper will recall to your minds and teach you everything else.[1231]

"I leave you in peace," Jesus announces, "my peace I leave with you—peace such as the world cannot give.[1232] Set your troubled hearts at ease and don't be afraid.[1233] You heard me say that I was going away and will return to you. If you love me, rejoice that I am going to the Father,[1234] who is greater than I am. I will not speak with you much more because the ruler of the world is coming—but he has no power over me."[1235]

“SEEING ME IS LIKE SEEING THE FATHER HIMSELF!”—John 14:9

God’s firstborn Son is his Father’s image. (2 Corinthians 4:4; Colossians 1:15) Jesus fully reflected God’s qualities and personality. He faithfully represented his Father, spoke the Father’s words and did the Father’s works. Jesus was such a perfect reflection of his Father that observing the Son would be like seeing the Father. (John 1:18; 14:9-11) Thus, when we read in the gospels about Jesus—the powerful and winsome words that he used in his teaching, the compassion that moved him to heal others, the empathy that caused him to give way to tears—we might well picture his Father saying and doing those very things. (Matthew 7:28-29; Mark 1:40-42; John 11:32-36) The four gospels are not only biographies of Jesus—they are portraits of his heavenly Father. To study Jesus’ life and ministry is also to learn about the kind of person God is.

“Remain in My Love”
John 14:31-15:17

As they prepare to leave the upper room,[1236] Jesus presents to his apostles an illustration: “I am the true vine—my Father is the cultivator, and you are the branches.”

He elaborates, “Every barren branch my Father cuts off;[1237] every fruiting branch he prunes to make it more fruitful. You are pruned already with the teaching that I have given to you.[1238] Remain united with me, and I will remain united with you. As the branch cannot bear fruit unless it remains united with the vine, neither can you bear fruit unless you remain united with me. The one who remains united with me—and I united with that one—will bear much fruit. Apart from me you can produce nothing.[1239] Anyone who does not remain united with me is cut off like a dry branch. Withered branches are gathered, thrown onto the fire and burned up.[1240] If you remain united with me and keep my teaching, whatever you ask for will happen.[1241] That you keep bearing the fruit of discipleship brings glory to my Father.”

“The fruit of discipleship” is love, as Jesus explains: “As the Father has loved me, I have loved you; remain in my love. Observe my commandments and you will remain in my love, as I have observed the Father’s commandments and remain in his love. All this I have told you so that you may share my joy, making your joy complete.[1242] This is my commandment: love one another as I have loved you.[1243] To surrender one’s life for one’s friends—there is no greater love. You are my friends if you do as I command. I no longer call you servants[1244], because a servant is not in his master’s confidence. Now you are my friends, because I have shared with you everything my Father told me. You didn’t choose me; I chose you and appointed you to keep bearing fruit—fruit that lasts.[1245] Then the Father will give you whatever you ask in my name. I command that you love one another.”

"I AM THE TRUE VINE"—John 15:1.

By Noah's time, cultivated vineyards were popular in the land of Canaan. (Genesis 9:20) They often had protective walls, a watchtower and a winepress. To sit in one's own vineyard and to eat from it signified prosperity and security.—1 Kings 4:25; Micah 4:4; Zechariah 3:10.

Jesus' metaphor of a vine resembles word pictures found in the Old Testament where Israel is called God's vineyard. (Isaiah 5:1-7) The prophets referred to unfaithful Israel as an empty, degenerate vine. (Jeremiah 2:21; Hosea 10:1) Jesus, however, is "the true vine," and his Father is "the cultivator." When the apostles and others received the promised spirit of God at Pentecost, they became branches of the vine.

To bear fruit as Christians, the branches must remain united with Jesus, just as branches of a literal vine must remain attached to the trunk to be alive and fruitful. As a cultivator expects a vine to produce fruit, God expects those in union with Christ to produce spiritual fruitage. (Galatians 5:22-23; John 4:36) Jesus' illustration emphasizes the unity that exists between Christ and Christians and between Christians and the Father.

"I Have Conquered the World"!
John 15:18-16:33

Just as the world hates Jesus, the world hates his followers because they do not belong to the world.[1246] After all, as Jesus reminds the apostles, "a servant is not greater than his master. They have persecuted me, and they will persecute you on account of me[1247] because they don't know the One who sent me. They have no excuse for their sin. If I had not come and spoken to them and done among them the works that no one else did, they would not be guilty of rejecting me.[1248] But they have seen me and hated me—my Father as well, for whoever hates me hates my Father. However, what was written in Scripture had to come true, namely, they hate me for no reason."[1249]

When, however, "the Spirit of Truth" arrives, that helper will bear witness about Jesus. In the spirit's power, the apostles will also bear witness. (Acts 1:8) "I have said all this to keep you from falling away[1250]," Jesus warns his apostles. "You will be expelled from the synagogue.[1251] Those who execute you will think of it as sacred service to God."[1252] In view of his imminent departure, Jesus prepares his apostles for persecution. They are grief-stricken; however, it is for their benefit that Jesus is going away.[1253] "If I don't return to the One who sent me," he explains, "the Helper won't come to you." When, however, Jesus sends God's spirit to his followers, that helper will guide them into "the whole truth," and disclose to them "the things to come."[1254] Furthermore, the Spirit of Truth "will prove the world to be wrong about sin, righteousness and judgment."[1255]

Soon the apostles "will see [Jesus] no longer." However, he assures them that this is not good-bye. Knowing they wonder what he means, Jesus elaborates, "The world will rejoice as you grieve. However, your grief will be transformed into joy.[1256] A woman in labor has pain because her time has come, but when the baby is born, she forgets her pain because she has brought a life into the world.[1257] Now you have grief, but I will see you again. Your hearts will rejoice, and no one will take away your joy.[1258] At that time, you will ask nothing of me; but ask anything of the Father[1259] and he will give it to you in my name—that's the solemn truth. The Father loves you because you love me and accept me as his representative.[1260]

The apostles affirm, "We are certain that you know everything and don't need anyone to tell you anything. That's why we believe that you came from God."[1261]

Jesus assures them, "I have said all this so that you may have peace through me[1262]. In the world you will have tribulation but take courage! I have conquered the world."[1263]

'May We All Be One'
John 17:1-26

Jesus' "time has come."[1264] Finished speaking with the apostles, Jesus raises his eyes to Heaven and speaks to his Father.[1265] "Glorify your son so that your son may glorify you," Jesus prays, "just as you have given him authority over all humankind to grant eternal life to those whom you have given to him. Eternal life means knowing you as the only true God and Jesus Christ as your messenger.[1266] I have glorified you on Earth by finishing your work.[1267] Let me share with you again, Father, the glory we shared before the world was."[1268]

Jesus continues, making supplication for his followers: "I have revealed who you truly are[1269] to the ones you gave to me out of the world.[1270] They have done as you said, accepting my message as having come from you, and believing that you sent me. I pray for those who belong to you, not for those who belong to the world. Holy Father,[1271] keep the ones you gave to me true to your own name. Not one of them is lost, except the one who chose to be lost[1272]. The world hates them because they don't belong to the world, any more than I belong to the world. I ask, not that you take them out of the world, but that you protect them from the Evil One. Sanctify them[1273] through your word, which is Truth.[1274] So that they may be sanctified through the truth, I am keeping myself holy[1275] for them.

"For these I pray, and for those who are brought by their message to have faith in me.[1276] May they all be one. May they be in union with us—I in union with them and you in union with me. May they be so completely unified that the world realizes it was you who sent me and that you love them just as you love me.[1277] And I want the ones you gave to me to be by my side, where they will see the glory you have given me.[1278] You have loved me from before the founding of the world.[1279] The world does not know you, Righteous Father, but I know you, and the ones you gave to me know that you sent me. I have made your name known to them[1280] and will continue to make it known, so that your love for me may be in them and I may be in union with them."

"Let Your Will Be Done"

Matthew 26:30, 36-46; Mark 14:26, 32-42; Luke 22:39-46; John 18:1

After singing hymns Jesus and the apostles depart from the upper room.[1281] They cross the Kidron Valley[1282] to the Mount of Olives and enter the garden of Gethsemane.[1283] Jesus leaves behind eight of the apostles, admonishing them, "To avoid temptation, keep praying."[1284] With Peter, James and John,[1285] Jesus goes farther into the garden. "Stay here," he tells the trio, "and keep watch[1286] with me."

The anguish Jesus feels is crushing the life out of him. Some distance away from the three apostles, Jesus sinks to his knees and lies face down on the ground,[1287] beseeching his Father, "*Abba,*[1288] you can do anything—don't make me drink this cup![1289] But even so, let your will—not mine—be done."[1290] In answer to his Son's prayer, God sends Jesus an angel for strength. Jesus is in such agony that his sweat streams to the ground as drops of blood.[1291]

After praying at length, Jesus goes back to Peter, James and John—they are sleeping. "Couldn't you stay on the watch for a single hour with me?" he asks them. "Stand up—pray to avoid temptation. The spirit may be willing, but the flesh is weak."[1292]

Jesus goes away and continues his prayer: "My Father, if this cup cannot be emptied unless I drink it, let your will be done." On returning to the three apostles, he finds them fighting to keep their eyes open.[1293]

A third time Jesus departs for privacy and prayer.[1294] When he returns to the apostles, again, they are asleep. "At a time like this," says Jesus, "you sleep and rest?[1295] You are about to see the Son of Man betrayed into the hands of sinners." Indeed, the "betrayer is near."

Betrayed with a Kiss
Matthew 26:47-56; Mark 14:43-52; Luke 22:47-53; John 18:2-12

To Gethsemane Judas Iscariot leads a rabble of religious leaders, soldiers and others.[1296] He will identify Jesus for the soldiers. "The one I kiss," Judas says, "is the man. Take him into custody."[1297] Carrying lamps, torches and weapons, Iscariot and his gang enter the garden. Seeing Jesus with his apostles, Judas goes straight to him. "Hello, Teacher!" says the traitor, and he tenderly kisses Jesus.[1298]

"Man, why are you here?" Jesus asks rhetorically. "To betray the Son of Man with a kiss?"

Jesus steps forward and asks the soldiers who they are looking for. "Jesus the Nazarene," they answer. When Jesus identifies himself, the men—including the betrayer himself—fall to the ground, stunned.[1299]

"I told you that I am he," Jesus continues, and he insists that his apostles be allowed to go free. (Jesus remembers his recent words in prayer: "Of those whom you have given me, I have not lost a single one."—John 17:12; see John 6:39.)

As the soldiers recover and advance to Jesus, his loyal apostles realize what is happening. Before Jesus can stop him, Peter draws his sword and strikes one of the high priest's servants (named Malchus), taking off an ear.[1300] "Enough!" says Jesus. He touches the servant's wound and heals it.[1301] Then he orders Peter, "Sheath your sword. Those who draw the sword will die by the sword. I could ask my Father for tens of thousands[1302] of angels to protect me. Don't you know that?"

Jesus addresses the crowd: "You come here with swords and clubs as if I was an outlaw.[1303] Every day at the Temple I was within your reach, but you didn't lay a hand on me. You choose this hour and the cover of darkness[1304]." Jesus is willing to be taken into custody; otherwise, "how would the prophecies[1305] about this be fulfilled?" Jesus is arrested; the 11 apostles flee.[1306]

Peter's Denials and a Rooster's Crow
Matthew 26:57-75; Mark 14:53-72; Luke 22:54-65; John 18:13-27

Under arrest, Jesus is led to former high priest Annas.[1307] In the meantime, Annas' son-in-law Caiaphas, the current high priest, assembles the Sanhedrin. After the resurrection of Lazarus, Caiaphas had explained to the Sanhedrin the political necessity for the judicial murder of Christ.

Annas interrogates Jesus about his followers and what he teaches them.[1308] Jesus replies, "I always taught in public—in a synagogue and in the Temple, where all our people gather—nothing was said in secret. Why question me? Question those who have heard what I told them."

An officer standing by slaps Jesus in the face, as if Jesus had spoken disrespectfully.[1309] Annas sends Jesus to Caiaphas, who has brought the Sanhedrin together at his home.[1310]

As Jesus is led away, Peter and John follow at a distance. Known to the high priest and his household,[1311] John speaks to the doorkeeper—a servant girl—on Peter's behalf, and gains entrance for himself and Peter to the courtyard at Caiaphas' house.[1312]

The chief priests and the entire Sanhedrin are casting about for any allegation deserving the death penalty for Jesus.[1313] Two witnesses come forward and claim to have heard Jesus say, "I will destroy this Temple made by men and in three days build another with no help from anyone."[1314] But their evidence is contradictory.[1315]

Caiaphas asks Jesus, "Do you have no answer to the charges these men bring against you?" Jesus remains silent. Caiaphas demands, "By the living God, I charge you to answer: Are you the Messiah, the Son of God?"

Jesus responds, "As you say, I am. And to you all I say this: You will see the Son of Man sitting at the right hand of the Powerful One,[1316] coming on the clouds of Heaven."[1317]—Daniel 7:13-14.

Caiaphas rips his garments.[1318] "Blasphemy!"[1319] he shouts. "What do we need with more witnesses?" The high priest asks the court for its verdict, and the Sanhedrin pronounces judgment: death.[1320]

The attendants holding Jesus in custody cover his eyes and hit him, saying sarcastically, "Now, Messiah, play the prophet and tell us who hit you." The Messiah—the Son of God—is spat upon, slapped and insulted.[1321]

Meanwhile, in the courtyard, Peter awaits the trial's outcome. He and members of the high priest's staff surround a burning fire to warm themselves. In the firelight, Peter is recognized as Jesus' disciple by several officers and servants, including the girl at the gatehouse and a relative of the man whose ear Peter wounded.[1322] For over an hour Peter dodges accusations with denials, cursing and swearing.[1323] His Galilean accent gives him away as an associate of "Jesus of Galilee."[1324] When, for the third time, Peter insists he doesn't know Jesus, a rooster crows.[1325] His Lord's words echo in Peter's head: "Before a cock crows, you will disown me three times." As the realization of what he has done crashes down on him, Peter weeps bitterly.

Death of a Traitor
Matthew 27:1-10; Mark 15:1; Luke 22:66–23:1

At dawn, the council of elders reconvenes, and Jesus is brought before the Sanhedrin.[1326] Again, the court demands, "If you are the Messiah, tell us."

"You wouldn't believe it if I told you," Jesus responds. "And if I questioned you, you wouldn't answer. However, from now on the Son of Man will be seated at the right hand of the Powerful One[1327]."

The inquisitors persist: "Then are you the Son of God?"

"As you say: I am."

With that, the Sanhedrin declares there is no need to hear anything further.[1328] Jesus is bound and led away to Roman Governor Pontius Pilate.[1329]

Meanwhile, Judas Iscariot, motivated by a mix of despair and remorse,[1330] tries to return his thirty pieces of silver to the chief priests. "I sinned when I betrayed an innocent man," Judas tells them.

"What do we care"? the priests reply. "It's your problem."

Judas throws the thirty silver pieces into the Temple, then commits suicide.[1331] The priests conclude it is illegal to deposit "blood money"[1332] in the Temple coffers. Instead, they buy a potter's field, a so-called Field of Blood.[1333]

BIOGRAPHICAL SKETCH: PONTIUS PILATE

Little is known of Pontius Pilate's personal history. The name Pontius suggests that he belonged to a tribe of Samnite nobles from southern Italy called the Pontii. The family name Pilate (if drawn from the Latin *pilum*—meaning "javelin") could indicate descent from a military man or from a freed slave (if "Pilate" comes from the Latin *pileus*—a cap customarily worn by slaves who had been granted their freedom).

After Herod Archelaus was removed from his ethnarchy over Judea, provincial governors were appointed by the emperor of Rome to rule the province, Pilate evidently being the fifth of these. Prefects of Pilate's rank—the lower nobility, as opposed to aristocrats of senatorial status—were usually sent to barbarous territories like Judea.

Pilate had a knack for offending the religious sensibilities of his subjects. His predecessors, out of regard for Jewish scruples over the making of images, had avoided military standards bearing effigies of the emperor; Pilate, however, showed no such restraint. He placed in his quarters at Jerusalem gold shields bearing his own name and that of Tiberius Caesar. Outraged Judeans protested and declared their willingness to die when threatened with execution. Eventually, the emperor ordered Pilate to remove the shields.

Pilate used money from the Temple treasury to build an aqueduct for Jerusalem. Dedicated funds could legitimately be used for public works and Temple authorities apparently cooperated with Pilate. Nevertheless, thousands of Judeans protested when Pilate visited the city. When they refused to disperse, Pilate sent soldiers armed with clubs into their midst. Many protestors fell slain; others fled wounded. This incident may have been the basis for a complaint about Pilate brought to Jesus.—Luke 13:1.

The last recorded incident in Pilate's career was another bloody conflict. A multitude of armed Samaritans deluded by an impostor gathered on Mount Gerizim to uncover treasures supposedly buried by Moses. Pilate's troops killed several of the crowd. Samaritans complained to Pilate's superior, Lucius Vitellius, governor of Syria, who ordered Pilate to go to Rome. Before Pilate could present himself to the emperor, Tiberius died.

Pilate's fate is unknown. The historian Eusebius claimed that Pilate was obliged to commit suicide. Hundreds of years later, the Ethiopian Church canonized Pilate, claiming that he became a Christian.

The Governor of Judea Meets “the King of Israel”
Matthew 27:11-14; Mark 15:2-5; Luke 23:2-6; John 18:28-38

Outside Pontius Pilate’s royal residence, the accusers of Christ wait to hand over their prisoner.[1334] The governor emerges from his palace.[1335] “What charge do you bring against this man?” he asks.[1336] Claiming that it is illegal for them to execute wrongdoers, the Sanhedrists accuse Jesus of capital offenses:[1337] opposing payment of taxes to Caesar, and seditiously claiming to be their anointed ruler.[1338]

Pilate reenters the palace and summons Jesus. “You are the king of Israel?”[1339] Pilate inquires.

“As you say,” Jesus answers, then clarifies, “My kingdom does not belong to this world; if it did, the Judeans would not have arrested me. But really, the source of my kingdom is not here.[1340] I was born and came into the world to testify about the Truth.[1341] Everyone on the side of the Truth listens to me.”

Pilate wonders, “What is truth?”[1342] but he does not wait for further explanation. Returning to the crowd outside the palace, he announces, “I find no crime in that man.”

The mob insists: “He’s been a troublemaker from the day he came here from Galilee and started teaching throughout Judea.”[1343] Learning that Jesus is a Galilean, Pilate sees an opportunity to change the jurisdiction of this unwelcome case.

King Herod Meets the King of Kings
Luke 23:7-12

Having ascertained that Jesus is from Galilee, Pilate sends Jesus to Herod Antipas, the ruler of Galilee. Herod is in Jerusalem for Passover[1344] and is excited to meet Jesus, hoping to see him perform a miracle.[1345] But Herod’s curiosity will not be satisfied. Despite being questioned at length by the king and accused by the religious leaders who are present, Jesus says nothing. Herod and his guards discredit Jesus, contemptuously clothing him with a gorgeous robe and mocking him.[1346]

Herod sends Jesus back to Pilate. This incident dissolves the ill will between Herod and Pilate, and the two men become friends.[1347]

"The King of Israel" and His Crown of Thorns
Matthew 27:15-30; Mark 15:6-19; Luke 23:13-25; John 18:39–19:3

As Pilate sits on the judgment seat outside his palace,[1348] he receives a message from his wife regarding Jesus. "Leave that righteous man alone," she says. "Today I suffered much in a dream because of him."[1349]

Knowing it is out of envy that the priests have handed over Jesus, Pilate intends to release this "so-called Messiah." On Passover Pilate customarily frees a prisoner and he knows of a criminal in custody named Barabbas.[1350] Addressing the crowd, Pilate gives them a choice: "Jesus or Barabbas—which of the two shall I hand over to you?"

Incited by their religious and civic leaders, the people shout, "Barabbas!"[1351] When Pilate asks what he should do with Jesus, the people roar, "Execute him!"

Pilate pleads, "Why? What crime has he committed? I found in him nothing deserving of death—neither did Herod; I will therefore punish him and let him go."[1352] Again and again the enraged mob calls for Jesus' death;[1353] eventually, it will prevail.[1354] Pilate takes some water and washes his hands before the crowd, pronouncing himself innocent of bloodguilt. "This is your responsibility," he tells the people.

They respond, "Let his blood come upon our heads and those of our children."[1355]

Barabbas—a robber, seditionist and murderer—is set free. Jesus is stripped, then scourged.[1356] After this bloody beating, soldiers lead Jesus into the palace courtyard where a body of troops heaps further abuse on him.[1357] The men braid a wreath of thorns and push it down on Jesus' head,[1358] put a reed in his right hand and drape him with a scarlet-colored robe.[1359] In mockery they kneel and say, "Long live the King of Israel!"[1360] They spit on Jesus and repeatedly slap his face.[1361] Taking the reed, they hit him on the head with it, driving deeper into his scalp the sharp thorns of his "crown."

"Behold the Man!"
Matthew 27:31-32; Mark 15:20-21; Luke 23:26-31; John 19:4-16

Crowned with the braid of thorns and cloaked with the scarlet robe, Jesus is presented to the crowd by Pilate, who proclaims, "Behold the man!"[1362] and reiterates, "I find him guilty of no crime."

The chief priests and their henchmen repeat their demand for Jesus' execution, falling back on the charge of blasphemy. "We have a law," they say, "and according to the law he must die, because he claimed to be the Son of God."[1363]—Leviticus 24:16.

With increasing alarm, Pilate asks Jesus, "Who are you, really?" Jesus remains silent. "Do you refuse to speak to me," Pilate demands, "knowing that I have the authority to release you or to execute you?"

"Your authority over me comes from Heaven,"[1364] says Jesus, "so the greater guilt is borne by the ones who delivered me to you."[1365]

When the governor tries again to free Jesus, the crowd attacks Pilate's patriotism. "If you release him," they threaten, "you are no Friend of Caesar.[1366] Anyone who claims to be a king defies the emperor."[1367]

Pilate remonstrates, "This is your king!"

The chief priests assert, "Caesar is our king."

"Take him away!" the crowd cries. Finally, Pilate relents and hands Jesus over to be executed.[1368] The soldiers strip off the scarlet cloak and redress Jesus with his own clothes. As he is led away, Jesus must bear the instrument of his own death. Eventually, a passerby, Simon from Cyrene, is pressed into service.[1369]

Many people, some beating themselves in grief, follow Jesus to the site of execution. Jesus tells the "daughters of Jerusalem" to stop weeping for him.[1370] "Weep instead for yourselves and for your children," he says. "The time will come when people say, 'Happy are the childless women!'[1371] Then they will beg the mountains to fall on them and the hills to hide them.[1372] If things go this hard when the tree is green, what will happen when it withers?"[1373]

'This Man Was God's Son'
Matthew 27:33-56; Mark 15:22-41; Luke 23:32-49; John 19:17-30

Along with two criminals,[1374] Jesus is led to Golgotha,[1375] a location not far from Jerusalem.[1376] The three condemned men are stripped of their clothing.[1377] Soldiers notice that Jesus' tunic has no seam, being woven from top to bottom.[1378] Rather than tear this quality clothing and divide it among themselves, the soldiers cast lots to decide whose it will be.[1379] Their actions fulfill a prophecy concerning the Messiah: "They *make a game out of* dividing my clothes among themselves; they cast lots for the clothes on my back."—Psalm 22:18, *The Voice Bible.*

Wine drugged with myrrh and bitter gall is provided for the condemned; tasting it, Jesus refuses to drink. This offering (and a later, second one) was foretold in prophecy: "They gave me bitter drink in my food. And because I was thirsty they gave me sour wine."—Psalm 69:21, *New Life Version.*[1380]

Jesus is stretched out on the instrument of death; Roman soldiers pound nails into his hands and his feet.[1381] Jesus prays, "Father, forgive them—they don't realize what they're doing."[1382]

The soldiers see the sign above Jesus' head: "The King of Israel,"[1383] it reads. They taunt, "Save yourself, king!"

Passersby shake their heads[1384] and shout at Jesus, "You—the one who would destroy the Temple and rebuild it in three days—save yourself!" Enraged priests repeat the false testimony that was given earlier at the Sanhedrin trials.

At first, both criminals hanging on either side of Jesus rail against him. Eventually, however, one of the men rebukes the other, then beseeches Jesus to remember him favorably. To this penitent thief Jesus promises, "You will be with me in Paradise."[1385]

A mysterious darkness falls over all the land, lasting for three hours.[1386] During this period, five people approach the scene of execution: Mary Magdalene; Mary the mother of the apostle James the Less; and Jesus' mother Mary, accompanied by her sister Salome[1387] and her son the beloved apostle John.[1388] To his mother Jesus says, "There is your son"; to John, "There is your mother." John takes Mary home.[1389]

As the darkness ends, Jesus calls out, *"Eli, Eli, lama sabachthani?"*[1390] which means, "My God, my God, why have you forsaken me?"[1391] Some standing nearby misunderstand him to be calling for Elijah.[1392] Jesus says, "I'm thirsty."[1393] A bystander places a sponge soaked with sour wine[1394] on the end of a hyssop stalk and extends it to Jesus.[1395]

"Wait!" others say. "Let's see if Elijah comes to save him."

Finally, Jesus speaks his last words: "It is finished! Father, I place my life in your hands."[1396] Then he bows his head, stops breathing and expires. At that, a violent earthquake occurs. Rocks split; tombs outside Jerusalem[1397] break open and corpses are ejected.[1398] (Passersby who see the bodies enter the city and report it.) The dividing curtain in Jerusalem's Temple is ripped in two, from top to bottom.[1399]

People return to their homes, beating their chests in grief and shame. Observing at a distance are many female disciples who sometimes traveled with Jesus, deeply moved by all these momentous events. The army officer in charge at the execution proclaims, "Certainly, this man was the Son of God!"[1400]

A New Tomb
Matthew 27:57–66; Mark 15:42–47; Luke 23:50–56; John 19:31–42

Israel's law requires that bodies of the executed be buried on the day of death. (Deuteronomy 21:22-23; Joshua 8:29; 10:26-27) Soldiers break the two criminals' legs to hasten their demise.[1401] Jesus, however, appears to be dead. Instead of breaking Jesus' legs, a soldier jabs his spear into Jesus' side—blood and water ooze from the wound.[1402] What the soldiers do and refrain from doing to Jesus fulfill prophecy.—Psalm 34:20; Zechariah 12:10.[1403]

A wealthy man from the Judean city of Arimathea presents himself to Pontius Pilate. Joseph, a reputable member of the Sanhedrin, is also a secret disciple who did not support the council's action against Jesus.[1404] Now he asks the governor for Jesus' body.[1405] From the officer in charge at the execution, Pilate confirms that Jesus is dead;[1406] he grants Joseph's request.

Joseph prepares Jesus for burial assisted by Nicodemus, another member of the Sanhedrin who is sympathetic to Jesus. They wrap the body in clean, fine linen, bandage it and scent it with myrrh and aloes.[1407] Joseph owns an unused tomb in a nearby garden[1408]—there he lays Jesus to rest. A large stone is rolled in front of the tomb.[1409] All this is hastily done before the Sabbath begins.[1410] Mary Magdalene and Mary the mother of James the Less linger outside the tomb on that bitter afternoon.[1411]

The next day, the chief priests and Pharisees approach Pilate and say, "We just remembered a claim that impostor once made: 'After three days I will rise.' Order his grave secured until that third day, lest his disciples steal the body and tell people he rose from the dead. That deception would be worse than the first."[1412]

Pilate replies, "Take a guard of soldiers and secure the sepulcher as best you can."[1413]

PART THREE
"THE RESURRECTION AND THE LIFE"

(JOHN 11:25)

An Empty Tomb!

Matthew 28:1-15; Mark 16:1-8 [9-11];[1414] *Luke 24:1-12; John 20:1-18*

"Who will roll the stone away from the entrance for us?" Women on their way to Jesus' tomb discuss this dilemma,[1415] for they intend to treat his body with spices they have prepared.[1416] When they come to the grave at sunrise on Sunday,[1417] Mary Magdalene,[1418] Mary the mother of James the Less, Joanna and Salome are shocked: the immense boulder has been removed! Moreover, the guards are gone, and the tomb appears empty.

Mary Magdalene runs to report what has happened to the apostles. To the women who stay behind appear two men in dazzling robes.[1419] "Don't be afraid," one of the men says. "Are you looking for Jesus the Nazarene, who was executed? He has risen—he's not here! See for yourselves the place where they laid him. Now be on your way and tell Peter and the rest that he will meet them in Galilee,[1420] as he said he would." Overwhelmed with fear and joy, the women run to tell the apostles what they have seen and heard.

By now, Mary Magdalene has found Peter and John.[1421] "Someone has taken the Lord away from the tomb," she reports, "and we don't know where he is!" Peter and John run to Jesus' tomb, John getting there first.[1422] He looks in and sees the linen wrappings but remains outside.[1423] When Peter arrives, he goes inside the tomb and finds the bandages and the cloth used to cover Jesus' head.[1424] Now John enters, and he realizes that Mary has told the truth. Nevertheless, he and Peter don't yet understand that Jesus had to rise from the dead, according to Scripture.[1425] The apostles leave; Mary, who has followed Peter and John to the tomb, remains.

As the three other women are enroute to tell the disciples that Jesus is alive, the Lord himself appears to them. "Good morning!" he says, and they bow down to him. "Have no fear!" Jesus continues. "Go and tell my brothers that I will meet them in Galilee."

Meanwhile, the soldiers who were guarding Jesus' tomb have returned to Jerusalem and reported to the chief priests. According to the guards, a great earthquake struck; then an angel came down from the sky and rolled away the stone securing the sepulcher. Now some members of the Sanhedrin bribe the soldiers to say that, while they slept, Jesus' body was stolen by his disciples. "And if Governor Pilate hears of this," the soldiers are assured, "we'll put it right with him, so you won't have to worry." For their complicity, the soldiers accept a considerable sum of money, and the lie that Jesus' body was stolen circulates widely.[1426]

At the empty tomb, Mary Magdalene grieves. Looking inside, she sees two angels—one at the head of where Jesus' body had been lying and the other at the foot. "Why are you crying?" they ask.

Mary answers, "They have taken away my Lord, and I don't know where he is." Then she turns around and sees a man whom she takes to be the gardener. "Sir, if you carried him off," she says, "tell me where he is and I will take him away." When he speaks her name, Mary recognizes Jesus' voice.[1427] *"Rabboni!"* Mary exclaims as she embraces her Teacher.

"Mary, you can't hold onto me," Jesus tells her. "I must rise above this world to be with my Father and your Father; my God and your God. Go, tell this to my brothers."[1428]

Mary runs to where the apostles and other disciples are gathered. "I have seen the Lord!" she tells them, adding her account to what they have heard from the other women. Yet, the reports seem like nonsense to most of the men.

On the Road to Emmaus

[Mark 16:12-13;] Luke 24:13-49; John 20:19-23

That same day, two disciples leave Jerusalem for Emmaus,[1429] a seven-mile trek. As they walk and talk, a stranger joins them and asks, "What are these matters that you debate between yourselves?"

One of the disciples, named Cleopas,[1430] replies, "You must be the only person in Jerusalem who doesn't know what has happened there recently."

"What do you mean?" the stranger asks.

"Jesus the Nazarene—a prophet powerful in word and deed in God's eyes and those of the people—was condemned and executed by our religious and civic leaders[1431]. We had hoped that he was the one destined to liberate Israel." Cleopas and his companion relate the events of that day: women went to the tomb where Jesus was buried, found it empty and saw two angels who said that Jesus is alive; others who went to the tomb "found it just as the women had said."

The stranger laments, "Too slow of wit and too dull of heart to trust in what the prophets spoke, are you? Was it not necessary for the Messiah to suffer these things and to enter his glory?" Then he takes them through the writings of Moses and the prophets, explaining scriptures pertaining to the Messiah.—See Psalms 16 & 100 and Isaiah chapter 53; compare Acts 2:14-36; 8:32-33.

Finally, the trio comes to Emmaus. The two disciples invite their fellow traveler to stay with them, and he accepts. When they sit down to supper, the stranger says a prayer, breaks bread and hands it to the disciples. As soon as they recognize Jesus, he vanishes. They exclaim, "Our hearts were on fire[1432] as he spoke to us on the road, opening up the meaning of the Scriptures to us!"

Cleopas and his companion rush back to Jerusalem, where they find the apostles and others with them. Before the two disciples can say a word, others tell them that the Lord has risen and appeared to Peter.[1433] Cleopas and his companion relate their experience traveling to and in Emaus.

Suddenly, Jesus himself appears in the room! Even though they locked the doors out of fear, Jesus is standing in their midst.[1434] But they are frightened, imagining that they are seeing things. Attempting to allay their doubts, Jesus invites, "Look at my hands and my feet[1435]—it is I; touch me and see. A vision[1436] doesn't have flesh and bones, as you can see that I have." His followers are amazed but unconvinced. After asking for food, Jesus accepts a piece of broiled fish and eats it.

"As I told you before," Jesus says, "everything written about me in the Law of Moses, the Prophets and Psalms must be fulfilled."[1437] Enlightening their understanding of the prophecies, he continues, "It was written that Messiah would suffer, then rise from the dead on the third day; and in his name repentance and forgiveness would be preached in all the nations—beginning at Jerusalem. About these matters you will bear testimony.[1438] Mark this: I am sending to you what my Father promised. But until you are invested with that power from above,[1439] stay in the City."[1440]

Seeing Is Believing
John 20:24-29

When Jesus appears to his sequestered followers, the apostle Thomas is not present. Afterward, others tell him, "We saw the Lord!"

Thomas responds, "I won't believe it unless I see and touch the mark of the nails in his hands and press my hand into his side."[1441]

Eight days later, the apostles—including Thomas—are again meeting behind locked doors.[1442] Jesus appears in their midst and greets them: "May you have peace." Turning to Thomas, Jesus says, "Put your finger here, and see my hands, and take your hand and put it into my side. Stop doubting—believe!"[1443]

Thomas exclaims, "My Lord! My God!"[1444]

"You believe it's me because you see me?" Jesus asks. "Those who believe without seeing are happy."[1445]

Breakfast on the Seashore
John 21:1-23

The third time Jesus appears to the apostles as a group after his resurrection is at the Sea of Galilee. Peter, Thomas, Nathanael, James and John and two others fish all night without catching anything.[1446] At daybreak, they see—but do not recognize—Jesus on the beach.[1447]

"Children,"[1448] Jesus calls, "you don't have any fish, do you?"

"No!" the men answer.

"Cast the net out to starboard," Jesus suggests, "and you'll find some." The fishermen do as Jesus says. They cannot draw in their net for the weight of the catch!

John[1449] tells Peter, "It's the Lord!" Peter plunges into the sea and swims about a hundred yards to shore. The others in the boat follow slowly, pulling the net filled with 153 large fish.[1450] Getting to shore, they see bread and a charcoal fire with fish already on it. Jesus invites them to bring some of their catch and have breakfast.

After the meal, Jesus takes a walk with John and Peter. Addressing him as "Simon son of Jonah," Jesus asks Peter, "Do you love me more than all else?"[1451]

"Yes, Lord," Peter replies. "You know that you are dear to me."

Jesus urges him, "Feed my lambs." Again, Jesus asks Peter, "Do you love me?"

"Yes, Lord," Peter answers earnestly. "You know that you are dear to me."

Jesus responds, "Shepherd my sheep." Now Jesus asks Peter, "Am I dear to you?"

Grieved at this persistent questioning, Peter says emphatically, "Lord, you are aware of all things; you know that you are dear to me."

Once again Jesus tells Peter what he must do: "Feed my sheep."[1452] Jesus reveals that Peter, in old age, will stretch out his hands and someone will dress him and carry him where he does not wish to go. Jesus thus indicates by what sort of death Peter will glorify God.[1453] "Keep following me," Jesus urges.

Peter looks at John[1454] and wonders aloud, "What about this man?"

"If I wanted him to remain until I return,"[1455] Jesus answers, "how would it concern you? Your concern is to follow me." Jesus' statement about John becomes popularly misunderstood to mean that the apostle would never die.

'You Will Be My Witnesses'
Matthew 28:16-20; [Mark 16:14-20;] Luke 24:50-53; Acts 1:1-12

For 40 days after his resurrection, Jesus appears to his disciples—presenting himself alive to them by many convincing demonstrations, teaching them about God's kingdom.[1456] (1 Corinthians 15:5-7) At a mountain in Galilee, Jesus meets with the 11 apostles (and likely other followers[1457]). He commissions them to "make disciples in every nation"[1458] by teaching and baptizing people. "I am with you always and forever[1459]," Jesus vows.

One final time, at Bethany, Jesus meets with his apostles. He directs them to remain in Jerusalem and wait there for the fulfillment of a "promise." This promise will be kept when, in a few days, Jesus' followers are baptized with God's spirit.[1460]

After Jesus blesses them, the apostles ask, "Lord, are you now going to restore sovereignty[1461] to Israel?"

He simply replies, "Don't concern yourselves with when things will happen—that's the Father's business.[1462] He will empower you with his spirit[1463] to be my witnesses[1464] in Jerusalem,[1465] throughout Judea and Samaria, even to the ends of the earth."

Jesus rises heavenward and disappears into a cloud.[1466] As the apostles watch Jesus' departure, two men in white garments appear.[1467] "Why are you looking into the sky[1468]?" they ask. "Jesus, who has ascended into Heaven, will return in the same manner as you have seen him rise into the sky."[1469] Rejoicing, the apostles return to Jerusalem where they spend all their time in the Temple praising God.[1470]

To the Ends of the Earth
Acts 1:13-15; 2:1-42; 9:1-20

Crowds of visitors from far-away places are in Jerusalem to celebrate Pentecost. (See "Pentecost.") About 120 people—including the apostles, Jesus' mother Mary and her four other sons[1471]—assemble in an upper room in a house (possibly near the Temple).[1472] Suddenly, the sound of a roaring windstorm fills the place.[1473] Upon each one present tongues as if of fire manifest,[1474] and everyone speaks in foreign languages. Ten days after Jesus ascended to Heaven, he has baptized his followers with God's spirit, and the Christian congregation is born.

Hearing "wonderful works of God" being spoken of in different languages, a crowd gathers. People are amazed that they can understand what the disciples are saying.[1475] Peter stands up and explains what has happened and why: "God resurrected Jesus; of this we are all witnesses. Exalted at God's right hand, he received from the Father the promise of His spirit and poured it forth, as you can see and hear."[1476]

Thus, the apostle to whom Jesus entrusted the keys of the Kingdom introduces Christianity to fellow Jews and Jewish converts. (Matthew 16:19) Later, Peter opens to Samaritans[1477] and Gentiles[1478] the opportunity to receive God's spirit and enter the kingdom of Heaven.—Acts 8:14-17; 10:44-45.

It is a man named Paul,[1479] however, who becomes known as "an apostle to the nations."[1480] (Romans 11:13) He steps into Christian history as a Pharisee who witnesses the stoning of Stephen, the new faith's first martyr. (Acts 7:58-8:3) With authorization from the high priest to arrest Jesus' followers and extradite them to Jerusalem[1481] Paul heads to Damascus.[1482] Near the city, a brilliant light flashes around Paul, causing him to collapse on the road. A voice from an invisible source calls to him: "I am Jesus, the one you are really persecuting."[1483] He tells Paul to await further instructions in Damascus. Jesus also appears to Ananias, one of his disciples in Damascus, and tells him that he has chosen Paul to bear His name "to the nations." After arriving in Damascus, Paul is baptized by Ananias and starts preaching about Jesus, the Son of God.

From a determined persecutor of Christians to one of Christianity's boldest defenders, Paul is transformed.[1484] About 25 years after Jesus appeared to Paul on the road to Damascus, the Apostle to the Nations[1485] writes that Gospel Truth has been "preached in all creation under heaven."[1486]—Colossians 1:5-6, 23.

PENTECOST...

...is the New Testament name for the Festival of Harvest/Weeks, which occurred at the end of a seven-week harvest period. (Exodus 23:16; 34:22) This annual festival marked the end of the barley harvest and the beginning of the wheat harvest. "Pentecost" means "the fiftieth day"; it was observed on the fiftieth day counted from Nisan 16, the day when a sheaf of the first fruits of the barley harvest was offered. *(The New Compact Bible Dictionary*, page 446; Leviticus 23:15-16) Instructions for this festival are found at Leviticus 23:15-21, Numbers 28:26-31 and Deuteronomy 16:9-12. The celebration drew great multitudes of worshipers from distant lands to Jerusalem, making it an ideal occasion for the birth of the Christian congregation with its mission to bear witness to all people. (Acts 1:8; 2:11) This Day of Pentecost began the great harvest of souls—the day of Christianity's first fruits—who would be joined together in the power of God's spirit.

EPILOGUE

John 20:30-31; 21:24-25

Certainly, Jesus performed many other signs in sight of his disciples that were not recorded. If everything Jesus did was written in full detail, the whole world would not have enough room for all the books.[1487] But what has been recorded suffices to prove that Jesus Christ is the Son of God, and to prove we will live forever if we demonstrate faith in his name.

From Heaven Jesus gave his beloved apostle John a series of visions, which are found in the Bible book of Revelation. Through these visions, John lived to see Jesus return.—John 21:22.

By inspiration John found himself in "the Lord's Day." (Revelation 1:10) In that time, God's salvation through the Messiah's rule will come to pass. Citizens of Heaven will rejoice! But to people of the world the Devil will come in great anger, knowing that he has little time left. Christians living then will know that Satan is destined to be abyssed and inactive for 1,000 years while Jesus rules the kingdom of Heaven. The faithful apostles and the rest of the "little flock" will rule with him.—Luke 12:32; Revelation 5:10; 12:9-10, 12; 20:1-2, 6.

John describes conditions on Earth during the Millennium: "God will dwell with humankind; he will be with them, and they will be his people. Yes, God himself will be with his people. From their eyes he will wipe every tear. Death will be no more, neither will mourning nor outcry nor pain be anymore—they are past and gone." (Revelation 21:3-4) The benefits of Jesus' ransom sacrifice will come to Adam's descendants on Earth and lift from them the curse of inherited sin. Christ and his corulers will raise humankind to perfection. At the end of his Millennial Reign, Jesus will hand over the Kingdom and the perfected human family to his Father. Finally, God will be all things to everyone.—1 Corinthians 15:28.

Christ/Messiah: Both titles mean "Anointed One." (Matthew 1:16; John 1:41) Old Testament "prophets, priests and kings were anointed with oil; Jesus Christ is God's Anointed One, who functions as prophet when he speaks God's word, as priest when he sacrifices himself and as king when he rules."—*The NIV Topical Study Bible,* page 1222.

Lord: This title designates Jesus as the Master and Owner of his followers. (John 13:13; Jude 4) "He wants us to confess him as Lord in our lives. Everyone will someday make this confession, whether willingly or not."—*The NIV Topical Study Bible,* page 66.

Savior: By giving his life as the redemption price for sinful humankind, Jesus became the Savior of the world.—John 4:42.

Son of David: This phrase identifies Jesus as the heir of the covenant that was to be fulfilled by one of King David's descendants.—Matthew 12:23; 21:9.

Son of God: The Son received his life from God as well as his commission. (Mark 1:11; John 1:14) Also, Jesus was "declared to be the Son of God with power, according to the spirit of holiness, by the resurrection from the dead."—Romans 1:4, *King James Version.*

Son of Man ("Human One," *Common English Bible):* By means of his birth to Mary, Jesus became human; he was not an incarnate spirit. This title also indicates that Jesus would fulfill the prophecy of Daniel 7:13-14.—Mark 13:26.

BIBLIOGRAPHY/RECOMMENDED READING

- Biblical Studies Press, L.L.C. *The NET Bible:* First Beta Edition (1996, 1997, 1998, 1999, 2000, 20001).
- Bryant T. Alton, ed. *New Compact Bible Dictionary, The* (1967) Zondervan Publishing House. Grand Rapids, Michigan. Seventh printing (1972).
- Buursma Dirk R., ed. *NIV Topical Study Bible, The* (1989) The Zondervan Corporation. Grand Rapids, Michigan.
- Cole Marley. *Living Destiny: The Man from Matthew Mark Luke John* (1984) Second edition (1987) Proguides Publishers. Knoxville, Tennessee.
- Douglas J.D., ed. *New Bible Dictionary, The:* Second edition (1982) Tyndale House Publishers, Inc. Wheaton, Illinois.
- Edersheim Alfred. *Life and Times of Jesus the Messiah, The: New Updated Edition. Complete and unabridged in one volume* (1993) Hendrickson Publishers, Inc. Seventh printing (2002).
- Jones Alexander, ed. *Jerusalem Bible, The* (1966) Darton, Longman & Todd, Ltd. And Doubleday & Company, Inc. Garden City, New York.
- Radmacher Earl D., ed. *Nelson Study Bible, The* (1997) Thomas Nelson Publishers. Nashville, Tennessee.
- Reese Edward. *Reese Chronological Bible, The* (1982) Bethany House Publishers. Minneapolis, Minnesota.
- Robertson A.T. *Harmony of the Gospels for Students of the Life of Christ, A* (1922) Harper & Row Publishers, Inc. New York, Hagerstown, San Francisco, London (1950) Citizens Fidelity Bank and Trust Co.
- Sandmel Samuel, ed. *New English Bible, The* (1961, 1970) Oxford University Press, New York.
- Watch Tower Bible and Tract Society of Pennsylvania. *Jesus—The Way, the Truth, the Life* (2015) Watchtower Bible and Tract Society of New York, Inc. Brooklyn, New York.

- Watch Tower Bible and Tract Society of Pennsylvania. *New World Translation of the Holy Scriptures—Study Edition*. (2019) Watchtower Bible and Tract Society of New York, Inc. Wallkill, New York.

ABOUT THE AUTHOR

Curtis "Corey" Garwood has been a student of the Bible for over 30 years. He is a small business owner living in Evansville, Indiana. This is his first book.

FOOTNOTES

[1] "For a time after Christ's ascension the account was kept alive by oral instruction from eyewitnesses. But details are prone to change with continued oral repetitions and accuracy tends to suffer in course of time. Hence many writers began setting themselves to writing the vital record. Jehovah's holy spirit particularly guided in the composition of four such written records, our present four Gospels that head the collection of books making up the Greek cannon."—*"Equipped for Every Good Work,"* page 275. Published in 1946 by the Watchtower Bible and Tract Society, Inc., Brooklyn, NY.

[2] "... eternal life consists in knowledge, or rather the *pursuit* of knowledge, since the present tense [of the verb in John 17:3] marks *a continuance, a progressive* perception."—Marvin R. Vincent's *Word Studies in the New Testament* (emphasis original); https://biblehub.com/commentaries/vws/john/17.htm

[3] In Heaven Jesus is known as the Word of God. (John 1:1, 14; Revelation 19:13) He was God's Spokesman during his ministry on Earth. (John 12:49-50) The Word has existed from "the beginning," since before other spirit beings and the physical universe were created.—John 1:2; Colossians 1:15-17; Revelation 3:14.

[4] By means of Jesus, all other forms of life came into existence. Furthermore, eternal life is obtainable only through Jesus, making him a beacon—or light—of hope.—John 8:12.

[5] Jesus came into the world of humankind when he was born, of course, and when he went out among people as the Light of the World.—John 1:9; 3:19; 8:12; 12:46.

[6] All descendants of Adam are born in sin. (Romans 5:12) Through Jesus' sin-atoning sacrifice, his "brothers" are adopted as God's children. (Romans 8:15; Galatians 4:5; Ephesians 1:5; Hebrews 2:10-13) God acknowledges them as his children from the time that he begets them by his spirit. (John 1:12-13; 1 John 3:1) They must remain faithful until the end of their mortal lives to receive the full realization of being adopted into God's family.—Romans 8:17; Revelation 21:7.

[7] On Earth Jesus was not an incarnate angel; he was a man, "made a little lower than the angels." (Hebrews 2:9, *King James Version)* He called himself "the Son of man" *(KJV)* or "the Human One" *(Common English Bible).*—Matthew 8:20; see "Jesus, A.K.A. ..."

[8] Other spirit beings are called God's "sons" (Genesis 6:2, 4; Job 1:6; 2:1; 38:7) but they were created by God through his only begotten Son. (Colossians 1:15-16; Hebrews 1:2) In relation to all of God's spirit sons, Jesus holds a unique position of preeminence and glory. (John 1:14; 3:16,18; Hebrews 1:5-6; 1 John 4:9) On Earth he reflected God's glorious qualities. His resurrection to Heaven fully revealed God's glory.—John 17:5.

[9] In Jesus' time, diners at meals would recline on couches in such a way that one could lean back on the bosom, or chest, of a close friend. (Luke 16:23; John 13:23) As the one closest to his Father, Jesus could explain God more fully and thoroughly than anyone else could.—Matthew 11:27; Luke 10:22; 1 John 5:20.

[10] In the Bible, names are important, often revealing something about the person's character, nature or reputation.

"Zechariah" is a Hebrew name meaning "Jehovah remembers." Elizabeth's name means "God is [my] oath."—*The New Compact Bible Dictionary*, pages 149, 614.

[11] King David organized Israel's priesthood into 24 divisions, each to serve at the sanctuary in Jerusalem for one week every six months. The paternal house of Abijah (a priestly descendant of Aaron) was chosen by lot to head the eighth division. Zechariah belonged to this division. (1 Chronicles 24:10; Nehemiah 12:17; Luke 1:5) The brazier that stood on the altar of incense in front of the Holy of Holies was kept burning by the priest on duty. He also supplied it with fresh incense, once before the morning sacrifice and again after the evening sacrifice. While the incense burned, worshipers gathered for prayer outside the sanctuary. (Exodus 30:7-8; compare Revelation 5:8) According to tradition, lots were drawn for this service but a priest who had previously officiated was not allowed to do so again before all others had performed the service. This tradition has influenced how Bible translators render Luke 1:9. *The Bible in Living English*, for example, speaks of "the customary drawing of lots for the priestly service." *The Message* version says that this was Zechariah's "one turn in life to enter the sanctuary of God and burn incense." See "The Temple—Center of Israel's Worship."

[12] Gabriel's name means "man of God." *(The New Compact Bible Dictionary*, page 184) He is the only angel named in the Bible other than Michael, and the only materialized angel to reveal his own name. Each time he appears in the Bible, Gabriel bears a momentous message.—Daniel 8:16-26; 9:21-27; Luke 1:11-20, 26-38.

[13] "John" is the English equivalent of the Hebrew name "Johanan," meaning "Jehovah has been gracious." *(The New Compact Bible Dictionary*, page 288) When God names a child, greatness usually follows.—Genesis 16:10-11; 1 Kings 13:1-2; Isaiah 7:14-15.

[14] John's mission was to prepare Israel for her savior, the Messiah. For those who responded to his call to repent, John promised reconciliation to God.—Mark 1:4; Luke 3:3.

[15] The worship service concluded when the priest emerged from the Temple and blessed the people. See Numbers 6:24-26.

[16] Children were a sign of God's blessing. (Genesis 1:28; Psalm 127:3-5; 128:3-6) For a married woman to be childless was viewed as a reproach. (Genesis 30:23; 1 Samuel 1:4-8; Psalm 113:9) Some rabbis considered it a husband's obligation to separate from a wife who could not give him children.

[17] According to tradition, Mary's mother and Elizabeth's mother were sisters, making Mary and Elizabeth first cousins. The Bible does not specify their exact relationship. Elizabeth was of the tribe of Levi and Mary was of the tribe of Judah, so they may not have been closely related.

[18] "Mary" corresponds to the Hebrew name "Miriam," the meaning of which is uncertain. Besides the mother of Jesus, five women in the New Testament are named Mary: (1) Mary Magdalene, (2) Mary the mother of James and Joses, (3) Mary the sister of Martha and Lazarus, (4) Mary the mother of John Mark and (5) Mary of Rome. (Matthew 27:56; John 11:1; Acts 12:12; Romans 16:6) In first-century Israel, Mary was one of the most common female names.—*Aid to Bible Understanding*, pages 1118-21. Published in 1971 by the Watchtower Bible and Tract Society, Inc., Brooklyn, NY.

[19] Human kings ruled Israel as God's anointed representatives. The promise that David's **throne**—his royal line—would endure forever was fulfilled in Jesus Christ, Son of David. (**Luke 1:32**; see 2 Samuel 7:16-17; Psalm 89:20-29, 34-37; 132:11-12; Isaiah 9:6-7; Jeremiah 23:5-6) Most first-century Israelites, expecting a political Messiah, did not recognize Jesus as David's heir.

[20] God's spirit made possible Jesus' miraculous conception. Jesus' holiness refers to his sinless nature.—Hebrews 4:15; 1 Peter 2:22.

[21] Mary's response, unlike that of Zechariah, betrayed no lack of faith. (Luke 1:18, 45) She unquestioningly accepted her role in the outworking of God's purpose. Also, Mary "willingly submitted to what her heart would feel hardest to bear—that of incurring suspicion of her purity in the sight of all, but especially in that of her betrothed," Joseph.—*The Life and Times of Jesus the Messiah: New Updated Edition* (page 107 note 28) by Alfred Edersheim.

[22] This trip might have taken several days. The distance between Nazareth and Ain Karim, the traditional hometown of Zechariah and Elizabeth, is 80 miles (128 km).

[23] Under the influence of God's spirit, John gave his first testimony about Jesus from his mother's womb.—Luke 1:15.

[24] Mary's song (her *magnificat*, as some call it) is a recital of what God had done for her and for other Israelites in the past; it gives evidence of her spirituality and her knowledge of the Scriptures. Compare Luke 1:46-49 with Genesis 30:13; Deuteronomy 10:21; Psalm 34:3; 35:9; 69:30; 119:9; Isaiah 61:10; Habakkuk 3:18; Malachi 3:12; and Luke 1:52-55 with 2 Samuel 22:51; Job 12:19; Psalm 98:3; 107:9; Isaiah 41:8-9; Micah 7:20.

[25] The administration of Judea as a Roman province from A.D. 6 to 135 was carried out primarily by a series of prefects, procurators and legates. See "Biographical Sketch: Pontius Pilate."

[26] The apostle Paul was mobbed in the Temple because of a rumor that he had brought a Gentile within the forbidden area. (Acts 21:27-32) Jesus' death broke down the "wall" between Jews and Gentiles.—Ephesians 2:14.

[27] The Ark of the Covenant was a chest made of acacia wood and overlaid with gold; it was kept in the Most Holy compartment of the tabernacle and later in the Most Holy of Solomon's temple. The ark had a solid gold cover with two cherubs facing each other; its principal contents were the two tablets of the Ten Commandments. (Deuteronomy 31:26; 1 Kings 6:19; Hebrews 9:4) When the ark disappeared and under what circumstances are unknown.

[28] God instituted circumcision as a sign of his covenant with Abraham. Traditionally, boys were circumcised and named at eight days old. (Genesis 17:10-14; Leviticus 12:3) According to Edersheim, "a benediction was spoken before circumcision, and ... the ceremony closed with the usual grace over the cup of wine, when the child received his name in a prayer."—page 111.

[29] Zechariah may have used a wooden tablet like the ones in use for centuries throughout the ancient Middle East. The recessed portion of the tablet was filled with a thin layer of wax. The soft surface was written on with a stylus made of iron, bronze or ivory. A typical stylus was pointed on one end and flattened into a chisel shape on the other. The flattened end was used to smooth mistakes out of the wax.

[30] Zechariah's question of unbelief had struck him speechless, but his answer of faith restored his voice. Unbelief cannot speak whereas faith loosens the tongue.

[31] Zechariah's *Benedictus* (its first word in the Latin Vulgate translation) is a praise psalm, one that calls for God to be praised ("Blessed be...") and then states why. (Luke 1:68, *King James Version)* Zechariah's *Benedictus* includes all three types of biblical prophecy: foretelling future events, forthtelling the Word of God, and praising God.

[32] Or "horn of salvation," namely, Jesus. (Luke 1:69, *King James Version)* Animals with horns use them to attack and defend. In the Bible, horns often represent strength, conquest and victory.—Deuteronomy 33:17; 1 Samuel 2:10; 2 Samuel 22:3; Psalm 75:4-5, 10; 132:17; Ezekiel 29:21; Daniel 7:24; 8:3-9, 20-22; Micah 4:13; Zechariah 1:18-21.

[33] **The house of his servant David** is a reference to the Messiah's descent from King David.—**Luke 1:69**; see 2 Samuel 7:12-13.

[34] God's power through his Son was aimed at greater enemies than mere human warriors. Jesus the Liberator provided the way to freedom from the chief source of oppression, the Devil and his demons. (Hebrews 2:14-15) Jesus freed many people from demonic possession and opened the gates of freedom to all those wishing to cast off the oppressions of false religion. (Matthew 23:4; Luke 4:18, 33-36; John 8:31-32) By his course of integrity he conquered, not just a city or an empire, but the world. (John 14:30; 16:33) Salvation through Christ frees believers to serve God without fear through a life of ethical integrity.

[35] Finally able to speak, Zechariah proclaimed what Gabriel told him in the Temple. (Luke 1:16-18) Both alluded to the prophecies of Isaiah 40:3 and Malachi 3:1. John the Baptist would be the forerunner of Jesus and prepare Israel for the Messiah by telling them of their need to repent. (Matthew 3:1-3; Mark 1:2-4; Luke 3:3-4) The coming Dayspring would provide enlightenment and forgiveness to sinners in spiritual darkness.—Luke 1:77-79.

[36] How Joseph discovered Mary was pregnant is not disclosed. In Israel engagement was a legally binding arrangement. A "betrothal" period of no longer than one year preceded the marriage. "At the betrothal, the bridegroom, personally or by deputy, handed to the bride a piece of money or a letter, it being expressly stated in each case that the man thereby espoused the woman. From the moment of betrothal both parties were regarded, and treated in law (as to inheritance, adultery, need of formal divorce), as if they had been actually married, except as regarded their living together." (Edersheim, page 245) Under Israel's law, indecency was grounds for divorce or annulment, and an engaged woman who slept with another man was stoned to death.—Deuteronomy 22:23-24; 24:1.

[37] To prepare Joseph for what he was about to hear, the angel called him **son of David**, reminding him of the promise in God's covenant with King David. (**Matthew 1:20**; see Psalm 89:3-4) Jesus is the heir of the kingship promised in that covenant.—Matthew 1:1.

[38] Wedding formalities ended with the husband taking his bride to live in his home, thereby publicly declaring her to be his marriage partner.—Genesis 24:67.

[39] Jesus' name means "Jehovah is salvation"; it was not an unusual name in Israel.—*The New Compact Bible Dictionary*, p. 106; Colossians 4:11.

[40] "Immanuel" was one of the prophetic title-names by which Messiah (Christ) would be identified. "Matthew considers Jesus' virgin birth as the ultimate fulfillment of the sign God told Isaiah to give to King Ahaz in Isa 7:14." (Verlyn D. Verbrugge: *The NIV Topical Study Bible*, page 1044) King Ahaz of Judah was opposed by King Rezin of Aram and King Pekah of Israel. "As a sign to Ahaz, a son would be born of a woman, and before that boy reached the age where he could tell right from wrong, the two kings would no longer be a threat to Ahaz. ... Since the Hebrew noun translated virgin in Is. 7:14 can also mean 'young woman,' some have suggested that Isaiah was prophesying about a son born during the lifetime of Ahaz—perhaps Isaiah's son Maher-Shalal-Hash-Baz (Is. 8:3)." (Matthew 1:23 footnote, *The Nelson Study Bible*. Copyright © 1997 by Thomas Nelson, Inc. Used by permission.) Other proposed identifications of the young woman and her son are (1) Ahaz' wife and her son Hezekiah the future king and (2) the "virgin" Israel and her people.—Jeremiah 14:17; Amos 5:2.

[41] Matthew's and Luke's genealogies of Jesus vary from that found in 1 Chronicles chapter 3. Such differences likely reflected those in the genealogical registers which were then in use and fully accepted by the Israelites.

[42] The second Cainan between Arphaxad and Shelah is regarded by most scholars as a copyist's error. (Luke 3:35-36; compare Genesis 10:24; 11:12; 1 Chronicles 1:18, 24) Another possibility is that "Cainan" is a variant of "Chaldean." Hence, the Greek text may have read, "the son of the Chaldean Arphaxad."

[43] Augustus evidently fulfilled Daniel 11:20, a prophecy about a ruler who sends an exactor through the kingdom. The gospel account adds a detail which helps to date this event. According to Luke 2:2, this registration took place when Quirinius was governor over the Roman province of Syria. Publius Sulpicius Quirinius, a distinguished Roman senator, served two non-consecutive terms as Syria's governor. The Bible's internal chronology harmonizes with Jesus' being born during Quirinius' first term, 3-2 B.C.

[44] This registration made it possible for Jesus to be born in Bethlehem, the hometown of his ancestor King David. There was a town named Bethlehem just 7 miles (11 km) from Nazareth, but prophecy specified that the Messiah would come from Bethlehem-Ephrathah. (Micah 5:2) That Bethlehem, known as the city of David, was in Judea, in the south. (Luke 2:4) The actual travel distance through Samaria (based on present-day roads) may have been up to 93 miles (150 km). The route passes through hilly country, and the arduous journey would have taken several days. Mary would soon become a mother but that did not exempt her and Joseph from making this trip.

[45] Apparently, Mary had no human help in delivering her child; it was she who swaddled the boy and laid him in the manger. Swaddling dates to antiquity. (Job 38:9) At Luke 2:4 the Greek word for "manger" may refer to the stall in which animals were kept or to their feeding place. (Luke 13:15) It may also be that, as in more recent times, mangers were cut in the rock walls of caves that were used for sheltering animals. "Justin Martyr wrote about A.D. 100 that the stall [where Jesus was born] was in a cave adjoining an inn which was used for livestock." *(The New Compact Bible Dictionary*, page 342) In view of the significance of Jesus' birth, its humble surroundings are ironic.

[46] A large number of sheep were regularly needed for offerings at Jerusalem's Temple; probably some of the sheep raised around Bethlehem were for this purpose. Sheep may be led out to pasture during the daytime in any season of the year. However, these shepherds were spending the night out in the fields with their flocks. This fact suggests that Jesus was born prior to the start of the rains in mid-October. By December, Bethlehem frequently experiences frost at night. (The Emperor would not likely have required people who were already inclined to revolt against him to travel in winter to register.) Because it was only at lambing time that shepherds stood guard over their flocks in the field, it has been suggested that Jesus was born in early spring. On the other hand, if Jesus was baptized on or around his thirtieth birthday (as Luke 3:23 implies) in the Jordan River, he was probably born in a warmer time of the year.

[47] **Luke 2:11** is the first reference in the New Testament to Jesus as **Savior**. See "Jesus, A.K.A. ..."

[48] Or "Christ the Lord." (Luke 2:11, *King James Version*; compare verse 26) The angel's use of the title Christ was evidently prophetic. At the time of his baptism, Jesus was anointed Lord and Christ by God's spirit. (Matthew 3:16-17; Mark 1:9-11; Luke 3:21-22; Acts 2:36) The term Christ ("anointed") was originally an adjective that came to be "a technical term referring to the hoped-for anointed one, that is, a specific individual. In the N[ew] T[estament] the development starts there ..., is so used in the gospels, and then develops in [the letters of] Paul to mean virtually Jesus' last name."—Luke 2:11 footnote, *The NET Bible*. Copyright © 2001 by Biblical Studies Press, L.L.C.

[49] When Jesus was baptized, God expressed goodwill to his Son with words of approval. (Mark 1:11; Luke 3:22) God expresses his goodwill also to those who demonstrate faith in him and become followers of his Son.—Ephesians 1:5, 9; Philippians 2:13; 2 Thessalonians 1:11.

[50] Edersheim speculates that "the shepherds told what had been spoken to them about this Child" to people in the Temple "to which they would bring their flocks" for sacrificial purposes. (See note above) "This may have prepared not only those who welcomed Jesus on His presentation in the Temple"—namely, Simeon and Anna—"but filled many others with expectancy."—page 133 note 26; Luke 2:25-38.

[51] Mary must have been a thoughtful, meditative person. She stored away the angel's words in her heart so that she could ponder over them and draw strength from them. Compare Luke 2:51.

[52] See Leviticus 12:3; compare Genesis 17:12. God's law to Moses, also called the Mosaic Law, refers to Israel's legal code given by God through Moses in the sixteenth century B.C.

[53] God's law by Moses required that a mother undergo purification for 40 days after giving birth to a male. (Leviticus 12:1-4) Through the process of childbirth, the sin of Adam is transmitted from one generation to the next. Mary was no exception, contrary to claims made by some theologians.—Romans 3:23; 5:12.

[54] Exodus 13:12, *New World Translation of the Holy Scriptures* (2013). As the firstborn son, Jesus was holy to God and belonged to him. For this reason, the Law required that Jesus be redeemed by Joseph and Mary. "The ceremony at the redemption of a firstborn son," says Edersheim, "consisted of the formal presentation of the child to the priest, accompanied by two short 'benedictions'—the one for the law of redemption, the other for the gift of a firstborn son, after which the redemption money was paid." (page 136) Parents of a firstborn son had to pay five silver shekels when the child was at least one month old. (Exodus 13:2; Numbers 18:15-16) Joseph would have been allowed to pay the five shekels while Mary made her purification offering, that is, 40 days after Jesus' birth. See note above.

[55] Under the Mosaic Law, a woman who had given birth was to offer a young ram as a burnt offering. If the family could not afford a ram, as was evidently the case with Mary and Joseph, two turtledoves or two young pigeons were acceptable. (Leviticus 12:6-8) There was a "superintendent of turtledoves and pigeons," with whom those who brought the poor's offering would deal. In the Court of Women ("so called because the women occupied in it two elevated and separated galleries"), according to Edersheim, the superintending priest was stationed by the third of thirteen trumpet-shaped contribution chests "to inform the offerer of the price of the turtledoves, and to see that all was in order." (pages 137, 170) Had Joseph and Mary already received the costly gifts brought by the Magi, the couple could have afforded a sheep for sacrifice when they went to the Temple. (Matthew 2:9-11) The Magi visited, not when Jesus was a newborn as depicted in Nativity scenes, but when he was older.

[56] According to Orthodox Church tradition, Simeon had been one of the translators of the Greek Septuagint version of the Old Testament. As he translated Isaiah 7:14 an angel appeared and promised that he would not die until he had seen the Messiah born of a virgin. This would make him well over 200 years old at the time of the meeting described in Luke 2:25-35.

[57] For a person to **die in peace** could mean his dying a tranquil death after having enjoyed a full life or after the realization of a cherished hope. (Genesis 15:15; 1 Kings 2:6) Being God's slave or **servant** was not a drudgery, but an honor and a privilege.—**Luke 2:29**; compare Joshua 14:7; 2 Samuel 7:5, 8; 2 Kings 10:10; Psalm 89:3; Isaiah 43:10.

[58] Spiritual enlightenment from the Messiah would benefit, not just the Israelites and Jewish converts, but the Gentile **nations** as well. (**Luke 2:32**; see Isaiah 42:6; 49:6; 52:10; 60:3; Luke 1:79) Jesus was, after all, the Light of the World.—John 8:12; 9:5.

[59] As foretold, Jesus proved to be a stumbling stone to many of his own countrymen. (Isaiah 8:14) Others, however, would put faith in Jesus, figuratively rising from a spiritually dead state to a righteous standing with God. (Isaiah 28:16; Ephesians 2:1) Simeon's prophecy was a grim reminder that the innocent child would become an object of hatred, and this hatred was already at work.—Matthew 2:13.

[60] Evidently Simeon foretold the pain and sorrow that Mary would suffer in connection with her son's death.—John 19:25.

[61] "Jesus is a litmus test for where people stand before God. He is a Judge who will expose the thoughts of all people (see Acts 10:42, 43; 17:30, 31)."—Luke 2:35 footnote, *The Nelson Study Bible.* Copyright © 1997 by Thomas Nelson, Inc. Used by permission.

[62] Anna's fasts and prayers indicated that she mourned over prevailing conditions and longed for change. (compare Nehemiah 1:4) For centuries Israel had been subject to foreign powers and deteriorating religious conditions had reached even to the Temple and its priesthood. By speaking about little Jesus to all those—like herself and Simeon—"waiting expectantly for God to rescue Jerusalem," Anna acted as a prophet. (Luke 2:38, *New Living Translation;* also verse 25) Basically, prophesying is declaring inspired messages from God, revealing the divine will; doing so may or may not involve foretelling the future.—Acts 2:17-18.

[63] Professor E.E. Ellis describes the magi as "religious astrologers." *(The New Bible Dictionary*—2nd edition, page 722) The Bible does not reveal their names or the number of them.

[64] Only the magi saw the **star**, so it was probably not a real star or a conjunction of planets. (**Matthew 2:2**) Contrary to what Christmas carols say, the "star" did not guide the magi directly to Jesus in Bethlehem. First, it led them to Jerusalem, where they met King Herod. The appearance of the "star" set in motion events that threatened the life of Jesus; it also resulted in the murder of innocent children. Far from being a sign from God, the "star" was of diabolical origin.—2 Corinthians 11:14.

[65] Chief priests were principal men of the priesthood, including former high priests and, possibly, the heads of the 24 priestly divisions. During Jesus' time, scholars (or scribes) were teachers of the Law. Originally, however, they were copyists of the Scriptures.

[66] See Micah 5:2. The village of Bethlehem, although insignificant in population and governing power, would become very significant because the greatest ruler would come from there to lead God's people. Bethlehem was King David's hometown and was sometimes called the City of David. (Luke 2:4, 11; John 7:42) This Bethlehem was in the territory of Judah (Judea) and not to be confused with the Bethlehem in Zebulun's territory. (Joshua 19:10, 15; Judges 17:7; 19:1) Bethlehem was earlier known as Ephrath, or Ephrathah.—Genesis 35:19; 48:7.

[67] After presenting Jesus at the Temple in Jerusalem, his parents apparently returned to Bethlehem and there were visited by the magi. By virtue of their long journey from the East, the magi did not arrive in time to visit Jesus in the stable where he was born. They visited Jesus when he was a child living in a house, contrary to what is depicted in Nativity scenes.

[68] Both frankincense (olibanum) and myrrh came from resinous gum that was obtained by making incisions in the bark of small trees or thorny shrubs. The frankincense tree grew along the southern coast of Arabia, and the myrrh bush thrived in the semidesert countries of present-day Somalia and Yemen. Both spices were highly esteemed for their fragrance. Frankincense was an ingredient of the holy incense burned at Israel's Tabernacle and Temple; it also accompanied grain offerings and was placed on each row of the Showbread inside the Holy Place. (Exodus 30:34-36; Leviticus 2:1; 24:7) Myrrh was one of the ingredients of the holy anointing oil and was used to scent such things as garments or beds; it was added to oil for massages and body lotions and was also used to prepare bodies for burial. (Exodus 20:23; Proverbs 7:17; John 19:39) Specimens of the products of their country, the offerings of frankincense and myrrh expressed the magi's homage of their land to the newborn king of Israel. "In this sense," says Edersheim,"the

Magi may truly be regarded as the representatives of the Gentile world." (page 149; see Psalm 72:10-11; Isaiah 49:23; 60:3, 10-11) The gift of gold was appropriate and timely. Jesus' family—evidently of little means—were soon forced to flee as refugees.

[69] Egypt was then a Roman province and home to a large Jewish population. Bethlehem was about 6 miles (9 km) south/southwest of Jerusalem, so Joseph and Mary could travel southwest to Egypt without passing through Jerusalem, where Herod issued his murderous edict. From Bethlehem to Egypt was probably a distance of at least 75 miles (120 km).

[70] "Considering the population of Bethlehem, their number could only have been small," Edersheim estimates, "probably twenty at the most. But the deed was none the less [sic] atrocious; and these infants may justly be regarded as the 'protomartyrs,' the first witnesses, of Christ, 'the blossom of martyrdom' .... The slaughter was entirely in accordance with the character and former measures of Herod."—page 149; see "Biographical Sketch: Herod the Great."

[71] The magi must have told Herod that they had been watching the so-called star for at least two years.—Matthew 2:7, 16.

[72] Jeremiah 31:15, *New Heart English Bible*—Jehovah Edition. In Jeremiah's prophecy, "Rachel," a symbol of all mothers in Israel, figuratively weeps over her sons taken into exile to the land of the enemy. Jeremiah's prophecy also contains the comforting promise of a return from enemy territory. (Verse 16) The application of this prophecy according to Matthew 2:17-18 refers to a return from enemy Death by means of a resurrection.—1 Corinthians 15:26.

[73] As the "son" of the prophet's text, Israel prefigured the Messiah.—Hosea 11:1; Matthew 2:15.

[74] Mary was living in Nazareth when Gabriel visited her.—Luke 1:26.

[75] "Nazarene" became an epithet applied to Jesus (and later to his followers). "The allusions to [Nazarene] as a title given to the Messiah in prophecy (Mt. 2:23) has been frequently taken as a reference to the 'Branch' ... of Is. 11:1 and similar passages ... ." (A.F. Walls: *The New Bible Dictionary*—2nd edition, page 818) Isaiah (11:1) referred to the promised Messiah as a Branch "out of [David's father Jesse's] roots." *(King James Version)* Jeremiah (23:5; 33:15) wrote about a righteous Branch as an offshoot of David. Zechariah (3:8; 6:12-13) described a king-priest named Branch (capitalized in the *KJV*).

[76] James may have been next to Jesus in age, being the first named of Mary's four other sons. (Matthew 13:55; Mark 6:3) After his resurrection, Jesus appeared to James. (1 Corinthians 15:7) James and his brothers may have been among the thousands who were baptized at Pentecost. (Acts 1:13-14; 2:1, 41) James became a prominent member of the congregation in Jerusalem and wrote the Bible book bearing his name. (Acts 15:13; 21:18; Galatians 1:19; 2:9, 12; James 1:1) Jesus' half-brother Jude evidently wrote the Bible book by that name. (Jude 1) Jesus had at least two half-sisters. (Matthew 13:55; Mark 6:33) Regarding the supposition that James, Joseph, Simon and Jude were Joseph's children from a previous marriage, Edersheim asks: "How could our Lord have been, through Joseph, the heir of David's throne (according to the genealogies), if Joseph had elder sons? And again, What became of the six young motherless children when Joseph and the Virgin went first to Bethlehem, and then into Egypt, and why are the elder sons not mentioned on the occasion of the visit to the Temple?"—page 252, note 2.

[77] Heli's wife, the mother of Mary, was Anna, whose sister had a daughter named Elizabeth, the mother of John the Baptizer. This tradition would make Elizabeth the first cousin of Mary.—Luke 1:36, *King James Version*.

[78] A comparison of Matthew 27:56 with Mark 15:40 indicates that Salome was the mother of the sons of Zebedee—James and John. John 19:25 suggests that Salome was also the fleshly sister of Mary, the mother of Jesus. Salome was a disciple of Jesus, among the women accompanying him and ministering to him from their belongings.—Luke 8:3.

[79] "The other Mary" was the wife of one whose name in Aramaic was Clopas but whose name in Greek was, supposedly, Alphaeus. (Matthew 27:61; 28:1; Mark 16:1; Luke 6:15; John 19:25, *American Standard Version)* She was present at the execution of Jesus in company with his mother Mary and Salome. Two days later, this "other Mary" and Mary Magdalene were the first ones to talk with the resurrected Christ. (Matthew 27:56; 28:1-10) If her husband was, as tradition claims, the brother of Joseph the foster father of Jesus, then Clopas' and Mary's sons James and Joses were Jesus' cousins. (Mark 15:40) James, also known as "James the Less" to distinguish him from the apostle James, the son of Zebedee, was appointed as one of Jesus' twelve apostles. James had a son named Judas who likewise was designated an apostle. This Judas was known as Thaddaeus, or the "son of James," to differentiate him from Judas Iscariot.—Luke 6:16, *ASV;* Matthew 10:3; John 14:22.

[80] Such an apprenticeship would typically have begun when a boy was about 12 to 15 years of age and would stretch over many years.

[81] This caravan traveled together for protection and fellowship. The journey through hilly and mountainous terrain may have been a round-trip of nearly 190 miles (300 km). The entire excursion—traveling from Nazareth, the stay in Jerusalem and the return trip—would take about two weeks. Although women were not required to attend the Passover celebration, Mary accompanied Joseph on the journey to Jerusalem. (Exodus 23:17; 34:23; Deuteronomy 16:16; see "Passover.") This may have been Jesus' first visit to the Temple since infancy. Attendance at the feasts in Jerusalem was not required until a young man came of age at 13.

[82] Although the celebration was a week-long affair (Exodus 23:15) personal attendance in the Temple was necessary only on the first two days of Passover; afterward, says Edersheim, "it was lawful to return to one's home—a provision of which, no doubt, many availed themselves."—page 170; see "Passover."

[83] On Sabbaths and feast-days members of the Sanhedrin taught on the terrace of the Temple.

[84] On Jesus' childhood education, Edersheim speculates that he went to a "Synagogue School" in Nazareth. Additionally, Jesus attended synagogue services, where Moses and the prophets were read, and occasional addresses were delivered. "From his intimate familiarity with Holy Scripture, in its every detail, we may be allowed to infer that the home of Nazareth, however humble, possessed a precious copy of the Sacred Volume in its entirety."—page 162; see Luke 4:16-17.

[85] The Greek text of Luke 2:49 is elliptical, reading: "I must be in the ... of my Father." An activity or a place is not specified. Jesus said he was "about [his] Father's business" *(King James Version)* or "in [his] Father's house." *(American Standard Version)* In his Father's house was where Jesus conducted his Father's business, so the two possibilities are not very different. (John 2:16) These are Jesus' earliest recorded words; they indicate that he to some

extent understood the miraculous nature of his birth and his special personal relationship with his heavenly Father. Probably, Joseph and Mary had passed on to him the information received during angelic visitations as well as through the prophecies of Simeon and Anna. (Matthew 1:20-21; 2:13, 19-20; Luke 1:30-37; 2:10-19, 29-35, 38) And yet, "Joseph and Mary did not comprehend the full import of Jesus' words which were the first recorded sign of his growing independence (cf. Jn 2:4)." However, "Jesus' independence was not rebellion. He returned to Nazareth and remained with the family until the beginning of his public ministry. ... Though she did not understand what he meant, Mary did not forget his words. Perhaps Luke learned of them directly from her."—Merrill C. Tenney: *The Wycliffe Bible Commentary*, page 1033. Copyright © 1962 by The Moody Bible Institute of Chicago, IL. See Luke 2:50-51.

[86] This obedience was more significant than that of any other child; it was part of his fulfilling God's law in every detail.—Exodus 20:12; Galatians 4:4.

[87] Or "the Immerser." (Mark 1:4, *The Emphasized Bible* by Joseph Bryant Rotherham) The designations "Baptist" and "Baptizer" are used in Mark interchangeably (6:14, 24-25), while John is always called "the Baptist" in Matthew and Luke. He is referred to simply as John in the Gospel of John.

[88] This desert region north of the Dead Sea where John lived and preached is also where Jesus was tempted by the Devil. Generally uninhabited, this barren eastern slope of mountains stretches down—a drop of some 3,900 feet (1,200 m)—toward the western bank of the Jordan River and the Dead Sea.

[89] The heavenly kingdom had drawn near in the sense that Jesus Christ, its future ruler, was about to appear. John was preparing God's people to see His means of salvation. (Luke 1:76-77; 2:30) Those baptized by John publicly repented over sins against God's law. Their change of mind and heart helped lead them to the Messiah.—Galatians 3:24.

[90] Isaiah 40:3, *A Literal Translation of the Bible* by Jay P. Green, Sr. (See also Malachi 3:1) "In ancient times, a messenger was sent ahead to announce the coming of the king. Local communities would often repair rough roads to ensure the comfort of the king as he traveled." (Mark 1:2-3 footnote, *The Nelson Study Bible*. Copyright © 1997 by Thomas Nelson, Inc. Used by permission.) John the Baptist 'prepared the way' as the forerunner of Jesus, who would come in his Father's name as Jehovah's representative.—John 5:43; 8:29.

[91] Desert locusts (or grasshoppers) are mostly protein. When used for food today, only the thorax is eaten (raw or cooked). They are said to taste something like shrimp or crab. God's law to Israel designated these insects as clean for food. (Leviticus 11:21- 22) Eating locusts and wild honey was not unusual for people living in the desert. The honey that John ate may have been produced by the Syrian (or Palestine) honeybee, a wild species that is native to the area and acclimated to the desert.

[92] While many of Jerusalem's religious leaders lived in ease and luxury, John lived in the desert. His lifestyle, as well as his clothing and diet, depicted him in his role as God's prophet. John's garment of woven camel's hair and his leather belt were reminiscent of the dress of the prophet Elijah, who prefigured John. (2 Kings 1:8; Matthew 17:12-13; compare Zechariah 13:4) Camel's haircloth was a rough fabric commonly worn by the poor. Because John was a Nazirite from birth, it is possible that his hair had never been cut. (Numbers 6:2-5; Luke 1:15) His dress and appearance likely made it immediately apparent that he lived a spartan life, completely devoted to doing God's will.

[93] "John's baptizing was a recurring popular event that attracted large crowds. ... One may visualize throngs making the trek to the wilderness, with people waiting in line to be baptized. As each person was baptized by John, he or she would admit to individual sin and the need for the Messiah." (Mark 1:5 footnote, *The Nelson Study Bible*. Copyright © 1997 by Thomas Nelson, Inc. Used by permission) John baptized people in symbol, or acknowledgment, of their heartfelt repentance for sins against God's law covenant. (Acts 19:4) Those baptized by John included cheating tax collectors and bully soldiers who blackmailed people. Tax collectors were generally shunned and classed with sinners and prostitutes. (Matthew 11:19; 21:32) If Israelite soldiers who were in a covenant relationship with God desired to be baptized in symbol of repentance of sins, they had to stop extorting others by false accusation. (Luke 3:12-14) John's baptism was directed, not to ritual purification like the baptism of proselytes to Judaism, but to moral purification.

[94] The wickedness of the religious leaders was spiritual poison to unsuspecting people. John compared them to snakes driven from their desert holes by the heat of a fire.

[95] In other words, "Let your change of heart be seen in your works," those works indicating heartfelt regret over a former way of life, wrongdoing or what one has failed to do. "Make clear by your acts that your hearts have been changed."—Matthew 3:8; Luke 3:8; *The Bible in Basic English;* see Acts 3:19; 26:20; 2 Peter 3:9.

[96] Unable to afford unfruitful trees taking up valuable space or a tree with unproductive branches, a fruit-grower would cut off what was dead. Placed and aimed, the ax of God's judgment was ready to begin cutting down **trees** that did not bear the fruit of repentance. (**Matthew 3:10**; **Luke 3:9**) Compare John's language and imagery with Psalm 74:5-6; Jeremiah 46:22-23.

[97] According to the Talmud, "everything that a servant will do for his master a scholar shall perform for his teacher, except the menial task of losing his sandal thong." (John 1:27 footnote, *The Nelson Study Bible*. Copyright © 1997 by Thomas Nelson, Inc. Used by permission) John the Baptist did not consider himself worthy to perform such a "menial task" for the Messiah.

[98] Or "will dip." (Matthew 3:11; Mark 1:8; Luke 3:16, *The Emphatic Diaglott* by Benjamin Wilson [interlinear reading]) "**Baptism** figuratively means 'to be identified with,' as an unbleached cloth is identified with the color in a vat of dye when it is dipped. As John the Baptist preached and the people identified with his message, they were baptized as an outward sign of their inward **repentance** or 'change of mind.'"—**Luke 3:3** footnote, *The Nelson Study Bible*. Copyright © 1997 by Thomas Nelson, Inc. Used by permission.

[99] Or "with divine power and judgment." (Luke 3:16 footnote, *The New English Bible)* John knew that the coming kingdom would be characterized by a great display of God's spirit in the lives of His people. (Joel 2:28-29) Those baptized with God's **spirit** become his spirit-begotten children, with the prospect of ruling in Heaven. (Revelation 5:9-10) This baptism would begin a few years later at Pentecost when Jesus poured out God's spirit on his followers. (Acts 1:5; 2:2-4, 33) The baptism with **fire** would occur in A.D. 70 when Roman armies destroyed Jerusalem and its Temple. (**Matthew 3:11**; **Luke 3:16**) There will be another destructive baptism by fire at the Last Judgment.—2 Peter 3:3-13; Revelation 20:9.

[100] A farmer would spread sheaves of grain on a threshing floor, stand on the sledge, and have an animal—such as a bull—pull him across the grain. The hooves of the animal and the sharp stones on the underside of the sledge would cut and break down the grain stalks, releasing the grain. The farmer would then use a winnowing fork, or shovel, to throw the threshed grain into the air. The wind would carry off the chaff, leaving the heavier grain to fall to the ground. He repeated the action until all the grain was separated. The chaff—the thin protective covering or husk on the kernels of cereal grains—was often gathered and burned to prevent it from blowing into the piles of grain and contaminating them. John the Baptist used threshing to illustrate how righteous people would be separated from the wicked.—Matthew 3:12; Luke 3:17; compare Matthew 13:24-30, 37-42.

[101] Although the Pharisees were popular, they looked down on the people. (John 7:49) The Sadducees were wealthy and favored the rich and, therefore, had little influence with the common folk.

[102] The precise time of the Sadducees' emergence as a religious sect is not known. The first historical mention of them by name appears in the writings of Josephus (A.D. ca. 37-ca. 100).

[103] While the Pharisees endeavored to please people by mitigating the Law's penalties with specious reasoning, the Sadducees interpreted God's law conservatively and applied its penalties with rigor. The Sadducees, for example, forbade the rendering of conjugal dues for forty days after the birth of a male infant and for eighty days after the birth of a female because the Law spoke of a woman as being unclean for such periods of time. (Leviticus 12:2-8) They even went so far as to forbid marital relations on the Sabbath because of the exertion involved.

[104] John's baptism was for those repenting of their sins. Jesus had no sin. (2 Corinthians 5:21; Hebrews 4:15; 7:22; 1 Peter 2:22) Jesus' baptism symbolized the presentation of himself to do God's will, in fulfillment of prophecy.—Psalm 40:7-8; Hebrews 10:5-9.

[105] Perhaps "coming down like a dove to enter into him." (Mark 1:10, *The New Testament: An American Translation* by Edgar J. Goodspeed) Jesus was the first person to be baptized with God's spirit; it anointed Jesus for and guided his messianic mission. (Matthew 4:1; 12:18, 28; Luke 4:14, 18; Acts 10:38) As God's spirit came down upon Jesus it may have looked like a fluttering dove approaching its perch. Doves, symbolizing innocence and purity, were offered as sacrifices to God. (Leviticus 1:14; 5:7; 12:8; 14:22; 15:14-15; Matthew 10:16; 21:12; Mark 11:15; Luke 2:24; John 2:14, 16) A dove released by Noah brought an olive branch back to the ark, indicating that the floodwaters were receding, and a time of rest and peace was at hand. (Genesis 8:8-22) Thus, at Jesus' baptism, the dove called attention to the role of Jesus as the Messiah, the pure and sinless Son of God who would sacrifice his life for humankind and lay the basis for a period of rest and peace during his rule as Messiah-King.

[106] Some of the significant words of Jesus' prayer were apparently later recorded at Hebrews 10:5-7. The Gospel of Luke gives the matter of prayer special attention. See "The Gospel According to..."

[107] Memories of his pre-human existence in Heaven may have been restored to Jesus at the time of his baptism and anointing.—John 6:46; 8:38; 17:5.

[108] To help us understand Jesus' relationship to God theirs is compared to a human son's relationship to his father.—Psalm 2:7; Matthew 11:27; Mark 13:32; Luke 9:26; John 1:14; 3:35; 5:19-23, 26; 8:28; 14:13; Hebrews 1:5-6; 2 Peter 1:17; 1 John 1:3; 2 John 3. See "Jesus, A.K.A..."

[109] This is the first of three instances in the gospels where God is reported as speaking audibly to humans. (Matthew 3:17; 17:5; Mark 1:11; 9:7; Luke 3:22; 9:35; John 12:28) By this declaration accompanied by the outpouring of God's spirit, Jesus was begotten as His spiritual Son, "born again" with the hope of returning to heavenly life and anointed by spirit to be God's appointed King and High Priest. (John 3:3, *King James Version;* see Luke 1:32-33; Hebrews 5:5) These events also identified Jesus as the Christ, the promised Messiah. (See "Jesus, A.K.A. ...") Jesus began his ministry knowing that he had his Father's approval and the power of His spirit upon him.

[110] The Bible describes certain individuals—including Jesus—as being filled with God's spirit. (Luke 4:1; Ephesians 5:18) This suggests that a person full of God's spirit might need a special filling for a particular task or challenge. See Exodus 31:2-5; 35:30-33; Luke 1:15, 67; Acts 2:4; 4:31; 6:3, 5; 7:55-60; 9:17-20; 11:24; 13:9-11, 51-14:1.

[111] Only Mark (1:13) mentions the wild beasts in this wilderness, apparently for the benefit of readers unfamiliar with Israel's geography. (See "The Gospel According to...") The area was the habitat of boars, hyenas, leopards, lions and wolves.

[112] The Hebrew word transliterated "Satan" and the Greek word for "Devil" mean, respectively, "adversary" and "slanderer."—*The New Compact Bible Dictionary*, pages 132, 526.

[113] Deuteronomy 8:3, *The Bible in Living English* by Steven T. Byington. Jesus knew that it would be wrong to use his miraculous powers to satisfy personal desires. He also demonstrated his dependence on God by refusing to eat at Satan's command. Meeting all three tests with quotation from Scripture, Jesus showed the power of the written Word to fight temptation. With consistent, meaningful use of Scripture, Jesus resisted and defeated Satan. By adopting this spiritual battle strategy, Christians can successfully meet the Devil's temptations.—Ephesians 6:17; James 4:7.

[114] From the southeastern corner of the Temple precinct, there was a drop of some 450 feet (137 m) to the floor of the Kidron Valley. The southeast structure had a flat roof with a parapet and was the highest in the Temple. Jesus and Satan may have gone to the Temple in Jerusalem by means of a vision.

[115] Psalm 91:11-12, *A Literal Translation of the Bible*. From his quotation Satan significantly omitted the words "to keep you in all your ways." (Matthew 4:6; Luke 4:10) "Satan tempted Jesus to gain public attention through spectacle rather than through His righteous life and message."—Matthew 4:6 footnote, *The Nelson Study Bible*. Copyright © 1997 by Thomas Nelson, Inc. Used by permission.

[116] Deuteronomy 6:16, *A Literal Translation of the Bible*. Malachi 3:10 explains the scriptural way to test Jehovah.

[117] The Devil apparently caused Jesus to see a vision that appeared to be real, as there is no literal mountaintop from which all the kingdoms of humankind can be seen.

[118] "Jesus was faced with the idea of being a material and political Messiah with its accompanying human privileges of wealth, glory, power. He chose instead utter dependence on God, humility, obedience to God's will."—Matthew chapter 4 note a, *The Jerusalem Bible*: Edited by Alexander Jones. See Luke 17:25; Hebrews 5:8.

[119] Or "fall down and do an act of worship to me." (Matthew 4:9, *New World Translation*) The Greek verb for "worship" is in the aorist tense, which indicates a single action. The Devil was not asking Jesus for ongoing adoration but for just one "act of worship."

[120] Deuteronomy 6:13, *New Heart English Bible*—Jehovah Edition. Jesus would not and could not serve Satan; he served Jehovah, and "no man can serve two masters."—Matthew 6:24, *King James Version*.

[121] The site of this community east of the Jordan, also called Bethabara, is unknown (John 1:28, *King James Version*); it is not the Bethany located near Jerusalem.—Matthew 21:17; Mark 11:1; Luke 19:29; John 11:1.

[122] The group included priests, Levites and possibly Pharisees. (John 1:19, 24) Priests oversaw Temple worship; Levites assisted them. (1 Chronicles 23:24, 28, 32) These men may have been on an informal mission from the Sanhedrin to learn more of what they heard from the Pharisees and the Sadducees.—Matthew 3:7.

[123] Concerned about maintaining peace under Rome's watch, Israel's rulers kept a close eye on professed messiahs. John showed awareness of the popular opinion that he might have been the Christ.—Luke 3:15.

[124] Some first century rabbis deduced from 2 Kings 2:11 that Elijah was still alive; others expected the resurrection of the prophet, based on Malachi 4:5. John the Baptist did not view himself as Elijah in person or as a reincarnation. The angel Gabriel told John's father Zechariah that John would accomplish his mission with "Elijah's spirit and power." (Luke 1:17; compare Matthew 17:10-13) "The history of John the Baptist," says Edersheim, "was the fulfilment *[sic]* of that of Elijah." Edersheim notes the similarities between the men and their times. "It was to a society secure, prosperous, and luxurious, yet in imminent danger of perishing from hidden, festering disease; and to a religious community which presented the appearance of helpless perversion, and yet contained the germs of a possible regeneration, that both Elijah and John the Baptist came. Both suddenly appeared to threaten terrible judgment, but also to open unthought-of possibilities of good. And, as if to deepen still more the impression of this contrast, both appeared in a manner unexpected, and even antithetic to the habits of their contemporaries. John came suddenly out of the wilderness of Judaea, as Elijah from the wilds of Gilead; John bore the same strange ascetic appearance as his predecessor; the message of John was the counterpart of that of Elijah; his baptism that of Elijah's novel rite on Mount Carmel."—page 177.

[125] Based on Deuteronomy 18:15, 18 the Israelites expected Messiah to be another Moses, prophet *par excellence*. (Numbers 12:7; John 6:14, 31-32; 7:40) Acts 3:20-22 identifies this prophet as Jesus.

[126] Isaiah 40:3, *New Heart English Bible*—Jehovah Edition. John identified himself as the fulfillment of Isaiah's prophecy, as his father Zechariah had. (Luke 1:76) This identification was confirmed by three gospel writers and by Jesus Christ.—Matthew 3:3; 11:7-10; Mark 1:3; Luke 3:4; 7:24-27.

[127] The clergymen wanted to know by what authority John was performing a religious rite.

[128] John acknowledged that he was preparing the way by getting people in a proper heart condition to accept the foretold Messiah. Thus, John's message served as a public notice that the ministry of his successor Jesus Christ was about to begin. John was born before Jesus and started his ministry before Jesus started his own. Jesus, however, did far greater works than John, in that sense surpassing him.

[129] The expression **Lamb of God** occurs only at John 1:29, 36 (although Jesus is spoken of figuratively as the Lamb almost thirty times in Revelation) and could reflect a number of passages in the Old Testament: the ram that Abraham offered up instead of his son Isaac (Genesis 22:13), the Passover lamb that was slaughtered in Egypt for the deliverance of the enslaved Israelites (Exodus 12:3-13), the male lamb that was offered on God's altar in Jerusalem each morning and evening (Exodus 29:38-39) or God's Servant brought to slaughter like a lamb. (Isaiah 53:7) Israelites offered sheep in recognition of sin and to gain an approach to God. These offerings foreshadowed the sacrifice that Jesus would make when he surrendered his perfect human life on behalf of **the world** of humankind who are guilty of sin inherited from Adam.—**John 1:29**; see 1 Corinthians 5:7; 1 Peter 1:19.

[130] Jesus is in permanent possession of God's spirit; it remains on him. Compare Isaiah 42:1.

[131] The other disciple might have been John the son of Zebedee, the traditional author of the fourth gospel. (Matthew 4:21; Mark 1:19; Luke 5:10) The writer never identifies himself by name, never mentions the apostle John by name, and always refers to John the Baptist simply as "John."

[132] Later events suggest that John the son of Zebedee likewise found his brother James and brought him to Jesus; yet, the Gospel of John does not include this personal detail.

[133] **John 1:41** explains that the title **Messiah** is translated "Christ," both meaning "Anointed One." (*The New Compact Bible Dictionary*, pages 106, 358; Matthew 1:1; see "Jesus, A.K.A. ...") In Bible times, priests, rulers and prophets were ceremonially anointed with oil.—Leviticus 4:3; 1 Kings 19:16.

[134] As **John 1:42** explains, **Cephas** is translated "Peter," a Greek name that means "rock." (*The New Compact Bible Dictionary*, page 448) In the Scriptures, Simon alone bears these names. After Jesus' death and resurrection, Peter lived up to the meaning of his name as a "rock" of strength for his fellow Christians. See Luke 22:32.

[135] Presumably to attend a wedding in Cana (roughly a two-day journey).—John 2:1.

[136] Philip was from Bethsaida, as were Andrew and Peter, who may have had something to do with Jesus finding Philip. (John 1:44-45) Bethsaida lay north of the Sea of Galilee and east of the Jordan River; it had a large Gentile population, which may explain Andrew and Philip's non-Jewish names.

[137] A comparison of Matthew 10:3, Mark 3:18 and Luke 6:14 with John 1:45-46 shows that Nathanael was also called Bartholomew. As seen in the case of Peter and others, it was not uncommon for a person to be known by more than one name.

[138] **The Law** refers to the Bible books of Genesis through Deuteronomy. **The Prophets** refers to the prophetic books of the Old Testament. (**John 1:45**) The entire OT bears witness about Jesus. (Matthew 5:17; Luke 24:27, 44; John 5:39; Acts 10:43; Revelation 19:10) Interestingly, prophecy associated the fig tree with messianic peace and plenty.—Micah 4:4; Zechariah 3:10.

[139] Nazareth stood in a mountain basin, surrounded by hills overlooking the plain of Esdraelon (Jezreel). The area was well-populated, with a number of cities and towns nearby. Nazareth was located close to important trade routes, so its inhabitants would have had access to information about the social, religious and political goings-on of the time. Nazareth also had its own synagogue. (Luke 4:16, 23) The gospels consistently call Nazareth a "city," denoting a population center larger than a village. (Matthew 2:23; Luke 1:26; 2:4, 39; 4:29) Although Nathanael's question is commonly understood as a rhetorical comment on Nazareth's insignificance, he may simply have been expressing surprise that Philip seemed to think that the Promised One was coming from a city in Galilee, since the Scriptures had foretold that the Messiah would come from the Judean town of Bethlehem.—Micah 5:2; John 7:42, 52.

[140] There was nothing hypocritical or devious about Nathanael. Jesus' words may reflect Psalm 32:2.

[141] Nathanael's exclamation amounted to a confession of Jesus' messiahship. Compare Psalm 2:6-7.

[142] Nathanael and the other apostles saw Jesus heal the sick, expel demons and raise the dead. They themselves were empowered to perform miracles.—Matthew 10:1, 8.

[143] In an important way angels minister between God and humans who have his approval. (Compare Genesis 28:12) Those who walked with Jesus had evidence that God's angels ministered to him and that he was under the special care and guidance of his Father. This was the first time that Jesus referred to himself as the Son of Man. See "Jesus, A.K.A. ..."

[144] Such an event was held, says Edersheim, in a "spacious, lofty dining-room, which would be brilliantly lit with lamps and candlesticks." Guests would be "disposed round tables on couches, soft with cushions or covered with tapestry, or seated on chairs."—page 248.

[145] Located in the hills north of Nazareth, Cana was about a three-day walk from where John was baptizing. (John 1:43; 2:1) Favored by many scholars as the location for Cana is Khirbet Qana, about 8 miles (13 km) north of Nazareth. In Arabic the place is known as Qana el-Jelil, the equivalent of Cana of Galilee. Religious tradition favors identification with Kafr Kanna, located 4 miles (6.5 km) northeast of Nazareth, possibly because it is easily accessible to pilgrims from Nazareth.

[146] No mention is made of Joseph, suggesting that Mary was by this time a widow. Tradition holds that Joseph was significantly older than Mary. Her suggestion that Jesus do something about the lack of wine implies that Mary was related to the bride or groom. To run out of wine at a wedding (a feast that often lasted for a week) would have been a humiliation in a culture that viewed hospitality as a sacred duty. Was Mary asking Jesus to give some godly exhortations to the guests and thus relieve the bridegroom's embarrassment? Was she merely reporting the situation to Jesus? Or was she asking him for a miracle? Jesus had performed no miracles up to this point. However, Mary had every reason to believe that her son was the Messiah, and now his public ministry had begun.

[147] The Son of God's activities were directed by his heavenly Father, not by family or friends. Besides, the **time** for Jesus to publicly identify himself as the Messiah had not yet come. **(John 2:4**; compare John 7:30; 8:20; 12:23, 27; 13:1; 17:1) Despite this gentle rebuke, Mary sensed that Jesus was not opposed to providing help, as her reaction showed.

[148] These vessels would have contained water for foot washing and handwashing. Israelites washed their hands before, during and after meals. Water was also needed for purifying cups and vessels. (Mark 7:3-4; compare Matthew 23:25; Luke 11:39) Unlike vessels made of other materials, such as clay, vessels of stone were not considered susceptible to ceremonial defilement. (Leviticus 11:33) This may explain the stone vessels' connection with "the Jewish manner of purifying."—John 2:6, *New Heart English Bible*.

[149] The director was responsible for seating guests and the overall running of matters, a combination of head waiter and master of ceremonies.

[150] Customarily, the everyday wine was served after the guests' palates were dulled with the better wine. Jesus' wine was so fine it astonished the director to see it being served late in the celebration.

[151] Performing miracles (also called "signs" in the Gospel of John) was one way Jesus demonstrated his credentials as the Messiah.—John 2:11, 23; 3:2; 6:2, 14, 26; 7:31; 12:17-18; 20:30-31.

[152] Capernaum was a center of Jesus' Galilean ministry. (Matthew 9:1) The royal official whose son Jesus healed was from Capernaum. (John 4:46-54) He may have heard Jesus speak there or picked up the story about the miracle at Cana from one of Jesus' disciples. Capernaum sat on the northwest shore of the Sea of Galilee, 680 feet (204 m) below sea level. This city was more prominently situated than Nazareth or Cana and evidently larger. (The first century population would have been around 1,500.) Capernaum was a major trade and economic center in the North Galilean region. Today Capernaum is a favorite tourist destination of visitors to Galilee.

[153] John 2:13 is the first of three or four references to Passover in that gospel. There is clear mention of a second (or third) Passover in John 6:4, and a third (or fourth) in 11:55; 12:1; 13:1; 18:28, 39 and 19:14. It is possible, if not probable, that the unidentified festival referred to in John 5:1 was a Passover.

[154] God's law required the Israelites to make sacrifices at the Temple, and pilgrims—some of whom traveled long distances—needed provisions while in Jerusalem. The Law allowed them to sell their produce and animals, bring the money to Jerusalem, and buy offerings and what was needed for their stay in the city. (Deuteronomy 14:23-26) Inside the Temple complex (probably in the Court of the Gentiles) merchants set up shop to sell sacrificial animals. These businessmen had a reputation for taking advantage of people.

[155] The sale of sacrifices within the Temple grounds was one of the chief sources of income for the wealthy and powerful family of the chief priest. Edersheim describes "the scene around the table of an Eastern money-changer—the weighing of the coins, deductions for loss of weight, arguing, disputing, bargaining." Truly, as Jesus said, "they had made the Father's House a mart and place of traffic."—page 255.

[156] Israel's law required males over 19 years old to pay a Temple tax. Only a half-shekel coin could be used to buy sacrificial animals, and Roman coins were unacceptable because of their imperial portraits—idolatrous images to the Israelites. Pilgrims had to exchange their currency for money that would be accepted at the Temple. Jesus evidently felt that the fees charged by the moneychangers were exorbitant and that their actions amounted to extortion.

[157] Jesus' actions fulfilled Zechariah 14:21: "And there is no merchant any more in the house of Jehovah of Hosts on that day!"—*Literal Translation of the Holy Bible* by Robert Young.

[158] Or "zeal," defined as "an intense, positive, burning interest, marked by a sense of dedication."—John 2:17 & note, *New World Translation of the Holy Scriptures* (Study Edition).

[159] This challenge, says Edersheim, "marked two things: the essential opposition between the Jewish authorities and Jesus, and the manner in which they would carry on the contest, which was henceforth to be waged between Him and the rulers of the people." (page 259) The only **sign** that Jesus' religious enemies will see is the raising of his **temple** (the Sign of Jonah).—**John 2:18-19**; see Matthew 12:39-40; 16:4; Luke 11:29-30.

[160] As "the way" to "worship the Father in spirit and in truth," Jesus supplanted the Temple as the "place" for believers to worship God acceptably. (John 4:20-24; 14:6; Revelation 21:22) The Messiah was the foretold cornerstone of the Christian congregation. (Psalm 118:22; Isaiah 28:16; Ephesians 2:20-21; 1 Peter 2:5-8) Figurative use of a temple being applied to people is not unusual in the Bible.

[161] "Nicodemus appears as an exception to the statement of [John] 2:24, as one whom Jesus did trust, and who amid all difficulties of temperament and station proved not unworthy of the trust." (*A Harmony of the Gospels for Students of the Life of Christ* by A.T. Robertson, page 25) Religious representatives from the Pharisees had investigated John the Baptist. From them Nicodemus likely learned that John, while denying that he was the Messiah, said that the Messiah was present. (John 1:20, 24, 26-27) Edersheim speculates that Nicodemus visited Jesus at the apostle John's residence in Jerusalem. (John 19:27) Likely, Nicodemus wanted "to shroud his first visit in the utmost possible secrecy. It was a most compromising step for a Sanhedrist to take. With that first bold purgation of the Temple a deadly feud between Jesus and the Jewish authorities had begun, of which the sequel could not be doubtful."—Edersheim, pages 263-64.

[162] Nicodemus was not speaking for the whole Sanhedrin but at least one other member, Joseph of Arimathea, believed in Jesus. (Luke 23:50-51) The popularity of Jesus damaged the prestige of the Sanhedrin, in particular the Pharisees. "They were the ones most people thought would be able to identify the long-awaited Messiah and announce Him to the people. Unfortunately, the Pharisees had begun to think of the coming Messiah as one who would elevate and honor them when He came. But Jesus showed no inclination to do this. Instead, He called all to repentance, even the Pharisees. He made it painfully clear to the Pharisees that their devotion to Scripture was undermined by their tendency to apply it wrongly and to exalt themselves over others. Although they had diligently studied the Scriptures, they had not learned the central truths of Scripture: justice, mercy, and faith (Matt. 23:23)." (*The Nelson Bible*, page 1762. Copyright © 1997 by Thomas Nelson, Inc. Used by permission) Nicodemus, a teacher, was willing to be taught.

[163] Or "born from above." (John 3:3, *The Emphasized Bible)* A new birth "from God" is from Heaven above. (John 1:13, *The Bible in Basic English;* 1 John 3:9; see 1 Peter 1:3, 23) This birth Jesus contrasted with being born of the flesh.—John 3:6-8; 6:63.

[164] When Jesus was baptized in water, God's spirit descended upon him. Jesus was thus **born from water and spirit**. **(John 3:5)** At that time, God announced that he had brought forth Jesus as a spiritual son. (Matthew 3:16-17; Mark 1:11; Luke 3:21-22) Others would eventually receive God's spirit and thus be born again as his spirit-begotten children. A born-again Christian is a baptized believer, begotten by God to be his child with the prospect of eternal life in Heaven.—Romans 8:14-18.

[165] Nicodemus could hear, feel and see the effects of the wind, but he could not know its origin or destination. Similarly, those who have not been **born from water and spirit** would find it difficult to understand how God's spirit could cause a person to be born again; nor could they grasp the glorious future that lies ahead for such a person. (**John 3:5**) "Wind" and "spirit" are two meanings of one Greek word.

[166] Or "Amen, amen, I say to you." (John 3:11, *Catholic Public Domain Version)* Jesus frequently used the term *amen* to emphasize the absolute truthfulness and reliability of a statement, a promise or a prophecy. This use of *amen* is said to be unique in sacred literature. Only the Gospel of John repeats the term in succession, doing so in all 25 occurrences.

[167] Isaiah 44:3-5 and Ezekiel 37:9-10 are pertinent examples of water and wind as life-giving symbols of God's spirit. Nicodemus had enough information at his disposal to have understood Jesus' statements about the necessity of being born from above by the regenerating work of God's spirit. See also Proverbs 30:4-5.

[168] In order to live, Israelites bitten by poisonous snakes had to gaze at the copper serpent put up by Moses. Similarly, sinful humans who desire to gain eternal life must look to Jesus and demonstrate faith in him.—Numbers 21:5-9; Hebrews 12:2.

[169] Going beyond mere belief or recognition that someone exists, genuine faith is demonstrated through obedience. (Hebrews 11:1; James 2:19-22) In John 3:36, demonstrating faith in the Son is contrasted with disobeying the Son.

[170] John 3:15 contains the first mention of eternal life in that gospel. Eternal life through Jesus is a gift from God. (Romans 6:23) Jesus offered humankind the Water of life (John 4:14; 7:37-38), the Bread of life (John 6:33, 35, 48, 51, 53-54) and the Light of life (John 8:12).

[171] Or "For God loved the world in this way..." (John 3:16, *Christian Standard Bible)* Jesus' words emphasize (1) the degree to which God loved the world of redeemable humankind and (2) the way he expressed that love.

[172] Other spirit beings are God's "sons," but they were created by God by means of his **unique**, "only-begotten Son."—**John 3:16**, *King James Version;* see Genesis 6:2, 4; Job 1:6; 2:1; 38:7; Colossians 1:16.

[173] God did not send his Son to "condemn the world" of humankind. (John 3:17, *King James Version)* He sent Jesus on a loving mission to save those who showed faith.—2 Peter 3:9.

[174] Jesus personified light in his life and teachings and reflected understanding and enlightenment from God. (John 1:7-9) The expression **come into the world** seems to refer primarily to Jesus' ministry as a light-bearer to the world of humankind rather than to his birth.—**John 3:19**; see John 12:46.

[175] "Since God is light and his first act in creation was to dispel darkness, understandably darkness became a symbol of sin and evil. Living in sin is walking in darkness, and one controlled by sin is under the influence of the powers of darkness. ... But Christ came as the light of the world to release people from darkness; those who believe in him must put off the deeds of darkness and become lights in this dark world. Those who do not believe face the judgment day as a day of darkness and gloom..." (Verlyn D. Verbrugge: *The NIV Topical Study Bible*, page 972. See 1 John 1:5) Nicodemus, out of the darkness of his life and religion, came to the Light of the world.

[176] At this point, both Jesus and John are baptizing Israelites who are repentant over their sins against God's law covenant. (Acts 19:4) Jesus, after his resurrection, instructed his disciples to do baptizing of a different significance.—Matthew 28:19.

[177] John baptized Jesus at Bethany, which is on the eastern side of the Jordan. Aenon and Salim were west of the river. (John 1:28; 3:23, 26) The exact locations of these places, mentioned in the Bible only at John 3:23, are uncertain. They were "in the neighborhood" of where Jesus was. (Edersheim, page 450) In Aramaic, Aenon means "springs" and Salem means "peace." John was, allegorically speaking, near salvation.

[178] John's disciples exaggerated their concern that another of his disciples (Jesus) was competing with him, telling John that he was losing his audience to this other preacher.

[179] In Bible times, a close acquaintance of the bridegroom acted as his legal representative and played a key role in making arrangements for the marriage. Usually, he was the one who brought the couple together. After the wedding, the bridegroom's friend, knowing he had successfully done his duty, got out of the way. Jesus was **the bridegroom** and John the Baptist was **the bridegroom's friend.** John accomplished his objective by introducing the first disciples—the symbolic **bride**—to Jesus. (John 1:29, 36; 2 Corinthians 11:2; Revelation 19:7; 21:2, 9) After that he 'decreased' in importance as Jesus 'increased.'—**John 3:29-30**.

[180] John corrected Antipas for marrying his sister-in-law. (Mark 6:17-18) Antipas was nominally Jewish and professedly under Israel's law. See Leviticus 18:16; 20:21.

[181] Perhaps Jesus did not want to provoke a premature confrontation with the Pharisees. They may have turned their attention to Jesus because John the Baptist had been thrown into prison.

[182] From Judea to Galilee was about a three-day journey on the direct route through Samaria. Most Israelites, however, took the long way around along the Jordan River.

[183] Sychar has been identified with the village of ʿAskar at the foot of Mount Ebal, about 0.4 miles (0.7 km) north-northeast of Jacob's Well.

[184] The journey from the Jordan Valley in Judea to Sychar in Samaria is a steep ascent of 3,000 feet (almost 900 m). John 4:6 is the only place in the Bible where Jesus is said to be tired.

[185] The patriarch owned property in nearby Shechem. (Genesis 33:18-19; Joshua 24:32) Perhaps Jacob dug this well (or had it dug) to provide water for his large household and flocks and thereby prevent trouble with Amorites who owned other water sources in the region; or he may have needed another water supply when other wells in the area dried up. The traditional site of this well is Bir Yaʿqub (Be'er Yaʿaqov), situated 1.5 miles (about 2.5 km) southeast of modern-day Nablus, not far from Tell Balata, the site of Shechem. As the Samaritan woman observed, the well is deep; its water level never rises to the top. In the nineteenth century the well was measured to a depth of 75 feet (about 23 m). There is debris at the bottom, so the well might have been twice as deep in ancient times. Because the well is usually dry from about the end of May until the autumn rains, its water may come from rain and percolation; or the well may be spring-fed. Interestingly, two Greek words—one meaning fountain, the other meaning cistern—are used interchangeably in John chapter 4 for Jacob's Well; compare verses 12 and 14.

[186] This account is unique to the Gospel of John. "Because the whole narrative reads like that of one who had been present at what passed," Edersheim suggests that the apostle John remained with Jesus. (page 281) Of course, the details of the conversation could have been related to John by the woman or Jesus.

[187] Israelites assumed that "Samaritans were ritually impure or unclean. Thus, an Israelite who used a drinking vessel after a Samaritan had touched it would become ceremonially unclean."—John 4:9 footnote, *The NET Bible.*

[188] Edersheim suggests that the woman could have recognized Jesus as an Israelite by his manner of dress and his accent.

[189] In John chapter 4 and elsewhere in the Bible, water symbolizes God's provisions (foremost of which is Jesus) for restoring humankind to sinless life.—Isaiah 12:3; Jeremiah 2:13; Ezekiel 47:1-12; Zechariah 14:8; Revelation 7:17; 21:6; 22:1-2, 17.

[190] Perhaps sensing sarcasm in the woman's response, Jesus changed the subject.

[191] The woman passed Jesus' test of her honesty. This test was also an opportunity to carry truth to her mind and reach her heart.

[192] According to Edersheim, there was another well nearer to Sychar on the eastern side of the village. Perhaps this woman went to Jacob's Well "because, if her character was what seems implied in verse 18, the concourse of the more common women at the village-well of an evening might scarcely be a pleasant place of resort to one with her history."—page 283.

[193] Since Samaritans acknowledged no prophets after Moses, it must have occurred to the woman that this prophet was the Messiah. (John 4:20) A discussion of what constituted true worship naturally followed. The woman may have thought that Jesus was going to tell her to go to a place of worship and make a sacrifice for her sins.

[194] Mount Gerizim is situated in the heart of the district of Samaria; its summit rises over 2,800 feet (850 m) above the Mediterranean Sea. For the importance of Mount Gerizim to the Samaritans, see "Samaria and Samaritans."

[195] Or "the Messiah who brings salvation comes through the Jews." (John 4:22, *The Expanded Bible)* Jesus shifted the direction of the conversation from the "where" of true worship to the "what" of true worship. The Jews, chosen as the people from whom the Messiah would come, had been entrusted with true worship; only though them could one learn about the Messiah. (Romans 3:1-2) Anyone who wished to serve the God of Israel had to do so in association with his chosen nation.

[196] That is, a spirit person, or being. Spirits (including the glorified Jesus and the angels) have a spiritual body, far superior to a physical body. (1 Corinthians 15:44-45; 2 Corinthians 3:17; Hebrews 1:14) To help us understand what God is like, Bible writers use anthropomorphisms. Interestingly, "most of the alterations in the Samaritan Pentateuch are with the view of removing anthropomorphisms."—Edersheim, page 289.

[197] Today true worship no longer revolves around a physical location. Worshiping **with spirit** involves more than being sincere and enthusiastic. Such worship is guided by God's spirit, which would help one who reads Scripture be attuned to God's thinking. Worship that is acceptable to God cannot be based on imagination, myths or lies. True worship is in harmony with facts and consistent with the **truth** revealed in God's written Word.—**John 4:23-24**; 16:13; 17:17.

[198] Because they accepted Moses' writings, Samaritans looked forward to the coming of the Messiah, the prophet greater than Moses. (Deuteronomy 18:15, 18) See "Jesus, A.K.A. ..."

[199] Most Israelites disdained Samaritans, and many Israelite men looked down on women. The first time that Jesus openly identified himself as the Messiah was to a Samaritan woman.

[200] The woman misunderstood Jesus' remarks about "living water" and thought he was referring to H^2O. Likewise, the disciples thought Jesus was talking about physical food, while he was really speaking figuratively and spiritually again. His explanation that his food was his ministry led naturally into the metaphor of the harvest. The fruit of his ministry was represented by the Samaritans who were coming to him.

[201] Or "white already to harvest." (John 4:35, *King James Version)* Jesus may have referred to an approaching crowd of Samaritans ready to accept his message; or perhaps they were wearing white robes.—John 4:41-42; compare Matthew 9:35-38.

[202] Harvesting was usually a communal work, with groups of reapers collecting ripe grain from a field. (Ruth 2:3; 2 Kings 4:18) King Solomon, the prophet Hosea and the apostle Paul used the work of reaping to illustrate important truths. (Proverbs 22:8; Hosea 8:7; Galatians 6:7-9) Jesus also used this familiar occupation to illustrate the role that the angels and Christians would play in the discipling work. (Matthew 13:24-30, 39) "In this case, Jesus sowed by giving the message to the woman. He was about to reap because He would see the whole city saved. Also, the disciples were going to reap the harvest that Christ had sown."—John 4:36 footnote, *The Nelson Study Bible.* Copyright © 1997 by Thomas Nelson, Inc. Used by permission.

[203] While the initial spiritual harvest took place mainly among the Israelites, an even greater harvest that included the Samaritans would soon become a reality.—Acts 1:8; 8:1, 14-17.

[204] Jesus "came into his own world, but his own nation did not welcome him." (John 1:11, *Contemporary English Version)* The Samaritans not only welcomed Jesus but proclaimed him to be the Savior of the world. The Messiah saves from sin those of the world of humankind who demonstrate faith in him.—John 1:29; 3:16-17; 1 John 2:2; 4:14.

[205] To emphasize the Samaritans' descent from foreigners, some Israelites called Samaritans "Cuthim," or "Cuthaeans," that is, people of Cuth and Cuthah. The king of Assyria moved people from Cuth and Cuthah to Samaria after Israel went into exile in the eighth century B.C. (2 Kings 17:24) For their part, Samaritans claimed descent from Jacob through Joseph, a claim that many Israelites would likely have disputed.—John 4:12.

[206] The Samaritans accepted only the first five books of the Bible (and possibly the book of Joshua) but only their revision, the Samaritan Pentateuch; it was written in their own characters, derived from ancient Hebrew. The text differs from the Masoretic text of the Hebrew Bible in some 6,000 instances. Most variances are minor details, but there are some major differences. To give credence to the Samaritans' belief that Gerizim was the holy mountain of God, "Gerizim" is substituted for "Ebal" as the mountain where the Law of Moses was to be written on plastered stones. (Deuteronomy 27:4, 8) Their acceptance of the Pentateuch nevertheless gave Samaritans a basis for believing in the Prophet greater than Moses. (Deuteronomy 18:15, 18; John 4:25) First-century Samaritans were looking for the coming of the Messiah; some, like the woman at the well and her neighbors, recognized him but other Samaritans rejected him.—Luke 9:52-53; 17:16; John 4:39.

[207] The synagogue was the building or place for non-sacrificial worship: Scripture reading, instruction, preaching and prayer. (Acts 13:14-15; see "A Typical Synagogue Service.") Ten was the minimum number of members that could establish a synagogue. In Jesus' day, each sizable town in Israel had a synagogue; larger cities had more than one.—Luke 4:16.

[208] John the Baptist started to proclaim a similar message about six months prior to Jesus' baptism. (Matthew 3:1-2) Jesus could say with added meaning that the Kingdom was near because he was present as its future king.

[209] Or "Repent and believe in the Gospel." (Mark 1:15, *Catholic Public Domain Version)* "The Gospel" is the message about God's kingdom and of salvation by faith in Christ. The Greek word for repentance means to change one's mind, motivated by remorse and desire to turn away from sin.

[210] Unlike the Samaritans, Jesus' own countrymen required miraculous proof that he was worthy of their belief. (John 4:39, 42, 48) A superficial welcome based on enthusiasm for miracles was no real honor at all.

[211] This man was connected by blood or by office with Herod Antipas, the tetrarch of Galilee and Perea. Doubtless there were many administrative officials living in Capernaum, it being a border town.

[212] In ancient times, a road led past Cana down to the shores of the Sea of Galilee and along the shoreline to Capernaum. The distance by road between Cana and Capernaum is 25 miles (about 40 km). Jesus apparently visited Cana the second time alone. By this time, the disciples had returned to Capernaum and their occupations.

[213] According to Roman time, **the seventh hour** was 7 p.m., meaning the official spent the night due to the late hour and encountered his servants the next day; it was 1 p.m. according to Jewish time, meaning these servants met their master that evening after sundown (which started the new day).—**John 4:52**.

[214] The weekly day of rest began at sunset on Friday. Tradition dates this visit of Jesus to Nazareth's synagogue on the Day of Atonement *(Yom Kippur*, September/October). "On His entrance into the Synagogue, or perhaps before that, the chief ruler would request Jesus to act for that Sabbath as the [delegate of the congregation]. ... [T]he person who read in the Synagogue the portion from the Prophets was also expected to conduct the devotions." (Edersheim, pages 298, 304) Such devotions included leading the congregation in prayer and reciting the *Shema*, the creed of faith consisting of three passages from the Pentateuch: Deuteronomy 6:4-9; 11:13-21 and Numbers 15:37-41. Some commentators and Bible versions suggest that Jesus was a regular reader at his hometown synagogue's services. Luke 4:22 seems to contradict this, however.

[215] Without the help of chapter and verse numbers (these aids were added centuries later), Jesus demonstrated his thorough familiarity with God's written Word.

[216] Jesus received this anointing with God's spirit at his baptism. (Matthew 3:16; Mark 1:9-10; Luke 3:21-22) His message appealed to humble people. Jesus reached out to those the world tends to forget.—Matthew 5:3; Luke 6:20.

[217] Jesus' miracles achieved physical release for the ill and disabled. Although some Israelites might have applied Isaiah's prophecy literally, the liberation announced by Jesus was a spiritual one, from bondage to sin. (Matthew 26:27-28; Luke 1:77; 7:47; 24:47; Acts 2:38; 5:30-31; 10:43; 13:38; 26:18; Ephesians 1:7; Colossians 1:13-14; 2:13) This prophecy and Jesus' application of it to his ministry are evidently allusions to the Jubilee, a year of fresh starts. (Leviticus 25:10) Every fiftieth year in Israel, debts were forgiven, slaves were freed, and ancestral lands were returned to the original owners. To those who respond to his message Jesus offered a fresh start with the cancellation of spiritual debt and freedom from enslavement to death. Christ's kingdom will one day make the earth a paradise, humankind's original home environment.

[218] Isaiah 61:1-2, *New Heart English Bible:* Jehovah Edition. Jesus' ministry of salvation marked the beginning of this time of goodwill. His reading stopped short of what Isaiah said concerning God's relatively short "day of vengeance," apparently to keep the focus on that longer "year of Jehovah's favor" toward those turning to him for salvation.

[219] "The reading of the section from the Prophets," says Edersheim, "was in olden times immediately followed by an address, discourse, or sermon." (page 308) Out of respect, one stood up to read. The reader/speaker then sat down in view of the congregation to expound upon what he read. (Compare Matthew 5:1) Interestingly, the preacher usually referred to Israel's Messianic hope at the close of his address.

[220] News of the miraculous healing of a sick child in Capernaum evidently spread quickly to neighboring towns.—John 4:46-54.

[221] Israel had a long history of rejecting God's prophets, her native sons.—Luke 11:47-51; Acts 7:52-53.

[222] For her unfaithfulness to God, Israel received judgment in the form of famine. At that time, only Gentiles—such as the widow in Zarephath—received healing. The Phoenician town of Zarephath was located on the Mediterranean Coast outside Israel's territory. Zarephath's Greek name Sarepta is preserved in that of Sarafand in modern-day Lebanon, located 8 miles (about 13 km) south-southwest of Sidon.

[223] Nazareth was built on the brow of a mountain. (Luke 4:29) To the southwest of the modern city is a 40-foot (12 m) cliff where this incident may have occurred. The Nazarenes may have seen Jesus as a false prophet deserving to be stoned. (Deuteronomy 13:5) The place of execution was to be outside the city and witnesses to the wrongdoing threw the first stone at the condemned. (Leviticus 24:14; Numbers 15:35-36; Deuteronomy 13:1-10; 17:2-7; Acts 7:57-59) According to the Talmud, the victim was first thrown over the brow of a hill or precipice and thereafter was pelted with stones until dead. Edersheim believed that the Nazarenes "intended accidentally to crowd [Jesus] over" the cliff. (page 316) Whatever plan the mob had in mind, they certainly intended to kill Jesus, his unflattering comparison of them to faithless Gentiles so angered them. In the days of Elijah and Elisha, the Israelites had apostatized to Baal worship and were persecuting the prophets. Elijah was fleeing from his own countrymen when the widow in Zarephath took him in and fed him. (1 Kings 17:8-24) Israel was still riddled with Baal worship when Elisha healed the Syrian army chief Naaman of his leprosy.—2 Kings 5:1-14.

[224] "The road by the brow of the hill," says Edersheim, "bifurcates, and we can conceive how Jesus ... passed through their midst."—page 316.

[225] Jesus spent most of his ministry in and around Galilee with Capernaum the center of his activity. (Matthew 9:1) Capernaum was not far from Nazareth (where he grew up), from Cana (where he turned water into wine), from Nain (where he resurrected the son of a widow) and

from the vicinity of Bethsaida (where he miraculously fed about 5,000 men and restored sight to a blind man).

[226] Isaiah 9:1-2, *The Living Bible.* As it approaches, death casts a figurative shadow over its victims. Jesus brought spiritual enlightenment that could remove the shadow and rescue believers from death.— Luke 2:32; John 12:46.

[227] What Matthew (4:18) and Mark (1:16) call the Sea of Galilee, Luke (5:1) calls the Lake of Gennesaret, after a small plain bordering the northwest shore of the lake. (The Greek word translated "sea" may also mean "lake.") In the Gospel of John (6:1; 21:1) this body of water is called the Sea of Tiberias. This freshwater inland lake in northern Israel lies on average 700 feet (210 m) below sea level; it is 13 miles (21 km) long from north to south and 8 miles (12 km) wide from east to west, and its greatest depth is about 160 feet (48 m).

[228] The presence of a third man—likely Andrew—in the boat with Jesus and Peter is implied by the plural pronouns in Luke 5:6-7.

[229] Along the shore of the Sea of Galilee near Capernaum there is a spot that forms a natural amphitheater. The acoustics of this location would have allowed a large crowd to hear Jesus speaking from a boat.

[230] In the presence of a holy man working with divine backing, Peter, **a sinful man**, felt unworthy and feared his sinfulness might lead to judgment.—**Luke 5:8**.

[231] "Jesus does not drive away the sinner who recognizes his or her wretched condition. He accepts the confessing sinner and offers that person the opportunity of reconciliation with God. Then He sends the forgiven sinner out to do the work of God."—Luke 5:10 footnote, *The Nelson Study Bible.* Copyright © 1997 by Thomas Nelson, Inc. Used by permission.

[232] Or "men who catch people for God." (Matthew 4:19, *The Passion Translation)* Whereas fish are caught, killed, cooked and eaten, human souls are caught from the prospect of eternal death and given new life. Peter, Andrew, James and John had been Jesus' disciples for some six months to a year. After witnessing a miraculous catch of fish, they accepted Jesus' invitation to leave their business and follow him continuously. Galilean fishermen did not cast lure and line into the water and wait for fish to strike; they pursued fish with nets. Like fishing, discipling would be strenuous, labor-intensive work that required initiative and perseverance but sometimes produced few results.

[233] Not included in the commercially important groups was the catfish, the largest fish in the Sea of Galilee. Having no scales, it was unclean according to the Mosaic Law and would have been discarded.—Leviticus 11:9-12.

[234] The appellation "St. Peter's fish" is drawn from Matthew 17:27. *Tilapia galilaea*, or musht, is commonly accepted to be St. Peter's fish, and it is served as such in restaurants near the Sea of Galilee.

[235] Rather than quote revered rabbis as authoritative, as was the scholars' custom, Jesus spoke as Heaven's representative, basing his teachings on the Word of God. (John 7:16) On this occasion Jesus likely spoke about his ministry and its relationship to Old Testament fulfillment.

[236] Demons are invisible, wicked spirit creatures with superhuman powers. Called "sons" of God at Genesis 6:2 and "angels" at Jude 6, they were not created evil; rather, they were angels who made themselves God's enemies by disobeying him and joining Satan in rebellion.—1 Peter 3:19-20; 2 Peter 2:4; compare Revelation 12:3-4.

[237] God is the Holy One *par excellence*. (Leviticus 11:44; 19:2; 20:26; Psalm 99:5; Isaiah 6:3; 1 Peter 1:15-16; Revelation 4:8) All that belongs to him—especially his Son—is holy.—Luke 1:35; John 6:69; Acts 3:14; 4:27, 30; Revelation 3:7.

[238] The demon controlling the man evidently spoke in the plural with reference to his fellow demons and in the singular with reference to himself alone. Jesus was a threat to all demons, not just the ones tormenting this man.

[239] This expression "stills the raging of the powers of evil just as, characteristically, it is again employed in the stilling of the storm, Mark 4:39." (Edersheim, page 335) It was the man who shouted but Jesus reprimanded the demon, the source of the man's words.

[240] A demon or demons in control of someone could cause much suffering. (Matthew 17:15; Mark 9:18; Luke 9:39) But upon being freed of the paranormal possession, the person returned to a normal state of mind and body.

[241] Or "foul." (Mark 1:27, *An American Translation)* The demons are morally and spiritually unclean and have a defiling influence on humans. Jesus, **the Holy One of God**, fought this uncleanness and unholiness.—**Mark 1:24**.

[242] The physician's gospel classifies the fever as "high," drawing attention to the seriousness of the condition. (Luke 4:38; Colossians 4:14) Peter's mother-in-law evidently lived in his home, one he shared with his brother Andrew. First Corinthians 9:5 confirms that Peter (Cephas) was married.

[243] In each case the same Greek word is used. (Luke 4:35, 39, 41) On the Sea of Galilee, Jesus rebuked the violent winds and raging sea. (Matthew 8:26; Mark 4:39; Luke 8:24) In every one of these instances, a rebuke from Jesus put a stop to some kind of threat.

[244] With the Sabbath day ended, people could bring their sick ones to be cured without fear of criticism. See Matthew 12:10; John 5:15-16; 7:23; 9:16.

[245] See Isaiah 53:4-5; compare 1 Peter 2:24. "It was to take on himself the expiation of sin that Jesus ... came on earth; that is why he could relieve men of their bodily ills which are the consequence and the penalty of sin."—Matthew chapter 8 note f, *The Jerusalem Bible:* Edited by Alexander Jones.

[246] Demons at times caused the people they controlled to suffer from physical disorders. (Matthew 12:22; 17:14-18) However, the Scriptures differentiate between ordinary sickness and the harm caused by demon possession. (Matthew 4:24) Regardless of the cause of people's suffering, Jesus cured them.

[247] These apostate spirits shall not have the honor of speaking about the Son of God. "They know He is the Anointed One, *but He doesn't want to be acclaimed in this way*." (Luke 4:41, *The Voice Bible)* Had Jesus allowed the demons to testify that he was the Messiah, it could have given credence to the Pharisees' accusation that he cast out demons by the power of their Prince.—Matthew 9:34; 12:24; Mark 3:22; Luke 11:15.

[248] The Decapolis was a loose federation of ten towns with their surrounding territories. Most of these cities were located east of the Sea of Galilee and the Jordan River, and as far northeast as to include Damascus. They were centers of Hellenistic culture and trade. There is no record of Jesus having visited any of the cities.

[249] Also called Transjordan, the region east of the Jordan River was known as Perea (from a Greek word meaning "the other side; beyond").—*The New English Bible;* note on Matthew 4:25, *New World Translation* (Study Edition).

[250] The Gentile region of Syria lay north of Galilee, between Damascus and the Mediterranean Sea.

[251] According to the physician's gospel, the man had "an advanced case of leprosy." (Luke 5:12, *New Living Translation;* compare Matthew 8:2; Mark 1:40) What the Bible called leprosy included but was not restricted to the condition known today as Hansen's disease; it could affect clothing and houses as well as people.

[252] Or "cleanse me." (Mathew 8:2, *The Emphasized Bible)* According to Israel's law, a leper had to call out in warning, "Unclean," to protect others from coming too close and risking infection. The Law also viewed lepers as ceremonially unclean and required that they be quarantined.—Leviticus 13:45-46, *King James Version;* Numbers 5:2-3.

[253] In addition to what Jesus did, Mark records how Jesus felt. (1:41; compare Matthew 8:3; Luke 5:13; see "The Gospel According to...") Some Bible manuscripts and versions say that Jesus was "moved with anger"—not at the leper but at the heartless way other people probably treated him. *(New Living Translation,* Mark 1:41 footnote) Religious tradition speaks favorably of a rabbi who hid from lepers and of another who threw stones to keep them away.

[254] No one was to come within four cubits (6 feet; 1.8 meters) of a leper; on windy days, 100 cubits (150 feet; 45 meters). Such extra-biblical rules led to heartless treatment of lepers. By contrast, Jesus was so moved by the leper's plight that he touched the man, even though he could have cured him with just a word. See Matthew 8:8, 13; Mark 7:29-30; Luke 7:7, 10; John 4:49-51.

[255] Until, that is, after the man's healing was completed. The report of Jesus healing the leper might have prejudiced the priest who had to pronounce the man clean, and the former leper's testimony might have hastened the confrontation between Jesus and the religious leaders.

[256] In accord with the Law, a priest had to verify that a leper had been healed. The cured leper was required to go to the Temple in Jerusalem and bring as an offering (or gift) two live clean birds, cedarwood, scarlet and hyssop. Afterward, the former leper was restored to the community.—Leviticus 14:2-32.

[257] Luke 5:16 is one of several instances in which that gospel alone mentions that Jesus was praying. (Luke 3:21; 6:12; 9:18; 11:1; 23:46; see "The Gospel According to...") For anyone who seeks a sense of peace in our troubled world, wants to develop a close relationship with God, prepare for important decisions, gain strength for Christian living and receive God's direction, Jesus' example is worthy of imitation.

[258] Possibly the home of Peter; it must have been a sizable house to accommodate Peter, his wife, his mother-in-law and his brother Andrew.—Mark 1:29.

[259] Also called scribes, scholars were a class of men learned in the Law of Moses. They were originally copyists of the Scriptures.

[260] The men may have reached the roof by means of outside stairs, "or else reached it by what the Rabbis called 'the road of the roofs', passing from roof to roof, if the house adjoined others in the same street." (Edersheim, page 347) Roofs were often constructed of wooden beams covered with branches, reeds and a layer of earth, which was plastered. Individual tiles may have been put on the mud roof or somehow embedded in it. However, the roof through which the paralytic was lowered Edersheim regards as, not the house's main roof, "but as that of the covered gallery under which we are supposing the Lord to have stood. This could, of course, have been readily reached from above. In such case it would have been comparatively easy to 'unroof' the covering of 'tiles,' and then, 'having dug out' an opening through the lighter framework which supported the men, would be but the work of a few minutes."—page 348; Mark 2:4; Luke 5:19.

[261] A blasphemer is one who insults God—directly or indirectly, in speech or action. The Bible prohibits blasphemy, prescribing severe punishment for it. (Leviticus 24:14-16; 1 Timothy 1:20) On this occasion, the religious leaders charged Jesus with blasphemy for claiming authority to forgive sins, a prerogative of God alone. Later, they judged his identification as the Son of God as the ultimate blasphemy, deserving of death.—Matthew 26:65-66.

[262] By his "spirit"—perceptive powers—Jesus was able to discern the thinking, reasoning and motives of others.—Mark 2:8; Luke 6:8; 9:47; John 2:25.

[263] It would be easier for someone to say that he could forgive sins, since there would be no visible evidence to substantiate such a claim. But to say, **Get up and walk** required a miracle that would prove to witnesses that Jesus also had the authority to forgive sins. On the other hand, it is harder to say someone's **sins are forgiven** because one must possess the authority to forgive sins for the declaration to be true. (**Matthew 9:5**; **Mark 2:9**; **Luke 5:23**) This account links sin to sickness. Adam's descendants have inherited the consequences of his sin, namely, sickness and death. (Romans 5:12) Humankind needs not only physical and emotional healing but especially spiritual healing. Jesus forgives the sins of all who love and serve God. One day, sickness will be removed forever.—Isaiah 33:24.

[264] Matthew was better known as Levi before his selection as one of the 12 apostles. (Luke 5:27, 29) The gospel bearing Matthew's name never refers to him as Levi. His father's name was Alphaeus, evidently not the Alphaeus who was the father of the apostle James. (Matthew 10:3; Mark 2:14; 3:18; Luke 6:15) Israelites who collected taxes for Rome were despised by fellow Jews. (Matthew 11:19; 21:32) There were two classes of tax collectors: "the tax-gatherer in general" and "the custom house official." The latter, according to Edersheim, was "the object of chief execration ... because his exactions were the more vexatious and gave more scope to rapacity." (Compare Luke 3:12-13) Matthew was a custom house official, a publican "of the worst kind."—pages 357, 358; .

[265] Custom houses were small buildings or booths located at a port or on the edge of a city or town. The collected taxes "were a form of customs duty or toll applied to the movement of goods and produce brought into an area for sale. As such these tolls were a sort of 'sales tax' paid by the seller but obviously passed on to the purchaser in the form of increased prices ... . The system as a whole is sometimes referred to as 'tax farming' because a contract to collect these taxes for an entire district would be sold to the highest bidder, who would pay up front, hire employees to do the work of collection, and then recoup the investment and overhead by charging commissions on top of the taxes. Although rates and commissions were regulated by law, there was plenty of room for abuse in the system through the subjective valuation of goods by the tax collectors, and even through outright bribery."—Matthew 9:9 footnote, *The NET Bible*.

[266] For a teacher to gather around himself a circle of pupils was not just a common practice but, according to Edersheim, "a sacred duty." Edersheim speculated: "How often, as [Matthew] sat at the receipt of custom, must he have seen Jesus passing by; how often must he have heard His Words, some, perhaps, spoken to himself, but all falling like good seed into the field of his heart and preparing him at once and joyously to obey the summons when it came: *Follow Me!*"—page 328.

[267] Matthew showed concern for the spirituality of his colleagues and others by inviting them to his home for a meal with Jesus.

[268] The question bordered on an accusation that Jesus was ritually unclean by his choice of dining companions. As a matter of ritual cleanliness Israelites were very careful about personal associations and contact. They would not eat with sinners because sharing a meal with someone indicated close fellowship with that person. Eating with a sinner might have conveyed acceptance of that one's sins. (Acts 11:2-3; 1 Corinthians 5:11) Since all humans are **sinners** (Romans 3:23; 5:12) the term is used in this context more specifically.—**Matthew 9:11**; **Mark 2:16**; **Luke 5:30**; see Luke 7:37, 39; 19:7.

[269] Because of their piety and scrupulous law-keeping, the scholars and the Pharisees thought they were righteous. (Compare Philippians 3:6) They certainly needed spiritual healing but were too self-righteous to accept aid from anyone, especially Jesus. Only those who humbly recognize their spiritual need can be treated.—Matthew 5:3.

[270] John's disciples could have been fasting to mourn his imprisonment. Matthew might have hosted his feast on one of the Jewish fast days. (Luke 18:12) These are possible reasons for the complaint of John's disciples and the Pharisees.

[271] Israel's prophets used the image of a wedding to describe God's relationship to his people and as a metaphor for the messianic age. (Isaiah 54:5-6; 62:4-5; Jeremiah 2:2; Hosea 2:16-20) John the Baptist spoke of Jesus as a bridegroom. (John 3:28-29) Accordingly, while Jesus was present, Jesus' disciples did not fast. After Jesus died, his disciples mourned and had no desire to eat. Although first-century Christians fasted, the practice was not required or regulated as it was in Judaism.—Acts 13:2; 14:23.

[272] Wine (also milk, butter, cheese, oil and water) was sometimes stored in bottles made from animal hides—sheep, goats or cattle. A dead animal's head and feet were cut off, and the carcass was carefully removed from the skin to avoid opening its belly. After the hide was tanned, the openings were sewed up. The neck or a leg of the animal was left unsewn to serve as the bottle's opening, which was closed with a stopper or tied with a string. Over time, the skin would harden and lose its elasticity. New wine in such a bottle might continue to ferment, creating pressure that could burst the old, hardened skin.—Joshua 9:4.

[273] John 5:1 does not specify which holy day and it cannot be positively identified; it could have been one of the three annual festivals—Passover, Pentecost, Tabernacles—that male Israelites were required to attend in Jerusalem. (Deuteronomy 16:16) In context this unnamed festival takes place shortly after Jesus said that the harvest was four months away (although some scholars regard his words as proverbial, suggesting nothing about the season when spoken; John 4:35). The harvest season, particularly the barley harvest, got underway about Passover time. However, Jesus seems to have attended this festival alone, and his disciples would have gone with him for a festival requiring their presence in Jerusalem. Another popular suggestion for the feast of John 5:1 is Purim, which occurs a month before Passover. But Purim was celebrated in homes and synagogues, not in the Temple and never on the Sabbath. Furthermore, the weather at that time of year would not have been warm enough for sick ones to be outside in the porticoes of Bethzatha. Edersheim suggests the Feast of Trumpets or the so-called Feast of Wood-offering. (Leviticus 23:24; Nehemiah 10:34). Neither of these celebrations, however, would require Jesus' presence in Jerusalem.

[274] The Sheep Gate was rebuilt by High Priest Eliashib and his associates, which suggests that the gate was near the Temple. (Nehemiah 3:1, 32; 12:39) The gate was probably located in the wall of the second quarter, the part built by King Manasseh, at or near the northeast corner of the city. The Sheep Gate may have been so named because through it were brought sheep and goats for sacrifice or perhaps for a market that was located nearby.

[275] The pool of Bethzatha (or "Bethesda"; "Bethsaida"; "Place of Mercy") was located at the Sheep Gate in the northeast corner of Jerusalem. (John 5:2, *King James Version; Douay-Rheims; Catholic Public Domain Version)* The pool's five porticoes "were *covered walkways* formed by rows of columns supporting a roof and open on the side facing the pool. People could stand, sit, or walk on these colonnaded porches, protected from the weather and the heat of the sun." (John 5:2 footnote, *The NET Bible)* North of the Temple mount, archaeologists discovered the remains of a large pool consisting of two basins and embracing an overall area of about 150 by 300 feet (46 by 92 m). The wall separating the northern and southern basins likely included one of the five colonnades, and the other four likely lined the outer perimeter of the pool area.

[276] Edersheim attributes the "bubbling up of the water ... not to supernatural but to physical causes. Such intermittent springs are not uncommon, and to this day the so-called 'Fountain of the Virgin' in Jerusalem exhibits the phenomenon." Edersheim points out that "the Gospel-narrative does not ascribe this 'troubling of the waters' to Angelic agency, nor endorses the belief, that only the first who afterwards entered them, could be healed. This was evidently the belief of the impotent man, as of all the waiting multitude (John 5:7). But the words in Verse 4 of our Authorized [King James] Version, and perhaps, also, the last clause of verse 3, are admittedly an interpolation." (page 321 note 8) The legend that an angel healed just the first sick person who

went into the pool recalls the unbiblical aphorism, "God helps those who help themselves."

[277] "Sabbath" comes from a Hebrew word meaning "to desist, cease, rest"; it was the seventh day of the Jewish week, beginning at sunset on Friday and ending at sunset on Saturday. *(The New Compact Bible Dictionary*, page 512) Except priestly service in the sanctuary, no work was allowed on the Sabbath. Jesus taught that the sabbath was for people's benefit, and that human needs took precedence over sabbath law. This brought him into regular conflict with the religious leaders.—Matthew 12:1-14; Mark 2:23-3:6; Luke 6:1-11.

[278] This mat ("bed" in the *King James Version)* would have been made of straw or rushes, perhaps with quilting or a mattress of some sort added for comfort. (John 5:8) When not in use, the mat could be rolled up and stored away. At Mark 2:4-12, the same Greek word refers to some kind of stretcher on which a paralyzed man was carried.

[279] The sick man did not enter the water; yet he was instantly cured. Jesus, not an angel, performed a miracle at the pool.—Matthew 11:5; Luke 7:22.

[280] "The Jews" or "Judeans," referring to "Jewish leaders" or possibly others who were zealous for the traditions.—John 5:10, *King James Version; The Holy Bible in Modern English* (Revised Edition) by Ferar Fenton; *New Heart English Bible.*

[281] "Over the years, the Jewish leaders had amassed thousands of rules and regulations concerning the Sabbath. By Jesus' day, they had 39 different classifications of work. According to them, carrying furniture and even providing medical treatment on the Sabbath were forbidden."—John 5:10 footnote, *The Nelson Study Bible.* Copyright © 1997 by Thomas Nelson, Inc. Used by permission. Compare Jeremiah 17:21-22.

[282] Significantly, the Judeans did not ask the man, 'Who healed you?' They asked him, "Who is the man who said to you, 'Take up your mat and walk'?"—John 5:12, *World English Bible.*

[283] The man had been sick for 38 years due to inherited imperfection, not because of a sin he had committed. (John 5:5; see Romans 5:12) Now that the man had been shown mercy and was healed, Jesus urged him to follow the way of salvation and avoid willful sin that could result in something worse than sickness, that is, everlasting destruction.—Hebrews 10:26-27.

"Jesus' admonition ... teaches that the purpose of the healing is to lead to a new life." (David M. Stanley: John 5:14 footnote, *The New English Bible)* The paralyzed man's physical restoration was also a spiritual resurrection. See John 5:24.

[284] Jesus' work of preaching and healing was in imitation of God's good works and therefore not forbidden by Sabbath laws. "In claiming the right to work even as his Father worked, Jesus was claiming a divine prerogative" because "the Sabbath privilege was peculiar to God, and no one was equal to God." (John 5:17 footnote, *The NET Bible)* Jesus was making himself God's equal, as far as his listeners were concerned.

[285] In response to allegations of blasphemy and Sabbath-breaking, Jesus repeatedly declared himself to be the Son of God and the appointed judge of humankind. He also said that Moses wrote about him. "All this indicated that he was the Messiah, but he did not here expressly assert it as he did in Samaria (John 4:26). That would have precipitated the collision, for to claim to be the Messiah would in the view of the Jewish rulers involve political consequences. Comp. John 11:48."—Robertson, page 43.

[286] The spiritually dead who put faith in Jesus' words and discontinued walking in their sinful course passed over from death to life. (Ephsians 2:5; compare Luke 9:60) The condemnation of death was lifted, and they were given the hope of eternal life because of their faith in God.—Romans 5:12; 6:23.

[287] Jesus has in himself **the gift of life** in the sense that his Father granted him powers that originally only the Father had, including the power to resurrect the dead.—**John 5:26**.

[288] Or "all those in the memorial tombs." (John 5:28, *New World Translation)* The term "memorial tombs" carries the implication of preserving the memory of the deceased person, suggesting that the person who died is remembered by God. See Job 14:13; Luke 23:42.

[289] Or "Those who did good things will come out into the resurrection of life, and those who did wicked things into the resurrection of judgment." (John 5:29, *Common English Bible)* Compare Acts 24:15; Romans 6:7.

[290] On Earth Jesus used authority received from God to cast out demons, to preach and teach, to forgive sins, to control the forces of nature, to raise the dead and to judge. (Matthew 7:29; 9:6; Mark 1:22; 2:10; Luke 4:36; 5:24; John 5:27) The resurrected and ascended Lord now rules at God's right hand with "all authority in heaven and on earth."—Matthew 28:18, Young's *Literal Translation*.

[291] A man's testimony about himself was not accepted in Israel's courts.

[292] For example, God bore witness about Jesus at his baptism.—Matthew 3:17; Mark 1:11; Luke 3:22.

[293] His critics could have discerned that Jesus was the Messiah by comparing his life and teachings with what "Moses and all the prophets" foretold. (Luke 24:27, *King James Version*; see Acts 10:43; compare Revelation 19:10) But they refused to make a sincere examination of the abundant biblical evidence that Jesus was the promised Messiah.—Deuteronomy 18:15, 18; John 7:48.

[294] Perhaps Jesus and his disciples walked on footpaths that separated one tract of land from another. Had they walked through a field, trampling the grain as they went along, the Pharisees undoubtedly would have taken issue with this as well.

[295] The Law allowed a hungry Israelite to enter the field or vineyard of another and eat of its produce to satisfaction.—Deuteronomy 23:24-25.

[296] Reaping was forbidden on the Sabbath, but the disciples were picking grain to eat, not to sell. (Exodus 34:21) No work—including food preparation—was to be done on the Sabbath except priestly service. (Exodus 31:15) Israel's religious leaders, claiming the right to determine what constituted work, made the Sabbath difficult for people to observe.—Exodus 20:9-10; Luke 13:14.

[297] Literally "bread of the face" in Hebrew. Also called "layer bread" and "loaves of presentation," the **Showbread** was figuratively before God as a constant offering to him. Twelve loaves of bread were placed in two stacks of six each on the table in the Holy of the Tabernacle and of the Temple. This offering to God was replaced with fresh bread every Sabbath. The removed bread was normally eaten only by the priests.—Note on **Matthew 12:4**; Glossary: "Showbread," *New World Translation* (Study Edition); Exodus 25:30; 40:22-23; Leviticus 24:5-9.

[298] Priests treat the Sabbath as any other day by carrying on butchering and other work in connection with the animal sacrifices. The work of their sacred ministry, far from stopping, actually increased on the Sabbath.—Numbers 28:9-10.

[299] Edersheim explains why David was blameless in eating the showbread and why the Sabbath-labor of the priests was lawful: "The Sabbath-Law was not one merely of rest, but of rest for worship. The Service of the Lord was the object in view. The priests worked on the Sabbath, because this service was the object of the Sabbath; and David was allowed to eat of the shewbread, not because there was danger to life from starvation, but because he pleaded that he was on the service of the Lord and needed this provision. The disciples, when following the Lord, were similarly on the service of

the Lord; ministering to Him was more than ministering in the Temple, for He was greater than the Temple."—pages 513-14.

[300] Or "The Sabbath was made to meet the needs of people, and not people to meet the requirements of the Sabbath."—Mark 2:27, *New Living Translation.*

[301] Jesus claimed authority over one of Israel's God-given institutions. The Sabbath was "at his disposal" for doing the works of his Father.—Matthew 12:8, *The New Testament in the Translation of Monsignor Ronald Knox*. See also John 5:17-19.

[302] Only Luke mentions which of the man's hands was paralyzed. The physician's gospel often supplies medical details that the others do not. (Colossians 4:6; see "The Gospel According to...") The man may have been put forward by Jesus' enemies to test/trap him. But commentator Jerome claimed that the man was a mason and sought Jesus out for a cure so that he would not have to beg for a living.

[303] The religious leaders believed that healing was lawful on the Sabbath only if the life of an Israelite (not of a foreigner) was in danger.

[304] That is, in the middle of the room. "Most likely synagogues were arranged with benches along the walls and open space in the center for seating on the floor."—Mark 3:3 footnote, *The NET Bible.*

[305] A sheep left in a pit until the next day might die and cause financial loss. (See also Proverbs 12:10) Clearly, it was allowable on the Sabbath to do what was necessary to save life or prevent death.

[306] Knowing that they would condemn themselves with a response, the Pharisees kept quiet. They could not and would not admit that it was more consistent with the intention of the Sabbath law to restore this man's afflicted hand—even on the day of rest—than to destroy his hopes for the sake of keeping human tradition.

[307] Instead of rejoicing in a miracle, the religious leaders reacted with rage to a supposed violation of the Law.

[308] Israelites who supported Herod's dynasty and enjoyed his favor were known as Herodians. This political party evidently included members of the Sadducees. (See "Who Were the Pharisees and the Sadducees?") This was the first of two occasions when the Herodians and the Pharisees colluded to do away with Jesus. The second occasion was just three days before Jesus was executed. Apparently, they plotted together over an extended period of time.—Matthew 22:15-16.

[309] Jesus' quiet withdrawal was in keeping with the prophet Isaiah's description of the Messiah (42:1-4). See "In His Name Nations Will Hope."

[310] By this time Jesus' reputation had expanded into regions outside Israel's territory.

[311] In Jesus' day, Idumea was the southernmost region of the Roman province of Judea. Descendants of Isaac's son Esau—known as Edomites—originally occupied territory south of the Dead Sea. In the fourth century before Christ, the Nabataean Arabs occupied their land and the Edomites moved north into the Negeb, as far as the region around Hebron—that territory was called Idumea, the Land of the Edomites. They were conquered by the Hasmoneans (Maccabees) and forced to be circumcised and live by Jewish law or be expelled. Among those who submitted were the forefathers of the Herods.

[312] This was probably a boat owned by one of the four former fishermen among the apostles. Jesus taught from the boat and could move to another area along the shore to help more people.

[313] An "apostle" is one who is sent forth. (Matthew 10:5; Mark 3:14) However, since the apostles continued to be Jesus' pupils, they were still called disciples. A "disciple" is one who is taught, a learner who is personally attached to his or her teacher—an attachment that shapes the disciple's whole life.

[314] This name comes from an Aramaic word meaning "Twin." The apostle Thomas was known by another Greek name, *Didymos* ("Didymus" in some English Bibles), which also means "Twin." (John 11:16; 20:24) Tradition—not Scripture—identifies Thomas with Jesus' half-brother Jude, and Jesus as his symbolic twin.

[315] "Iscariot" possibly means "a man of Kerioth," suggesting that Judas and his father Simon were from the Judean town of Kerioth-hezron.—*The New Compact Bible Dictionary*, page 298; Joshua 15:25; John 6:71.

[316] Jesus gave James and John the name "Boanerges" (a Semitic expression found only in Mark), meaning "Sons of Thunder" (For Gentile readers Mark explains or translates terms that Jewish readers would have been familiar with.—See "The Gospel According to..."); it likely reflected their fiery enthusiasm. (Luke 9:54) In Hebrew, Aramaic and Greek, the phrase "son(s) of" can highlight a distinguishing quality or characteristic. See Acts 4:36.

[317] Known as James the Less, he was perhaps smaller in physical stature or younger in age than James the son of Zebedee. (Mark 15:40) James the Less was also known as the Son of Alphaeus, but not the Alphaeus who was Matthew Levi's father. (Mark 2:14; 3:18; Luke 6:15) It is generally thought that James' father was the same person as Clopas. (Matthew 27:56; 28:1; Mark 15:40; 16:1; Luke 24:10; John 19:25) Probably to avoid confusion with Judas Iscariot, the name Thaddaeus is sometimes used. (John 14:22) In the listings of the apostles at Luke 6:16 and Acts 1:13, Judas Thaddaeus is called the son of James (the Less). In some translations Judas is "the brother of James," since their exact relationship is not specified in Greek.

[318] Simon was also known as "the Cananean," (Matthew 10:4; Mark 3:18, *Douay-Rheims Challoner Revision)* a Hebrew or Aramaic term corresponding to the Greek word for zealot; it distinguished this apostle from Simon Peter. (Luke 6:15; Acts 1:13) Simon may have been known as the Zealot because he was zealous for Israel's independence from Rome and possibly a one-time member of a Jewish party known as the Zealots. In another time, he might have been called Simon the Patriot. The term could also refer to his general temperament.

[319] Luke records an abbreviated version of the Sermon to which Matthew devotes three chapters. Accounting in part for Luke's brevity is the omission of portions of seeming interest to Israelites only. (Matthew 5:17-27; 6:1-18; see "The Gospel According to...") Several portions of the Sermon that do not appear in Luke's account are repeated by Jesus on other occasions. Compare Matthew 6:9-13, 25-34 with Luke 11:1-4; 12:22-31.

[320] The seaport town of Sidon was for many years the principal city of the Phoenicians. Named after Canaan's firstborn son Sidon, the city is known today as Saida in Lebanon. A colony of Sidonians settled about 22 miles (35 km) south of Sidon and called the place Tyre, which is modern-day Sur in Oman. In time Tyre became the principal Phoenician seaport. During Jesus' Galilean ministry, many people from around Tyre and Sidon (Jews or proselytes, no doubt) came to hear his message and to be cured of their diseases. (Mark 3:8-10; Luke 6:17-19) Jesus traveled through the district around Sidon, where he met a Phoenician woman who believed in him.—Matthew 15:21-28; Mark 7:24-31.

[321] Some commentators refer to the discourse in Matthew as the Sermon on the Mount and to the one in Luke as the Sermon on the Plain. What Luke calls a plain might be a level spot on a mountain. (Matthew 5:1; Luke 6:17) Robertson harmonizes the two accounts this way: "Jesus first went up into the mountain to pray (Luke 6:12) and selected and instructed the Twelve. Afterwards he came down to a level place on the mountain side whither the crowds had gathered and stood there and wrought miracles (Luke 6:17). He then went up a little higher into the mountain where he could sit down and see and teach the multitudes (Matt. 5:1). Matthew gives the multitudes as the reason for his going up into the mountain. By this arrangement any discrepancy between 'sat' in Matthew and 'stood' in Luke disappears. ... Many writers affirm that the tradition mentioned by Jerome, making the Horns of Hattin the place where the Sermon on the Mount was delivered, suits this explanation exactly. There is a level place on it where the crowds could have assembled."—pages 48, 274.

[322] Although large crowds were gathered to listen to Jesus, it seems that he spoke mainly for the benefit of his disciples.—Matthew 4:25-5:1; Luke 6:17, 20.

[323] Genuine happiness involves contentment, satisfaction and fulfillment. Each beatitude is introduced with "happy" (or "blessed"). Next a quality of life is mentioned, painting part of a picture of the people who will be blessed by God's kingdom. Each beatitude concludes with a look ahead to an aspect of the Kingdom.

[324] The Greek phrase in Matthew 5:3 popularly rendered "poor in spirit" conveys the idea of being painfully aware of one's spiritual poverty and need for God. (*King James Version*; see *The Berkeley Version of the New Testament* and *An American Translation)* Luke simply refers to the poor (6:20), who are often more fully aware of their dependence on God because they recognize their spiritual need. (James 2:5) However, being poor does not in itself merit God's blessing.

[325] "... the rewards are related to God's coming kingdom and the beatitudes become conditions for admission to the kingdom."—M. Jack Suggs: Matthew 5:3-10 footnote, *The New English Bible*.

[326] Those who mourn their sinful state are happy to know that they can be forgiven by repenting of their sins and demonstrating faith in Christ. (John 3:16; 2 Corinthians 7:10) "The promise *they will be comforted* is the first of several 'reversals' noted in these promises. The beatitudes and the reversals that accompany them serve in the sermon as an invitation to enter into God's care, because one can know God cares for those who turn to him."—Matthew 5:4 footnote, *The NET Bible*.

[327] Those who **weep now will laugh**, not out of amusement, but because they experience joy, which is a fruit of God's spirit.—**Luke 6:21**; Romans 14:17; Galatians 5:22-23; 1 Thessalonians 1:6.

[328] Humble (meek) ones willingly submit to God's will and guidance and do not try to dominate others. Jesus, the foremost example of humility, would inherit authority over the entire Earth. (Matthew 11:29; 28:18) Humble believers share in this inheritance, some of them ruling as kings over the earth and others living on it as subjects.—Psalm 37:29; Matthew 25:34; Revelation 5:10.

[329] Righteousness is what is right according to God's standard of right and wrong. (Genesis 15:6; Deuteronomy 6:25; Zephaniah 2:3; Matthew 6:33) God promises to satisfy those who long for righteousness and strive to conform to his standard. (Compare Psalm 107:9) In contrast, the Pharisees and scholars had their own standard of righteousness.—Matthew 5:20.

[330] Not limited to forgiveness or leniency in judgment (James 2:13), **mercy** is the compassion and pity that move a person to take the initiative to assist those in need.—**Matthew 5:7**; compare Proverbs 11:17.

[331] Human eyes cannot see God. (Exodus 33:20) But **the pure in heart** can **see God** with their minds and hearts. (**Matthew 5:8**; Ephesians 1:18; compare Hebrews 11:27) Purity in heart refers to moral and spiritual cleanness, including one's affections, desires and motives. Believers who are resurrected to Heaven actually see God.—1 John 3:2.

[332] Or "the makers *and* maintainers of peace."—Matthew 5:9, *The Amplified Bible.*

[333] In **Matthew 5:3, 10** and **Luke 6:20, 23** the present tense **belongs** is significant. "Jesus makes the kingdom and its blessings currently available. ... Jesus was saying, in effect, 'the kingdom belongs even now to people like you.'"—Luke 6:20 footnote,

The NET Bible.

[334] Even amidst persecution and suffering, Christians are "happy," or "blessed." (Matthew 5:11-12, Young's *Literal Translation*; *King James Version)* The ultimate happiness for Christians will be realized in the New Heaven and New Earth to come.—2 Peter 3:13; Revelation 21:1-4.

[335] The word Beatitude comes from the Latin *beati*, meaning "Blessedness." (Matthew 5:3 footnote, *New World Translation of the Holy Scriptures—with References.* Published in 1984 by the Watchtower Bible and Tract Society of New York, Inc. Wallkill, NY; *The New Compact Bible Dictionary*, page 72) Luke's version of Jesus' sermon includes four woes, which are the antithesis of four beatitudes. "A **woe** is a cry of pain that results from misfortune. Just as God presented blessings for obedience and curses for disobedience in Deut. 28, Jesus presented blessings and woes to His disciples who were anticipating the kingdom. The same blessings and woes apply to believers today when their works are evaluated (see 1 Cor. 3:12-15; 2 Cor. 5:10; 1 John 2:28; Rev. 22:12)."—Luke 6:24 footnote, *The Nelson Study Bible.* Copyright © 1997 by Thomas Nelson, Inc. Used with permission.

[336] What the rich acquire on Earth is all that they receive. (Matthew 6:19-21) Wealth can blind one to his or her spiritual poverty and need for God.—Deuteronomy 8:17-18; Job 31:24-25, 28; Psalm 52:6-7; Proverbs 11:28; Luke 12:20-21; 16:25; 18:22-25; 1 Timothy 6:17.

[337] Salt, a preservative, symbolizes freedom from corruption or decay. Gospel truth can preserve the lives of those who respond to it, thereby avoiding moral corruption and spiritual decay.—Mark 9:50.

[338] "Pure salt maintains its flavor. In Israel, some salt was mixed with other ingredients. When it was exposed to the elements, the salt would be 'leached out.'" (Matthew 5:13 footnote, *The Nelson Study Bible.* Copyright © 1997 by Thomas Nelson, Inc. Used with permission.) Useless salt was thrown away. Something similar could happen to a disciple who stops following Jesus.

[339] In Bible times, a common household lamp was a small earthenware vessel filled with olive oil. A wick was used to draw up the oil to feed the flame. Lampstands in wealthy households were made of clay or metal. In poorer homes, lamps were set on earthenware or wood stands. Lamps could also be hung from the ceiling by a cord or placed in a niche in the wall.

[340] Believers behold God's glory and reflect it (**your light** is reflective, not inherent; see 2 Corinthians 3:18; Philippians 2:15) Part of a Christian's witness to the world is an exemplary life, a living expression of the God and Father of Christ. Jesus' listeners would have understood the term "Father" in relation to God by its use in the Old Testament. (Deuteronomy 32:6; Psalm 89:26; Isaiah 63:16) Jesus' frequent use of **Father** highlights God's intimacy with his worshipers.—**Matthew 5:16**.

[341] A builder fulfills a contract to build a structure by finishing the building, not by ripping up the contract. When the work is finished, the contract is fulfilled. Jesus did not break, or rip up, the Law; he fulfilled its purpose—to identify the Messiah—by keeping it. (Galatians 3:24) And as a

perfect man, he kept God's laws perfectly. In his Sermon on the Mount, "Jesus clarified both the heart of the law and the nature of true religion in God's kingdom (see Mic. 6:8). In a sense, Jesus turned the law, which was mainly negative, inside out to show its positive core ...."—Matthew 5:2 footnote, *The Nelson Study Bible*. Copyright © 1997 by Thomas Nelson, Inc. Used with permission.

342 Or "one smallest letter ["iota," *Revised Standard Version]* or one stroke of a letter ["dot," *RSV]*." (Matthew 5:18, *New World Translation)* In the Hebrew alphabet used in Jesus' time, the smallest letter was *yod* (י). Certain Hebrew characters had a tiny stroke, apex or "tittle" that differentiated one letter from another. Jesus' hyperbole emphasized that God's Word would be fulfilled down to the most minute detail.

343 The so-called righteousness of the religious leaders was nothing more than rule-following. Only "the righteousness of God through faith in Jesus Christ" is acceptable according to Kingdom standards.—Romans 3:21-22, *The Bible in Basic English*.

344 Continued looking (more than just a passing immoral thought) often arouses passionate desire. Then, if an opportunity arises, it can result in adultery. Compare James 1:14-15.

345 To save their life, some people have willingly sacrificed a gangrenous limb. It is more important to sacrifice anything, even something as precious as an eye or a hand, to avoid immoral thinking and its resulting actions. Compare Proverbs 23:2.

346 Or "It is more profitable for you that one of your members should perish, than for your whole body to be cast into Gehenna," or "Hell." (Matthew 5:29-30 & footnote, *World English Bible)* Gehenna, also known as the Valley of Hinnom, was prophetically spoken of as a place where dead bodies would be strewn. (Jeremiah 7:31-32; 19:6) By Jesus' day, it had become a place for burning Jerusalem's garbage, making it a fitting symbol of complete destruction.—Matthew 10:28.

347 God hates divorce and his law to Israel did not encourage it. (Malachi 2:16) Divorce was nevertheless allowable but regulated. Legalities such as a **certificate** were deterrents to hasty breakups as well as protection for wives.—**Matthew 5:31**.

348 Heard, that is, "in the synagogues, where the teachings of tradition were given orally."—Matthew chapter 5 note h, *The Jerusalem Bible:* Edited by Alexander Jones.

349 Or "fornication," all sexual intercourse that is unlawful according to the Bible.—Matthew 5:32, *King James Version*; see Leviticus 20:10-21; Deuteronomy 23:17-18; Romans 1:26-27; 1 Corinthians 6:9.

350 After a divorce on grounds **other than unfaithfulness,** the remarriage of either partner would constitute **adultery**. A man or woman who marries such a divorced person would also be guilty of adultery.—**Matthew 5:31-32**; 19:9; Luke 16:18; Romans 7:3.

351 That is, subject to trial in one of the courts located throughout Israel. (Deuteronomy 16:18; Matthew 10:17; Mark 13:9) Local **courts** had authority to try cases of **murder**.—**Matthew 5:21**; see Deuteronomy 19:11-12; 21:1-9.

352 Jesus condemned even attitudes that contribute to breaking God's law. Continued wrath could lead to murder.—1 John 3:15.

353 Depending on the context, the Greek word for "brother" may refer to a family relationship, a spiritual relationship or to one's fellow man.—Matthew 5:22-24; 7:3-5, *King James Version*

354 Someone addressing a fellow worshiper with such a derogatory term as *raca* ("empty, vain, or worthless" person) would not only be nurturing hatred in the heart but also be giving vent to it by contemptible speech.—Matthew 5:22, *King James Version; The New Compact Bible Dictionary*, page 486.

355 Israel's **High Court** was the Sanhedrin—the judicial body in Jerusalem made up of the high priest and 70 elders and scholars; its rulings were final.—**Matthew 5:22.** See "The Sanhedrin—Theocracy's High Court."

[356] To call a fellow believer a "fool," in the scriptural sense of the term, is to judge them unworthy of eternal life and thus decree their destruction. (Matthew 5:22, *King James Version)* From God's standpoint, one who desires destruction for a fellow believer would be deserving of just such a judgment. Compare Deuteronomy 19:17-21.

[357] The **altar** refers to the altar of burnt offering in the Temple's courtyard for priests, where ordinary Israelites were not allowed. In the scene Jesus describes, a worshiper is at the very point of handing over a sacrificial offering to the priest. Before offering this **gift** in a way that would be acceptable to God, the worshiper needed to go away and find the offended fellow believer, who was likely among the many thousands of pilgrims who came to Jerusalem for the seasonal festivals, the usual time for bringing such sacrifices to the Temple. (Deuteronomy 16:16) The goal would be to effect a change by removing, if possible, ill will from the offended person's heart. (Romans 12:18) Maintaining **peace** with others is a prerequisite for enjoying peace with God.—**Matthew 5:23-24**.

[358] This rule "was necessary to restrain the human desire to retaliate beyond the injury inflicted." (Verlyn D. Verbrugge: *The NIV Topical Study Bible*, page 83; Exodus 21:24; Leviticus 24:20) In Jesus' day, the rule was misapplied to condone personal vengeance; it was properly applied only after cases came to trial and the appointed judges determined the appropriate punishment.—Deuteronomy 19:16-21.

[359] Following Jesus' teaching and example, Christians should be willing to endure personal insult without retaliating. (John 18:22-23) The intention behind a slap is provocation and not injury, so Jesus' words do not prohibit self-defense. Metaphorically, the slap means rejection. For Christians, risk is involved in reaching out to people in the way that Jesus did. When one's efforts are rejected, a Christian must persist in trying to reach others with gospel truth.

[360] Anciently, it was customary for people to give a garment in pledge to guarantee payment of a debt. (Job 22:6) If a debtor was unable to pay, a court could award that garment to the creditor. (Proverbs 20:16; 27:13) For the sake of peace, Jesus' followers should be willing to give up not only their "inner garment" (a shirt-like tunic with long sleeves or half sleeves, reaching to the knees or ankles and worn next to the skin) but also their more valuable "outer garment" (a loose robe or coat, or just a simple rectangular piece of material).—Matthew 5:40, *21st Century New Testament* by Vivian Capel. Compare 1 Corinthians 6:7.

[361] Roman authorities could, for example, press men or animals into service or commandeer whatever was considered necessary to expedite official business.—Matthew 27:32.

[362] Some rabbis narrowed the meaning of "neighbor" to fellow Israelites, especially those who kept the oral traditions; all other people were enemies to be hated. Contrary to what Jesus' listeners may have been taught, the Law contained no command to hate one's enemies. (Leviticus 19:18) "God's approach is to transform enemies into friends because of what Christ has done—and he asks us to do the same. He asks us to be agents of reconciliation who respond to hostility not with more hostility but with love. God's people are called to love their enemies and do good to them, and even to pray for them."—Verlyn D. Verbrugge: *The NIV Topical Study Bible*, page 705.

[363] Jesus' counsel is in harmony with the spirit of the Old Testament.—Exodus 23:4-5; Job 31:29-30; Proverbs 24:17; 25:21.

[364] Tax collectors were generally shunned by fellow Israelites because they collaborated with a resented foreign power and extorted more than the official rate. (Luke 3:12-13; 19:8) Luke 6:32-34 replaces the expression **tax collectors** (which in this context would be meaningful only to Israelites) with the more general term "sinners," people unconcerned with observing details of Israel's law.—**Matthew 5:46**; see "The Gospel According to..."

[365] Or "brothers," referring to the entire nation of Israel. (Matthew 5:47, *King James Version)* Israelites were offspring of one common father, Jacob (Israel), and they were united in worship of the True God.—Psalm 133:1.

[366] Gentiles had no relationship with God. Israelites viewed them as godless and unclean people to be avoided. Luke 6:32-34 replaces the expression **pagans** (which in this context would be meaningful only to Israelites) with the more general term "sinners."—**Matthew 5:47**; see "The Gospel According to..."

[367] Or "sons of the Most High." (Luke 6:35, *New English Translation)* In Jesus' time and culture, sons had privileges that daughters did not. "However, Jesus is most likely addressing both men and women in this context, so women too would receive these same privileges."—Luke 6:35 footnote, *The NET Bible.*

[368] In imitation of God, love must be displayed without discrimination and expanded to embrace even one's enemies.

[369] For Israelites, good works that made someone righteous in God's eyes were principally almsgiving, prayer and fasting.—Deuteronomy 15:7-11.

[370] Or "give money to the poor."—Matthew 6:2, *The Bible in Basic English.*

[371] Literally, "playactors." (Matthew 6:1-18 footnote, *The New English Bible)* The English word "hypocrite" comes from a Greek word that originally referred to stage actors who wore large masks designed to amplify the voice. The term came to be a metaphor for anyone masking their real intentions or personality by playing false or putting on a pretense.—Matthew 6:2, 5, 16; 7:5; Luke 6:42.

[372] Contribution boxes in the Temple were shaped like trumpets. (Jesus, it appears, had an ironic sense of humor!)

[373] The hypocrites gave in order to be seen by others, and they were seen and glorified by others for their charity. That was their **full** reward. They could expect nothing from God.—**Matthew 6:2**.

[374] This figure of speech denotes the utmost discretion or secrecy. Jesus' followers are not to advertise their charity even to intimate friends, to those who are as close to them as the left hand is to the right.

[375] This was not a blanket condemnation of public prayer. Jesus denounced prayers said in a way to impress listeners and draw admiring compliments.

[376] Jesus did not mean that repeatedly praying about the same subject was wrong. (See Matthew 26:39, 42, 44) He disapproved of praying by rote like pagans who prayed without thinking and babbled mindlessly.

[377] **This way** in contrast with the practice of those who were accustomed to saying the same things over and over. (**Matthew 6:9**) Jesus did not provide a model prayer to be repeated by rote. He gave it for the purpose of centering attention on the most important things—God's reputation and rulership. His model prayer was also to serve as a deterrent to materialism, to encourage a loving and forgiving spirit and to be a protection against temptation.

[378] By using the plural pronoun **our**, the one praying acknowledges that others too have a close relationship with the **Father** and are part of His family of worshipers.—**Matthew 6:9**; also, Matthew 5:16; Romans 8:15.

[379] Or "may your name be kept holy." (Matthew 6:9, *World English Bible)* In the Bible "name" at times means "reputation." (Jeremiah 32:20, *Free Bible Version)* By means of his coming Kingdom God will **vindicate** his **reputation** and clear it of reproach.—**Matthew 6:9**.

[380] A petition for God to take decisive action to rule the earth.—Daniel 2:44; compare Psalms 2 & 110.

[381] This petition could be understood in two possible ways: (1) asking that God's **will be done on Earth** as it is already being done in Heaven; (2) requesting that God's will be done fully both in Heaven and on Earth. (**Matthew 6:10**) Like Christ, Christians prefer and submit to God's will.—Matthew 26:39; Mark 14:36; Luke 22:42; John 5:30.

[382] Those who serve God can confidently ask him to supply them, not with excessive provisions, but with their "daily bread." (Matthew 6:11; Luke 11:3, *King James Version)* This request is a reminder that God commanded the Israelites to gather the miraculously provided manna in daily amounts.—Exodus 16:4.

[383] Receiving God's forgiveness depends on whether the person has forgiven his personal "debtors," (Matthew 6:12, *King James Version)* that is, those who have sinned against him. (Matthew 6:14-15; 18:35; Luke 11:4) In Biblical Greek, to forgive can mean to cancel a debt.—Matthew 18:27, 32.

[384] Jesus encouraged his followers to pray for God's help to avoid or endure temptation. (1 Corinthians 10:13) God does not lead people into temptation in the sense of tempting them to sin. (James 1:13) The request "lead us not into temptation" is a rhetorical way to ask for protection from sin.

[385] Israelites abstained from food on the Day of Atonement, in times of distress and when in need of divine guidance. They established four annual fasts to mark calamitous events in their history. Fasting could be done sincerely (1 Samuel 7:6; 2 Chronicles 20:3; Ezra 8:21) or hypocritically (Isaiah 58:3-5; Luke 18:12). Jesus neither commanded nor discouraged fasting. See "Feast or Fast?"

[386] Or "and to-morrow is cast into the oven." (Matthew 6:30, *American Standard Version)* Withered flower stalks and grass were collected from the fields as fuel for baking ovens.

[387] The belief or trust of Jesus' listeners (primarily his disciples) was not strong. **Little** implied a deficiency—not an absence—of **faith**.—**Matthew 6:30**; 8:26; 14:31; 16:8; Luke 12:28.

[388] Worrying cannot add even a little to the length of our life; rather, it can distract us and steal our joy. Undue anxiety about what may happen in the future can cause us to rely on ourselves rather than on God. (Proverbs 3:5-6) God has promised to take care of all our needs, just as he fully provides for the needs of his animal creation.—Matthew 6:11, 26; see Psalm 136:25; 147:9; Luke 12:24.

[389] There is no need to be anxious for material needs if God's service is put first. Christians must always make seeking the Kingdom their paramount concern in life. Those who keep seeking God's righteousness readily do his will and conform to his standards of right and wrong.

[390] Or "Set free, and you will be set free." (Luke 6:37, *World English Bible)* In Biblical Greek forgiveness means to release from punishment, even when retribution might seem warranted.

[391] God holds us to the standards that we apply to others.—Matthew 7:2; Luke 6:38; also Proverbs 19:17; 21:13; 28:27; Matthew 6:14-15; 18:35; Mark 11:25-26; James 2:13.

[392] It is dangerous to follow the lead of judgmental, hyper-critical people. The Pharisees, for example, harshly judged unbelievers who did not live by Israel's law and also fellow Israelites who did not follow the Pharisees' extra-biblical traditions. Christians, instead of continually finding fault, should continue forgiving the shortcomings of fellow believers, thereby encouraging others to show the same forgiving attitude.

[393] The critic implies that a fellow believer's spiritual vision—moral perception and judgment—is defective, when it is the critic's own spiritual vision that is impaired. This powerful (even humorous) hyperbole suggests that Jesus was familiar with the work done in a carpenter's shop.—Mark 6:3.

[394] Jesus applied this term to the religious leaders at Matthew 6:2, 5, 16, but at Matthew 7:5 and Luke 6:42 it applies to a disciple who fixates on another's faults while ignoring their own.

[395] The continuous action indicated by the Greek verb form used at Matthew 7:7 shows the need for perseverance in prayer. Jesus' illustration at Luke 11:5-10 makes a similar point. Compare 1 Chronicles 16:11.

[396] The rhetorical question implies that it would be unthinkable for a loving parent to do such a thing. Bread and fish were staples in the diet of people living around the Sea of Galilee. The size and shape of loaves could have reminded people of stones, and small serpents may have looked like fish that were often eaten with bread.

[397] Because of inherited sin, all humans are imperfect and, consequently, comparatively wicked.—Psalm 51:5; Ecclesiastes 7:20; Romans 3:23; 5:12.

[398] Arguing from the lesser to the greater, Jesus first presented an obvious fact or a familiar truth, then drew an even more convincing conclusion based on that fact. Jesus often used this line of reasoning.—Matthew 10:25; 12:12; Luke 11:13; 12:28.

[399] God gives us, not all we want, but the good we need, such as the gifts of wisdom and guidance.—James 1:17.

[400] The two roads picture contrasting ways of life, either approved or disapproved by God, determining whether one enters God's kingdom.—Psalm 1:6; Jeremiah 21:8.

[401] Animals—their characteristics and habits—are often applied in a figurative sense in the Bible. The wolf can picture such undesirable qualities as ferocity, greed, viciousness and craftiness. (Matthew 10:16; Luke 10:3; John 10:12; Acts 20:29) Jesus compared false prophets to ravenous wolves who exploit others for personal gain and are extremely covetous. A wolf in sheep's clothing exhibits sheeplike qualities to give the impression of being a harmless member of God's flock of worshipers.—Matthew 7:15; Acts 20:28.

[402] Or "By what they produce." (Matthew 7:16, *The Names of God Bible)* Words and deeds reveal the motives of the heart. (Compare James 3:10-12) The **fruits** of false prophets include their doctrine. (**Matthew 7:16**; 16:12) Whatever is spoken or taught in God's name should be tested against the truths in God's written Word.—1 John 4:1-3.

[403] In this context, **lawbreakers** are people with contempt for laws (God's laws in particular) and who act as if there were no laws.—**Matthew 7:23**; 1 John 3:4.

[404] Or "Master." (Luke 6:46, *The New Testament in Modern Speech*; see "Jesus, A.K.A. ...") "Jesus pointed out that those who called Him by this title of respect acknowledge submission to Him. However, when these same people ignored His teaching, they were guilty of hypocrisy."—Luke 6:46 footnote, *The Nelson Study Bible*. Copyright © 1997 by Thomas Nelson, Inc. Used with permission.

[405] "The key difference in the two houses is not their external appearance. Pharisees and scribes may seem to be as righteous as the heirs of the kingdom. The key in the story is the foundations." The **solid foundation** "pictures a life founded on a proper relationship to Christ ([Matt.] 16:18; 1 Cor. 10:4; 1 Pet. 2:4-8)."—**Matthew 7:24-27** footnote, *The Nelson Study Bible*. Copyright © 1997 by Thomas Nelson, Inc. Used with permission.

[406] One who hears Jesus' words **and acts on them** can face any difficult circumstance. One who hears Jesus' words but **does nothing** may be overwhelmed by circumstances and experience total loss. (**Matthew 7:24, 26**; compare 1 Corinthians 3:12-15) Sudden winter storms are not uncommon in Israel, especially during the month of Tebeth (corresponding to December/January). Storms bring high winds, torrential rains and destructive flash floods.

[407] Jesus did not cite a list of authorities, like the rabbis did, nor did he need to. His words were self-authenticating.—Matthew 5:20, 22, 28, 32, 34, 39, 44.

[408] *Letters of John Quincy Adams to His Son on the Bible and Its Teachings*, page 9. Copyright © 2012 Forgotten Books. Originally published in 1850.

[409] Centurion was the highest rank that the common soldier could reach in Rome's army. In command of about 100 men, centurions drilled the soldiers and regulated their conduct. They also inspected arms, supplies and food. Centurions were among the most experienced and valuable men in the army, making the humility and faith of the officer who approached Jesus even more impressive. (Matthew 8:5 says that the centurion came to Jesus. According to Luke 7:3, the officer sent Jewish elders to act as his intermediaries.) Like Cornelius, this Gentile was evidently in sympathy with Judaism, although not necessarily a proselyte. (Acts 10:1-2) Edersheim suggests that it was from the ailing servant, possibly an Israelite, that the Roman officer came to know Israel's God.

[410] Or "child." (Matthew 8:6, 8, 13; Luke 7:7, *Wycliffe Bible* by Terrence P. Noble) The servant was regarded as a member of the centurion's family. Compare Luke 7:3, 10.

[411] The centurion had the synagogue built or donated the cost of its construction. Rome supported a stable religious community, seeing it as politically advantageous. Synagogues were valued as preservers of order through their emphasis on morals.

[412] The centurion was no doubt aware that Israelites avoided association with Gentiles. (Acts 10:28) Israel's religious leaders taught that anyone who entered a foreigner's home would become ceremonially unclean. (John 18:28) Against such association Moses' law made no ruling.

[413] This commendation of a Gentile's faith was a strong rebuke of Israel, who thought she would have priority in the Kingdom arrangement. (Zechariah 8:23) As Jesus went on to show, being a descendant of Abraham was no guarantee of a place in the Kingdom.

[414] "It was a common belief," according to Edersheim, "that in the day of the Messiah redeemed Israel would be gathered to a great feast, together with the patriarchs and heroes of the Jewish faith. (Isa. 25:6) ... Gentiles could have no part in that feast." (page 379) But Gentiles will be welcomed to dine **in the kingdom of Heaven.—Matthew 8:11**; 22:2-14; Luke 13:28-30; compare Psalm 107:2-3.

[415] Grinding the teeth is a metaphor for sorrow and anger, especially "for the dismay and frustration of the wicked at seeing the virtuous rewarded." (Matthew chapter 8 note e, *The Jerusalem Bible:* Edited by Alexander Jones; see Psalm 112:10) Jesus' contemporaries believed that Gentiles would be consigned to "a place of darkness" on Judgment Day, whereas Jewish sinners would be saved by "the merit of circumcision." (Amos 5:20) "Never, surely, could the Judaism of [Jesus'] hearers have received more rude shock than by this inversion of all their cherished beliefs."—Edersheim, pages 379, 380.

[416] Nain was over 20 miles (32 km) southwest of Capernaum, about a day's journey. Overlooking the Plain of Jezreel and located in an attractive natural setting, the modern-day village of Nein sits on the northwest side of the hill of Moreh, about 6 miles (10 km) south-southeast of Nazareth. Ruins in the area show that the small village was larger in earlier centuries, fitting its description at Luke 7:11-12 as a "city."

[417] Jesus and his disciples may have met the funeral procession at a "gate" at Nain's eastern entrance, which was in the direction of the hillside tombs lying to the southeast. (Luke 7:12) The crowd may have included mourners chanting lamentations and musicians playing mournful tunes.—Jeremiah 9:17-18; Matthew 9:23.

[418] The woman was now socially alone and without protection.

[419] "Although sometimes translated 'coffin,' the *bier* was actually a stretcher or wooden plank on which the corpse was transported to the place of burial." (Luke 7:14 footnote, *The NET Bible)* The bier had poles projecting from its corners that allowed four men to bear it on their shoulders.

[420] Perhaps the people were thinking of the miracles wrought by the prophets Elijah and Elisha.—1 Kings 17:17-23; 2 Kings 4:32-35.

[421] According to Josephus, John the Baptist met his death at Machaerus fortress, located on the Perean side of the Dead Sea. Possibly John spent time in that prison. However, it is likely that at the time of his death, John was held in Tiberias, a city on the western shore of the Sea of Galilee, much closer to Nain than Machaerus.

[422] Jesus had thus far proven to be a different sort of Messiah from what John (and Israelites in general) had expected. (Matthew 3:10-12; Mark 1:7-8; Luke 3:16-17) John's question might imply an expectation that Jesus (or **another**, a successor) will complete the fulfillment of all that the Messiah was foretold to accomplish and perhaps free John from prison.—**Matthew 11:3; Luke 7:19**.

[423] If John's query caused some to question his commitment to Jesus, their doubts should have been erased by Jesus' supportive statements of the Baptist. John carried on where Malachi, the last of the Old Testament prophets, left off, and fulfilled Malachi's final prophecy.—Malachi 3:1; 4:5-6; Luke 1:17.

[424] John prepared the way for Jesus but died before Christ opened the way to Heaven. (Hebrews 10:19-20) If a lesser one in the Kingdom is greater than John, then John's eternal reward lies outside Heaven. (Psalm 37:9, 11, 22, 29, 34) John held open the door to the Kingdom but he did not enter it. (John 10:3) As the bridegroom's "friend," John did not expect to be part of the spiritual "bride" of Christ. (John 3:28-29) Jesus' words also contrast the era of Heaven's kingdom with that of the Mosaic Law, which preceded and prepared for it. John stood at the end of the old era and proclaimed the new, an era so great that its least important member was greater than the most important one of the previous era, John himself.

[425] John's life of self-denial included fasting and abstaining from alcohol. (Matthew 11:18; Luke 1:15) For his asceticism, he was accused of being influenced by evil spirits. People were equally critical of Jesus who, unlike John, freely associated with others—including the despised tax collectors and sinners.

[426] Professional mourners were often accompanied by flutists playing mournful tunes. Flutes were also played on joyous occasions, such as at banquets and weddings (1 Kings 1:40-41; Isaiah 5:12; 30:29), a custom imitated by children in public places. The Israelites, like petulant children, were complaining that John and Jesus did not dance to their tune. That generation wanted things their way, not God's.

[427] Or "wisdom is shown to be right by the lives of those who follow it." (Luke 7:35, *New Living Translation)* By the way they lived their lives, John and Jesus proved that the accusations against them were untrue. Wisdom had other **children**: those who responded to John and Jesus, unlike most of **the adults of [that] generation.**—**Luke 7:29, 35**.

[428] The towns of Chorazin and Bethsaida were near Capernaum, the city that Jesus apparently used as a home base in Galilee. In the area of Bethsaida, Jesus will miraculously feed more than 5,000 people and cure a blind man. (Mark 8:22; Luke 9:10-17) Since these events had not happened yet, Jesus was exercising his power of foreknowledge, predicting the reaction of the general populace to his miracles.

[429] Sackcloth was a coarse cloth used in making sacks, or bags, such as those for containing grain; it was usually woven from dark-colored goat's hair and was the traditional garment of mourning. (Genesis 37:34) Sackcloth and ashes were sometimes associated with fasting, weeping or sorrow. (Esther 4:3; Isaiah 58:5; Ezekiel 27:30-31; Daniel 9:3) Nineveh was a national example of humiliation and repentance; even her king covered himself with sackcloth and sat down in the ashes.—Jonah 3:5-6.

[430] The prophets of old repeatedly pronounced woe against Tyre and Sidon. (Isaiah 23:1-18; Jeremiah 25:17, 22, 27-28; 47:4; Ezekiel 26:1-28:26; Joel 3:4; Zechariah 9:2-4) However, these Gentile cities will come off better than the cities of Galilee on Judgment Day.

[431] **Heaven** metaphorically denotes a highly favored position; **Hades** (or "the grave") figuratively represents debasement.—**Matthew 11:23**, *The Holy Bible in Modern English* (Revised Edition). Compare Isaiah 14:14-15.

[432] What happened to ancient Sodom had become proverbial and was often mentioned in connection with God's anger and judgment. (Genesis 19:24; Deuteronomy 29:23; Isaiah 1:9; Lamentations 4:6) Jesus' comparison emphasized how unresponsive and culpable most people were in Chorazin, Bethsaida and Capernaum.—Luke 10:13-15.

[433] Such spiritual truths include the secrets of the Kingdom, which God revealed to Jesus' disciples but concealed from Israel's religious leaders.

[434] Or "meek"; "mild." (Mt 11:29, *King James Version; Wycliffe Bible)* "Meekness is a quality closely connected with humility and gentleness .... It does not denote weakness but strength; a meek person is in control of himself, not insisting on his own way but reaching out in kindness for the good of others. It is a quality that Jesus exhibited and one he expects of us; it is one aspect of the fruit of the Spirit ...."—Verlyn D. Verbrugge: *The NIV Topical Study Bible,* page 1295. See Matthew 5:5; 21:5; Galatians 5:22.

[435] One who is **lowly in heart** is humble and unpretentious. (**Matthew 11:29**; James 4:6; 1 Peter 5:5-6) The condition of a person's figurative heart is reflected in one's disposition or one's attitude toward God and other people.

[436] One type of wooden yoke was a bar or frame fitted to a person's shoulders, and loads were suspended from it on each side of the body. Another type of yoke was a wooden bar or frame that was placed over the necks of two draft animals when they pulled a load. If Jesus had in mind a double

yoke, then he would be inviting his disciples to get under the yoke with him and he would assist them. If the yoke is one that Jesus puts on others, then the reference is to submission to Christ's authority and direction. Taking on Jesus' **yoke** would involve service, not rest. (Compare **Matthew 11:28**, *King James Version)* Unfaithful Israelites viewed the keeping of the Law as a burdensome yoke. (Jeremiah 5:5) People in Jesus' day labored under a load of religious requirements laid upon them by their leaders. (Matthew 23:4; Luke 11:46) Jesus' kindly yoke is refreshingly light, for the load of Christian requirements is not burdensome.—1 John 5:3.

[437] A token of affection or respect, a kiss might have included touching one's lips to those of another, another person's cheek or, in an exceptional case, even the feet. (Proverbs 24:26) Kissing was common not only between male and female relatives (Genesis 29:11; 31:28) but also between male relatives (Genesis 27:26-27; 45:15; Exodus 18:7; 2 Samuel 14:33); it was likewise a gesture of affection between close friends.—1 Samuel 20:41-42; 2 Samuel 19:39.

[438] In ancient times, walking was the main way of traveling. Those who did not go barefoot wore sandals consisting of little more than a sole and leather straps. On entering a house, the guest's sandals were removed. Foot-washing was performed either by the householder or by a servant. At the very least, water was provided for that purpose.—Genesis 18:4; 19:2; 24:32; Judges 19:21; 1 Samuel 25:41.

[439] Luke 7:37 says that the woman learned of Jesus' whereabouts and went to see him. Perhaps she had heard his invitation, "Come to me..." and was responding to it. (Matthew 11:28-30) Without proof, some identify her with Mary Magdalene, and from this identification comes the equally unprovable claim that Mary Magdalene was a prostitute. (Compare this account with Mary Magdalene's introduction at Luke 8:2.) Edersheim insinuates that this unnamed immoral woman was admitted to the party because she was known—in the biblical sense—to Simon. This is "by no means inconsistent with what we know of the morality of some of these Rabbis," Edersheim claims.—page 389 note 9.

[440] Alabaster jars were small vase-like vessels for perfume originally made of stone found near Alabastron, Egypt. The stone itself, a form of calcium carbonate, came to be known by the name Alabastron. A less costly material, such as gypsum, was used to make similar jars; these too were called alabasters because of the use to which they were put. However, genuine alabaster cases were used for the more costly ointments and perfumes, like those with which Jesus was anointed.—Matthew 26:7; Mark 14:3.

[441] Simon used the term **sinner** in a specific way, inferring that the woman lived a "sinful life," practicing sin of a moral or a criminal nature. (Luke 7:39, *Today's English Version)* What she did for Jesus, however, said much about her contrite heart. Also, for her to appear before people who knew her reputation took humility and courage.

[442] Jesus based some of his illustrations on the relationship between creditors and debtors. (Matthew 18:23-35; Luke 16:1-8) Only Luke records this illustration of two debtors, in which Jesus likens sin to a debt too big to be repaid. In Luke's recording of Jesus' model prayer, the term "debts" instead of sins is used.—11:4; compare Matthew 6:12.

[443] Lit., "five hundred denarii." (Luke 7:41, *The Darby Bible* by John Nelson Darby) A denarius was a Roman silver coin. Agricultural laborers in Jesus' day commonly received a denarius for a 12-hour workday.—Matthew 20:2.

[444] Or "her great love proves that her many sins have been forgiven; where little has been forgiven, little love is shown."—Luke 7:47, *The New English Bible.*

[445] Mary's epithet suggests that Magdala was her hometown or place of residence. This town was located on the western shore of the Sea of Galilee, about halfway between Capernaum and Tiberias. Ancient rabbinic sources describe Magdala as materially wealthy but morally bankrupt.

[446] Joanna is a shortened feminine form of the Hebrew name Jehohanan, meaning "Jehovah is gracious." *(The New Compact Bible Dictionary,* page 268) Her husband Chuza was a steward (in domestic or governmental affairs) to Herod Antipas. Little is known of Joanna, as she is mentioned only twice in the New Testament—both times in the Gospel of Luke (8:3; 24:10). Perhaps she was a source of information for the author.

[447] This suggests that they were relatively wealthy. Inscriptions from a synagogue in Aphrodisias in Asia Minor from around the same period reveal that many of the congregation's major donors were women.

[448] Also, Jesus' family may be concerned for his safety as opposition to his ministry increases.

[449] The phrase **Son of David** was often applied to Jesus; it identified the descendant of King David who was the Heir of the Kingdom covenant.—**Matthew 12:23**. See "Jesus, A.K.A. ..."

[450] News of the resurrection in Nain had reached Judea (Luke 7:17) and, probably, the religious leaders in Jerusalem.

[451] The name **Beelzebub** may be an alteration of Baalzebub (meaning "lord of flies"), the Baal worshiped by the Philistines at Ekron. (2 Kings 1:2-3, 6, 16; *The New Compact Bible Dictionary*, page 66) To monotheistic Israelites, any lord (baal) opposed to the true Lord of Israel was an embodiment of the Devil. Jesus' critics recognized his work as supernatural but called it diabolical. For attributing to Satan, the work of God's spirit they would be held accountable.

[452] **House** could refer to an individual family or to an extended household.—**Matthew 12:25**; **Mark 3:25**; Acts 7:10; Philippians 4:22.

[453] Or "sons," referring either to Israelite exorcists or to the disciples of Jesus. (Matthew 12:27, *American Standard Version)* "If this is a reference to the disciples, then Jesus' point is that it is not only him, but those associated with him whose power the hearers must assess."—Matthew 12:27 footnote, *The NET Bible.*

[454] Or "the kingdom of God has come upon you [before you expected it]." (**Matthew 12:28**, *Amplified Bible)* The presence of God's authority has come because Jesus does indeed **expel demons by the power of God's spirit.**

[455] Since it is by his spirit that God gives life and teaches people about Christ, sinning against God's spirit involves consciously and willfully resisting the operation of his spirit to draw people to Christ. Persistent unbelief, then, is the unforgivable sin.—Hebrews 10:26-31.

[456] The influence of these religious leaders is spiritual poison. They are against Jesus, scattering people away from the Son of God.—Matthew 12:30; also, Matthew 3:7; 23:33; Luke 3:7.

[457] The Pharisees' **fruit**—their absurd accusations against Jesus—prove that they are **rotten**. **Words** reflect the condition of one's **heart** and thus provide a basis for judgment.—**Matthew 12:33-37**.

[458] Or "adulterous"; in a spiritual sense, unfaithful to God. (**Matthew 12:39**, *King James Version*; see James 4:4) Israel's false religious practices were acts of spiritual adultery against her "husband." (Isaiah 54:5; Jeremiah 31:32 *KJV;* also, Jeremiah 3:14, 20; 5:7-8; 9:2; 13:27; 23:10; Hosea 7:4) For similar reasons, Jesus denounced his contemporaries as **unfaithful**.—Matthew 16:4.

[459] Or "whale"; "sea-monster." (**Matthew 12:40** & footnote, *American Standard Version;* compare Jonah 1:17) The seaport of ancient Joppa may have been a headquarters for whalers. (Jonah 1:3) However, our knowledge of the creatures inhabiting the seas and oceans is too incomplete to determine just what **fish** might have been involved; it is almost certainly extinct.

[460] Fittingly, the only proof for faithless ones will be what seems to be the absence of proof: Jesus' death and burial. Jonah compared his deliverance from the belly of the great fish to being raised from the dead. (Jonah 2:1-2) Jesus' resurrection from the dead was to be just as real as Jonah's deliverance. Unlike Jesus' faithless contemporaries, the Ninevites repented after Jonah preached to them. (Jonah 3:5) As if witnesses at a trial, they "will rise up in the judgment with this generation, and will condemn it," said Jesus. By her example, the queen of Sheba, who came from afar to hear Solomon's wisdom, will likewise "arise in the judgment with this generation and will condemn it."—Matthew 12:41-42, *The Emphasized Bible.* See 1 Kings 10:1-10.

[461] Israel had been cleansed and had reformed—much like the person from whom the unclean spirit came out. But the nation rejected God's prophets, culminating in its opposing Jesus. Israel's condition—like that of the possessed person—became worse than at its start.

[462] The Gospels distinguish Jesus' natural (half) brothers—at least some of whom lacked faith in him—from his spiritual brothers, his disciples. (John 2:12; 7:5) After becoming a Christian, Jesus' half-brother James wrote about the importance of hearing God's word and acting upon it.—James 1:22-25.

[463] Jesus' parables and illustrations were short and usually fictitious narratives from which a moral or spiritual truth could be drawn.

[464] Sowers would carry a bag of seed tied across the shoulder and around the waist or form a pouch for the seed in a part of their cloak. They would then disperse the seed by hand with long sweeping motions. Because fields were cut through with hard-packed footpaths, a sower had to make sure that the seed landed on good soil. As soon as possible the seed was covered to protect it from hungry birds.

[465] Referring to a limestone base immediately beneath the soil.

[466] Palestinian weeds have a major root system and can grow up to 6 feet (1.8 m) tall.

[467] The parable of the sower illustrates various lifelong responses (not individual moments of decision) to the Kingdom gospel. "The background for this well-known parable, drawn from a typical scene in the Palestinian countryside, is a field through which a well-worn path runs. ... The use of seed as a figure for God's giving life has OT roots (Isa 55:10-11)."—Matthew 13:3 footnote, *The NET Bible*.

[468] Bearded darnel is a species of the grass family. Not until it reaches maturity can this poisonous plant be distinguished from wheat. "Sowing darnel in a field for purposes of revenge (cf. Mt. 13:25f.) was a crime under Roman legislation," says *The New Bible Dictionary*. "The necessity for a law on the subject suggests that the action was not infrequent."—2nd edition, page 948.

[469] Even if the weeds were identified, uprooting them would result in loss of the wheat because the roots of both plants would have become intertwined.

[470] Reapers sometimes simply pulled the stalks of grain from the ground. Typically, however, they would harvest the grain by cutting the stalks with a sickle.—Deuteronomy 16:9.

[471] Storehouses for threshed grain could be found throughout Israel. Some facilities might also be used to hold oil and wine or even precious metals or stones.

[472] Jesus' use of parables fulfilled a prophecy about the Messiah: "I will open my mouth in parables; I will utter things which have been kept secret from the foundation of the world." As the psalmist ("the prophet") used illustrative language to recount much of the history of God's dealings with Israel, Jesus used figurative language in the many illustrations he used to teach his followers.—Matthew 13:35, *King James Version*. See Psalm 78:2.

[473] **Hidden truths** (or "sacred secrets," *The Emphasized Bible*; "mysteries," *King James Version)* are aspects of God's purpose withheld until God reveals them to those whom he chooses. (**Matthew 13:11**; **Luke 8:10**; Romans 16:25-26; Colossians 1:26-27) They can mean a new revelation or a revealing interpretation of existing revelation. (Daniel chapter 2) Once revealed, these truths are given the widest possible proclamation. (Ephesians 3:2-10) With his Kingdom parables, Jesus was explaining how current events developed old promises. The New Testament consistently links the events of Jesus' ministry and message with Old Testament promises. (Luke 1:69-70; Hebrews 1:1-2) The most important of all hidden truths centers on the role of Jesus in God's eternal purpose.—Colossians 4:3.

[474] Those who accept Jesus' teaching receive a share in the Kingdom now and more in the future. As for those who reject Jesus' words, their opportunities with respect to the Kingdom will someday be taken away. Those who do not heed his word Jesus described as having nothing—**what they think they have** is nothing at all. It is not what one thinks one has that is important but whether one actually has something or not.—**Luke 8:18**.

[475] Jesus' parables revealed Kingdom truths to those who would accept them and concealed them from those who would reject them, a fact that fulfilled prophecy. (Isaiah 6:9-10) "Those who saw so dimly could only be further blinded by the light of full revelation .... Jesus, therefore, does not reveal with complete clarity the true nature of the messianic kingdom which is unostentatious. Instead, he filters the light through symbols, the resulting half-light is nevertheless a grace from God, an invitation to ask for something better and accept something greater."—Matthew chapter 13 note e, *The Jerusalem Bible:* Edited by Alexander Jones.

[476] The pathway soil is hard and unresponsive, like the hearts of those willingly blinded by Satan from understanding the Kingdom message.—2 Corinthians 4:4.

[477] Some seem eager to accept the Kingdom message but their commitment to Christ is superficial. "A person needs to meditate on the truths in Scripture and establish them as principles for living in order to withstand the trials and temptations that will inevitably come."—Luke 8:13 footnote, *The Nelson Study Bible.* Copyright © 1997 by Thomas Nelson, Inc. Used with permission.

[478] Some who have heard the Kingdom message lack single-mindedness and become unproductive. They succumb to worry or pleasure-seeking, both of which produce spiritual apathy.—2 Timothy 2:4; 4:10.

[479] A person who recognizes the ring of truth in the Kingdom message determines to follow God's call and experiences a genuine transformation. In the **rich soil** of **the heart** the message is implanted and becomes fruitful.—**Luke 8:15**; John 15:2-3; James 1:21.

[480] The apostles requested an explanation of this one parable out of all the parables they had heard that day. And fittingly so, for they were "wheat" in whose midst there was a 'weed,' Judas Iscariot.

[481] The final gathering of Christian **wheat** is described as a **harvest**, as is the final judgment of counterfeit Christian **weeds**. The **end of an age** is a period of time leading up to the conclusion of a state of affairs.—**Matthew 13:38-39**; 24:3; 28:20; Hebrews 9:26.

[482] "The Jewish teacher who becomes a disciple of Christ has at his disposal all the wealth of the Old Testament as well as the perfection of the New, v. 12."—Matthew chapter 13 note l, *The Jerusalem Bible.* Edited by Alexander Jones.

[483] "Some understand the parable as a reference to evangelism. While this is certainly involved, it does not seem to be the central idea. In contrast to the parable of the sower which emphasizes the quality of the different soils, this parable emphasizes the power of the seed to cause growth (with the clear implication that the mysterious growth of the kingdom is accomplished by God), apart from human understanding and observation."—Mark 4:29 footnote, *The NET Bible.*

[484] Fish without fins and scales were unclean according to the Mosaic Law and could not be eaten.—Leviticus 11:12; Deuteronomy 14:10.

[485] "Observe Jesus in the forenoon teaching a crowded audience (Mark 3:19), some of whom insult and blaspheme him, and others demand a sign, and at length his mother and brethren try to carry him off as insane (comp. Mark 3:21); in the afternoon giving a group of most remarkable parables, several of which he interprets; towards night crossing the Lake in a boat, so tired and worn that he sleeps soundly amid the alarming storm..." For Jesus it had been "a day of toil and trial." (Robertson, page 61) The so-called pillow was probably part of the boat's equipment; it may have been a sack of sand kept as ballast beneath the stern deck, a leather-covered seat for the helmsman or a cushion on which an oarsman could sit.

[486] When cold air from the surrounding mountains rushes down and collides with warm air above the water's surface, the resulting turbulence creates sudden windstorms on the Sea of Galilee.

[487] This region, extending from the Sea of Galilee to Gadara, included the town of Sennabris on the southern shore, most likely the town that the herdsmen entered after the swine drowned. Some link the Gerasenes region with the large district radiating from the city of Gerasa (Jarash), which was 34 miles (55 km) south-southeast of the sea. This location, says Edersheim, "entirely meets the requirement of the narrative. About a quarter of an hour to the south of Gersa *[sic]* is a steep bluff, which descends abruptly on a narrow ledge of shore. ... Again, the whole country around is burrowed with limestone caverns and rock-chambers for the dead, such as those which were the dwelling of the demonized [sic]." (pages 418-19) Gerasa was one of the ten towns of the Decapolis.—Matthew 4:25.

[488] Matthew (8:28) mentions two men; Mark (5:2) and Luke (8:27) refer to one. Perhaps Mark and Luke draw attention to just one of the men because Jesus spoke to him, and his case was more outstanding. It could also be that after both men were healed (as implied by Matthew 8:33), only one of them wanted to accompany Jesus.

[489] Burial places were usually located outside the cities and avoided by Israelites because of their ceremonial uncleanness, making them an ideal haunt for disturbed or demonized people. "According to common Jewish superstition," says Edersheim, "the evil spirits dwelt especially in lonely desolate places, and also among tombs. ... [I]t was chiefly at night that evil spirits were wont to haunt burying-places."—page 419.

[490] Humans may refuse to recognize Jesus' power over the demons but the demons themselves are well aware of it. (Matthew 9:34; 12:24; Mark 1:24; 3:11, 22; Luke 4:41; 11:15) The **torment** seems to refer to restraint or confinement to "the Abyss." (**Matthew 8:29**; **Mark 5:7**, 10; **Luke 8:28,** 31, *Free Bible Version)* The demons may have had in mind the imprisonment of Satan for 1,000 years. (Revelation 20:1-3) Their question reveals an understanding that there was an appointed **time** for them to face their judgment. (**Matthew 8:29**; 25:41; James 2:19; 2 Peter 2:4; Jude 6; Revelation 12:7-9) Perhaps they feared that Jesus' arrival on the scene portended a change in when their sentence would be carried out.

[491] A typical first-century Roman legion consisted of 6,000 soldiers; hence, many demons were battling with this man for control of his mind and body. Possibly, the chief one of these demons caused this man to say that his name was **Legion**.—**Mark 5:9**; **Luke 8:30**.

[492] Economic reasons might have motivated their request. There was a market for pork among the Gentiles living in the Decapolis region. Whereas it was unclean for Israelites, Greeks and Romans considered pork a delicacy (Leviticus 11:7; Deuteronomy 14:8) The financial loss of such a large herd as 2,000 hogs could amount to a quarter of a million dollars in today's economy.

[493] Jesus usually instructs those whom he heals not to tell anyone because he does not want people to reach conclusions about him on the basis of second-hand stories. In this case, the former demoniac is living proof of Jesus' power and can witness to people whom Jesus may not reach personally. It was less likely that people in the Gentile Decapolis would misunderstand the messianic mission of Jesus as a political one. The man's testimony may also counteract any unfavorable report about the loss of the swine.

[494] Jairus was the main elder at the synagogue; as such, he was responsible for organizing the services. Possibly, Jairus and Jesus knew one another. "How often Jesus must, with consent and by invitation of this Ruler, have spoken in the Synagogue," Edersheim suggests, "and what irresistible impression His words had made."—page 426.

[495] Much of what then passed for medical treatment would today be dismissed as quackery. The Talmud proposed several different remedies for menstrual hemorrhage, for example: burning up an ostrich egg and carrying the ashes in a cloth—linen in summer, cotton in winter.

[496] Or "the edge of his cloak," referring to the blue tassel on the clothing that signified a male Israelite's obedience to God's law. (Matthew 9:21, *New English Translation;* Numbers 15:38-39) The ritually impure woman touched the part of Jesus' garment that symbolized his ritual purity. Perhaps she had heard of someone doing something similar and being healed. Understandably, she did not want to reveal her condition to the crowd. If she came into contact with others that would make them unclean as well. (Leviticus 15:19-31) God's law taught respect for the sanctity of blood and reminded the Israelites that they (and all humankind) were born in a sinful state in need of a redeemer.—Leviticus 17:10-14.

[497] "The woman had no idea that Jesus had consciously healed her. ... He wanted to correct any mistaken notion she may have had about her healing," says Nelson. "It was not any magical quality of His clothing, but His divine will that had made her well."—Mark 5:29-30 footnote, *The Nelson Study Bible.* Copyright © 1997 by Thomas Nelson, Inc. Used with permission.

[498] This is the only recorded instance in which Jesus directly addressed a woman as **Daughter**. (**Mattthew 9:22**; **Mark 5:34**; **Luke 8:48**) By using this term of endearment, a form of address that signifies nothing about the woman's age, Jesus emphasized his tender concern for her.

[499] "To have faith is to relinquish trust in oneself and to put that trust in another. The woman who had the hemorrhage had put her trust in physicians but to no avail. Now she put all her trust in Jesus, believing He could cure her. According to Jesus, it was her faith that made her well. This was a proclamation Jesus made many times (Matt. 8:10; 9:22, 29; 15:28; Luke 7:50; 8:48)." However, "faith itself does not heal; rather, it is the proper object of that faith, Jesus, who heals."—Mark 5:34 footnote, *The Nelson Study Bible.* Copyright © 1997 by Thomas Nelson, Inc. Used with permission.

[500] The Greek word Jesus used literally means "scourging" and refers to a form of whipping often used as torture.—Note on Mark 5:34, *New World Translation* (Study Edition). See Acts 22:24; Hebrews 11:36.

[501] "Brief as is the record of this occurrence; it must have caused considerable delay in the progress of our Lord to the house of Jairus. For in the interval the maiden, who had been at the last gasp when her father went to entreat the help of Jesus, had not only died, but the house of mourning was already filled with relatives, hired mourners, wailing women, and musicians, in preparation for the funeral."—Edersheim, page 432.

[502] The Bible likens death to sleep.—Job 14:12; Psalm 13:3; Jeremiah 51:39, 57; John 11:11-14; Acts 7:59-8:1; 1 Corinthians 15:51-52; 1 Thessalonians 4:13-16.

[503] The use of force may have been necessary to evict the raucous crowd. Jesus "drove them all out," according to Goodspeed's translation.—Mark 5:40.

[504] Jesus "may have left the nine Apostles with the people, or outside the house, or parted from them in the courtyard of Jairus' house before he entered the inner apartment."—Edersheim, page 433; compare Mark 5:37-40; Luke 8:51.

[505] Mark 5:41 records Jesus' exact words and translates them. *"Talitha cumi"* could be either Hebrew or Aramaic. Like the expression *"Ephphatha,"* this is one of the few times that Jesus is quoted verbatim.—Mark 7:34.

[506] Certainly, the girl's reappearance could not remain a secret. The command to not make it known, albeit a temporary measure, would permit Jesus to leave quietly. Jesus discouraged publicity and did not want to be known primarily for his miracles lest people seek him solely for selfish reasons. Furthermore, he wanted people to see and hear for themselves and make their decision regarding him based on personal experience with him, not on the basis of second-hand information.

[507] These men express their belief that Jesus is heir to the throne of David and thus the Messiah. See Psalm 89:3-4; Luke 1:31-33.

[508] The Pharisees denied, not that Jesus performed a miracle, but that he did so with God's power.—Matthew 12:28.

[509] The accounts do not refer to Nazareth by name but as "his own city"; literally, "his father's place," the area from which his immediate family came.—Note on Matthew 13:54, *New World Translation* (Study Edition); Mark 6:1, *The Emphasized Bible.*

[510] He taught in that synagogue many months earlier. People initially marveled at what he said but later took offense and tried to kill him. (Luke 4:16-30) "It was intolerable, that He should not only claim equality with an Elijah or an Elisha, but place them, the burghers of Nazareth as it were, outside the pale of Israel, below a heathen man or woman. ... And now He had come back to them, after nine or ten months, in totally different circumstances. No one could any longer question His claims, whether for good or for evil."—Edersheim, page 439.

[511] His fellow Nazarenes recognized Jesus, not as a prophet, but as a common laborer like themselves. Jesus learned carpentry from his adoptive father, Joseph. Since Joseph is not mentioned by name, he may already have died.

[512] Believers in the perpetual virginity of Mary claim that the brothers referred to are actually Jesus' cousins. However, terms denoting familial relationships are not used loosely or indiscriminately in the New Testament. See Luke 21:16; Acts 23:16; Colossians 4:10.

[513] Or "are not his sisters here with us?" (Mark 6:3, *King James Version)* While Jesus' mother and brothers had apparently left Nazareth (and possibly settled in Capernaum), his sisters seem to have remained there, probably married to Nazarenes. See "Jesus' Early Family Life."

[514] The people feel that Jesus is just a local man and reject the evidence that he is the Messiah? Because of their familiarity with Jesus, even his relatives stumble at him.

[515] "It is perfectly natural that after a long interval he should give the Nazarenes another opportunity to hear his teaching, and to witness miracles, which he would not work for them when demanded, but now voluntarily works in a few cases, so far as their now wonderful unbelief left it appropriate." (Robertson, page 77) On unreceptive skeptics Jesus did not waste his divine power. "He will not return again to Nazareth. Henceforth He will make commencement of sending forth His disciples, partly to disarm prejudices of a personal character, partly to spread the Gospel-tidings farther and wider than he alone could have carried them."—Edersheim, page 440.

[516] At the hands of unfaithful shepherds or leaders, the Israelites as God's sheep suffered greatly. (Ezekiel 34:2-16) They were "torn and thrown down," said Jesus. (Matthew 9:36, *The Emphasized Bible)* The Greek word for "torn" originally meant "to flay, lacerate," conveying an image of sheep with their skin ripped apart by wild animals or torn as they wandered among brambles and sharp rocks. Used figuratively, the term conveys the idea of being dejected, neglected and helpless—"thrown down."—https://www.billmounce.com/greek-dictionary/skyllo.

[517] The Kingdom was near in the sense that its designated King, Jesus Christ, was present.

[518] "... the Gospels present the career of Jesus as the proclamation of the kingdom joined with healing activity." (M. Jack Suggs: Matthew 10:8 footnote, *The New English Bible*; see Matthew 12:28; Luke 11:20) Like their Master's ministry , the apostles' missions involved words and deeds; the message was supported by miracles.—Luke 9:2; 10:9.

[519] "In temporary accommodation to the prejudices of His disciples and of the Jews," Jesus' apostles "were not to touch either Gentile or Samaritan territory" on this short-term mission. (Edersheim, page 442) This was "a national religious survey to determine the people's response to Jesus as Messiah. For the Twelve to cover an area that is at most 75 miles by 125 miles would not take very

long. Thus, they did not need extensive provisions."—Matthew 10:9-10 footnote, *The Nelson Study Bible*. Copyright © 1997 by Thomas Nelson, Inc. Used with permission.

[520] In contrast with religious philosophers who went from house-to-house begging, material comforts were unimportant to the apostles compared with their ministry.

[521] "The oriental greeting is a wish of peace. In [Matthew chapter 10] v. 13 this wish is treated in concrete fashion as an entity which, if it fails to secure its effect, nevertheless remains in being and returns to its original owner."—Matthew chapter 10 note e, *The Jerusalem Bible:* Edited by Alexander Jones. See Judges 19:20.

[522] Any dust except that of the Holy Land was reckoned unclean by Israelites. Shaking dust from their feet would signify that the apostles disclaimed responsibility for the consequences that would come from God. Compare Acts 13:51; 18:6.

[523] To reject the apostles' message was more serious than the worst sins of the most wicked cities and would result in more severe judgment.

[524] In the Bible, animals and their characteristics and habits are often applied in a figurative sense, picturing both desirable and undesirable traits. Sheep often denote the defenseless, innocent and, at times, abused people of God. (2 Samuel 24:17; Psalm 44:11, 22; 95:7; 119:176; John 10:7-16; 21:15-17; Romans 8:36) The wolf, in most occurrences, pictures ferocity, greed, viciousness and craftiness. (Matthew 7:15; John 10:12; Acts 20:29) Snakes are wary, preferring to flee rather than attack. (Compare Genesis 3:1) The apostles must be so cautious toward opposers and avoid possible dangers. Yet they are to be **innocent as doves**. (**Matthew 10:16**) The dove sometimes symbolizes innocence and purity. (Song of Solomon 5:2; Matthew 3:16; Mark 1:10) "The position of Israel in a hostile world" is described in the Midrash as "sheep in the midst of wolves"; it also describes Israel as "harmless as the dove towards God, and wise as serpents towards the hostile Gentile nations. Such an even greater would be the enmity which the disciples, as the true Israel, would have to encounter from Israel after the flesh." (Edersheim, page 443) Jesus' followers needed to combine the characteristics of serpents and doves by being prudent, sensible, shrewd, pure of heart, blameless and innocent.

[525] Local courts were attached to synagogues and had the power to inflict the penalties of scourging and excommunication.—Matthew 23:34; Mark 13:9; Luke 21:12; John 9:22; 12:42; 16:2.

[526] Or "whoever will have persevered, even to the end." (Matthew 10:22, *Catholic Public Domain Version)* The discourse recorded in Matthew chapter 10 "goes far beyond that Mission of the Twelve, beyond even that of the Early Church." Jesus' discourse "sketches the history of the Church's Mission in a hostile world up 'to the end.'" (Matthew 10:22) His words "contain references to division in families, persecutions, and conflict with the civil power (vv. 16-18), such as belong to a much later period in the history of the Church." Early Christians "would be brought before governors and kings—primarily the Roman governors and the Herodian princes (v. 18)." Jesus' words "contain also that prediction which could not have applied to this first Mission of the Apostles, 'Ye shall not have gone over the cities of Israel, till the Son of Man be come' (v. 23)." According to Daniel 7:13 the coming of the Son of Man is a coming for judgment. For Jerusalem and its Temple, the end came with judgment and destruction in A.D. 70. (Mark 13:9-13) "To the Jewish persecuting authorities, who had rejected the Christ, in order, as they imagined, to save their City and Temple from the Romans (John 11:48), and to whom Christ had testified that He would come again this judgment on their city and state, this destruction of their polity, was 'the Coming of the Son of Man' in judgment, and the only coming which the Jews, as a state, could expect, the only one meet for them."—Edersheim, pages 440-41, 443, 444.

[527] "But they were not to fear such misrepresentations. In due time the Lord would make manifest both His and their true character (Matt. 10:26). Nor were they to be deterred from announcing in the clearest and most public manner, in broad daylight and from the roofs of houses, that which had been first told them in the darkness, as Jewish teachers communicated the deepest and

highest doctrines in secret to their disciples, or as the preacher would whisper his discourse into the ear of the interpreter. The deepest truths concerning His Person, and the announcement of His Kingdom and Work, were to be fully revealed, and loudly proclaimed."—Edersheim, page 446.

[528] In Bible times, houses had flat roofs from which announcements could be made and certain actions could become widely known.—2 Samuel 16:22.

[529] At **Matthew 10:28** the **soul** is referred to as destructible. (See also Acts 3:23) Almighty God can destroy a person's soul—future life prospects—or can resurrect him or her to enjoy eternal life. For other examples of "soul" meaning a person's life, see Mark 8:35-37; Luke 12:20.

[530] Literally, "Gehenna," meaning "valley of Hinnom," which lies to the south and southwest of ancient Jerusalem. (**Matthew 10:28**, *World English Bible; The New Compact Bible Dictionary*, page 191) By Jesus' day, the valley had become a place for burning refuse, so "Gehenna" was a fitting symbol of **annihilation**.

[531] Taking on the responsibilities and consequences connected with becoming a disciple of Jesus can mean suffering, shame, torture and even death.

[532] Those who recognize and support true messengers from God will be richly rewarded.—Mark 9:41; Hebrews 6:10; see 1 Kings 17:8-24.

[533] The occasion was either Herod's birthday or the anniversary of his ascension to the throne (the "birthday" of his reign). The Greek word describing the occasion allows for either possibility.—Matthew 14:6; Mark 6:21.

[534] According to some Bible manuscripts and versions, the daughter was "also named Herodias." (Mark 6:22, *New Living Translation*) The name Salome is preserved in the writings of Josephus. Antipas married Salome's mother Herodias, having taken her from his half-brother Herod Philip. This adulterous and incestuous union was contrary to God's law (Leviticus 18:16; 20:21); for criticizing it John the Baptist was arrested. See "Biographical Sketch: Herod Antipas."

[535] **Half my kingdom** is a figure of speech for great wealth.—**Mark 6:23**.

[536] Herod respected John but feared losing the respect of his guests. This fear and a lack of faith allowed Herod to murder a righteous man.

[537] Although the Bible does not mention where John was imprisoned, it seems to have been near where Jesus was carrying out his ministry in Galilee. (Matthew 11:1-3) The most prominent men of Galilee were in attendance at Herod's party (Mark 6:21), indicating that it was held at Herod's residence in Tiberias, a city located on the western shore of the Sea of Galilee. John was evidently in captivity near to where the party took place.

[538] Herodias was a granddaughter of Herod the Great and a sister of Herod Agrippa I. (Acts 12:1-4, 6, 11, 19-23) Her daughter Salome married Philip the tetrarch, her father's half-brother. Intermarriage was common among the Herods.

[539] The only miracle of Jesus recorded in all four Gospels.

[540] This large boat, always at Jesus' service, was probably owned by the sons of Jonah (Andrew and Peter) or the sons of Zebedee (James and John).—Matthew 8:23; Mark 4:1, 36; Luke 8:22.

[541] In the *King James Version* at Mark 6:45 Jesus instructed his apostles "to go [by boat] to the other side before unto Bethsaida," while the parallel passage at John 6:17 gives their destination as Capernaum. Modern Bible translations, however, allow for the understanding that the apostles began their trip toward Capernaum by first going coastwise "toward Bethsaida" (the point from which they left Jesus evidently being near the site of the miraculous feeding of the 5,000, likely some distance south of Bethsaida and on the opposite side of the sea from Capernaum) and thereafter crossing over the northern end of the sea, heading for the ultimate destination, Capernaum. (Mark 6:45, *Common English Bible, Disciples' Literal New Testament, Living Oracles New Testament, New American Bible—Revised Edition, New Testament for Everyone*, Moffatt's *New*

Translation, New World Translation, Open English Bible) They landed on the shores of the land of Gennesaret, apparently somewhat S of Capernaum.—Mark 6:53.

[542] The apostles thought Jesus was suggesting they spend "two hundred denarii"—about eight months' pay for a laborer—on food for everyone. (Mark 6:37; John 6:7, *The Darby Bible*; Luke 9:13) To purchase bread for thousands of people and bring it to an isolated location would have been an expensive feat. However, Jesus did not expect the (nearly) impossible of his apostles. His request was an encouragement to trust him as part of their spiritual growth.

[543] About 5,000 "men" were present but the total number of "people" could have been 10,000 to 15,000. (Matthew 14:21; John 6:10, *American Standard Version)* Most of those present were Passover pilgrims on their way to Jerusalem. They may also have heard of John the Baptist's execution and been in a ready frame of mind to hear Jesus.

[544] "Barley bread was, almost proverbially, the meanest. Hence, as the Mishnah puts it, while all other meat-offerings were of wheat, that brought by the woman accused of adultery was to be of barley because ..., 'as her deed is that of animals, so her offering is also the food of animals.'" (Edersheim, page 467; 1 Kings 4:28; Revelation 6:6) The Gospel of John uses a unique Greek word for fish that refers to a small, generally dried or pickled fish eaten with bread, like a sardine.—6:9, 11; 21:9-10, 13.

[545] Fish were commonly prepared by broiling or by salting and drying and were usually eaten with bread. (See "Fish and Fishing in the Sea of Galilee.") Often the bread was unleavened (*matstsah'* in Hebrew), made by mixing water and freshly ground wheat or barley flour without adding leaven before kneading the dough. Loaves were made flat and baked hard; breaking them to eat was customary.—Matthew 15:36; 26:26; Mark 8:6; 1 Corinthians 10:16.

[546] These baskets may have been made of wicker with a cord handle for carrying them. They had an approximate volume of 2 gallons (7.5 L).

[547] Many of Jesus' contemporaries expected that the prophet like Moses would be the Messiah (although some made a distinction between the two; John 1:21) The multiplying of the loaves may have reminded its beneficiaries of Moses and the manna. Perhaps they thought this new "Moses" would deliver them from bondage to Rome, as the original Moses had led his people out of Egypt. Jesus' miracle aroused such a popular response that there was danger of an uprising, which would have created a pretext for Jesus' arrest. Having no intention of ruling as a king on Earth, Jesus withdrew from the people into the mountains.

[548] "The fourth watch" (Matthew 14:25; Mark 6:48, *King James Version)* lasted from about 3:00 a.m. until sunrise at about 6:00 a.m. The Israelites formerly divided the night into three watches of about four hours each. (Exodus 14:24; Judges 7:19) By Jesus' time, they had apparently adopted the Greek and Roman system of four three-hour watches.

[549] By the bright light of a Passover-season moon Jesus could see the boat even from a distance. Since the Sea of Galilee is about 8 miles (12 km) wide, the apostles may have been in about the middle of the lake.

[550] "When Jesus 'constrained the disciples to enter into the boat, and to go before Him unto the other side' (Matt. 14:22), they must have thought, that His purpose was to join them by land, since there was no other boat there, save that in which they crossed the Lake (John 6:22). And possibly such had been his intention, till He saw their difficulty, if not danger, so this miracle also was not a mere display of power, but, being caused by their need, had a moral object."—Edersheim, page 473.

[551] It may have only seemed to the apostles that Jesus was passing them by. Alternatively, Jesus may have passed by to assure the apostles of his presence, as God "passed by" Moses at Mt. Sinai.—Exodus 33:19, 22, *American Standard Version*.

[552] Gennesaret is a small plain measuring about 3 by 1.5 miles (5 by 2.5 km) bordering the northwest shore of the Sea of Galilee, just west of Capernaum. If Capernaum had been their destination (John 6:17), the storm blew them off course.

[553] The people had commandeered boats from Tiberias, a city on the western shore of the Sea of Galilee, about 9.5 miles (15 km) south of Capernaum. Herod Antipas built Tiberias as his new capital and residence, naming it in honor of Tiberius Caesar. The largest city in the region, Tiberias is mentioned in the Bible only at John 6:23. As far as is known, Jesus never visited Tiberias, perhaps because of its strong foreign influence. Compare Matthew 10:5-6.

[554] Or "food which remains to everlasting life." (John 6:27, *New Heart English Bible)* Physical food sustains people day by day, but "food" from God's Word makes it possible for believers to live forever.—Matthew 4:4; Luke 4:4.

[555] Eternal life is a gift. (John 4:29; Romans 6:23) Nevertheless, demonstrating faith in Jesus requires work; it means putting one's life into the Christian faith, activating it and making it produce good works. Compare James 2:18-26.

[556] Taking Jesus' words for a claim to messiahship, the people asked for proof—despite having just witnessed the miraculous feeding of thousands of people. These Israelites wanted a Messiah who could supply them with physical sustenance. (John 6:14-15) As a justification, they reminded Jesus that Moses (the Messiah's prototype) had given their forefathers manna in the Sinai desert. According to tradition, the Messiah would cause manna to fall from Heaven as Moses had.—Exodus 16:4, 15.

[557] Manna from Heaven satisfied the physical needs of the Israelites temporarily. **The Bread of God**, the channel of blessing to the **world** of humankind, satisfies spiritual hunger forever.—**John 6:33**.

[558] Or "the last day." (John 6:39, *King James Version;* also verses 40, 44, 54) Throughout the Bible, the resurrection is associated with Judgment Day.—Daniel 12:13; John 12:48; Revelation 20:4-6.

[559] Humans have free will, and everyone has a choice when it comes to serving God. (Deuteronomy 30:19) The Father draws to himself those whose hearts are rightly disposed.—Proverbs 21:2; Jeremiah 31:3; Acts 13:48.

[560] Isaiah 54:13, *New Heart English Bible*—Jehovah Edition. By teaching people, God draws them to himself.

[561] This discussion regarding the bread from Heaven reached its climax while Jesus taught in a synagogue in Capernaum. Edersheim suggests the following succession of events: "... part of what is here recorded by St. John (John 6:25-65) had taken place when those from across the Lake had first met Jesus (John 6:25-36); part on the way to, and entering, the Synagogue (John 6:41-52); and part as what He spoke in His Discourse, (John 6:52-58), and then after the defection of some of His former disciples (John 6:61-65). ... [I]t would have been quite consistent with Jewish practice, that the greater part should have taken place in the Synagogue itself, the Jewish questions and objections representing either an irregular running commentary on His Words, or expressions during breaks in, or at the conclusion of, His teaching."—page 493.

[562] Feeding on Jesus' flesh and drinking his blood means demonstrating faith in him. (Compare John 6:40) He made this declaration just prior to the Passover (John 6:4), so his listeners should have thought of the impending festival and the significance of the lamb's blood in saving lives on the night that their forefathers left Egypt. (Exodus 12:21-23) Jesus' **blood** would likewise play an essential role in gaining **eternal life**.—**John 6:53**.

[563] Or "Does this cause you to stumble?" (John 6:61, *World English Bible)* Stumbling may involve breaking one of God's laws on morals, losing faith, accepting false teachings or taking offense.

[564] Edersheim suggests that Jesus' resistance to the attempt to make him the Messiah-King turned the tide of popular enthusiasm. (John 6:15) "At last, by some miracle more notable even than the giving of the Manna in the wilderness, enthusiasm has been raised to the highest pitch, and thousands were determined to give up their pilgrimage to the Passover, and then and there proclaim the Galilean Teacher Israel's King. If He were the Messiah, such was His rightful title. Why then did He so strenuously and effectually resist it? In ignorance of His real views concerning the Kingship, they would naturally conclude that it must have been from fear, from misgiving, from want of belief in Himself. At any rate, He could not be the Messiah."—page 492.

[565] Or "an adversary." (John 6:70, *The Emphasized Bible)* From inspired prophecy Jesus knew that he would be betrayed by a close associate. (Psalm 41:9; John 13:18) This does not mean that Judas' failure was predestined. When Judas started to go bad, Jesus, who could read hearts and thoughts, detected this change.—Matthew 9:4; Mark 2:8; John 2:25; 6:64; Revelation 2:23.

[566] These men were probably emissaries from the Sanhedrin, sent to determine Jesus' position on issues of importance to them. **The elders' teaching** put eating with unwashed hands on the same level as having relations with a prostitute. (**Matthew 15:2; Mark 7:5**; see the Babylonian Talmud, Sotah 4b.) When Pharisees ceremonially cleansed themselves, they washed up to the elbow. They 'baptized' themselves and their eating utensils before meals. (Mark 7:4, Young's *Literal Translation)* Instead of directly answering the hypocrites' question, Jesus addressed two issues of deeper significance: (1) the superiority of God's law over human tradition; (2) the difference between ritual defilement and moral defilement.

[567] "In earlier times, the Hebrews held the written Law of God, the Torah, in such esteem that they would not write down their reflections on it, lest they should tempt later generations to consider their words as important as God's Law. But as time went on, written commentaries on the Law, collected in the Talmud, assumed greater authority than the Torah itself." (Mark 7:8-9 footnote, *The Nelson Study Bible*. Copyright © 1997 by Thomas Nelson, Inc. Used by permission.) "The ordinances of the Scribes were declared more precious, and of more binding importance than those of Holy Scripture itself."—Edersheim, page 485.

[568] The Pharisees claimed that money, property or anything dedicated as a gift to God belonged to the Temple and could not be used for a different purpose. The possessor still had what was pledged, which made the vow a legal fiction involving no sacrifice of ownership. Adult children could excuse themselves from helping needy parents by claiming that their resources were already dedicated to God. This was no more than a despicable evasion of filial duty.

[569] The mind may be the center of human activity, but the Bible describes the heart as the seat of intellect, emotions and will—"the wellspring of all of life." Due to inherited sin and imperfection, "the human heart is wicked and produces all sorts of evil actions. But the believer's heart, softened, recreated and purified by God, produces good fruit and a life of obedience to God's will."—Verlyn D. Verbrugge: *The NIV Topical Study Bible*, page 683. See Genesis 6:5; Deuteronomy 11:18; Proverbs 4:23; 7:2-3; Jeremiah 17:9; 24:7; 31:33; 32:39; Ezekiel 11:19-20; Romans 2:29.

[570] What we take into our mind and allow to settle in our heart is the raw material of our actions. See Psalm 101:3; 119:11; 2 Corinthians 10:5.

[571] Jesus was more concerned with holiness than hygiene. He did not discourage washing hands before eating a meal. Rather, he condemned the religious leaders who tried to bypass God's righteous laws by resorting to human traditions. To them legal purity was more important than moral purity.

[572] Phoenicia was part of the Roman province of Syria. This apparently was Jesus' only journey beyond the borders of Israel.

[573] This Gentile woman called Jesus **Son of David** without knowledge of God's promises to King David. (**Matthew 15:22**; see 2 Samuel 7:12; Psalm 89:3-4) She was addressing a miracle-worker, not her Messiah. "To have granted her the help she so entreated, would have been ... to make His works of healing merely works of power. ... And yet he could not refuse her petition."—Edersheim, page 501; see "Jesus, A.K.A. ..."

[574] Initially limited to Israel, gospel truth eventually extended to all nations.—Matthew 10:5-6; 28:19; Acts 1:8.

[575] Or "little dogs." (Matthew 15:26-27; Mark 7:27-28, *The Emphasized Bible)* According to Israel's law, dogs were unclean, and the Scriptures often use the term in a derogatory sense. (Leviticus 11:27; Matthew 7:6; Philippians 3:2; Revelation 22:15) However, in both Mark's and Matthew's account of Jesus' conversation, the diminutive form (the form of a noun that generally denotes smallness) of the term meaning "house dog" or "pup" is used, softening the comparison. Perhaps Jesus was suggesting an affectionate term for household pets in Gentile homes, and in such households, the children would be fed first. Jesus' comparison was not an insult but a test of the woman's faith.

[576] With Abraham, Isaac and Jacob, all nations will be blessed by the Messiah. (Matthew 8:11; Luke 13:28-29) "Heathenism may be like the dogs, when compared with the children's place and privileges; but He is their Master still, and they under His table; and when He breaks the bread there is enough and to spare for them—even under the table they eat of the children's crumbs."—Edersheim, page 503.

[577] The Decapolis region was wedged in between the dominion of Philip and that of Antipas. Robertson suggests that Jesus was avoiding Galilee, "the territory ruled by Herod Antipas. The tetrarch Philip, who governed the districts east of the Lake of Galilee and of the upper Jordan, was a better man than Antipas, and moreover had no cause to feel uneasy about Jesus." Furthermore, "the moment [Jesus] returns to Galilee the Jewish leaders begin to attack him."—pages 95, 97.

[578] These Israelites brought with them large baskets—or hampers—customarily used to carry provisions when traveling through Gentile areas.—Matthew 15:37; Mark 8:8.

[579] The man was not mute, but his speech had, in consequence of his hearing loss, "been so affected as practically to deprive him of its power. This circumstance, and that he is not spoken of as so afflicted from his birth, leads us to infer that the affliction was—as not unfrequently—the result of disease, and not congenital."—Edersheim, page 505.

[580] This was not something Jesus usually did. However, the deaf can be easily embarrassed, especially in a crowd. Jesus desired to help the man, whose nervousness may have been apparent, in the kindest way possible.

[581] Although "the use of saliva for cures [was] universally recognized by the Rabbis," Jesus was not using his saliva as a natural healing agent. (Edersheim, page 506 note 10) Says *The Pulpit Commentary*, "these signs used by our Lord were intended to awaken the afflicted man's faith, and to stir up in him the lively expectation of a blessing." Interestingly, priests in the Latin Church touch the nostrils and ears of those they are baptizing with saliva from their own mouths.—https://biblehub.com/commentaries/pulpit/mark/7.htm.

[582] Like the expression *"Talitha cumi,"* Jesus' use of the Semitic expression *"Ephphatha,"* (**Open**) is one of the few times that he is quoted verbatim.—**Mark 7:34**; 5:41.

[583] Jesus knew that curiosity seekers could hamper his freedom to move about.

[584] These were Gentiles glorifying Israel's God, while many Israelites were willingly deaf to the Messiah's message.

[585] Only Matthew (15:38) mentions the women and the young children in addition to the 4,000 men. Possibly, the total number of those miraculously fed was over 12,000.

[586] Some scholars identify Magadan with Magdala, which is believed to have been located on the site of the depopulated village of Khirbet Majdal (Migdal), about 3.5 miles (6 km) north-northwest of Tiberias and about 5 miles (8 km) southwest of Capernaum.

[587] This strong emotional reaction may have reflected Jesus' exasperation over the Pharisees' demand for a sign while they stubbornly ignored the evident demonstrations of power that they had already seen. It was "a sigh that came straight from his heart."—Mark 8:12, *Complete Jewish Bible;* see "The Gospel According to..."

[588] The Pharisees and Sadducees did not heed the signs already performed by Jesus, so it is doubtful that seeing another sign would have produced faith in them. (Compare John 20:30-31) The only sign to Nineveh was Jonah's solemn warning of near judgment and his call to repentance. Likewise, the only sign to this **wicked and unfaithful generation** was the warning cry of judgment and the loving call to repentance.—**Matthew 16:4**; Luke 19:41-44.

[589] "Leaven was a common Jewish metaphor for an invisible, pervasive influence." *(The Nelson Study Bible,* page 1658. Copyright © 1997 by Thomas Nelson, Inc. Used with permission.) "As leaven ferments the dough, ... but can also make it go bad, ... so the perverse doctrine of the Jewish leaders threatens to misguide those for whom they are responsible." (Matthew chapter 16 note b, *The Jerusalem Bible:* Edited by Alexander Jones. See Matthew 13:33; 15:14; 1 Corinthians 5:6-8; Galatians 5:9) In the account of Mark (8:15), Jesus' warning included the leaven of Herod, referring to the Herodians. An example of their nationalistic "leaven" was the question about the paying of taxes that Jesus' enemies used in an attempt to trap him.—Matthew 22:16-17; Mark 12:13-14.

[590] "They thought the words of Christ implied, that in His view they had not forgotten to bring bread, but purposely omitted to do so, in order, like the Pharisees and Sadducees, to 'seek of Him a sign' of His Divine Messiahship—nay, to oblige Him to show such—that of miraculous provision in their want."—Edersheim, page 522; Mark 8:11.

[591] In the original Greek (and some Bible versions) the accounts of Matthew and Mark consistently distinguish between the types of baskets used for collecting leftovers on the two occasions when Jesus miraculously fed the crowds. (Matthew 14:20; 15:37; 16:9-10; Mark 6:43; 8:8, 19-20) The 12 vessels used to gather leftovers after Jesus fed about 5,000 men may have been small wicker hand baskets. The seven baskets that contained the leftovers from Jesus' feeding of the 4,000 men were likely large hampers (similar perhaps to the "basket" in which Paul was lowered to the ground; Acts 9:25). This indicates that the writers were present or had received the facts from reliable eyewitnesses. Furthermore, Matthew and Mark record the feeding of the 5,000 and the feeding of the 4,000 and put Jesus on record referring to both incidents. Some critics accuse Matthew and Mark of confusing the two incidents but there is no reason why both could not have occurred.

[592] "Jesus asks the disciples to forget their material needs and give their minds to the spiritual nature of his mission to which the miracles point."—Mark chapter 8 note b, *The Jerusalem Bible:* Edited by Alexander Jones.

[593] **The leaven of the Pharisees and the Sadducees** was, specifically, lack of faith, which was behind the demand of a sign from Jesus. (**Matthew 16:6, 11**) "In this context, the leaven of the Pharisees must be linked with their desire to see a sign, because they did not believe in Jesus' identity. Herod also wanted a sign (Luke 23:8). This unbelieving attitude, like leaven, had started to permeate the general population."—*The Nelson Study Bible,* page 1658. Copyright © 1997 by Thomas Nelson, Inc. Used with permission.

[594] Gradual healing allowed the man's eyes and brain time to adapt to the new sensation of sight. Figuratively speaking, the eyes of Jesus' disciples were gradually opened to his identity as the Messiah.

[595] Bethsaida was notorious for its unbelief.—Matthew 11:21-22; Luke 10:13-14.

[596] Jesus and his disciples probably spent some days making the ascent of 25 miles (40 km) to Caesarea Philippi (today called Banias), which was located on Mount Hermon at an elevation of 1,150 feet (350 m) above sea level. It was a place "where no hostility had been aroused, and [Jesus] could quietly instruct the Twelve." (Robertson, page 98) Caesarea Philippi had long been associated with idol worship. At least a hundred feet above the village rose a large rocky cliff, and into the facade many idols were carved. Jesus may have referred to this in his play on words in Matthew 16:18.

[597] Apparently, some saw in Jesus the continuation of John's work (or that of Elijah, if they did not believe in John) of heralding the Messiah. To others Jesus seemed a second Jeremiah, denouncing woe on Israel and calling sinners to repentance; or else one of those old prophets, who had spoken either of the near judgment or of the coming glory. On one point, however, all agreed: Jesus was not an ordinary man or teacher; yet he was not accepted as the Messiah.

[598] Or "Christ," both meaning "Anointed One." (**Matthew 16:16**, *The Voice Bible;* see "Jesus, A.K.A. ...") Because the title **Messiah** was misunderstood by the Israelites and the Roman authorities, Jesus was careful not to use it publicly.—**Mark 8:29**; **Luke 9:20**.

[599] The true God is alive and active in contrast with the lifeless gods of the nations, such as the gods worshiped in the region of Caesarea Philippi. (Deuteronomy 5:26; Joshua 3:10; Jeremiah 10:10; Daniel 6:26; Acts 14:15) To believe that Jesus is the Messiah is to believe that he is the Son of God—the former title designating his holy office, the latter his divine nature.

[600] Or "flesh and blood." (Matthew 16:17, *King James Version)* This common Hebrew expression refers to fleshly or human thinking. (1 Corinthians 15:50; Galatians 1:16; Ephesians 6:12) To such thinking Peter would shortly succumb in trying to dissuade Jesus from accepting his destiny.

[601] Jesus foretold the formation of the Christian **congregation**, or "church." (**Matthew 16:18**, *King James Version)* The Greek word for congregation refers to a group of people 'called out' for a particular purpose. (1 Peter 2:9) In the *Septuagint* it often refers to the entire nation of God's people. Compare Deuteronomy 31:30 with Acts 7:38.

[602] "Peter is but a fragment of the whole, while Christ Himself is the entire rock. Thus, it could be said that the church would be built on Christ, the Rock. Be that as it may, at least it can be said that the context allows that the rock upon which the church is built is Peter's confession that Jesus is the Son of God."—*The Nelson Study Bible,* page 1604. Copyright © 1997 by Thomas Nelson, Inc. Used with permission.

[603] Or "gates of the grave"; "might of Hades." (Matthew 16:18, *A Faithful Version; The New Testament in Modern Speech* by Richard Francis Weymouth) By means of a resurrection the gates will open to release the dead from Hades. Jesus' own resurrection confirmed this promise.—Revelation 1:18; 20:13.

[604] The imagery used by Jesus interestingly compares to that used in the 89th Psalm, a Messianic psalm based on 2 Samuel chapter 7. Psalm 89 "discusses the perpetuity of the Davidic throne (Kingdom). Jesus applies this imagery to the spiritual Kingdom that He is building."—Robertson, page 100; Psalm 89:4, 26, 38, 48.

[605] To be given keys was to be entrusted with a degree of authority. (Isaiah 22:20-22; Revelation 3:7) The term "key" came to symbolize authority and responsibility. Peter will have the privilege of unlocking, as it were, opportunities for groups of people to enter the kingdom of Heaven. (Acts 2:36-42; 8:14-17; 10:44-48) Locking and unlocking evidently refers to decisions forbidding or allowing certain actions or developments made after the corresponding decision was made in

Heaven. (Compare Matthew 18:18) The idea that Heaven would abide by any decision made by an ecclesiastical court on Earth is not what Jesus had in mind. Judaism believed something similar. "One of the powers claimed by the Rabbis [was] ... to say that 'the Sanhedrin above' confirmed what 'the Sanhedrin beneath' had done."—Edersheim, page 532.

[606] Because a suffering messiah did not square with popular expectation, Jesus' identity could not be openly proclaimed until the Messiah's true nature was revealed.

[607] At this crucial moment, after Jesus elicited from his disciples their first explicit profession of faith in him as the Messiah, he told them for the first time of his coming death. This was Jesus' way of bracing the apostles' faith for the approaching crisis of his execution.

[608] Jesus was not identifying Peter with Satan the Devil but was referring to him as an "enemy or adversary," which is the meaning of the Hebrew noun *satan'. (The New Compact Bible Dictionary,* page 526) Peter had allowed himself to be influenced by Satan. Refusing to let anything hinder him from fulfilling his Father's will, Jesus strongly rebuked Peter.

[609] Peter was to be a "rock" of supportive strength, not **a stumbling-stone**. (**Matthew 16:**18, **23; Mark 8:33**) A stumbling-stone is an action or a circumstance that leads a person to follow an improper course, to stumble or fall morally or to fall into sin.

[610] "... by this time the crowd had followed and found him, and he addressed them, or this could be construed as a separate occasion from the discussion with the disciples in [Luke] 9:18-22. The cost of discipleship is something Jesus was willing to tell both insiders and outsiders about. The rejection he felt would also fall on his followers."—Luke 9:23 footnote, *The NET Bible*.

[611] The burnt offerings, sin offerings and guilt offerings of the Old Testament did not actually take away sin; they foreshadowed the perfect sacrifice of Christ. Of Christians God expects, not animal sacrifices, but self-sacrifice—in imitation of Jesus. One motivated by self-protection will not respond to Jesus. Willingness to risk rejection by the world of unbelievers is necessary to gain eternal life. The investment of all one's resources (time, talent, wealth, even life itself) in what is eternal will produce returns forever.—Matthew 6:19-20; 19:27-29; 25:14-30; Mark 10:28-30; Luke 18:28-30; Philippians 3:8.

[612] "The glory of God is rooted in his very nature—majestic, awesome, holy. ... God reveals his glory to humanity both directly and through his works .... Jesus Christ is the glory of God in human flesh .... He revealed God's glory by what he did and especially through his death and resurrection. He is now exalted in glory and will someday return in glory."—Verlyn D. Verbrugge: *The NIV Topical Study Bible*, page 672.

[613] Judgment by the Son of Man will be based upon how individuals responded to Jesus and his teachings. (2 Corinthians 5:10; 1 John 2:28; Revelation 22:12) To be **ashamed** of Jesus and his teachings would be tantamount to denying him. (**Mark 8:38**; **Luke 9:26**; compare Matthew 10:33; Luke 12:9) Confession of Christ will be rewarded before the Father in Heaven.—Matthew 5:11-12; 2 Timothy 2:11-12; Revelation 2:26-27.

[614] Son of Man is "a special title for a ruler enthroned over the whole earth with power and glory, a title that Jesus chose to apply to himself. Central to his task as Son of Man was his life of suffering and his death, though he also knew that as Son of Man he would rise again, ascend into heaven to sit at God's right hand and return on the clouds of heaven." (Verlyn D. Verbrugge: *The NIV Topical Study Bible,* page 950; see Psalm 110:1; Daniel 7:13-14; Acts 1:9-11; "Jesus, A.K.A. ...") **Certain ones** would **see the Son of Man coming in his kingdom** by means of his Transfiguration. (**Matthew 16:28**) Some believe this prediction included the descent of God's spirit at Pentecost and the destruction of Jerusalem.

[615] The Transfiguration may have taken place on one of the spurs of Mount Hermon, which is near Caesarea Philippi.

[616] Moses was similarly described after being in God's presence.—Exodus 34:29-35.

[617] These two figures personify the Old Covenant. Moses, representing the Law, and Elijah, representing the Prophets, appeared in homage to "the Mediator of the New Covenant."—Hebrews 12:24, *Montgomery New Testament* by Helen Barrett Montgomery.

[618] That is, his **departure** from earthly life. (**Luke 9:31**) The Greek word is *exodus*, inviting a comparison between Jesus' death and Israel's journey to salvation.

[619] Or "tabernacles." (Matthew 17:4; Mark 9:5; Luke 9:33, *King James Version)* Robertson suggests that the Transfiguration took place "probably not long before the feast of tabernacles (near the end of September) and Peter may have meant that they celebrate the feast on the mountains instead of going to Jerusalem."—page 103.

[620] "A strange peculiarity has been noticed about Hermon in 'the extreme rapidity of the formation of cloud[s] on the summit. In a few minutes a thick cap forms over the top of the mountain, and [just] as quickly disperses and entirely disappears.'"—Edersheim, page 541.

[621] The same expression is used at Matthew 12:18, which is a quotation from Isaiah 42:1 regarding the promised Messiah.

[622] Jesus' followers still had much to learn from him, the prophet like Moses. (Deuteronomy 18:15, 18) This was the second time that God's voice was heard during Christ's ministry. The first instance occurred at Jesus' baptism. (Matthew 3:16-17; Mark 1:11; Luke 3:22) The third instance happened shortly before Jesus' last Passover.—John 12:28.

[623] From Luke 9:32, 37 it appears that the vision took place at night. This would make the Transfiguration of Christ so much more striking and memorable, for it was intended to be something truly outstanding.

[624] Or "Tell the vision to no one." (Matthew 17:9, *The Darby Bible)* Like most Israelites, the apostles entertained incorrect expectations of the Messiah. They needed to correctly understand who the Christ was and what he would do before they were ready to proclaim Jesus as such.

[625] Evidently, the apostles knew as yet nothing of Jesus' personal resurrection. They may have understood **raised from the dead** as a figurative expression for his triumph and vindication. (**Matthew 17:9; Mark 9:9**) "Since death did not fit the conception held of the Son of Man ([Mark] 8:32), it seemed impossible to think of his resurrection."—M. Jack Suggs: Mark 9:9-10 footnote,

The New English Bible.

[626] Even though Jesus had just foretold his death, the Transfiguration reassured Peter, John and James that Jesus was the Messiah. However, according to what Israel's scholars taught, an appearance by Elijah would precede the resurrection of the dead that would inaugurate Messiah's reign. Having just seen the Messiah in his glory, the apostles were surprised that Elijah had not appeared as the Messiah's forerunner. Assuming that the scholars were correct, why should the apostles not tell everyone about Elijah's appearance on the mountain? This uncertainty prompted their question concerning the scholars' teaching.

[627] "Elijah had come; if the people had received his message, there would have been the promised restoration of all things. ... (Matt. 11:14) ... But Israel did not know their Elijah and did unto him whatsoever they listed; and so, in logical sequence, would the Son of Man also suffer of them." (Edersheim, page 546) "The Baptist's disclaimer about being Elijah (John 1:21) means only that he was not Elijah in person come back to earth according to popular expectation."—Robertson, page 104.

[628] On other occasions, Jesus refused challenges to work a miracle. (Matthew 12:38-39; 16:1, 4; Mark 8:11-12; Luke 11:16, 29; John 2:18; 6:30) Apparently, his disciples accepted a similar challenge and failed.

[629] This reproof is directed to all of the people, the disciples in particular.

[630] "Demons controlled an individual's total being, expressing their influence in various physical or mental illnesses .... Some consider demon possession to be the Biblical terminology for epilepsy and mental illness and psychological maladies not known by the first-century mind." (Verlyn D. Verbrugge: *The NIV Topical Study Bible,* page 1099) However, note the distinction between possession and epilepsy and other afflictions in Matthew 4:24.

[631] Or "I believe. Help my unbelief." (Mark 9:24, *World English Bible)* Even a believer can be nagged by hopelessness and doubt.—Matthew 8:26; 14:31; 28:16-17; Luke 24:38; John 20:27.

[632] Or "You, spirit, who are the cause of his loss of voice and hearing."—Mark 9:25, *The Bible in Basic English.*

[633] Or "because of your little faith." (Matthew 17:20, *The Emphasized Bible)* Strong faith along with prayer for God's empowering help was needed to expel the unusually strong demon.

[634] This alone time gives Jesus further opportunity to prepare the apostles for his death and for the work they will do thereafter. They "still had much to learn. Their fear shows that they understood something about what Jesus said, but they did not understand how and why Jesus could say such things about Himself, since He was the Messiah. The suffering of the Messiah was something the disciples did not yet understand. They would continue to be confused in their understanding of how such suffering fit into God's plan until Jesus' death and resurrection ([Luke] 24:25, 26, 43-49)."—Luke 9:45 footnote, *The Nelson Study Bible.* Copyright © 1997 by Thomas Nelson, Inc. Used with permission.

[635] Or "the half shekel." (Matthew 17:24, *American Standard Version)* This contribution was an annual obligation for all male Israelites at least 20 years old. Various Temple services were maintained through taxation. (Exodus 30:13-16) The collectors of the Temple tax may have been trying to involve Jesus in a breach of this well-known requirement.

[636] Perhaps it was for fear of offending those at whose hands-Jesus had told him-Christ would suffer, that Peter answered as he did, without consulting with his Master.

[637] In Jesus' day, members of the imperial family were tax-exempt. The Son of God—the God who is worshiped at the Temple—is not legally required to pay the Temple tax. His disciples, furthermore, are his brothers and sons of the same Father.—Romans 8:29; Hebrews 2:11.

[638] This coin—a stater, or tetradrachma—was worth four drachmas, the equivalent of a shekel, which was exactly the amount required to pay the Temple tax for two.—Exodus 30:13.

[639] "It was the common Jewish view, that there would be distinctions of rank in the Kingdom of Heaven," and the apostles grew up in a religious climate that stressed position and privilege. From Jesus' announcement of his resurrection on the third day, the apostles might have expected the Kingdom—and their exaltation—to come soon. The distinction of witnessing the Transfiguration bestowed on Peter, James and John "may have roused feelings of jealousy in the others, [and] perhaps of self-exaltation in the three."—Edersheim, page 553.

[640] Edersheim imagines this scene as set in Peter's house in Capernaum (Matthew 17:25; Mark 9:33), and the child to be a son of Peter. Children have a trusting spirit and are willingly dependent on others. In ancient culture, they were insignificant. A child would therefore be the perfect object lesson to counter ambition.

[641] Matthew chapter 18 outlines four reasons for the necessity of humility: (1) for entry into and greatness in the Kingdom (verses 2-4); (2) to prevent offenses (verses 5-11); (3) to conduct discipline in the congregation (verses 5-20); (4) for forgiving one another (verses 21-35).

[642] Whether or not one physically followed Jesus, one who "owned Jesus in the face of the Jewish world" was certainly not his enemy and could say nothing against him. "Not, that it is unimportant to follow with the disciples, but that it is not ours to forbid any work done, however

imperfectly, in His Name, and that only one question is really vital—whether or not a man is decidedly with Christ."—Edersheim, page 555.

643 Or "shall offend," that is, figuratively stumble one who would otherwise follow Jesus and believe in him.--Matthew 18:6; Mark 9:42, *King James Version*.

644 Or "little ones." (Matthew 18:6, 14; Mark 9:42, *King James Version)* Jesus' followers may have seemed of little importance from the world's standpoint but they were precious in God's eyes.

645 Literally, "millstone of a donkey." (Matthew 18:6; Mark 9:42, *The Expanded Bible)* Some millstones were small enough to be turned by hand but others (such as those for grinding grain or pressing olives) were turned by a beast of burden. An upper millstone might be as much as 5 feet (1.5 m) in diameter and would be turned on an even larger lower stone. It may have been such a large millstone that Samson was forced to turn for the Philistines. (Judges 16:21) The animal-powered mill was common in Israel and throughout much of the Roman Empire. "According to St. Jerome, the punishment which seems alluded to in the words of Christ, and which we know to have been inflicted by Augustus, was actually practised *[sic]* by the Romans in Galilee on some of the leaders of the insurrection under Judas of Galilee." (Edersheim, page 557; see Acts 5:37) The gruesome punishment of drowning reflects Jesus' feelings about one who stumbles a believer into sin.

646 Or "behold the face of." (Matthew 18:10, *King James Version)* This biblical phrase means that "the courtier is in the king's presence." (Matthew chapter 18 note e, *The Jerusalem Bible:* Edited by Alexander Jones; see 2 Samuel 14:24) Because they have access to the very presence of God, only spirit beings can see God's face. (Exodus 33:20) Angels take an interest in each believer and look out for the spiritual welfare of believers as a whole.—Psalm 34:7; Hebrews 1:14.

647 The comparison illustrates God's pursuit of the sinner. The shepherd was of modest means—flocks often had up to two hundred heads of sheep.

648 Jesus was not encouraging self-mutilation or implying that a person was subservient to the will of the limbs or eyes. He meant that a person should deaden a body member or treat it as if it were severed from the body rather than use it to commit a sin. Compare Colossians 3:5.

649 The New Testament paints a beautiful picture of unity in the early Christian congregation with its images of believers praying, worshiping and coming to decisions in the harmony of shared lives. Based on God's gift of unity, Christians are encouraged to work towards unity within the congregation. This does not presume that Christians will agree on all matters of faith and life, but it does require that believers love one another in Christ.—Ephesians 4:13.

650 Or "brother." (Matthew 18:15, 21, 35, *King James Version)* Jesus was discussing the spiritual relationship between two believers of either gender.

651 They would be witnesses to any agreement and to the fact that the offended believer acted in good faith to attempt a reconciliation.

652 Under the Mosaic Law, judges and officers represented Israel in judicial matters. (Deuteronomy 16:18) In Jesus' day, offenders answered to local councils made up of Israel's elders. (Matthew 5:22) In the early Christian congregation, discipline was sometimes administered through direct measures against straying members with the loving purpose of restoration. See 1 Corinthians 5:1-13; 2 Corinthians 2:5-11.

653 Or "as the Gentile and the publican." (Matthew 18:17, *American Standard Version)* Israelites did not associate with Gentiles. Israelites who paid the Romans for the right to collect taxes were hated by other Israelites who thought of them as traitors to their country and to their religion.

[654] Any decision made by the congregation would follow Heaven's decision, not precede it, and the congregation would make decisions based on principles already laid down in Heaven. Matthew 18:18 does not refer to heavenly support or validation of a decision made on Earth. Instead, it means that the congregation would receive direction from Heaven, highlighting the need for such guidance to ensure that decisions made on Earth harmonize with the decision that has already been made in Heaven. Compare Matthew 16:19.

[655] Some rabbis taught that one should grant forgiveness up to three times. (Compare Amos 1:3, 6, 9, 11, 13; 2:1, 4, 6) It must have seemed to Peter quite a stretch of generosity to extend forgiveness to seven offenses. But forgiveness, as Edersheim puts it, "must not be computed by numbers. It is qualitative, not quantitative: Christ forgives sin, not sins."—page 560; John 1:29.

[656] "Or seventy-seven times; the Greek can mean either 490 or 77; the point is unlimited forgiveness."—Comment on Matthew 18:22, *The Expanded Bible*.

[657] Ten thousand talents, to be exact. Just one talent would have been the equivalent of about 20 years' wages for a common laborer, so it would have taken the average worker thousands of lifetimes of work to repay a debt of 10,000 talents. The magnitude of his debt suggests that the servant was a high-ranking official.

[658] That amount was 100 denarii, the wages of 100 days of work for a laborer—small compared to 10,000 talents (=60,000,000 denarii).—Matthew 20:2.

[659] In a figurative sense, debts can refer to sins, and therefore can be canceled, or forgiven.—Matthew 6:12.

[660] This was essentially a life sentence. How could the prisoner earn money with which to satisfy his debt? His predicament became more hopeless than it was when he owed sixty million days' wages but was free to work for it.

[661] God forgives sins and forgets them. (Jeremiah 31:34; Hebrews 8:12; 10:17) Jesus' parable illustrates the obligation of one who has been forgiven to forgive others. (Matthew 6:12, 14-15; Mark 11:25; Ephesians 4:32; Colossians 3:13) "If our forgiveness should be in direct proportion to the incredible amount that we have been forgiven ..., then we must always be willing to forgive."—Matthew 18:35 footnote, *The Nelson Study Bible*. Copyright © 1997 by Thomas Nelson, Inc. Used with permission.

[662] During the celebration, Israelites lived in makeshift shelters of branches and leaves to remind them of their exodus in the wilderness where they lived in tents. (Leviticus 23:40-43) The Festival of Tabernacles (Booths) was celebrated for seven days (Ethanim 15-21; late September-early October), followed by a solemn assembly on the eighth day. (Leviticus 23:34, 36) Also called the Feast of Ingathering, the autumn festival marked the end of the agricultural year; it was one of the three festivals that required of-age males to observe in Jerusalem. John 7:2 is the only mention of this festival in the New Testament.

[663] Jerusalem, the religious center of the country, was crowded during the three annual festivals. Jesus' unbelieving brothers sarcastically urged him to work miracles before the largest audience possible. Of course, they shared the common apocalyptic expectation of a Messiah who would rule the world from Jerusalem.

[664] Or "my time is not yet fulfilled"—the **time** of Jesus' death at Jerusalem, followed by his resurrection and ascension to the Father.—**John 7:8**, *The Darby Bible*. See John 2:4; 7:30; 8:20; compare John 12:23; 17:1.

[665] "When the noise and publicity that he wished to avoid had subsided, Jesus went to Jerusalem, but privately, not publicly as his brothers had suggested. ... The first purpose of Christ seems to have been to take the more direct road to Jerusalem, through Samaria, and not to follow that of the festive pilgrim-bands, which travelled *[sic]* to Jerusalem, through Peraea, in order to avoid the band of their hated rivals." (Edersheim, page 564) "The enmity between Jews and *Samaritans* was ancient and deep, of the sort possible only where there are rival claims to being the true guardians of a common tradition (the Law of Moses)."—M. Jack Suggs: Luke 9:52 footnote, *The New English Bible.*

[666] This was a time for patience, not judgment. (Compare 2 Peter 3:9) In the recent Transfiguration vision, James and John had seen the prophet Elijah, who called down fire from Heaven.—1 Kings 18:38; 2 Kings 1:10-14.

[667] Edersheim identifies this scholar, who "broke into a spontaneous declaration of readiness to follow Him absolutely and everywhere," as "'one' of the company" traveling with Jesus. He was "perhaps, stimulated by the wrong of the Samaritans, perhaps, touched by the love which would rebuke the zeal of the disciples, but had no word of blame for the unkindness of others."—page 565; Luke 9:57, *The Darby Bible*; Young's *Literal Translation.*

[668] Unlike animals that were created to live on Earth, Jesus had no permanent home in the world of unbelieving humankind. The scholar would experience rejection and hardship if he followed Jesus, and he may have been too proud to accept such a way of life.

[669] See "Jesus, A.K.A. ..." Sometimes Jesus called himself the Son of Man "to express his lowly state, ... especially the humiliation of the Passion ... ." At other times Jesus used the title "to proclaim the definitive triumph of his resurrection, ... of his return in glory, ... of his coming in judgment." (Matthew chapter 8 note h, *The Jerusalem Bible:* Edited by Alexander Jones) Matthew 8:20 is the title's first occurrence in the gospels.

[670] Or "Let those without eternal life concern themselves with things like that." Jesus was evidently saying, "Let the spiritually dead bury their own dead," meaning that the man should not wait to make his decision to follow Jesus. (Luke 9:60, *The Living Bible; New Living Translation)* First-century burial customs in Israel "involved a reinterment of the bones a year after the initial burial, once the flesh had rotted away. At that point the son would have placed his father's bones in a special box known as an ossuary to be set into the wall of the tomb. ... Thus, Jesus could well be rebuking the man for wanting to wait around for as much as a year before making a commitment to follow him. In 1st century Jewish culture, to have followed Jesus rather than burying one's father would have seriously dishonored one's father (cf. Tobit 4:3-4)." (Matthew 8:22 footnote, *The NET Bible)* Nevertheless, "there are higher duties than either those of the Jewish Law, or even of natural reverence, and a higher call than that of man. ... When the direct call of Christ to any work comes ... then every other call must give way. ... [T]his duty about the living and life must take precedence of that about death and the dead. ... [T]o postpone the immediate call, is really to reject it." (Edersheim, page 566) By following Jesus, the man would put himself on the way to eternal life, not among those who were spiritually dead in God's eyes. However, he was not prepared to put the Kingdom first in his life, which is essential to remaining spiritually alive.—Matthew 6:33.

[671] The familiar work of plowing was often alluded to in Old Testament illustrations. (Judges 14:18; Isaiah 2:4; Jeremiah 4:3; Micah 4:3) Jesus' reference to plowing emphasized the importance of wholehearted discipleship. Distraction from the work at hand would make crooked furrows. Looking back would cause the work in the field to fall behind. Similarly, the invitee to Christian discipleship cannot be double minded. If distracted from the responsibilities of discipleship, one could become unfit for God's kingdom.

[672] Or "untrained." (John 7:15, *The New English Bible*) "To the Jews there was only one kind of learning—that of Theology; and only one road to it—the Schools of the Rabbis."—Edersheim, page 578. Compare Acts 4:13.

[673] "Among the Jews a Rabbi's teaching derived authority from the fact of its accordance with tradition—that it accurately represented what had been received from a previous great teacher, and so on upwards to Moses, and to God Himself. On this ground Christ claimed the highest authority. His doctrine was not His own invention—it was the teaching of Him that sent Him. The doctrine was God-received, and Christ was sent direct[ly] from God to bring it. He was God's messenger of it to them." (Edersheim: 578)

[674] "The test of a teacher is whether or not he delivers God's message. Jesus gave God's message; so, did Moses. The religious leaders were breaking Moses' law by seeking to kill Jesus." (John 7:18-19 footnote, *The Nelson Study Bible.* Copyright © 1997 by Thomas Nelson, Inc. Use with permission.) Their wicked plot was apparently an open secret.—John 7:25.

[675] Under Moses' law, a male infant was to be circumcised on the eighth day, even if that eighth day was a sabbath. (Leviticus 12:3; Philippians 3:5) Every argument for or against circumcision on the Sabbath would be an argument for or against healing on the Sabbath.

[676] First-century messianic expectations were not monolithic. Israelites knew from Scripture that the Messiah was to be born in Bethlehem; some, however, believed that he would lie hidden in secret—in Heaven, possibly—until the day of his coming. (Daniel 9:25; Malachi 3:1; Matthew 2:4-5; 24:26; John 7:42) This belief was vindicated by Christ's heavenly origin, but his audience did not recognize it. He may have come from Galilee, but his origin was with God.—Micah 5:2; John 1:1.

[677] Non-priestly members of the tribe of Levi formed what may be likened to a police force. This force was under the direction of the captain of the Temple. (Luke 22:52; Acts 4:1; 5:22-26) Some of these Levites were stationed as guards at the entrances to the Temple, others patrolled around it keeping watch. This force was the only armed corps of Israelites permitted by Rome.

[678] Jesus is speaking of his death and resurrection to Heaven, and his enemies cannot follow him there. "Christ, like God himself, must be sought while there is still time to find him. But the Jews will let this 'time' slip by and instead of coming to them, salvation will come to the pagans (the 'Greeks')."—John chapter 7 note n, *The Jerusalem Bible:* Edited by Alexander Jones. See John 12:20-21, 32; compare Hebrews 2:9.

[679] When their homeland was conquered by other nations—first the Assyrians, then the Babylonians—the Israelites were dispersed. (2 Kings 17:23; 24:14-15; Jeremiah 52:28-30) Only a remnant of the exiles returned to Israel. (Isaiah 10:21-22) By the fifth century before Christ, Hebrew communities were apparently found in the 127 provinces of the Persian Empire. (Esther 1:1; 3:8) In the first century of the Christian era, there were Jewish populations in many Greek-speaking communities outside of Israel—for example, in Syria, Asia Minor and Egypt—as well as in the European part of the Roman Empire, including Greece and Rome. Efforts to win converts to Judaism resulted in many people gaining knowledge of Israel's God and law.—Matthew 23:15.

[680] Scripture uses the imagery of hunger and thirst to teach spiritual truths. God promises to satisfy the spiritually hungry and thirsty. (Isaiah 41:17; 55:1; Joel 3:18; Matthew 5:6; Revelation 21:6; 22:17) Jesus, the Bread of Life and the Living Water, is the ultimate spiritual sustenance.—John 4:10, 14; 6:35, 48.

[681] Jesus may have alluded to one of the festival's rituals. Each morning a priest would pour out water collected from the Pool of Siloam in a golden pitcher into a basin leading to the base of the Temple's altar. (Because the festival's first day was a sabbath, water had been brought to the Temple on the preceding day.) He would time his return from the Pool of Siloam to the Temple so that he arrived just as the priests were ready to lay the pieces of the sacrifice on the altar. As he came through the Water Gate and into the Court of the Priests, his entry was announced by a threefold blast from the priests' trumpets. As the water was poured, wine was poured into a different basin. This rite "commemorated the Mosaic water-miracle." Also included in the liturgy of the feast were "prayers for rain ... and reading from biblical passages foretelling lifegiving water for Zion." (John chapter 7 note r, *The Jerusalem Bible:* Edited by Alexander Jones. See Exodus 17:1-6; Isaiah 44:3; 58:11; Ezekiel 47:1-12; Zechariah 13:1; 14:8) When Jesus earlier spoke with a Samaritan woman about "living water," he focused on the benefits of receiving this water. (John 4:10, 14, *King James Version)* At the Festival of Tabernacles, Jesus indicated that **living water** would **flow** from his followers who put faith in him as they shared it with others. Jesus—not the believer—is the source of this life-giving water, a symbol of God's spirit. (**John 7:38**-39) Beginning on the day of Pentecost the following year, anointed Christians started to share waters of truth with others. Compare Revelation 22:17.

[682] At Pentecost the following year, God poured out his spirit on Jesus' followers, giving them the hope of immortal life in Heaven. (Acts 2:4, 33) Having this anointing, the Christians were able to grasp the meaning of many things that they had not understood before. Compare Acts 19:2.

[683] It was common knowledge that Jesus was from Galilee. He was well-known as Jesus of Nazareth. (Matthew 21:11; 26:71; Mark 10:47; 14:67; Luke 18:37; John 1:45) However, people were generally unaware of Jesus' birth in Bethlehem. (Micah 5:2; Luke 2:11) They knew the Scriptures, but they did not know the Messiah.—John 5:39.

[684] Jesus' speaking and teaching abilities were a gift from God.—Isaiah 50:4. See Matthew 7:28-29; Mark 1:22; 12:37; Luke 4:22, 32; 19:48; 21:38; 24:19.

[685] A term of contempt implying that those so described were a "cursed people."—John 7:49, *Holy Bible from the Ancient Eastern Texts: Aramaic of the Peshitta* by George M. Lamsa.

[686] This rhetorical question/insult reflects the contempt that these Judeans felt toward Galileans. Since the Sanhedrin and the Temple were in Jerusalem, no doubt a great concentration of teachers of the Law was to be found there, which likely gave rise to the proverb: "Go north [to Galilee] for riches, go south [to Judea] for wisdom." But there were teachers of the Law as well as synagogues that served as educational centers throughout Galilee.—Luke 5:17.

[687] Or "Search and see; the Prophet doesn't come from Galilee." (John 7:52, *The New Testament in the Language of Today* by William F. Beck; Deuteronomy 18:15, 18) The Sanhedrists forgot (or refused to admit) that the prophet Jonah was from the Galilean town of Gath-hepher (2 Kings 14:25), and that Isaiah (9:1-2) prophesied that Light would be seen in Galilee. (Matthew 4:12-16) Jesus grew up in Galilee but was born in Bethlehem and was a descendant of David. From the beginning, wrong ideas about Jesus grew from willful ignorance or misunderstandings of Scripture.

[688] Based on John 7:53-8:11, this account is missing from most ancient Greek manuscripts.

[689] The Law held both parties to the adultery equally guilty, which makes one wonder why the man was not brought to Jesus also.

[690] "On this occasion we find Christ, first in 'The Treasury' (John 8:20), and then (John 8:21) in some unnamed part of the sacred building, in all probability one of the 'Porches.' Greater freedom could be here enjoyed, since these 'Porches,' which enclosed the Court of the Gentiles, did not form part of the Sanctuary in the stricter senses. Discussions might take place, in which not, as in 'the Treasury,' only 'the Pharisees' (John 8:13), but the people generally, might propound

questions, answer, or assent. ... [In] 'the Treasury,' ... 'the Pharisees'—or leaders—would alone venture to speak."—Edersheim, page 588.

691 This was another way of saying, "I am the Messiah." In the Court of Women four great golden lampstands stood, each having four golden bowls. At night during the Festival of Tabernacles, four youths of priestly descent would climb ladders with large pitchers of oil, filling the 16 bowls. Old clothing of the priests was used as wicks for the lamps. These lamps made a brilliant light that could be seen at a considerable distance, lighting up the courts of the houses in Jerusalem. Certain men, including some of the elders, danced with flaming torches in their hands and sang songs of praise, accompanied by musical instruments. "This 'festive joy,' ... was no doubt connected with the hope of earth's great harvest-joy in the conversion of the heathen world, and so pointed to 'the days of the Messiah.' ... [T]he Pharisees could not have mistaken the Messianic meaning in the words of Jesus."—Edersheim, page 589. See Isaiah 9:2; 42:6; 49:6; Matthew 4:13-16.

692 In Israel's courts, no one was allowed to testify on their own behalf. (Deuteronomy 17:6; 19:15) Invoking this fundamental principle implied that these Pharisees sat in judgment of Jesus. "Their demand for a witness had proceeded on the assumption of their being the judges." (Edersheim, page 591) Jesus condemned the Pharisees for judging "from a human standpoint."—John 8:15, *The Holy Bible in Modern English* (Revised Edition).

693 This was a reference to Jesus' pre-human existence in Heaven and to his being the promised Messiah, whom these religious leaders should have been expecting. When they died in their sin of unbelief, they could not follow Jesus to Heaven.

694 Or "When you have killed the Messiah."—John 8:28, *The Living Bible*; compare John 3:14; 12:32.

695 According to Jewish tradition, only one who labored in the study of the Law was free. Jesus did not refer to "truth" in an intellectual or philosophical sense, or even in a political sense (as his listeners apparently thought). Jesus referred to **the truth** that saves humans from sin. And the freedom Jesus spoke of comes through continuing in his teaching.—**John 8:32**.

696 The Israelites had been in bondage to Egypt, Assyria and Babylon, and were then under the authority of Rome; yet they refused to be called slaves.

697 A slave has no rights to an inheritance and may be dismissed at any time. Only the son born (or adopted) into the household remains for as long as he lives. (Compare Hebrews 3:5-6) The truth about the Son is the truth that sets people free from bondage to sin and death forever.

698 Unlike Isaac, these unbelieving Israelites were not really Abraham's children; they were merely of his race, like Ishmael. Those who truly believe in Christ are the true children of Abraham. (Galatians 4:29-31) The New Testament holds up Abraham as an example of persistent faith and one who lived his faith. (Romans 4:11; Galatians 3:7-9, 16, 29; Hebrews 11:8-10, 17-19; James 2:21-23) His **deeds** included paying homage to God's representatives.—**John 8:39**; see Genesis 14:20; 18:2; Hebrews 7:4.

699 Or "We were not born from fornication." (John 8:41, *American Standard Version)* The Israelites were claiming to be legitimate children of God and of Abraham and, thus, heirs of the promises made to Abraham. They also objected to the insinuation of spiritual adultery, being unfaithful to their covenant with God. Compare Hosea 1:2.

700 Their descent was of the Devil, morally speaking, because they cherished murderous designs and refused to accept Jesus' message.

701 That is, from the **start** of the Devil's course as a murderer, a liar and a slanderer of God. (**John 8:44**; 1 John 3:8) The angel who became Satan the Devil was not created evil.

[702] Essentially, the Pharisees called Jesus a "heretic ... Child of the Devil." (Edersheim, page 595) In other words, they told him,

'You are the one who is not a child of Abraham!' See "Samaria and Samaritans."

[703] Those who continued in Jesus' teaching passed over from death to life. (John 5:24) Jesus was not saying that he would prevent physical death; he was saying that he could give eternal life.

[704] With eyes of faith, Abraham looked forward to the Messiah's arrival. (Hebrews 11:13; 1 Peter 1:11) In another sense, Abraham saw Jesus' **day** when his son Isaac was born. Jesus, the ultimate fulfillment of the Abrahamic promise, was the Greater Isaac. (**John 8:56**; Galatians 3:16) Furthermore, tradition says that "Abraham had, in vision, been shown ... the coming world—and not only all events in the present 'age,' but also those in Messianic times."—Edersheim, page 596.

[705] Or "I am who I am long before Abraham was anything." (John 8:58, *The Message)* Jesus referred to his pre-human existence in Heaven. (John 1:1-2; 17:5) The Pharisees took this for blasphemy, the punishment for which was stoning.—Leviticus 24:16; John 10:33.

[706] "[S]ince the Porches opened upon the Court [of the Gentiles], the Jews might there pick up stones to cast at Him (which would have been impossible in any part of the Sanctuary itself), while lastly, Jesus might easily pass out of the Temple in the crowd that moved through the Porches to the outer gates."—Edersheim, page 588.

[707] The likely setting for this scene, Edersheim suggests, is the entrance to the Temple (or its Courts), then the chosen spot for those objects of pity who solicited charity. (See Acts 3:2) Although the blind man would not ask for or receive alms on the Sabbath, his presence in the wonted place would secure wider notice and perhaps lead to many private gifts.

[708] Jesus' contemporaries believed that certain sins in the parents would manifest in specific diseases in their children. Also, rabbis taught that an unborn child was capable of sinning. For example, "when a pregnant woman worshiped in a heathen temple the unborn child also committed idolatry." (John 9:2 footnote, *The NET Bible)* Jesus rejected such unscriptural notions. The Bible teaches that, because of Adam's sin, all humans are born imperfect and therefore subject to physical defects.—Romans 5:12.

[709] The figurative **nighttime** that Jesus referred to was the time of his trial, execution and death when he would be unable to perform **the work of God**.—**John 9:3-4**; see Luke 22:53; compare Job 10:21-22; Ecclesiastes 9:10.

[710] "Except when danger to life or the loss of an organ was involved," the application of remedies was a violation of Sabbath law, according to the interpretation of tradition. Applying saliva to the eye was "expressly forbidden, on the ground that it was evidently intended as a remedy." (Edersheim, page 600) Saliva was commonly used in folk remedies but Jesus' miracles were performed with God's power; it was not his saliva that healed people.—Mark 7:32-35; 8:22-25.

[711] Whether the man made his way to the pool with or without assistance is not stated. To go to Siloam and wash off the clay was an opportunity for the man to demonstrate his faith, just as bathing in the Jordan River was required of Naaman before he was cured of his leprosy. (2 Kings 5:9-14) Siloam, meaning "sender," was supplied with water from the Gihon Spring, which intermittently gushes, or sends forth, water. *(The New Bible Dictionary,* page 1112) Water drawn from Siloam during the Festival of Tabernacles symbolized the blessings of the Messianic Age, and Jesus—the one sent by God—is the source of these blessings. (John 3:17, 34; 5:36; 9:4; compare Isaiah 42:6-7) The location of Siloam was identified with a small pool in Jerusalem called Birket Silwan until the remains of a larger pool were discovered less than 330 feet (100 m) southeast of the smaller pool. Coins found during the excavation date back to Israel's revolt against Rome (A.D. 66-70), suggesting that the pool was in use until Jerusalem's destruction. This larger pool is now generally recognized as the pool of Siloam.

[712] This is an exceptional instance in the New Testament where a healing took place with no reference to the faith of the person healed or prayers offered up on his behalf (unless Jesus prayed silently for the man).

[713] The Sanhedrin would not hold a formal meeting on the Sabbath. Even if this was such a meeting, the testimony of only one witness would be insufficient for proceeding further. Nevertheless, the Pharisees continued with their inquiry.

[714] This could be a tacit admission that Jesus actually healed the man, or a reference to Jesus' work in making mud.

[715] This form of excommunication may have been "adopted as a contingency to deal with those who were proclaiming Jesus to be the Messiah. ... It was probably local, limited to the area around Jerusalem." (John 9:22 footnote, *The NET Bible)* Nevertheless, "to persons so wretchedly poor as to allow their son to live by begging, the consequence of being ... put outside the congregation ... would have been dreadful."—Edersheim, page 601.

[716] The age of legal maturity in Israel was 13. Some consider the expression **of age** as referring to the qualifying age for military service, which was 20.—**John 9:21**; Numbers 1:3.

[717] "They said, He was 'a sinner'—and yet there was no principle more frequently repeated by the Rabbis, than that answers to prayer depended on a man being 'devout' and doing the Will of God. There could therefore be only one inference: If Jesus had not Divine Authority, He could not have had Divine Power."—Edersheim, page 603; John 9:24.

[718] Or "'From birth you have been evil.' The implication of this insult, in the context of John 9, is that the man whom Jesus caused to see had not previously adhered rigorously to all the conventional requirements of the OT law as interpreted by the Pharisees. Thus, he had no right to instruct them about who Jesus was."—John 9:34 footnote, *The NET Bible.*

[719] Evidently the man was banned from the synagogue. There were different degrees of excommunication. The first and lightest was a rebuke, a punishment that lasted from one to thirty days, during which the person could not come within six feet of another Israelite. (Compare 1 Timothy 5:20) The second degree of excommunication lasted for at least thirty days, followed by a second admonition, which lasted another thirty days; during this time the person was excluded from all fellowship and worship. (Compare Titus 3:10) If the wrongdoer was still unrepentant, the final excommunication was pronounced. This was a ban of indefinite duration. Henceforth, the disfellowshipped one was as good as dead to fellow Israelites. No conversation was to be held with him, and it was forbidden to eat or drink with him. (Compare 1 Corinthians 5:11) "The Rabbinists enumerate twenty-four grounds for excommunication .... But in general, to resist the authority of the Scribes, or any of their decrees, or to lead others either away from 'the Commandments,' or to what was regarded as profanation of the Divine Name, was sufficient to incur the ban."—Edersheim, pages 601, 602.

[720] The beggar recognized Jesus as the foretold **Son of Man** ("Son of God" in the *King James Version)*, the Messiah with divine authority. (**John 9:35**) He bowed down to Jesus, similar to how people bowed down to prophets, kings or other representatives of God. On many occasions, the obeisance done to Jesus expressed a gratitude for divine revelation or recognition of divine favor like that expressed in earlier times.—Matthew 8:2; Mark 1:40; Luke 5:12; compare 2 Samuel 14:4.

[721] Although Jesus did not come into the world to judge it, the inevitable result of his coming was judgment against those who refused to believe in him. The Light of the World spiritually enlightened the blind and blinded the ones who thought they were enlightened.—Matthew 13:13-17; Mark 4:11-12; Luke 8:10; John 3:17-21.

[722] Perhaps some of the Pharisees followed the man to see if he led them to Jesus.

[723] The blind man received sight physically, and this led him to see spiritually as well. But the Pharisees, who claimed to be spiritually sighted, were spiritually blind. Those who claimed to **see**, or understand, were especially reprehensible because they had greater knowledge. (**John 9:41**; compare John 3:10) Had the religious leaders been just uninformed laymen with the normal burden of human sin, their rejection of Jesus might have been excused. However, it condemned them more than their inherited imperfection did. To receive Jesus was to receive the light of the world, to reject him was to reject the light, close one's eyes, and become blind. (John 8:24) The blindness of the Pharisees was incurable because they rejected the only cure.—John 12:37-40.

[724] "The Rabbinists also called their spiritual leaders 'feeders' .... They were, surely, not shepherds, who had cast out the healed blind man, or who so judged of the Christ, and would cast out all His disciples."—Edersheim, page 605; John 9:22, 34.

[725] The Israelites under the Mosaic Law covenant were like a flock of sheep. (Psalm 23:1-2; 95:6-7) The Law served as a fence, separating the **sheep** in this **sheepfold** from people not under this arrangement.—**John 10:1-2**.

[726] "Israel's rulers ... had climbed up to their place in the fold ... as a thief or a robber. They had wrongfully taken what did not belong to them—cunningly and undetected, like a thief; they had allotted it to themselves, and usurped it by violence, like a robber. What more accurate description could be given of the means by which the Pharisees and Sadducees had attained the rule over God's flock, and claimed it for themselves!"—Edersheim, pages 605-06.

[727] Flocks of sheep spent their nights in the safety of a sheepfold—roofless enclosures with stone walls and only one opening—protected from thieves and predators. A doorkeeper would keep watch overnight and open the door for the shepherds in the morning. Each shepherd would collect his flock by calling out to the sheep, and his sheep would recognize their shepherd's voice and respond. John the Baptist, like a doorkeeper, identified Jesus as the shepherd to follow into Messiah's kingdom.

[728] Amazingly, sheep can distinguish their shepherd's voice from that of others. Shepherds would name each sheep and use personalized sounds to distinguish themselves from other shepherds. They would teach the sheep from an early age to respond to different calls, or voice commands, to protect them from dangers or lead them to good pastures and water. Sheep can recognize their shepherd's tender care and protection for them individually and as a flock. In the Scriptures, shepherding is used in the figurative sense of caring for, protecting and nourishing the sheeplike servants of God.—Ezekiel 34:12-16; 1 Peter 5:2-4.

[729] "His flock know His Voice, and in vain would strangers seek to lead them away, as the Pharisees had tried. It was not the known Voice of their own Shepherd, and they would only flee from it."—Edersheim, page 606.

[730] Those **thieves and robbers** were counterfeit religious leaders, including false Messiahs.—**John 10:8**; see Matthew 23:2-35; Luke 11:39-52.

[731] To prevent wild beasts from entering the sheepfold and the sheep from leaving it, "some shepherds lay down across the entry of the sheepfold at night to sleep. ... Thus, the shepherd was also the door." (John 10:7 footnote, *The Nelson Study Bible*. Copyright © 1997 by Thomas Nelson, Inc. Use with permission.) Only those who enter through Jesus will be given authority to shepherd God's flock.—John 21:15-17.

[732] "In his mercy God provided leaders to shepherd his people; however, all too often these shepherds thought only of themselves and failed to take proper care of the flock. Thus, God himself promised to care for them and to provide a new shepherd, Jesus Christ." (Verlyn D. Verbrugge: *The NIV Topical Study Bible,* page 921; Ezekiel 34:23; 37:24) He is the "model" Shepherd who knows his sheep, searches for those who are wandering and lost, and is willing to die for them. "For a literal shepherd with a literal flock, the shepherd's death would have spelled disaster for the sheep; in this instance it spells life for them (Compare the worthless shepherd of Zech 11:17, by contrast)."—John 10:11 & footnote, *The NET Bible.*

[733] Shepherds were well-aware of the danger posed by wolves. In the Bible, the wolf symbolizes ferocity, greed, viciousness and craftiness. Those compared to wolves include false prophets, opposers of gospel truth, and false teachers who would endanger the Christian congregation from within.—Matthew 7:15; 10:16-17; Luke 10:3; Acts 20:28-30.

[734] Hired hands were often motivated by the wages they received rather than by loyalty to the owner or concern for the sheep. Compare Job 7:2.

[735] No one could rob Jesus of the life he had in himself because it was given to him by God. (John 5:26; 7:30, 44; 8:20; 10:39) He surrendered his life willingly and then received it again by resurrection.—Acts 2:24.

[736] Jesus' instructions to the 70 (or 72, depending on the Bible version and the manuscripts from which it was translated) in almost every particular "are the same as those formerly given to the Twelve." However, "both the introductory and the concluding words addressed to the Apostles are wanting in what was said to the Seventy. It was not necessary to warn them against going to the Samaritans, since the direction of the Seventy was to those cities of Peraea and Judea .... Nor were they armed with precisely the same supernatural powers as the Twelve (Matt. 10:7, 8; comp. Luke 10:9)."—Edersheim, page 568.

[737] The disciples were to go as they were and not be distracted by procuring anything extra; God would provide for them.

[738] Such greetings could have included embraces and long conversation. Jesus was emphasizing that his followers should avoid unnecessary distractions and make the most of their time. His direction "was suitable to a temporary and rapid mission, which might have been sadly interrupted by making or renewing acquaintances." (Edersheim, page 568) The prophet Elisha gave similar instructions to his servant Gehazi. (2 Kings 4:29) In both cases, the mission was urgent, so there was no time for delay.

[739] **A child of peace** is someone who desires to be reconciled with God and who listens to and embraces gospel truth, giving him or her peace with God. (**Luke 10:6**; compare Acts 10:36) The expression "refers to the character of the head of the house and the tone of the household."—Edersheim, page 569.

[740] That is, in search of a place that could provide better material comforts. Such things were of secondary importance to the disciples when compared to their mission.

[741] Wiping the dirt or the dust from one's feet indicated a disclaiming of responsibility. The disciples were peacefully departing and leaving that house or that city to the consequences that would come from God.—Matthew 10:14-15; Luke 9:5; Acts 13:50-51.

[742] Jesus' **name** indicated the sphere of authority for the disciples' exorcisms, which foreshadowed the Devil's final defeat.—**Luke 10:17**-18; Revelation 12:10.

[743] A metaphor for divine remembrance and approval; see Exodus 32:32; Isaiah 4:3.

[744] The disciples' healing ministry meant the reversal of the effects of sin and death, introduced by Satan. (Genesis 3:1-19) This reversal is "portrayed graphically as Satan falling from heaven. Jesus' ministry and what grows out of it represents the defeat of Satan, sin and death."—Luke

10:18 footnote, *The Nelson Study Bible.* Copyright © 1997 by Thomas Nelson, Inc. Used with permission. See Revelation 12:7-9.

[745] Jesus' followers will be able to prevail over injurious things, symbolically trampling on **serpents and scorpions**. (**Luke 10:19**; compare Psalm 91:13; Ezekiel 2:6) Such is the power of God's kingdom come!—Luke 10:9, 11.

[746] "Revelation to the humble ..., rather than to the '*wise* of the world' was a familiar theme, common in NT times, but with ancient roots; see, e.g., Isa. 29.14; Prov. 26.12; 1 Cor. 1.19-20."—M. Jack Suggs: Luke 10:21-22 footnote, *The New English Bible.*

[747] This lawyer was "not one of the Jerusalem Scribes or Teachers, but probably an expert in Jewish Canon Law, who possibly made it more or less a profession in that district, though perhaps not for gain." He "put his question to 'tempt'—test, try—the great Rabbi of Nazareth. There are many similar instances in Rabbinic writings of meetings between great Teachers, when each tried to involve the other in dialectic difficulties and subtle disputations." (Luke 10:25) This lawyer's theoretical question was not a "matter of deep personal concern, as it was to the rich young ruler, who, not long afterwards, addressed a similar inquiry to the Lord (Luke 18:18-23)."—Edersheim, page 637; compare Luke 7:30.

[748] "To inherit something is to receive it. In other words, the man was asking, 'What must I do to share in the reward at the resurrection of the righteous at the end?' (see Phil. 3:11-14). The Old Testament basis of this question is the hope of resurrection in Dan. 12:2. Jesus countered the lawyer's test by having him answer his own question."—Luke 10:25-26 footnote, *The Nelson Study Bible.* Copyright © 1997 by Thomas Nelson, Inc. Used with permission.

[749] The first five books of the Bible—Genesis, Exodus, Leviticus, Numbers and Deuteronomy—are collectively known as the Torah; also called the Pentateuch.

[750] To do something with one's whole **soul** means to do it with one's whole life, wholeheartedly.—**Luke 10:27**.

[751] Emphasizing in the strongest possible way the need for complete and total love for God; see also Mark 12:30.

[752] This commandment, according to Paul, sums up the entire Mosaic Law.—Romans 13:9-10; Galatians 5:14; see also James 2:8.

[753] The road from Jerusalem to Jericho was over 12 miles (20 km) long and had a steep, .6 miles (1 km) descent. This road was notoriously dangerous because it ran through desert terrain and caves where robbers hid. Robberies were so frequent that eventually a garrison was stationed to protect travelers.

[754] A Levite was a member of the tribe of Levi, named for Jacob's third son with Leah. (Genesis 29:34) Levites assisted priests with their duties. (Numbers 3:6-8) The priest and Levite may have believed the man to be dead and avoided contact with his body for fear of becoming ritually unclean and therefore unfit for Temple service.

[755] The physician's gospel describes wound treatment consistent with medical methods of the day. (Luke 10:34; Colossians 4:6) Oil was sometimes used to soften wounds (Isaiah 1:6), and wine has certain medicinal value as an antiseptic and mild disinfectant. Luke also describes how the wounds were bound up, preventing further aggravation. Oil, wine and bandages—a traveler's first aid kit—were carried by the Samaritan because he was on a journey.

[756] These hostelries on unfrequented roads afforded lodging to travelers. For man and beast, bed was free of charge, but board was not. The innkeepers were commonly Gentile.

[757] Literally, "two denarii." (Luke 10:35, *The Darby Bible)* A denarius was a Roman silver coin that weighed about 0.124 ounces troy (3.85 g) and bore an image of Caesar on one side; it was the daily wage of a laborer and was the head tax coin exacted by the Romans from the Israelites.—Matthew 20:2; 22:17-21; Mark 12:14-16; Luke 20:22-24.

[758] Might this Israelite have been reluctant to say here, "the Samaritan"?

[759] Unnamed in Luke 10:38, Bethany was where Martha, Mary and their brother Lazarus lived. The village stood on the east-southeast slope of the Mount of Olives at about 2 miles (3 km) from Jerusalem. (John 11:1, 18; 12:1) Just as Capernaum was Jesus' home in Galilee (Matthew 4:13; 9:1; Mark 2:1), Bethany might be called his home in Judea.

[760] "It would have been no uncommon occurrence in Israel for a pious, wealthy lady to receive a great Rabbi into her house," says Edersheim. "But the present was not an ordinary case. Martha must have heard of Him, even if she had not seen Him. But, indeed, the whole narrative implies (comp. Luke 10:38), that Jesus had come to Bethany with the view of accepting the hospitality of Martha, which probably had been proffered when some of those 'Seventy,' sojourning in the worthiest house at Bethany, had announced the near arrival of the Master."—page 574; Luke 10:1.

[761] Martha generally took the lead, which suggests she was the older sister.—John 11:20.

[762] A disciple sits at the master's feet.—Luke 8:35; compare Acts 22:3.

[763] The repetition of her name suggests Jesus' affection for Martha in his admonition of her. Compare Luke 13:34; 22:31.

[764] By her anxious attention to the meal, Martha was missing out on spiritual nourishment from the Son of God. Jesus commended Mary for giving priority to **the most important thing**—listening to the word of God.—**Luke 10:42**.

[765] Prayer was a regular part of Jewish life and worship, and the Old Testament contains numerous prayers in the Psalms and elsewhere. The disciple was no doubt familiar with the formalistic prayers of the religious leaders of Judaism. But he had observed Jesus praying and likely sensed a difference from the sanctimonious prayers of the rabbis. Possibly this disciple was not present for Jesus' Sermon on the Mount, so Jesus repeated the essential points of his model prayer.—Matthew 6:9-13.

[766] Depending on the Bible version and the master text(s) from which it is translated, Luke 11:2 omits the petition for God's will to be done on Earth. (Compare Matthew 6:10) The omission is not significant because, when God's name is sanctified and his reign begins, his purpose for the earth will be accomplished. That Jesus did not repeat his model prayer verbatim indicates that it was not meant to be memorized and recited by rote.

[767] "God is addressed in terms of intimacy *(Father)*. The original Semitic term here was probably *Abba*. The term is a little unusual in a personal prayer, especially as it lacks qualification. Although it is a term of endearment used in the family circle, it is not the exact equivalent of 'Daddy' (as is sometimes popularly suggested). However, it does suggest a close, familial relationship."—Luke 11:2 footnote, *The NET Bible.*

[768] "The reference here is to God's program and progress. This is more affirmation than request, highlighting the petitioner's submission to God's will and the desire to see God's work come to pass."—Luke 11:2 footnote, *The Nelson Study Bible*. Copyright © 1997 by Thomas Nelson, Inc. Used with permission.

[769] Or "for we also forgive everyone who sins against us." (**Luke 11:4**, *New English Translation)* In his Sermon on the Mount, Jesus used the term "debts" instead of **sins**. (Matthew 6:12) The Greek word for **forgive** literally means to let go of a debt by not demanding repayment. One who sins against another incurs a figurative debt and must therefore seek that one's forgiveness.

[770] Homes in those days, especially those of the poor, often consisted of only one large room. If the man of the house was to get up, he would likely disturb the whole family, including sleeping children.

[771] The same blasphemous criticism was made in Galilee a year or so earlier. (The events of Luke chapter 11 are set in Judea or Perea.)—Matthew 9:34; 12:24; Mark 3:22.

[772] It is not clear what these fence-sitters expected to see. God's kingdom was "bursting upon them in the activity of Jesus." (M. Jack Suggs: Luke 11:16 footnote, *The New English Bible)* What more could Jesus have done that would have made them commit to him?

[773] Or "sons." (Luke 11:17, *King James Version)* "Jesus' question and the implied reply to it can be taken in one of two ways: (1) How did Jewish exorcists expel demons? If the answer is by God's power, then why not give Jesus the same credit? (2) How did Jesus' disciples, who were the 'sons' of Israel, drive out demons? The dissenters not only had to explain Jesus' miracles, but those of His followers. Most scholars prefer the former interpretation."—Luke 11:19 footnote, *The Nelson Study Bible.* Copyright © 1997 by Thomas Nelson, Inc. Used with permission.

[774] God's spirit (or "finger") enabled Jesus to expel demons and cure sick people. (Luke 11:20; compare Matthew 12:28; see Exodus 8:19; Deuteronomy 9:10; Psalm 8:3) Hence, the Kingdom had overtaken its opposers, because the King Jesus was there performing these works, which demonstrated God's victory over evil.

[775] Jesus is stronger than Satan and so does not need the Evil One's power to expel demons. According to popular belief, "the casting out of Satan was part of the work of the Messiah." In "mortal conflict with moral evil, and with Satan as its representative," Messiah, "as the Stronger, bindeth 'the strong one,' spoils his house (divideth his spoil), and takes from him the armour *[sic]* in which his strength lay ('he trusted') by taking away the power of sin (Matt. 12:29)."—Edersheim, page 612; Luke 11:21-22.

[776] Those who were against Jesus, by their accusations and criticisms, scattered others away from the Son of Man.

[777] In their culture, Jewish mothers were valued for their sons' accomplishments. Women hoped to be the mother of a prophet, particularly of the Messiah. Yet, Jesus never suggested that his own mother Mary should be given special honor. True happiness for anyone, man or woman, is found in being a faithful servant of God, not in any familial ties or accomplishments.

[778] On an earlier occasion, Jesus explained **the sign of Jonah** as referring to his death and resurrection. (**Luke 11:29**; Matthew 12:39-40) Jonah compared his deliverance from the belly of a fish to being raised from the dead. (Jonah 2:1-2) Jesus' resurrection was to be just as real as Jonah's deliverance. However, even when Jesus was resurrected, his hard-hearted critics still refused to demonstrate faith in him. Jonah also served as a sign by means of his call to repentance. Unlike the Ninevites, Jesus' hearers refused to heed the call to repentance. (Jonah 3:5-10; Matthew 12:41) As **one greater than Jonah,** Jesus should have been heard and obeyed.—**Luke 11:32**.

[779] A literal eye that functions properly is to the body like a lighted lamp in a dark place, enlightening the entire person. **Eye** is used in a figurative sense at **Luke 11:34**. See also Ephesians 1:18.

[780] Or "Your eye is like a lamp to the body, so if your eye is set on innocent things your whole existence will be enlightened, but if it is intent on what is wicked your whole existence will be dark." (Luke 11:34, *21st Century New Testament)* "Jesus addresses his message to all and if the mind is 'healthy', i.e., unclouded by selfish prejudice, ... it can be understood by all." (Luke chapter 11 note i, *The Jerusalem Bible:* Edited by Alexander Jones) As Edersheim puts it, "spiritual receptiveness is ever the condition of spiritual reception."—page 615;.compare John 3:19-21

[781] The meal referred to at Luke 11:37 was not the evening meal, but either breakfast *(New Testament in Modern Speech)* or the midday meal *(New American Standard Bible).* Commentators

have suggested that the Pharisee's invitation was given for the purpose of formulating an accusation against Christ. This, however, seems inconsistent with the unexpressed astonishment of the Pharisee when he saw Jesus sit down to eat without washing. This Pharisee, it seems, regarded Jesus as a celebrated Rabbi, albeit one who taught strange doctrine.

[782] Before eating, Pharisees washed their hands up to the elbow. (Mark 7:3-4) From the Talmud Edersheim draws the following account of a feast and its attendant rituals: "As the guests enter, they sit down on chairs, and water is brought to them with which they wash one hand. After this the cup is taken, when each speaks the blessing over the wine partaken of before dinner. Presently they all lie down at [the] table. Water is again brought [to] them, with which they now wash both hands, preparatory to the meal, when the blessing is spoken over the bread, and then over the cup by the chief person at the feast, or else by one selected by way of distinction. The company responded by Amen .... After dinner the crumbs, if any, are carefully gathered hands are again washed, and he who first had done so leads in the prayer of thanksgiving." (page 618) Washing to that extent would not violate God's law but it was not required.

[783] In the Bible, a fool is one who rejects reason and follows a morally insensible course that is out of harmony with holiness; not someone lacking intellectually but morally, blind to God.—Psalm 14:1; 53:1; 92:5-6.

[784] Or "give the things inside as alms." (Luke 11:41 footnote, *The NET Bible)* "Alms" refers to money or food given to relieve the poor. Israel's law gave specific directions to her people regarding their obligations toward the poor. (Leviticus 23:22; 25:25-28, 35-54; Deuteronomy 15:7-11) An act of genuine charity is a gift that comes from a willing heart. (2 Corinthians 9:7) Believing that almsgiving had merit in itself toward salvation, Pharisees gave of their possessions but not of themselves. They ritualistically washed their hands but failed to wash their hearts from wickedness. **To be completely clean**, the practice of one's religious duties (such as almsgiving) and the condition of one's heart (including love for God and the poor) must agree. (**Luke 11:41**) In addition to the outside of the cup and plate, the inside must be washed as well. "Religious duties are not to be performed hypocritically, i.e., for the applause and esteem of people, but rather *they are to be done* out of a deep love for God and a sensitivity to and concern for the needs of others."—Luke 11:42 footnote, *The NET Bible.*

[785] **Rue** and **mint** were cultivated for use in medicine and as a seasoning for food. Jesus did not condemn the tradition of tithing such herbs, but the Law did not explicitly command it. (Leviticus 27:30; Deuteronomy 14:22; Matthew 23:23) The Pharisees gave a tenth, not only of produce of their fields, but also of items acquired through purchase, trade or other business. (Luke 18:11-12) This was done for fear that the items had not been tithed properly by their original owners. In their scrupulous legalism, the Pharisees disregarded **God's love and justice**.—**Luke 11:42**; see MIcah 6:8; Zechariah 7:9-10.

[786] Or "uppermost seats." (Luke 11:43, *King James Version)* Evidently, the directors of the synagogue and distinguished guests sat near the Scripture rolls at the front of the synagogue, in full view of the congregation. These seats of honor were likely reserved for such prominent individuals.

[787] Or "the marketplaces." (Luke 11:43, *American Standard Version)* The proud scholars and Pharisees loved to be noticed and greeted in these busy centers of buying and selling.

[788] A person who walked on an inconspicuous grave became ceremonially unclean for seven days. (Numbers 19:16) One month before every Passover graves were whitewashed so that they could be easily discovered and avoided. Like unmarked graves, the unclean thinking of the Pharisees was not apparent. (Matthew 23:27-28) People who mixed freely with Pharisees, believing them to be good men, unwittingly became infected with their corrupt attitudes and unclean thinking. (Compare 1 Corinthians 15:33) How Jesus' rebuke must have stung the Pharisees, who thought of themselves as paragons of purity, to be told they caused uncleanness!

[789] By attacking, not merely the practices of the Pharisees, but also their principles, Jesus condemned the whole system of traditionalism, represented by the leaders—Pharisees and scholars (teachers of Mosaic Law).

[790] These **burdens** were the oral traditions and the Pharisees' interpretation of the Law. (**Luke 11:46**) The leaders had no compassion for those who tried to follow the rules, nor would they lift one regulation to lighten anyone's load, insisting that their manufactured customs must be followed.

[791] The current generation finished the job of killing the prophets started by previous generations. Their memorials actually honored their ancestors who murdered God's prophets. "They committed the murders, and you provide the tombs," said Jesus. (Luke 11:48, *The New English Bible)* The only prophet these hypocrites honored was a dead prophet.

[792] Jesus foretold a worse despoiling of his own generation because of its greater wickedness.—Luke 21:20-32; compare Revelation 18:24.

[793] Leaders who were versed in the Law took away divinely provided knowledge that was **key** to entering the Kingdom. (**Luke 11:52**; Matthew 23:13) Instead of unlocking the meaning of God's Word for people, they imposed burdensome traditions on them.

[794] "Here we have a series of discourses to the disciples ([Luke 12:]1-12), to one of the crowds (13-21), to the disciples (22-40), to Peter (41-53), to the multitudes (54-59). The constant interruption is typical of the teaching of Jesus. This address, as often, repeats some of Christ's favorite sayings." (Robertson, page 126) Compare Luke 12:2-9 with Matthew 10:26-33; Luke 12:10 with Matthew 12:31-32; Luke 12:11-12 with Matthew 10:18-20.

[795] Jesus had just exposed the Pharisees' system of worship for its outward show and inner worthlessness. His warning "naturally connects itself with what had passed at the Pharisee's table, an account of which must soon have spread. ... Pharisaism, while pretending to [be] what it was not, concealed what it was. And it was this which, like 'leaven,' pervaded the whole system of Pharisaism."—Edersheim, page 623; Luke 11:39-12:1.

[796] Specifically, "two assaria coins," (Luke 12:6, *Worldwide English Bible)* An assarion was worth about one-sixteenth of a day's wage, approximately 45 minutes' work. Previously, Jesus said that two sparrows—the cheapest of all birds sold as food—could be bought for one assarion. (Matthew 10:29) On this occasion, he said that five sparrows could be obtained for two assaria. Sparrows were of such little value that the fifth one was included free of charge.

[797] The number of hairs on the human head averages more than 100,000. God's intimate knowledge of such minute details guarantees that he is keenly interested in each one of us.

[798] Perhaps this man coveted more than his legal share of the inheritance. (Deuteronomy 21:17) This might explain such an inappropriate interruption of Jesus' spiritual discussion with his demand. Israel's elders arbitrated monetary disputes. Instead of involving himself in a divisive family problem, Jesus illustrated the danger of focusing on wealth.

[799] Or "avarice"; "covetousness." (Luke 12:15, footnote, *The NET Bible)* The warning covered more than money and got to the root attitude—a selfish desire to acquire more possessions, all of which are temporary and ultimately worthless.—Psalm 49:16-17; Proverbs 30:8-9; Ecclesiastes 5:15; Matthew 6:19-21; 1 Timothy 6:7-10, 17-19; James 5:1-5.

[800] Or "Unthinking one." (Luke 12:20, Young's *Literal Translation)* It was foolish of the rich man to make plans without taking God into account. He set his heart on acquiring riches, not on serving God.—James 4:13-15.

[801] As a materially wealthy person is enriched by material things, so a spiritually wealthy person—one who is rich **in God's eyes**—is enriched by spiritual things, that is, things that are important from God's perspective.—**Luke 12:21**; see Proverbs 22:4; Jeremiah 17:11; Philippians 3:7-8; 1 Timothy 6:17-19; James 2:5.

[802] Anxiety or worry can divide our mind and distract us, robbing us of joy. Compare Matthew 6:27-28, 31, 34; see 1 Corinthians 7:32-34; Philippians 4:6.

[803] Since God provides for the raven, a bird that was unclean according to the Law covenant, he will never forsake his holy people. (Leviticus 11:13, 15; Deuteronomy 14:12, 14; Psalm 147:9, 11) When Jesus gave similar admonition in the Sermon on the Mount, he did not refer to a specific bird.—Matthew 6:26.

[804] Or "Which of you by being anxious can add a cubit to his height?" (Luke 12:5, *World English Bible)* Anxiety cannot add to one's physical height or lifespan. Undue anxiety can, in fact, shorten one's life; it is useless and shows a lack of faith in God's ability to provide for his creatures.

[805] During the hot summer months, vegetation in Israel withered in as little as two days. Dried flower stalks and grass were collected from the fields as fuel for the baking ovens. Yet, God cares enough to beautify a part of his creation with such a short life. "The phrase *how much more* is a typical form of rabbinic argumentation, from the lesser to the greater. If God cares for the little things, surely he will care for the more important things."—Luke 12:28 footnote, *The NET Bible.*

[806] Or "'neither be ye uplifted,' in the sense of not aiming, or seeking after great things (comp. Jer. 14:5)," such as the Gentile world sought. (Edersheim, page 625; Luke 12:29-30) The materialistic world is comparable to passengers on a sinking ship who scurry about for the best deck chair. A life consumed with possessions has little room for God.

[807] Those who "seek the Kingdom of God above all else" enjoy "a rich relationship with God."—Luke 12:21, 31, *New Living Translation.*

[808] Being generous to others with what God gives is a way to store up for oneself treasure in heaven. (Philippians 4:17) A faithful first-century disciple was required to follow the Lord unencumbered by worldly cares or possessions. (Matthew 19:21; Mark 10:21; Luke 18:22) Today "the Christian should have as not holding and use what he has not for self nor sin, but for necessity."—Edersheim, page 625; compare 1 Corinthians 7:30-31.

[809] Wedding celebrations of that time could last for a week.—Tobit 11:18.

[810] What Jesus asked of others he was willing to do himself.—John 13:5, 14.

[811] Jesus will one day return to judge how professed Christians followed him. (Matthew 16:27; Romans 2:5-6; 14:10; 2 Corinthians 5:10; Revelation 22:12) However, this return could not be timed (Matthew 24:36; Mark 13:32; Luke 12:40); it might take so long that some would not be looking for him any longer. Attentive faithful ones will be rewarded with service at the Lord's table.—Luke 12:37-38.

[812] Is the parable only for the disciples or for the crowd or for all humankind? The mention of unfaithful slaves suggests that "the parable focuses on those who are associated with Jesus." (Luke 12:41 footnote, *The NET Bible)* "The issue is who lives life in a way that looks for, and takes seriously, the return of Jesus (see 1 John 2:28)."—Luke 12:41 footnote, *The Nelson Study Bible.* Copyright © 1997 by Thomas Nelson, Inc. Used with permission.

[813] "A steward with authority over other servants; Jesus, therefore, is speaking of the apostles (the 'us' of Peter's question)." (Luke chapter 12 note e, *The Jerusalem Bible:* Edited by Alexander Jones) The collective **servant** is **wise** in a practical sense, or "prudent."—**Luke 12:42**, *The Emphasized Bible.*

[814] **Domestics** refers to all individuals who serve in the master's household.

[815] **The master** is Jesus, "the Son of Man," and **the trustworthy and wise servant** involves his "little flock" of followers. (Luke 12:32) When **the master comes**, there will be a functioning arrangement for the spiritual feeding of Jesus' followers, his household. (**Luke 12:42-43**; compare Matthew 24:45-47) The appointed servant's happiness is illustrated in Jesus' parable of the talents.—Matthew 25:20-23.

[816] See Jeremiah 5:14; 23:29. "Jesus' coming brings judgment on those who refuse to accept Him and divides the believers from the faithless."—Luke 12:49 footnote, *The Nelson Study Bible*. Copyright © 1997 by Thomas Nelson, Inc. Used with permission.

[817] Perhaps these Galileans were the ones killed when thousands protested Pilate's use of money from the Temple treasury (money likely acquired with the cooperation of Temple authorities) to construct an aqueduct for bringing water into Jerusalem. (See "Biographical Sketch: Pontius Pilate.") The "narration of this event must be connected with the preceding Discourse of Jesus. He had asked them, whether they could not discern the signs of the terrible national storm that was nearing. And it was in reference to this ... that they repeated this story. ... It is as if these Jews had said to Jesus: Yes, signs of the times and of the coming storm!"—Edersheim, page 628.

[818] This tower was evidently near the Pool of Siloam in the southeast sector of Jerusalem. The tragedy Jesus referred to may have occurred recently and may have been related to the construction of Pilate's aqueduct.

[819] Such disasters were providential invitations to repentance. Sin was not the immediate cause of either calamity. Jesus' peers, however, connected specific punishments to specific sins. "They would probably think that the fall of the tower, which had buried in its ruins these eighteen persons, who were perhaps engaged in the building of that cursed structure, was a just judgment of God! ... But Christ argued that it was wrong to infer that Divine judgment had overtaken His Galilean countrymen, as it would be to judge that the Tower of Siloam had fallen to punish these Jerusalemites." (Edersheim, page 628) The view that judgment and death result directly from committed sin was common in Judaism but not always the correct conclusion.—John 9:1-3.

[820] Since its root structure was complex and took time to develop, a new fig tree was usually given two or three years to bear fruit, about the same amount of time Jesus had spent trying to cultivate faith among the Israelites. This parable illustrated the need and urgency of national repentance. (Compare Isaiah 51:1) Also, it suggested that Jesus was in the third year of his ministry and would soon begin his fourth and final year. Many New Testament scholars believe that Jesus' ministry was three and-a-half years long.

[821] An unproductive tree not only fills the place which a good tree might occupy, it also deteriorates the soil.

[822] The tree of Israel—barren of the fruit of faith—was cut down in A.D. 70.—Luke 13:35; 19:41-44; Galatians 5:22.

[823] Luke 13:11 attributes the woman's infirmity to "a spirit of weakness," that spirit evidently being a demon.—*The Emphasized Bible;* compare verse 16.

[824] Interestingly, the director did not deny Jesus' power to heal or that a miracle occurred. Jesus performed some of his most outstanding miraculous works on the Sabbath, restoring its proper spirit. (John 5:5-9; 9:1-14) Also, his Sabbath miracles demonstrated the kind of relief that his coming Millennial Reign—a period of sabbath rest for Earth and her inhabitants—will bring as he raises humankind to physical and spiritual perfection.—Revelation 21:1-4.

[825] Over time the Christian congregation would grow and swell, leavened with elements good and bad; all sorts of "birds" would claim shelter in its branches. Compare Matthew 13:31-33; Mark 4:30-32.

[826] Also called Hanukkah, the Festival of Dedication is an eight-day celebration in mid-December; it commemorates the rededication of the Temple. On the 25th day of the month of Chislev in 168 B.C. King Antiochus IV Epiphanes of Syria sacrificed swine to Zeus of Olympus on the Temple's altar. Two years later, Judas Maccabaeus recaptured Jerusalem and the Temple. After the Temple was cleansed, the rededication took place on Chislev 25, 165 B.C., exactly three years after Antiochus had made his disgusting sacrifice. Daily burnt offerings to the God of Israel resumed.—1 Maccabees 4:52-59.

[827] Located on the east side of the outer courtyard of the Temple in Jerusalem, Solomon's Colonnade was a spacious, covered passageway that offered protection from winter's strong east wind.—John 10:22-23; Acts 3:11; 5:12.

[828] Jesus and his Father are **one** in action and cooperation. (**John 10:30**, 37-38; 17:11, 21) This type of unity exists among Christians as they work with one another and with God.—1 Corinthians 3:8-9.

[829] Or "a god." (John 10:33, *The New English Bible*) "This exchange can call to mind the trial scene before the Sanhedrin (see Lk. 22.66-71). Here, too, the issue is raised whether Jesus claims to be the Messiah (vv. 24-31) or the Son of God (vv. 33-38)."—David M. Stanley: John 10:24-38 footnote, *The New English Bible*.

[830] Or "your law," referring to the entire Old Testament, not just to the Law of Moses.—John 10:34, *King James Version*.

[831] At Psalm 82:6 judges, in their capacity as representatives of and spokesmen for Jehovah, are called "gods." They were godlike in their exercise of judicial sovereignty. See also Exodus 4:16; 7:1.

[832] Until it was time for Jesus to die, his enemies were powerless to touch him.—Luke 22:53; John 7:30; 8:20.

[833] Religious leaders in Jesus' day debated over whether many will be saved or only a few. Jesus' questioner may have been a Pharisee or one of their representatives. While the question regarding salvation was broad and speculative (Will the saved be few?), Jesus' answer emphasized individual responsibility (Will you?).

[834] Or "Strive with earnestness." (Luke 13:24, *The Darby Bible*) The effort Jesus encouraged may be compared to an athlete's striving to win the prize of a contest.—1 Corinthians 9:24-25; Hebrews 12:1.

[835] Salvation is attainable only on God's terms. Those who seek to **enter through the narrow door** on their own merit will **fail**.—**Luke 13:24**.

[836] Those who do not know Jesus, even those who think they do, will not be acknowledged by him.—Matthew 7:21-23.

[837] This expression can include the idea of anguish, despair and anger, possibly accompanied by bitter words and violent action.

[838] Or "recline at table." (Luke 13:29, *Catholic Public Domain Version*) In Bible times, couches were often placed around a table at banquets or large meals. Those partaking of the meal reclined on a couch with their head toward the table, often resting their left elbow on a cushion. Food was usually taken with the right hand.

[839] The privileges of Israel's covenant relationship with God constituted, so she believed, a claim to the Kingdom. Her children will witness their own expulsion from the Kingdom. To dine with someone indicated close fellowship with that person. Israelites (**the first** ones to be invited **to dine in the Kingdom**) would never have done so with Gentiles (**the last** ones Israelites would expect **to dine in the Kingdom**).—**Luke 13:29-30**.

[840] Perhaps Herod himself started this rumor, slyly hoping to scare Jesus away. Jesus' ministry seems to have disturbed Herod. The king had been manipulated by his wife into executing John the Baptist, and he may have been afraid to kill another prophet of God. (Matthew 14:1-2; Mark 6:16-19) On the other hand, the Pharisees' suggestion that Jesus should depart could have been a ruse to get Him out of Perea, where, evidently, his miracles were attracting and influencing the people.

[841] The prophet Zechariah was martyred in Jerusalem. (2 Chronicles 24:20-21; Matthew 23:35; Luke 11:51) Jerusalem was the capital, where those accused of being false prophets were tried by the Sanhedrin, the high court. Furthermore, animal sacrifices were offered in Jerusalem, so it would be **unacceptable** (or inconceivable) for the Messiah to be killed elsewhere. (**Luke 13:33**; compare 1 Corinthians 5:7) Jesus was tried by the Sanhedrin and executed just beyond the city walls. While no Bible prophecy explicitly states that the Messiah would die in Jerusalem, this idea may be inferred from Daniel 9:24-26.

[842] Jesus' host may have been a director of the synagogue where they had worshiped that day and where Jesus may have taught.

[843] What the ancients called "dropsy," edema is a severe accumulation of fluid, often in the limbs. Dropsy, which may have been a symptom of advanced deterioration of the body's vital organs, was dreaded because it often indicated that the person would suffer a sudden death. The man with dropsy may have been invited to the meal for a treacherous purpose, although he might not have been aware of this. His is one of several miraculous healings mentioned only in the physician's gospel. See also Luke 13:11-13; 17:12-14; 22:50-51; see "The Gospel According to..."

[844] Compare Proverbs 25:6-7. At feasts or banquets in Jesus' day, guests reclined on couches placed along three sides of a table. The Romans called this dining arrangement with three couches a *triclinium*. One couch was the lowest place of honor, one was the middle, and one was the highest. A diner was above the person to the right and below the one to the left. At a formal banquet, the host typically sat at the first position on the lowest couch. The place of honor was the third position on the middle couch. Each position in the dining room was traditionally viewed as having a different degree of honor.

[845] God will not forget what his servants do to carry out his love and mercy. (Hebrews 6:10) If not in this life, the reward will come in the next.—Isaiah 26:9, 19; Acts 20:35; 24:15.

[846] Real estate and livestock are examined before purchase, not after. The invitees showed no interest in the occasion nor respect for their host, who had given them prior notice. "To them," says Edersheim, "it was not a feast at all, but something much less to be desired than what they had, and would have been obliged to give up, if they had complied with the invitation."—page 648.

[847] Israelites with certain physical defects and foreigners were disqualified from the priesthood. (Leviticus 21:17-23; Ezekiel 44:9) This invitation was extended to such disadvantaged ones of the Jewish nation (the City) and to proselytes.

[848] A final invitation was extended to people living outside Israel (the City), whom the Jews viewed as unworthy before God. (Acts 10:28) Israel as a nation rejected Jesus' invitation to dine in God's kingdom.

[849] Or "does not hate." (Luke 14:26, *New Heart English Bible)* In this context, "hate" means to love less. Compare Deuteronomy 21:15.

[850] This does not mean that Jesus' followers must get rid of personal possessions. Christians should see material things as secondary and let nothing stand in the way of worshiping God and serving his Son.—1 Timothy 6:17-19; Hebrews 13:5.

[851] It is practical wisdom first to sit down and calculate the expense of undertaking discipleship. One should be able to accept all that goes with discipleship and reckon that one can complete the course, even as a would-be builder of a tower wants to complete construction of it.

[852] Jesus used the peace-promoting work of an ambassador to illustrate our individual need to sue for peace with God and give up all to follow in the footsteps of his Son to get God's favor and everlasting life.—2 Corinthians 5:20.

[853] "God still wants our sacrifices today—not animals killed in an effort to honor or appease him, but the sacrifices of lives dedicated to him, lives poured out in praise and confession of him, lives

rich with deeds of kindness done to our fellow humans, and lives committed to using our resources in God's work."—Verlyn D. Verbrugge: *The NIV Topical Study Bible*, page 108.

[854] A faithless, salt-less disciple is useless to God. (Matthew 5:13) The kind of salt Jesus referred to is assumed to be "chemically impure salt, perhaps a natural salt which, when exposed to the elements, had all the genuine salt leached out, leaving only the sediment or impurities behind. Others have suggested the background of the saying is the use of salt blocks by Arab bakers to line the floor of their ovens: Under the intense heat these blocks would eventually crystallize and undergo a change in chemical composition, finally being thrown out as unserviceable." Genuine salt can never lose its flavor because its chemical properties cannot change. "In this case the saying by Jesus here may be similar to Matt 19:24, where it is likewise impossible for the camel to go through the eye of a sewing needle."—Luke 14:34 footnote, *The NET Bible*.

[855] The religious leaders criticized Jesus' choice of dining companions because table fellowship indicated acceptance of the other diners.—Matthew 9:11; Mark 2:16; Luke 5:30.

[856] This shepherd with 100 sheep is of modest means, as flocks often had up to twice as many heads of sheep. The shepherd spent sleepless nights protecting the flock from predators and thieves. (Genesis 31:39-40; 1 Samuel 17:34-35; Amos 3:12; Luke 2:8; John 10:10, 12-13) He kept the flock from scattering, looked for lost sheep, carried feeble or weary lambs in his bosom or on his shoulders and cared for the sick and injured. (1 Kings 22:17; Isaiah 40:11; Ezekiel 34:4-6; Zechariah 11:15-16; Luke 15:4-5) God and Jesus are figuratively referred to as shepherds, as are those who take the lead among Christians.—Psalm 23:1; 80:1; Hebrews 13:20; 1 Peter 2:25; 5:2, 4.

[857] Or "who repents," that is, changes his or her mind and ways.—Luke 15:7, *World English Bible*.

[858] **Ninety-nine righteous ones who never strayed** is a rhetorical way of describing the religious leaders, who believed they were "good people in no need of rescue."—**Luke 15:7**, *The Message*.

[859] Illumination was needed to search for the coin because the window in a home, if there was one, was usually small.

[860] Or "sweep." (Luke 15:8, *King James Version*) Houses at that time generally had clay floors, so the woman swept the floor with a broom made of palm twigs to help her find the lost coin.

[861] This lost coin (a "drachma," worth about a day's wage) may have had special value as one of a set of ten, perhaps an heirloom or part of a prized string of coins used for adornment.—Luke 15:8 footnote, *New Living Translation*.

[862] The younger son wanted his inheritance even though his father was still alive. The firstborn received a double share, according to Israel's law. (Deuteronomy 21:17) The inheritance of the younger son would have been half that of his older brother. Although fathers were cautious of breaking up an estate early, the father in Jesus' parable granted his son's request. This illustrates God's respect for free will; he allows all humans to go the way of their choosing. Choices, of course, have consequences.

[863] Or "living in debauchery."—Luke 15:13, *The Darby Bible*.

[864] The carob tree is an attractive evergreen found throughout the Mediterranean area. Inside its fruit, or pods, are several pea-like seeds separated from one another by a sweet, sticky, edible pulp. Carob pods are still widely used as food for livestock. The degradation to which the prodigal son had sunk was accentuated by his willingness to eat the food of unclean animals.—Leviticus 11:7-8.

[865] In Bible times, kissing was common between male relatives.—Genesis 27:26-27; 45:15; 48:9-10; 50:1; Exodus 18:7; 2 Samuel 14:33.

[866] A hired hand was not part of the estate, as were the servants, but was an outsider, hired usually for just a day's work.—Matthew 20:2.

[867] Accepting his son's confession, the father restored him to full family membership. The act of putting on the son's hand a **ring**—which may have borne the family seal—showed the father's favor and affection as well as the dignity, honor and status accorded his restored son. The **robe** may have been a richly embroidered vestment of the sort presented to an honored guest. The son was apparently so destitute that he was barefoot and therefore needed **sandals**. "The servants were not only to bring these articles, but themselves to 'put them on,' the son, so as thereby to own his mastership."—Edersheim, page 656; **Luke 15:22.**

[868] Or "bring the calf we have been fattening and kill it." (Luke 15:23, *Jerusalem Bible*) The father had been always on the outlook for his son, "an impression which is strengthened by the later command to the servants to 'bring the calf, the fatted one' ..., as if it had been specially fattened against his return."—Edersheim, page 655.

[869] "The father responded to his disgruntled older son by explaining that just because someone receives a blessing, that does not mean there is no blessing for others. The father also implied that the older son always had the opportunity to celebrate with a fattened calf, since the animals were his."—Luke 15:31 footnote, *The Nelson Study Bible*. Copyright © 1997 by Thomas Nelson, Inc. Used with permission.

[870] How the manager brought about this deflationary trend is debatable. Either he removed interest from the debt or his own commission. The latter is more likely, considering that his master commended the manager's actions.

[871] The possession of or desire for money "so easily tends to wrongdoing." (Luke 16:9, *The New Testament: A Private Translation in the Language of the People* by Charles B. Williams) Christians who "are rich in this world" should not "trust in uncertain riches, but in the living God." (1 Timothy 6:17, *King James Version*; see 1 Timothy 6:9-10; James 1:9-11; 5:1-5) However, if we use our **worldly wealth** to make **friends** with God and Jesus (with acts of charity, for example), we "will be welcomed into an eternal home."—**Luke 16:9**, *Contemporary English Version;* see 1 Timothy 6:18-19.

[872] "Small examples of selfishness now result in greater selfishness later. Likewise, small examples of generosity now result in greater generosity later. ... A person who cannot handle money certainly cannot handle spiritual matters that are of much more value."—Luke 16:10 & 11 footnotes, *The Nelson Study Bible*. Copyright © 1997 by Thomas Nelson, Inc. Used with permission.

[873] That is, be less devoted to.—Genesis 29:30-31; Deuteronomy 21:15; Matthew 6:24; Luke 14:26; John 12:25.

[874] Or "Riches." (Luke 16:13, *Emphasized Bible*) A servant of God cannot give him exclusive devotion and at the same time be devoted to gathering material possessions.

[875] Jesus' story about two men and their changes in circumstances underscored the magnitude of a change that was taking place: the old covenant had led to the Messiah, and the obligation to keep the Mosaic Law was ending. Whereas the Law allowed men to divorce their wives on various grounds, for example, Jesus said that adultery was the only acceptable basis on which to obtain a divorce.—Luke 16:16-18.

[876] Though the Bible does not name the man, he has become known as Dives, which is the Latin word for "rich." This adjective describes the man in the *Vulgate*.

[877] Purple dye was obtained from shellfish or mollusks found along the shores of the Mediterranean Sea. In the neck of these creatures is a small gland containing a single drop of fluid. When exposed to air and light, this fluid gradually changes color from cream to purple. Because the amount of fluid acquired from each shellfish was small, accumulating a large amount was costly. Hence, this dye was expensive, and garments dyed **purple** became the mark of wealthy people or those in high station.—**Luke 16:19**; Esther 8:15.

[878] To describe the **beggar**, **Luke 16:20** uses a Greek word that refers to one who is very poor, or destitute. The same word is used figuratively at Matthew 5:3 to convey the idea of people who are painfully aware of their spiritual poverty and of their need for God—"those who are beggars for the spirit."—Matthew 5:3 footnote, *New World Translation*.

[879] Dogs were unclean animals to the Israelites and have an unfavorable figurative sense in the Bible. (Leviticus 11:27; 1 Samuel 17:43; 24:14; 2 Samuel 9:8; 16:9; 2 Kings 8:13; Proverbs 26:11; Matthew 7:6; 15:26; Mark 7:27; 2 Peter 2:22; Revelation 22:15) The mention of **dogs** in this parable indicates the low state of the beggar.—**Luke 16:21**.

[880] Or "the rich man also died; and he was buried in hell ["Hades," *World English Bible;* "the grave," *A Faithful Version*]."—Luke 16:22, *Douay-Rheims Challoner Revision*.

[881] Or "bosom." (Luke 16:22-23, *King James Version*) The bosom position was one of special favor and close fellowship. (John 1:18) This figure of speech is drawn from the practice of reclining on couches at meals in such a way that one would lean back on the bosom, or chest, of a special friend.—John 13:23.

[882] The imagery suggests separation of the thirsty rich man from the presence of God. (Psalm 42:1-2; 63:1; Isaiah 5:13; 65:13) "The torment, especially of thirst, of the wicked, is repeatedly mentioned in Jewish writings." In one fable, "the righteous [man] is seen beside delicious springs, and the wicked [man] with his tongue parched at the brink of a river, the waves of which are constantly receding from him." In this legend, however, "the beatified is a Pharisee, while the sinner tormented with thirst is a Publican!"—Edersheim, page 669; contrast Luke 18:10-14.

[883] With Abraham, Lazarus received "the comfort which had been refused to him on earth, and the [rich] man who had made this world his good, and obtained there his portion, of which he had refused even the crumbs to the most needy, now received the meet reward of his unpitying, unloving, selfish life."—Edersheim, page 670.

[884] The Age of the Law and the Age of the Kingdom in Luke 16:16 "are suggested by the appeal, on the one hand to *Moses and the prophets*, and the hint, on the other hand, of one who will *rise from the dead*."—M. Jack Suggs: Luke 16:29, 31 footnote,

The New English Bible.

[885] Or "stumbling-blocks"; "snares," actions or circumstances leading one to follow an improper course, to stumble or fall morally or to fall into sin. (Luke 17:1, *The Holy Bible in Modern English—Revised Edition; Twentieth Century New Testament)* The Greek term originally referring to a trap (or perhaps the stick in the trap to which bait was attached) came to refer to any impediment that would cause one to stumble or fall.

[886] A large millstone would be turned by a domestic animal, such as a donkey, and be used to grind grain or crush olives. An upper millstone might be as much as 5 feet (1.5 m) in diameter and would be turned on an even larger lower stone.

[887] Or "lead astray"; "ensnare"; "trip up." (Luke 17:2, *Catholic Public Domain Version; Complete Jewish Bible; The New Testament in Modern English* by J.B. Phillips) See note above on **occasions for falling into sin.**—**Luke 17:1.**

[888] Jesus' humble followers were "little" in the world's estimation. (Luke 17:2, *King James Version)* The gruesome punishment of drowning reflects Jesus' feelings about those who stumble his followers into sin.

[889] Or "your brother," meaning a fellow believer, irrespective of gender. (Luke 17:3, *New Heart English Bible)* The responsibility for righting a wrong between believers lies with the one who is wronged.—Matthew 18:15.

[890] **Seven times** conveys the idea of an indefinite number of times.—**Luke 17:4**; compare Psalm 119:164; Matthew 18:22.

[891] God's servants view themselves modestly, "undeserving of special praise." (Luke 17:10, *New English Translation)* They put God's interests first and appreciate their privilege to worship as members of his household.

[892] A figure of speech for the very smallest measure of size. (See "A Mustard Seed, A Mountain & Faith.") Instead of miraculously increasing their faith, Jesus encouraged the disciples to put their faith into action. Like a muscle, faith gets stronger when exercised. With selfless devotion and discharge of duty, faith increases.—1 Corinthians 4:2.

[893] This tree, commonly cultivated in Israel, has an extensive root system, thus requiring great effort to uproot.

[894] Since leaving Jerusalem after the Feast of Dedication, Jesus has been in the area across the Jordan called Perea. (John 10:40) As he heads south toward Jerusalem, his disciples and large crowds—including tax collectors and sinners—travel with him. (Luke 14:25; 15:1; 17:11) In his parting words to his Perean followers are admonitions Jesus gave to his disciples in Galilee. Compare Luke 17:1-4 with Matthew 18:6-7, 21-22; Luke 17:6 with Matthew 17:20.

[895] A village on the east-southeast slope of the Mount of Olives, about 2 miles (3 km) from Jerusalem (Mark 11:1; Luke 19:29; John 11:18); home to Martha, Mary and Lazarus. Today the site is marked by the small village of el-ʿAzariyeh (El ʿEizariya), an Arabic name meaning "the Place of Lazarus," located 1.5 miles (2.5 km) east-southeast of the Temple Mount.

[896] From Jesus' answer the apostles "would naturally infer ... that Lazarus would not die, and that his restoration would glorify Christ, either as having foretold it, or prayed for it, or effected it by His Will." (Edersheim, page 691) "Jesus will be glorified by the miracle itself, ... but the miracle will bring about his [own] death, [John] 11:46-54, by which also he will be glorified."—John chapter 11 note b, *The Jerusalem Bible:* Edited by Alexander Jones.

[897] The disciples' fears for Jesus' safety in Judea would prove to be well-founded.—John 10:31-33; 11:53.

[898] The **hours of daylight** left for Jesus had not yet elapsed; until they did, no harm could come to him. (**John 11:9**; compare John 9:4) He will use to the full the short time (**twelve hours**, symbolically speaking) left for him; afterward will come the **night** when his enemies kill him.—**John 11:11**; compare Luke 22:53.

[899] Just as people can be awakened from a deep sleep, they can be resurrected from death.

[900] There would have been no miracle to confirm the apostles' faith had Lazarus not died.

[901] Burial was traditionally carried out on the day of death. (Acts 5:5-6, 10) Suggesting the significance of the four days is the rabbinic belief that "the soul hovered near the body of the deceased for three days, hoping to be able to return to the body. But on the fourth day it saw the beginning of decomposition and finally departed (*Leviticus Rabbah* 18.1). ... After this time, resurrection would be a first-order miracle, an unequivocal demonstration of the power of God."—John 11:17 footnote, *The NET Bible.*

[902] Martha and Mary "probably thought the message had reached Him too late, that Lazarus would have lived if Christ had been appealed to in time, or had been able to come—at any rate, if He had been there. Even in their keenest anguish, there was no failure of trust, no doubt, no close weighing of words on their part—only the confidence of love." (Edersheim, page 691) Knowing that the resurrection of the dead was yet to come, Martha, rather than asking for Lazarus to be brought back to life, affirmed her faith in Jesus.

[903] **Judgment Day** will apparently correspond to the Thousand Year Reign of Christ when he will judge humankind, including the resurrected dead.—**John 11:24**. See John 12:48; Revelation 20:4-6.

[904] Jesus is the hope of the living and the dead. (Revelation 1:18) His death and resurrection opened the way for the dead to return to life. After Jesus was resurrected, God granted him the power not only to resurrect the dead but also to impart eternal life.—John 5:26, 28-29.

[905] Demonstrating faith in Jesus leads to eternal life.—John 6:39-40, 44, 54.

[906] Especially during the first three days after death and burial, it was customary for mourners to visit the grave. It appears that "the burial of Lazarus did not take place in a common burying-ground," that is, in a cemetery, where the poor or strangers were laid to rest. (Jeremiah 26:23; Matthew 27:7) Being rich or at least well-to-do, Lazarus was interred "in his own private tomb in a cave—probably in a garden." Burial tombs were "acquired and prepared long before they were needed, and treated and inherited as private and personal property .... In such caves, or rock-hewn tombs, the bodies were laid, having been anointed with many spices ..., with myrtle ..., aloes, and, at a later period, also with hyssop, rose-oil, and rose-water. The body was dressed and, at a later period, wrapped, if possible, in the worn cloths in which originally a Roll of the Law had been held .... The 'tombs' were either 'rock-hewn' or natural 'caves' or else large walled vaults, with niches along the sides." The average-sized burial chamber accommodated eight bodies; larger caves or vaults, thirteen. "At the entrance to the vault was 'a court' ... to hold their bier and its bearers. ... Certain it is, that after a time the bones were collected and put into a box or coffin, having first been anointed with wine and oil, and being held together by wrappings of cloths."—Edersheim, pages 693, 694, 695, 698.

[907] "This was not personal grief over the loss of a friend (since Lazarus was about to be restored to life) but grief over the effects of sin, death, and the realm of Satan. It was a natural complement to the previous emotional expression of anger ([John] 11:33). It is also possible that Jesus wept at the tomb of Lazarus because he knew there was also a tomb for himself ahead."—John 11:35 footnote, *The NET Bible.*

[908] These people misinterpreted Jesus' tears as helplessness, complaining that he had healed others, but now was powerless.

[909] An embalmed body would not have been expected to smell. Hebrews had the custom of preparing bodies for burial by binding them with cloths of clean linen along with spices. This was not an elaborate embalming process designed to preserve the body for a long time such as practiced by the Egyptians. (Genesis 50:3; 2 Chronicles 16:14; Matthew 27:59; Mark 16:1; Luke 23:55-56; John 19:39-40) Jesus had already performed at least two resurrections (Luke 7:12-15, 22; 8:49-55) but he had not yet raised up someone who had been dead for four days and whose body had already begun to decompose. Even those who believed that the soul remained with a dead body for three days would be convinced that Jesus had performed an exceptional miracle in the case of Lazarus.—John 12:9-11, 17.

[910] How did Lazarus walk out of the tomb "bound hand and foot with graveclothes"? (John 11:44, *King James Version*) "If Lazarus' decomposing body was brought back to life by the power of God, then it could certainly have been moved out of the tomb by that same power. Others have suggested that the legs were bound separately, which would remove the difficulty, but the account gives no indication of this. What may be of more significance for the author is the comparison which this picture naturally evokes with the resurrection of Jesus, where the graveclothes stayed in the tomb neatly folded ([John] 20:6-7). Jesus, unlike Lazarus, would never need graveclothes again."—John 11:44 footnote, *The NET Bible.*

[911] Jesus' miracles, if genuine, had to be "of Satanic agency." All Sadducees (including High Priest Caiaphas) rejected belief in the resurrection of the dead. "If [Jesus] headed the Messianic movement of the Jews as a nation, alike the Jewish City and Temple, and Israel as a nation, would perish in the fight with Rome."—Edersheim, page 700.

[912] High Priest Caiaphas was a skillful diplomat who held his office longer than any of his immediate predecessors. He was appointed by the Romans about A.D. 18 and remained in office for about 18 years. Like most of the Sanhedrin, Caiaphas was bent on destroying Jesus. Nevertheless, in view of his sacred office, Caiaphas was used by God to prophesy about Jesus. (Caiaphas actually meant that Jesus should be killed to prevent Israel from plunging into chaos.)

[913] "It was on that occasion that the members of the Sanhedrin formally resolved on His Death. It now only remained to settle and carry out the plans for giving effect to their purpose. ... [Jesus] had, indeed, before this raised the dead; but it had been in far-off Galilee, and in circumstances essentially different. But now it would be one so well known as Lazarus, at the very gates of Jerusalem, in the sight of all men, and amidst surroundings which admitted not of mistake or doubt."—Edersheim, page 688.

[914] Also called Ephrain, Ephraim was a city captured by Judah's King Abijah from King Jeroboam of Israel. (2 Chronicles 13:19) The site commonly suggested is the village of et-Taiyiba (et-Taiyibeh), identified with ancient Ophrah (Joshua 18:23) or Ephron (Joshua 15:9); it is located near the wilderness, overlooking the desert plains of Jericho and the Dead Sea to the southeast.

[915] "Certain respected older men in Israel assisted Moses and served as judges, advisers and representatives of the tribes. In New Testament times these Jewish elders still functioned as leaders of the people, helping to carry on the religious traditions of the Jews."—Verlyn D. Verbrugge: *The NIV Topical Study Bible,* page 1358.

[916] As shown in connection with Jesus' trial, Rome seems to have guarded its power to inflict capital punishment.—John 18:31.

[917] When lower courts could not reach a decision in a civil case or that of minor crime, it was referred to the Sanhedrin, whose rulings were final. The high court also had officers at its disposal as well as the power of arrest and imprisonment. (Matthew 26:47; John 7:32; Acts 4:1-3; 9:1-2) Until Roman rule the Sanhedrin had authority to carry out the death penalty.

[918] One such case was the arrest of the apostle Paul.—Acts 21:27-36.

[919] The Sanhedrin had sole jurisdiction in issues of national importance, in dealing with judges who defied its decisions and in judging false prophets. Jesus and Stephen appeared before the court charged with blasphemy, Peter and John with subverting the nation, and Paul with profaning the Temple.—Mark 14:64; Acts 4:15-17; 6:11; 24:6.

[920] For example, the high priest and his council instructed leaders of the synagogues in Damascus to cooperate in the arrest of Christ's followers.—Acts 9:1-2; 22:4-5; 26:12.

[921] Paul took advantage of this rivalry between the Pharisees and the Sadducees and their differences in belief when he defended himself before the Sanhedrin.—Acts 23:6-10.

[922] Consider, in contrast, the Sanhedrin's dealings with Jesus, Stephen and Paul.—Matthew 26:3-4, 59-60, 67-68; Mark 14:56-57; John 11:47-53; Acts 6:12-13; 7:58-59; 23:12-15.

[923] The final destination of this journey was Jerusalem. (Luke 17:11) With Passover approaching, Jesus traveled north from Ephraim through Samaria and southern Galilee, where he would join pilgrims going through Perea to Jerusalem. This visit to Galilee was the last one prior to his death. Jesus encountered the lepers when entering a village either in Samaria or in Galilee.

[924] Lepers congregated together or lived in colonies, making it possible for them to help one another. (2 Kings 7:3) Israel's law required lepers to live in isolation and to publicly identify themselves as contagious. (Leviticus 13:45-46; Numbers 5:2-3) In some of its forms, leprosy can result in gradual loss of body tissue, including fingers, toes or ears. (Numbers 12:10-12) Leprosy in the Bible is not restricted to the disease known by that name today (Hansen's disease), for it could affect not only people but also clothing and houses.—Leviticus 13:47-58; 14:34-53.

[925] A priest had to verify that a leper was healed. (Matthew 8:4; Luke 5:14) The cured leper had to travel to the Temple and bring as a gift offering two live clean birds, cedarwood, scarlet material and hyssop.—Leviticus 13:9-17; 14:2-31.

[926] Had this man and his companions not believed in Jesus, they would not have approached him in the first place and, therefore, would not have received healing for themselves. (See Matthew 9:20-22; 14:35-36; Mark 6:56; 10:50-52) However, only the despised Samaritan thanked Jesus for healing him. (John 4:9; 8:48) The other nine lepers, presumably Israelites, failed to respond with gratitude.

[927] Or "with striking observableness." (Luke 17:20, *New World Translation)* The Kingdom is not coming in a way that is obvious to all, contrary to what the Pharisees seemed to expect.

[928] Or "is within you, ... is within your grasp, ... will be among you." (Luke 17:21 footnote, *The New English Bible)* Jesus could tell the Pharisees that the Kingdom was in their midst because he, the future king, was present.—Matthew 21:5.

[929] "This is a reference to the *days* of the full manifestation of Jesus' power in a fully established kingdom."—Luke 17:22 footnote, *The NET Bible.*

[930] To spiritually enlightened Christians, the evidence of Jesus' imminent return as a heavenly king would be as obvious as **lightning flashing from one horizon to another**.—**Luke 17:24**.

[931] **The days of Noah** actually covered a period of years. (Matthew 24:37-39) Similarly, the foretold **days of the Son of Man** would cover a period of time, climaxed by the destruction of those who do not seek deliverance.—**Luke 17:26**; compare Isaiah 1:1; Jeremiah 1:2-3.

[932] Or "box-shaped vessel." (Luke 17:27, *New Heart English Bible)* The ark was not a boat, as it is often depicted in storybook illustrations.

[933] Roofs were flat and used as extra rooms for various purposes, and so a guard rail was required. (Deuteronomy 22:8; Joshua 2:6; 1 Samuel 9:26; 2 Samuel 11:2; Nehemiah 8:16-18; Acts 10:9) An external stairway or ladder allowed a householder to leave the rooftop without having to enter the house. The swiftness of judgment would require a swift escape.

[934] In the Bible, remembering includes action.—Genesis 40:14-15; Luke 22:19; 1 Corinthians 11:24-25.

[935] "Those who invest their lives in advancing Christ's kingdom, even to the point of suffering and death, will receive great privilege and glory in the climactic reign of Christ (see Matt. 5:10-12; 19:27-30; 2 Tim. 2:12; Rev. 20:4-6)."—Luke 17:33 footnote, *The Nelson Study Bible.* Copyright © 1997 by Thomas Nelson, Inc. Used with permission.

[936] Those **taken along** receive a favorable standing with the Lord and are brought into a way of salvation; all others will be **abandoned** to destruction. This corresponds to Noah's entering the ark when the Flood began and to Lot's being led out of Sodom; it therefore precedes the execution of judgment. Those who will be taken along and those who will be abandoned could be close associates—working at the same place of employment or even living in the same home. (**Luke 17:34-35**) Individually, "we must all appear before the judgment seat of Christ."—2 Corinthians 5:10, *King James Version.*

[937] Christians who are like sharp-eyed eagles will not be fooled by false Messiahs. (Luke 17:23, 37) They are members of Christ's body and well-fed spiritually. Some say that Jesus was foretelling the destruction of Jerusalem in A.D. 70 by Roman legions, who had the figures of eagles emblazoned on their standards. Others contend that Jesus' words referred to saved ones feeding on his body as their Ransom. Neither of these explanations, however, takes into account that Jesus was discussing what will happen in **the days of the Son of Man**. (**Luke 17:22, 26**) At that time, according to Revelation 19:11-21, the Word of God will execute judgment against all having the mark of the beast, which will occasion a victory feast. The **eagles** represent those taken along by Christ who **gather** with him at the feast; all others will be left behind as part of the enemy **carcass**.—**Luke 17:37**.

[938] Persistence in prayer means, not praying continuously, but praying "under all circumstances, however apparently adverse, when it might seem as if an answer could not come, and we would therefore be in danger of 'fainting' or becoming weary." (Edersheim, page 673; Luke 18:1) Luke alone contains this parable, providing another example of how the third gospel emphasizes prayer.—Luke 1:10, 13; 2:37; 3:21; 6:12; 9:28-29; 11:1-2; 22:40-45; 23:46; see "The Gospel According to..."

[939] This judge was neither religious nor constrained by public opinion. Jesus apparently referred to a judge or police magistrate appointed by Rome, one that handled financial cases. (Israel's courts were officiated by tribunals.) Widows were usually dependent upon others for support. (Isaiah 1:17; Acts 6:1; 1 Timothy 5:3-16; James 1:27) This woman's case may have been one where money was at issue.

[940] Unlike the judge who kept putting off the widow, God will bring about swift justice **for his chosen ones who appeal to him day and night**. (**Luke 18:7**) Persistence in prayer is not the cause of its answer. But certainty of what is asked for should lead to persistence in prayer, even when everything seems to forbid the hope of an answer.

[941] Jesus referred to, not faith in general but a particular kind of faith, like that of the widow. This would include having faith in the power of prayer as well as faith that God will cause justice to be done for his chosen ones. Jesus left the question about faith unanswered, apparently so that his disciples would think about the quality of their own faith. The parable about prayer and faith was particularly appropriate because Jesus had just been describing the tests his disciples would face.—Luke 17:22-37.

[942] That is, to the Pharisees or to people with a Pharisaic spirit. The Pharisee in Jesus' story seemed to think "that God should be grateful to him for his commitment. The man obviously looked down on other people and was proud of his fasting and tithing."—Luke 18:11-12 footnote, *The Nelson Study Bible*. Copyright © 1997 by Thomas Nelson, Inc. Used with permission.

[943] "[B]oth in the time of public service, and still more at other times, the Temple was made the place of private prayer." (Edersheim, page 675) Those who went to the Temple to pray did not go into the Holy or the Most Holy but were permitted to enter the surrounding courtyards. Evidently, in this parable the two men are portrayed as standing in one of the courts.

[944] Fasting was required by law only on the Day of Atonement. (Leviticus 23:27-29; compare Isaiah 58:3, 5)) Pharisees customarily fasted on the second and fifth days of the week. They wanted their piety to be observed. (Matthew 6:16) According to extra-biblical sources, the days they chose for fasting were the regular market days, when many people would be in town. They also fasted when special services were held in the synagogues and when the local courts met.

[945] Under the Mosaic Law, the Israelites were to pay the tithe, or a tenth of their crops. (Leviticus 27:30; Deuteronomy 14:22) Jesus reproved the Pharisees and scholars for focusing on minor details of the Law while failing to promote its underlying principles, such as justice and love for God.—Matthew 23:23; Luke 11:42.

[946] Literally, "the sinner." (Luke 18:13, *The Emphasized Bible)* The tax collector felt as if he alone were a sinner, that no one was as sinful as he. The Pharisee, in contrast, considered himself to be the only one who was not a sinner.

[947] God heard and honored the prayer that was offered in humility (the tax collector's). Jesus often called for humility and condemned those who exalted themselves.—Matthew 23:12; Luke 10:15; 14:11.

[948] Galileans on their way to Jerusalem traveled through Perea, a region on the east side of the Jordan River bordering Judea.

[949] When Jesus and the Perean Pharisees last encountered one another, they clashed about divorce. (Luke 16:18) This seems to have stuck in the Pharisees' minds. "Probably they also imagined, it would be easy to show on this point a marked difference between the teaching of Jesus and that of Moses and the Rabbis, and to enlist popular feeling against Him. ... Perhaps it may also have been in the hope that, by getting Christ to commit Himself against divorce in Peraea—the territory of Herod—they might enlist against Him, as formerly against the Baptist, the implacable hatred of Herodias."—Edersheim, page 704.

[950] Requiring a man who intended to divorce his wife to prepare a legal document gave him time to reconsider his decision. The intent of the Law was evidently to prevent frivolous divorces and to provide women with a measure of legal protection. (Deuteronomy 24:1, 3) Moses did not specify what constituted grounds for divorce; on this rabbinic opinion was divided. Conservative interpreters of Moses' law accepted only moral transgressions such as unchastity as grounds for divorce. Free-thinking theologians "declared it sufficient ground for divorce if a woman had spoiled her husband's dinner."—Edersheim, page 705.

[951] "God hates divorce, for it is a sin that is contrary to his intention for marriage—a permanent, lifelong, exclusive union. Yet he allowed, and even regulated, divorce in the Old Testament (though only because of human stubbornness). In the New Testament, while strongly reaffirming the ideal of a permanent covenant relationship, Jesus recognized the hardness of the human heart and the devastating impact of sin within human relationships, and he permitted divorce in cases of marital unfaithfulness."—Verlyn D. Verbrugge: *The NIV Topical Study Bible,* page 1036. See Malachi 2:15-16.

[952] Jesus gave three reasons against divorce: (1) God created one woman—and one woman only—for Adam; (2) God ordained marriage to be the strongest of human bonds, stronger even than the parent-child relationship; (3) marriage is a covenant, or contract, between two people who become one flesh or "one body [as though they were one person ...]." (**Mark 10:8**, *Expanded Bible)* The expression **one flesh** describes the closest bond possible between two humans. (**Matthew 19:5**; Ephesians 5:31) It not only refers to sexual intercourse but extends to the whole relationship, making the two individuals faithful and inseparable companions. Such a union cannot be broken up without damaging the partners bound by it.

[953] Or "fornication," all sexual intercourse that is unlawful according to the Bible.—Matthew 19:9, *King James Version.*

[954] Adultery is voluntary sexual intercourse by a married person with someone other than his or her mate. (Exodus 20:14; Matthew 5:27) Divorce "had not been provided for in the original institution [of marriage], which was a union to unity. Only one thing could put an end to that unity—its absolute breach. Hence, to divorce one's wife (or husband) while this unity lasted, and to marry another, was adultery, because, as the divorce was null before God, the original marriage still subsisted—and, in that case, the Rabbinic Law would also have forbidden it.... Jewish Law, which regarded marriage with a woman divorced under any circumstances as unadvisable ..., absolutely forbade that of the adulterer with the adulteress...."—Edersheim, page 706.

[955] Jesus recognized the right of a woman to divorce an unfaithful husband—something that his male contemporaries could not accept. To Jewish men, a husband committing adultery against his wife was an alien concept. The Pharisees did not ask Jesus, 'Is it legal for a couple to divorce for any reason they want?' Their question was: **Is it legal for a man to divorce his wife for any reason he wants? (Matthew 19:3; Mark 10:2)** Rabbis taught that only a woman could be unfaithful. For that reason, and because divorce would leave a woman without financial support, few Jewish wives initiated such action against their husbands. In Christianity, however, the same standard would apply to men and women.

[956] Some men are born "incapable of marriage"; others are eunuchs "because they have been castrated." (Matthew 19:12, *New English Bible; Complete Jewish Bible)* Such men were often appointed in royal courts as attendants or caretakers of the queen and the concubines. The term also refers to a man who was, not a literal eunuch, but an official assigned to duties in the court of the king. (Esther 2:15; Acts 8:27) Jesus used the term figuratively for a Christian—male or female—who remains unmarried **for the Kingdom of Heaven**. (**Matthew 19:12**; compare 1 Corinthians 7:7-8) Jesus' words do not constitute a "command of celibacy"; they describe those persons "who in the active service of the Kingdom feel, that their every thought is so engrossed in the work, that wishes and impulses to marriage are no longer existent in them."—Edersheim, page 707.

[957] Jesus exceeded the expectations of the adults who brought these children to him so that he might merely touch them; Jesus embraced the children (a detail found only in Mark).

[958] Referred to as a "ruler" at Luke 18:18, the man may have been the director of a synagogue or a member of the Sanhedrin.

[959] "The command to love is the summary of the Ten Commandments."—Verlyn D. Verbrugge: *The NIV Topical Study Bible*, page 198. See Matthew 22:37-40; Romans 13:10; Galatians 5:14; James 2:8.

[960] The Rabbis described the miseries of poverty as "worse than all the plagues of Egypt put together." (Edersheim, page 710 note 9) Possibly Jesus realized that the man would need to cultivate a greater degree of self-sacrifice to become a disciple. For someone who obeyed all of God's laws—including the command to love one's neighbor—giving his wealth to needy people should not have been difficult. Divesting oneself of all material possessions is generally not a Christian requirement. Concern for the needy is, nevertheless, expected of Christians—especially wealthy ones.—1 Timothy 6:17-18.

[961] Jesus' call for sacrifice comes with the promise of **treasure in heaven**. Jesus was not introducing a new requirement for salvation in telling the man to sell everything he had and give all the money to poor people. Jesus was testing the man's responsiveness to God's direction through Him. (**Matthew 19:21; Mark 10:21; Luke 18:22**; compare Luke 19:8-10) While the rich man was probably sincere, he had confined his righteousness to external obedience. Internally he loved money more than God.

[962] Or "rope." (Matthew 19:24; Mark 10:25; Luke 18:25, *The Passion Translation)* In Jesus' day, the camel (probably the Arabian camel) was the largest domesticated animal in the region.

[963] As a literal camel cannot go through the eye of an actual needle, a wealthy person who puts riches ahead of a relationship with God cannot enter the Kingdom. Material possessions that the young ruler could not part with were preventing him from serving God completely. Instead of continuing to be a highly respected rich man, he would become a materially poor follower of the generally despised Jesus. That was too high a cost for gaining the perfection of which Jesus spoke. (Matthew 19:21) Nevertheless, **with God anything is possible**, so a wealthy person could inherit the Kingdom.—**Matthew 19:26**; **Mark 10:27**; **Luke 18:27**; compare 1 Timothy 6:17.

[964] At that time the ruling class was made up of rich people; their wealth was considered a sign of God's blessing. (Deuteronomy 28:11-12) The disciples were asking, in effect, 'If the rich can't get into the Kingdom, who can?'

[965] Or "In the re-creation (regeneration; renewal)." (Note on Matthew 19:28, *New World Translation—Study Edition)* References in the New Testament to renewal of the world include Acts 3:21; 2 Peter 3:13 and Revelation 21:1-5.

[966] Or "judging." (Matthew 19:28, *King James Version)* Those who will rule with Christ in Heaven will also share with him in judging.—1 Corinthians 6:2; Revelation 20:4.

[967] Jesus did not mean that his followers must give up their possessions and renounce their families; they must reorder their priorities and make sacrifices for him.

[968] By means of the Mosaic Law, God introduced the Israelite or Jewish Age. Jesus Christ introduced the Gospel Age. In **the age to come**, that which the young ruler asked about, **eternal life** is promised. The investment made by Peter and the other disciples would yield rich dividends. Jesus does not deny rewards in the present age to his followers, but they must expect **persecution**.—**Mark 10:30**; **Luke 18:30**. See Matthew 10:39; 16:25; Mark 8:35; Luke 9:24; 17:33; John 12:25; Acts 20:24; Revelation 12:11.

[969] The rich young man, as one of Israel's leaders, was among the so-called **first**. As one who observed God's commandments, he showed much promise, and much might be expected of him. Yet he put wealth and possessions ahead of all else in life. In contrast, the common people saw in Jesus' teaching the truth and the way to life. They had been **last**, so to speak, but came to be first.—**Matthew 19:30**; compare Luke 16:25. See "Into the Vineyard" for an alternate interpretation of Jesus' illustration.

[970] Specifically, a denarius. This Roman coin weighed about 0.124 ounces troy (3.85 g) and bore an image of Caesar on one side.

[971] Some marketplaces were located along a road where the unemployed could wait to be hired.

[972] Only the first-hired workers were promised a specific wage. Those subsequently hired were told only that they would receive what was **fair** for their work.—**Matthew 20:4**.

[973] Apparently satisfied with what they received, those hired at the third, sixth and ninth hours did not complain about their wages. They had made no bargain with the employer, trusting him to be fair.

[974] Spitting on a person or in the face was an act of extreme contempt, enmity or indignation, bringing humiliation on the victim. (Numbers 12:14; Deuteronomy 25:9) Such treatment had been foretold for the Messiah.—Isaiah 50:6; compare Mark 14:65; 15:19

[975] Or "flogging"; "scourging"; "torturing." (Luke 18:33, *English Standard Version; A Faithful Version; Common English Bible)* This punishment was inflicted with a flagellum, an instrument consisting of a handle into which several cords or leather thongs were fixed. These thongs were weighted with jagged pieces of bone or metal to make the blows more painful.

[976] Twice before Jesus foretold his death and resurrection. This time, however, he said that he would be executed. After the first prediction, Jesus rebuked Peter for being the Devil's advocate. (Matthew 16:21-23; Mark 8:31-33) After the second prediction, the apostles argued over which of them would be greatest in the Kingdom. (Matthew 17:22-23; 18:1; Mark 9:31-34) After the third prediction, James and John asked for positions of co-rulership with Christ over a restored kingdom of Israel (or the future Christian congregation, according to some scholars).—Luke 19:11; Acts 1:6.

[977] The apostles could not reconcile their expectations of a glorious Deliverer with the ignominious treatment foreseen by Jesus. They did not understand the implications of the Messiah's suffering and death until the resurrected Christ explained matters to them.—Luke 24:25-27, 32, 44-47.

[978] It would appear that James and John inherited their brazen zeal from their mother. (Mark 3:17; 9:38; Luke 9:54) Although the place of greatest honor is always on the right, both positions—on the right and on the left hand—indicate honor and authority.—1 Peter 3:22.

[979] In the Bible, "cup" is often used figuratively of God's will for a person, and to drink the cup means to submit to God's will. (Psalm 11:6; 16:5; 23:5; 75:8; Matthew 26:39, 42; Mark 14:36; Luke 22:42; John 18:11) Jesus' "cup" involved not only suffering and death under false charges but also resurrection to immortal life in Heaven. Jesus used the term **cup** in parallel with **baptism**. (**Mark 10:38-39**) He referred to baptism into death, not water baptism. (Romans 6:3-5) "[T]he phrase about *baptism* ... alludes to the ancient picture of the sufferer as a victim of overwhelming 'waves' of tribulation; compare Lk. 12.50."—M. Jack Suggs: *The New English Bible*, Mark 10:38 footnote.

[980] Whatever love Jesus may have had for John, he did not give him a favored position in his Kingdom. (John 21:20, 24) Unlike his brother James and most of the apostles, John was not martyred. (Acts 12:2) He nevertheless shared in his Master's sufferings.—Revelation 1:9.

[981] "Christ's mission on earth is not to apportion men's rewards but to suffer for man's salvation."—Matthew chapter 20 note f, *The Jerusalem Bible:* Edited by Alexander Jones. See John 3:17; 12:47.

[982] Or "minister," one who does not let up in humbly rendering service on behalf of others. (Matthew 20:26; Mark 10:43, *King James Version)* In the Christian congregation, "the key to true leadership is service. Jesus himself ruled out the abuse of power by the Christian leader; rather, leaders must see themselves as humble servants, imitating Christ who humbly served God and the human race. For their part, God's people ought to honor, obey and respect the leaders God has placed over them."—Verlyn D. Verbrugge: *The NIV Topical Study Bible*, page 1069. See 1 Corinthians 16:16; Hebrews 13:7, 17.

[983] Or "ransom," a price paid to release those under bond or in slavery or to free prisoners of war. (Matthew 20:28; Mark 10:45, *King James Version)* Jesus' life was the price paid to redeem all sinners who demonstrate faith in him.—John 3:16; 6:40, 47; 20:31; Romans 3:24-25; 1 John 5:13.

[984] "Jesus turned the values of his day upside down when he suggested that serving is the road to greatness. Jesus was obedient to his Father's will his entire life, even to his death .... His death paid the price for us, freeing us to give total obedience to the loving Lord of the universe. Jesus wants us to serve him by serving others, recognizing that whatever we do for one of God's children we do for him. In our service we are to have the same humble, gentle, giving attitude that characterized Jesus."—Verlyn D. Verbrugge: *The NIV Topical Study Bible*, page 790. See Matthew 25:40.

[985] Jericho is about a day's journey (17 mi; 27.3 km) from Jerusalem. About a mile (1.6 km) south of this ancient city was a newer Roman city also called Jericho. Perhaps Jesus performed the miracle while leaving one Jericho (per Matthew 20:29 and Mark 10:46) and approaching the other Jericho (says Luke 18:35). Another possible explanation for the seeming discrepancy: "... the blind men made application when he was approaching the city, but were not then healed, and only when he had left the city were then healed. (Comp. Matt. 15:23 ff., and Mark 8:22 f.)"—Robertson, page 149.

[986] **Nazarene** was a descriptive epithet applied to Jesus and later to his followers. (**Mark 10:47**; **Luke 18:37**; Acts 24:5) The practice of associating people with the places from which they came was customary in Bible times.

[987] Addressing Jesus as the **Son of David**, the two blind men openly acknowledged him as the Messiah. (**Matthew 20:30-31**; **Mark 10:47-48**; **Luke 18:38-39**; see "Jesus, A.K.A. ...") The blind men, with spiritual insight, could see in Jesus what most sighted persons could not.

[988] Or "your faith has delivered you [from your disability]."—Luke 18:42, *Open English Bible.*

[989] To begin following Jesus at this point, with his ordeal at Jerusalem so near, was an act of courageous discipleship.—Luke 19:11.

[990] The head tax collector oversaw other tax collectors in and around Jericho. The district around this city was fertile and productive, yielding considerable tax revenue. Zacchaeus became rich by extorting money in the performance of his duties.

[991] Luke 19:4 is the only mention of the sycamore tree (or fig-mulberry tree) in the New Testament. Sycamore trees were frequently planted along roadsides because their thick, wide-spreading foliage provide good shade. They have short, stout trunks with lower limbs that branch out close to the ground—an easy climb for a short-statured man like Zacchaeus.

[992] This was a common complaint against Jesus. (Matthew 9:11; Mark 2:16; Luke 7:37-39; 15:1-2) The people despised Zacchaeus, who had enriched himself at their expense. (Compare Luke 3:12-13) Israelites generally avoided voluntary association with tax collectors and classified them with prostitutes and foreigners. (Matthew 9:10; 11:19; 18:17; 21:32; Mark 2:15; Luke 5:30; 7:34) They also resented tax collectors for their service to a Gentile power (Rome).

[993] A fourfold restitution was more than Israel's law required. In such cases of repentance and admission of guilt, the defrauder had to pay back the full amount plus twenty percent. (Leviticus 6:4-5; Numbers 5:7) Zacchaeus demonstrated the sincerity of his repentance by showing love for the poor and justice toward the oppressed.

[994] Literally, "took by fig-showing." (Luke 19:8, *Kingdom Interlinear Translation of the Greek Scriptures)* Exporting figs was prohibited in ancient Athens. Someone who denounced others by accusing them of attempting to export figs was called a "fig-shower." The term came to designate a person who accused others falsely for the sake of gain, or a blackmailer. (Luke 3:14) Interestingly, the fig-shower Zacchaeus climbed a "fig-mulberry tree."—Luke 19:4, *New World Translation of the Holy Scriptures—with References.*

[995] The "specific design" of this parable was "to check the wild enthusiasm of the multitude to make Jesus King in Jerusalem as they had once planned a year ago (John 6:15)." (Robertson, page 150) Christ may have spoken this parable to his followers "to teach them that the relation in which Jerusalem stood towards Him, and its fate, were quite different from what they imagined, and that His Entrance into the City and the Advent of His Kingdom would be separated by a long distance of time. Hence the prospect before them was that of working, not of reigning; after that would the reckoning come, when the faithful worker would become the trusted ruler."—Edersheim, page 795.

[996] The parable had a popular plot. It was not uncommon in the Roman Empire for a person of noble birth to travel to Rome in quest for royal power. See "Biographical Sketch: Herod Archelaus."

[997] The piece of silver money was a mina—not a coin but a unit of weight of some 10.9 ounces troy (340 g). One silver mina amounted to three- or four-months' wages.

[998] "Faithfulness is commended and rewarded with greater opportunity," Nelson observes. "Unfaithfulness," however, "results in loss of reward." (Luke 19:17 & 19:26 footnotes, *The Nelson Study Bible*. Copyright © 1997 by Thomas Nelson, Inc. Used with permission.) See Revelation 3:11, 21.

[999] During the Roman siege and destruction of Jerusalem, 1,100,000 rebels lost their lives, and 97,000 survivors were led away captive. This foreshadowed the worldwide slaughter of all those who do not want Jesus as Earth's new king at his second presence. In fulfillment of his parable about the minas, the resurrected Christ will command the angels to bring his worldly enemies before him and to execute them as irreconcilable opposers to the Kingdom.—Psalm 110:1-2; Hebrews 10:12-13.

[1000] Perhaps they touched a dead body or did something else that made them ritually unclean according to Israel's law.—Numbers 9:6.

[1001] Perhaps Jesus' enemies were trying to ascertain where he was staying so they could arrest him before he appeared publicly in the Temple.—Matthew 26:5; Mark 14:2.

[1002] The trip from Jericho to Bethany involves a climb of some 12 miles (20 km) over difficult terrain. Jericho is about 820 feet (250 m) below sea level, and Bethany is about 2,000 feet (610 m) above sea level.

[1003] Perhaps Simon was a former leper whom Jesus had at some point healed. It has also been suggested that Simon was the father of Lazarus, Martha and Mary. Simon's home was chosen to hold this banquet for some unstated reason. Maybe his guest-chamber was the largest in Bethany, or his house was nearest to the Synagogue.

[1004] A Roman pound was about 11.5 ounces (327 g). Alabaster is a translucent stone still used to make valuable items such as ornamented jewelry boxes. Nard is a reddish-colored oil derived from the spikenard plant found in the Himalayas in India. (Song of Solomon 1:12; 4:13-14) Because it was expensive, nard was often adulterated with inferior oils and sometimes counterfeited. Mary's oil, however, was pure.

[1005] "To pour ointment on the *head* was common," according to *Barnes' Notes on the New Testament*. However, "to pour it on the *feet* was an act of distinguished *humility* and attachment to the Saviour, and therefore deserved to be particularly recorded." (https://biblehub.com/commentaries/barnes/matthew/26.htm) Anointing Jesus' feet was "the act of greatest humility and the mark of deepest veneration," says Edersheim. "She who had so often sat at His feet, now anoints them."—pages 721-22 note 18; Luke 10:39.

[1006] Alabaster cases were flasks with narrow necks that could be sealed to prevent the precious perfume from leaking. Instead of unsealing the top, Mary broke off the neck of the case. This released all the perfume at once, filling the house with fragrance.

[1007] Literally, "three hundred denarii." (Mark 14:5; John 12:5, *The Darby Bible)* This sizable amount of money (200 denarii nearly sufficed to provide bread for 5,000 men and their families; John 6:7) would have gone into the money box kept by the embezzler Judas Iscariot. Possibly for thematic reasons, in Matthew and Mark Judas' offer to betray Christ to the priests follows the episode of Simon's feast. One example of Judas' greed is thus linked with the ultimate expression of it.—Matthew 26:6-16; Mark 14:3-11.

[1008] Opportunities to help the poor are never lacking, and Jesus encouraged those who could do so to meet their needs. (Deuteronomy 15:11; Matthew 19:21; Mark 10:21; Luke 18:22) However, he wanted people to give freely and of their own volition—like Mary did.

[1009] Anointing the dead with perfumed oil and ointments was the first step in preparing the body for burial. (2 Chronicles 16:14; John 19:39-40) "Christ sees Mary's act as a gesture of respect offered to his dead body before the time; it is a symbol of his actual burial, [John] 19:38f." (John chapter 12 note b, *The Jerusalem Bible:* Edited by Alexander Jones) "Her faith made it a twofold anointing: that of the best Guest at the last feast, and that of preparation for that Burial which ... she apprehended as so terribly near." (Edersheim, page 721) "The expensive oil points to (1) the value of Jesus' death and (2) the high cost of devotion to him."—Matthew 26:12 footnote, *The Nelson Study Bible.* Copyright © 1997 by Thomas Nelson, Inc. Used by permission.

[1010] Or "What she has done for me is one of the good works indeed!" (Matthew 26:10, *The Jerusalem Bible)* "The Jews divided 'good works' into 'almsgiving' and 'charitable deeds'; the latter were reckoned superior and included, among other pious acts, the burial of the dead. The woman, therefore, by making provision for Christ's burial, has performed a 'work' greater than almsgiving. Jesus seems to suggest ... that some loving instinct has given her a presentiment of the real significance of her action."—Matthew chapter 26 note b, *The Jerusalem Bible:* Edited by Alexander Jones.

[1011] Later rabbinic literature states, "The fragrance of good oil is diffused from the bedroom to the dining hall, but a good name is diffused from one end of the world to the other." *(Ecclesiastes Rabbah* 7.1.1) Mary's act of devotion was renown by the end of the first century when the Gospel of John was most likely written.—John 11:2.

[1012] Lazarus was living proof of the resurrection doctrine that Sadducees denied. (Acts 23:8) "The raising of Lazarus is linked by these verses [John 12:9-11] to the messianic entry in vv. 12-19; in Jewish tradition, the advent of the Messiah was related to the resurrection of the dead." (David M. Stanley: John 12:9-11 footnote, *The New English Bible)* The Gospel of John makes no further mention of the plot against Lazarus; it apparently never got past the planning stage.

[1013] Zion is another name for Jerusalem.—Isaiah 62:11.

[1014] Tradition locates the village of Bethphage between Bethany and Jerusalem at et-Tur, on the southeast slope of the Mount of Olives. From this point it is a short distance to one of the peaks of the Mount of Olives. Descending from there, Jesus would have had the city of Jerusalem in full view.—Luke 19:41.

[1015] The impressment of animals for service to a significant person was allowed by Roman law. Also, the people of Bethany were evidently anticipating Jesus' arrival and expecting him to enter Jerusalem. For permission from the animals' owner for their use all the apostles had to say was, "The Lord needs them."—Matthew 21:3, *Free Bible Version;* Mark 11:5-6; Luke 19:33-34.

[1016] Solomon, the son of David, rode to his anointing on his father's mule. (1 Kings 1:33, 38) Jesus, the one greater than Solomon, fulfilled the prophecy of Zechariah 9:9 by riding on a young donkey. (Matthew 12:42; 21:4-5; Luke 11:31; John 12:14-15) This colt had never been ridden before, and so met "the general conditions of consecration to Jehovah (Num. 19:2; Deut. 21:3)."—Edersheim, page 726.

[1017] "The announcement, that disciples of Jesus had just fetched the beast of burden on which Jesus was about to enter Jerusalem, must have quickly spread among the crowds which thronged the Temple and the City. As the two disciples, accompanied, or immediately followed by the multitude, brought 'the colt' to Christ, 'two streams of people met'—the one coming from the City, the other from Bethany."—Edersheim, page 727; Mark 11:9.

[1018] Psalm 118:26, Young's *Literal Translation.* "This was a Day of Triumph that seemed to the excited crowds to mean the establishment of a political Messianic Kingdom." (Robertson, page 152) The action of spreading garments on the road was like that undertaken at King Jehu's anointing. (2 Kings 9:13) The use of palm branches by the crowd symbolized their praise for and submission to Jesus as Israel's king. (Compare Leviticus 23:40; Revelation 7:9-10) On this and other solemn occasions Psalm 118 was the last of the Hallel Psalms (113-118) chanted.

[1019] Even creation knew what was taking place, yet the Pharisees missed it. "Stones bearing witness when sin has been committed" was a common expression. (Edersheim, page 729; compare Habakkuk 2:11) If the disciples had been forced into silence at this time, the literal stones would have cried out to fulfill Psalm 118:26. God's words do not return to him unfulfilled. (Isaiah 55:11) At this time Jesus no longer discouraged or avoided public expressions of acclaim.—Matthew 8:4; 9:30; 12:16; 16:20; 17:9; Mark 1:44; 3:12; 5:43; 7:36; 8:30; 9:9; Luke 9:21; John 6:15; 7:2-9.

[1020] For failing to recognize God's "visitation" in Jesus, Jerusalem will receive divine "visitation" in judgment.—Luke 19:44, *King James Version;* compare Luke 1:68, 78.

[1021] Jesus' words came true in A.D. 70 when the Romans erected a siege wall, or palisade, around Jerusalem.

[1022] Jesus was probably in the part of the Temple called the Court of the Gentiles. Some claim that tradition barred blind and lame ones from access to certain parts of the Temple, although the Scriptures do not specifically mention such a prohibition.

[1023] These youngsters, perhaps children of the Levites, may have acted as choirsters in the Temple.

[1024] Literally, "Hosanna," a plea to God for salvation or victory; in time, it became an expression of both prayer and praise. (Matthew 21:9, 15; Mark 11:9; John 12:13, *King James Version)* The Hebrew expression—meaning, "save, now, pray"—is found at Psalm 118:25, which was part of the Hallel Psalms sung regularly during Passover season. Therefore, these words readily came to mind on this occasion. One way God answered this prayer to save the Son of David was by resurrecting him from the dead. At Matthew 21:42, Jesus quoted Psalm 118:22-23 and applied it to the Messiah.—*The New Compact Bible Dictionary,* page 233.

[1025] Passover season is too early for fig trees to bear fruit. However, small, edible buds appear in spring before the leaves sprout. This tree, like Jerusalem and its beautiful Temple, looked promising, but was empty. Interestingly, the name of nearby Bethphage means "house of unripe figs."—*The New Compact Bible Dictionary,* page 80.

[1026] During Passover week Jesus and the apostles spent their nights in Bethany, perhaps with Lazarus and his sisters or with Simon the Leper. At least on Sunday night, however, they may have camped outside, because Jesus apparently ate no breakfast Monday morning. Compare Luke 21:37.

[1027] The nation of Israel was in a covenant relationship with God but barren of the fruitage of faith in his Son. By causing the unproductive fig tree to wither, Jesus demonstrated the ultimate end for the fruitless, faithless nation. (Compare Luke 13:6-9) On the following day, Jesus used the withered tree as an object lesson in faith as the basis for answered prayer. Compare Matthew 17:20; Luke 17:6.

[1028] More specifically, the part of the complex called the Court of the Gentiles.

[1029] Evidently, some used the courtyard as a shortcut to transport items for personal or commercial use. This detracted from the sanctity of God's house. Evicting the merchants and their customers, Jesus again asserted his authority over the Temple as the Messiah, as he had at the beginning of his ministry. Again, his authority was challenged.—John 2:13-16.

[1030] Jerusalem's Temple was meant to be "a house of prayer for all peoples," where both Israelites and God-fearing foreigners could worship and pray to the True God. (Isaiah 56:7, *American Standard Version;* 1 Kings 8:41-43) The actions of those who used the Temple for commerce discouraged others from approaching God in his house of prayer, depriving them of the opportunity to come to know him.

[1031] Jesus' words alluded to Jeremiah 7:11: "Has this house, which is called by my name, become a den of robbers in your eyes? Behold, I, even I, have seen it, says Jehovah." *(A Conservative Version* by Dr. Walter L. Porter) The merchants and money changers were making unjust profit from selling animals for sacrifice and charging exorbitant fees for exchanging currencies. (Foreign monies with pagan symbols were unacceptable as donations to the Temple.) Jesus was indignant that this place of worship had been turned into a center for commercial activity.

[1032] These foreigners were "Greeks." (John 12:20, *King James Version)* The word has a broad meaning in the New Testament; it may refer to Gentiles or to Hellenists (those who were influenced by Greek language and culture) who converted to Judaism. Had they been proselytes, however, these "Greeks" would probably not have been referred to as such. Foreigners who were not proselytes attended Jerusalem's religious festivals. (Acts 8:27) Out of all the apostles, why did the Greeks approach Phillip? Perhaps they identified with his Hellenistic name.

[1033] "Perhaps we should regard the opening words as bearing reference to the request of the Greeks, and hence as primarily addressed to the disciples (John 12:23), but also as serving as introduction to the words that follow, which were spoken primarily to the Greeks (vv. 24-26), but secondarily also to the disciples and which bear on that terrible, ever near, mystery of His Death, and their Baptism into it. ... The hour of decision was about to strike. Not merely as the Messiah of Israel, but in His world-wide bearing as 'the Son of Man,' as He about to be glorified by receiving the homage of the Gentile world, of which the symbol and the first fruits were now before Him. But only in one way could He thus be glorified: by dying for the salvation of the world, and so opening the Kingdom of Heaven to all believers."—Edersheim, page 743.

[1034] If one grain of wheat is put into the soil and **dies** as a seed, it can germinate and in time grow into a productive stalk with many grains. Similarly, one man—Jesus—by his faithfulness to death, will become the means of imparting eternal life to those with a similar spirit of self-sacrifice. (**John 12:24**) Rather than satisfy the curiosity of the Greeks, Jesus recommended following his self-sacrificing course, refusing to be distracted from the more important matters that lay ahead. It may be assumed that Philip carried Jesus' positive message back to the inquirers.

[1035] This is the last of three instances in the gospels where God is reported as speaking directly to humans. The first instance occurred at Jesus' baptism. (Matthew 3:16-17; Mark 1:11; Luke 3:22) The second instance was in connection with Jesus' transfiguration. (Matthew 17:5; Mark 9:7; Luke 9:35) This third instance is mentioned only in the Gospel of John.

[1036] In essence, this is Jesus' answer to the Greeks' request to meet him. Jesus will draw to himself people of all backgrounds, regardless of nationality, race or economic status.—John 6:44; Acts 10:34-35; Revelation 7:9-10.

[1037] For Jesus' listeners (and for all who read his words) there is a finite period to accept him as the Messiah. (Compare Isaiah 55:6) When that time is up comes **darkness** (death). One's response to the **Light** determines if one will become one of **his children**, a person to whom God reveals the truth and who lives according to that truth.—**John 12:35-36.**

[1038] According to John 12:38-40 those who disregarded Jesus fulfilled ancient prophecy: "Jehovah, who has believed our message? And to whom has the arm of Jehovah been revealed?" "The heart of this people has grown dull, and their ears sluggish, and they have closed their eyes, otherwise they might see with their eyes, and hear with their ears, and understand with their heart, and turn back, and I would heal them." (Isaiah 6:10; 53:1, *New Heart English Bible*—Jehovah Edition) Even some members of the Sanhedrin believed in Jesus. (Luke 23:50-51; John 3:1-2; 19:38) But they would not acknowledge him for fear of being expelled from the synagogue. Those rulers esteemed praise from their peers more highly than glory from God.—John 12:42-43.

[1039] Tuesday, Nisan 11 was the last day of Christ's public ministry.

[1040] **This mountain** referred to the Mount of Olives, on which they were standing. (**Matthew 21:21; Mark 11:23**) Strictly speaking, the Mount of Olives is not a mountain but a ridge that runs north to south about 1.8 mi (3 km) across the Kidron Valley; its central elevation is 100 ft (30 m) higher than Jerusalem.

[1041] The Sanhedrin was composed of chief priests, scholars and community leaders (or elders). (Mark 11:27; Luke 20:1; see also Matthew 26:3, 47, 57; 27:1, 41; 28:11-12) Chief priests were principal men of the priesthood, including former high priests and, possibly, the heads of the 24 priestly divisions. Scholars, also called scribes, were teachers of and experts in the Law of Moses. Elders were active in public affairs, both on a community level (Luke 7:3-5) and on a national level.

[1042] In Jesus' day, no one without rabbinic authorization dared to teach. The day after Jesus cleansed the Temple of commercialism, these authorities sought to verify his credentials.

[1043] "And so, their cunning and cowardice stood out self-condemned, when they pleaded ignorance—a plea so grossly and manifestly dishonest, that Christ, having given what all must have felt to be a complete answer, could refuse further discussion with them on this point."—Edersheim, page 738.

[1044] Religious service of itself does not result in God's approval, nor does a past life of sin prevent a sinner from gaining God's approval. (Matthew 7:21-23; 1 Corinthians 6:9-11) As far as the self-righteous religious leaders were concerned, tax collectors and prostitutes were spiritually lost. They, however, showed a readiness to obey (like the second son), whereas the religious leaders (like the first son) did not. Repentant ones showed a willingness to serve God even before those who professed to be doing his work.—Matthew 23:2-3.

[1045] In Israel, gathered grapes were usually placed in limestone vats or troughs cut into rock. The wine vat consisted of two levels, the juice flowing from the upper one to the lower. Men normally crushed the grapes barefoot, singing songs as they trod the winepress.—Isaiah 16:10.

[1046] The vineyard would have been fenced in by a stone wall (Proverbs 24:30-31) or by a hedge. (Isaiah 5:5) The watchtower was used as a vantage point to guard vineyards against thieves and animals. (Isaiah 5:2) The vineyard's owner had done everything to ensure a good yield of fruit, making his expectation of a return even more reasonable.

[1047] Sometimes the cultivators received a portion of the fruits. In other cases, cultivators paid rent or gave the owner a portion of the produce, the latter apparently being the case in Jesus' illustration.

[1048] The vinedressers hoped that with the son dead and his father out of the country, the inheritance would fall to those who worked the property.

[1049] "The owner of the vineyard, God, had let out His Vineyard—the Theocracy—to His people of old. The covenant having been instituted, He withdrew, as it were—the former direct communication between Him and Israel ceased. Then in due season He sent 'His Servants,' the prophets, to gather His fruits—they had had theirs in all the temporal and spiritual advantages of the covenant. But, instead of returning the fruits meet unto repentance, they only ill-treated His messengers, and that increasingly, even unto death. [Matthew 21:34-36] In His longsuffering He next sent on the same errand 'greater' than them—John the Baptist (Luke 7:26). And when he also received the same treatment, He sent last His own Son, Jesus Christ. His appearance made them feel, that it was now a decisive struggle for the Vineyard—and so, in order to gain its possession for themselves, they cast the rightful heir out of His own possession, and then killed Him!"—Edersheim, page. 767.

[1050] Jesus ministered to people from Syria, Decapolis and Perea; he praised the faith of a Roman centurion and a Canaanite woman. He also foresaw a time when the Kingdom would be taken away from Israel and "given to a nation bringing forth its fruit." The apostle Peter identified that new nation as the worldwide Christian congregation, applying to his fellow believers words that had been directed to Israel. (1 Peter 2:9; compare Exodus 19:5-6) The Great Commission to "disciple all the nations" is as relevant today as it was 2,000 years ago.—Matthew 21:43; 28:19, Young's *Literal Translation*.

[1051] "The neglect and non-belief which had appeared in the former Parable [about the father with two sons] have now ripened into rebellion, deliberate, aggravated, and carried to its utmost consequences in the murder of the King's only and loved Son. Similarly, what formerly appeared as [the Israelite leaders'] loss, in that sinners went into the Kingdom of God before them, is now presented alike as their guilt and their judgment, both national and individual."—Edersheim, page 766.

[1052] As the topmost stone of a building is conspicuous, so Jesus Christ is the crowning stone of the Christian congregation, which is likened to a spiritual temple.—Acts 4:11; Ephesians 2:20-21; 1 Peter 2:5-7.

[1053] Since Jesus introduced his story by mentioning the kingdom of Heaven, the king must be God. The king's son is Jesus, and those invited are the ones who will be with the Son in the kingdom of Heaven. (Compare Matthew 25:1-10; Revelation 19:9) The first invitees were Israelites, to whom Jesus and the apostles had been preaching about the Kingdom. (Matthew 10:6-7; 15:24) Most Israelites were unwilling to accept Jesus as the Messiah. They spurned the opportunity to be in the Kingdom and abused Jesus' followers—servants of the king. Gentiles eventually came in line for a place in the Kingdom. (Acts 4:13-18; 10:45) In A.D. 70 the Romans destroyed Jerusalem, Israel's foremost city.

[1054] "The first invitation had been sent to selected guests—to the Jews—who might have been expected to be 'worthy,' but had proved themselves unworthy; the next was to be given, not to the chosen city or nation, but to all that travelled *[sic]* in whatever direction on the world's highway, reaching them where the roads of life meet and part." (Edersheim, page 770; Matthew 22:8) These repeated endeavors to call, to admonish and to invite are also characteristic of the two previous parables. One of the central objects of Jesus' teaching was to exhibit God's patience and goodness.

[1055] "The 'Servants'—that is, the New Testament messengers—had ... brought in as many as they found, both bad and good: that is, without respect to their previous history, or their moral and religious state up to the time of their call .... [W]e must not expect on earth—not even at the King's marriage table—a pure Church."—Edersheim, page 770.

[1056] Since this was a royal wedding, it may be that a special garment was provided by the royal host for his guests. Failure to wear it would show great disrespect for the host. The guest's unwillingness to dress properly for the occasion also showed his unwillingness to adorn his faith with good works.—Matthew 3:8; 5:20; 7:21.

[1057] "Many are called out of the world by God to partake of the Gospel-feast, but few out of the world—not, out of the called—are chosen by God to partake of it. The call to the feast and the choice for the feast are not identical. The call comes to all; but it may be outwardly accepted, and a man may sit down to the feast, and yet he may not be chosen to partake of the feast, because he has not the wedding-garment of converting, sanctifying grace. And so one may be thrust even from the marriage-board into the darkness without, with its sorrow and anguish."—Edersheim, page 771.

[1058] Herodians were "supporters of the Herodian dynasty, ... the most suitable people to report to the Roman authorities what they hoped to induce Jesus to say against Caesar." (Matthew chapter 22 note c, *The Jerusalem Bible:* Edited by Alexander Jones) "If it could have been proved, on undeniable testimony, that Jesus had declared Himself on the side of, or even encouraged, the so-called 'Nationalist' party, He would have quickly perished, like Judas of Galilee." (Edersheim, page 738; see Acts 5:37) The Herodians included Sadducees; they joined with the Pharisees—their political opposites—to oppose Jesus.—Mark 3:6. Compare Matthew 16:11 with Mark 8:15.

[1059] The Roman emperor during Jesus' earthly ministry was Tiberius. However, the term **Caesar** could refer to the Roman civil authority, or the State and its duly appointed representatives. (**Matthew 22:17**; **Mark 12:14**; **Luke 20:22**) The question referred to an annual poll tax (probably amounting to a denarius) which Rome levied on all her subjects who had been registered by census. (Luke 2:1-3) " ... the right of coinage implies the authority of levying taxes," says Edersheim, "and indeed constitutes such evidence of *de facto* government as to make it duty absolutely to submit to it." On the other hand, "there was a strong party in the land; with which, not only politically but religiously, many of the noblest spirits would sympathise *[sic]*, which maintained, that to pay the tribute-money to Caesar was virtually to own his royal authority, and so to disown that of Jehovah, Who alone was Israel's King." (Edersheim, page 739) Jesus was offered the alternative of popular disfavor or disloyalty to Rome.

[1060] For paying taxes to Rome, citizens used the silver denarius bearing the image of Caesar. On the front side of a common denarius of this time there was an image of the laurel-crowned head of Roman Emperor Tiberius and the inscription in Latin, "Tiberius Caesar, son of the Divine Augustus." On the reverse side appeared an image of Tiberius' mother Livia portrayed as a goddess of peace with the words "High Priest" (Pontifex Maximus). In accommodation to the Jewish conscience, the coins that the Roman emperors had struck specially for Palestine bore no image of any kind.—Mark 12:16 & Luke 20:24 footnotes, *The Nelson Study Bible*. Copyright © 1997 by Thomas Nelson, Inc. Used with permission.

[1061] Payment for services rendered by the secular government as well as the honor and relative subjection that is to be shown to such authorities belong to Caesar, the one whose image was imprinted on Roman currency. (Romans 13:1-7) However, Caesar did not have the right to ask anyone to dedicate or devote their life to him. Such dedication and devotion—wholehearted worship, whole-souled love, and complete, loyal obedience—belong to God, the one whose image is imprinted on humankind.—Genesis 1:26; Matthew 4:10; 22:37-38; Acts 5:29; Romans 14:8.

[1062] Nine resurrections are mentioned in the Bible, including the resurrection of Jesus. (1 Kings 17:21-22; 2 Kings 4:32-35; 13:20-21; Matthew 9:24-25; Luke 7:14-15; John 11:43-44; Acts 9:40; 20:9-12; 1 Corinthians 15:3-4) Before Christ was raised from the dead, the resurrection was "a matter of hope, not of faith: something to look forward to, not to look back upon. The isolated events recorded in the Old Testament, and the miracles of Christ ... were rather instances of resuscitation than of Resurrection." (Edersheim, page 748) Everyone besides Christ who rose from the dead died again.

[1063] This arrangement was known as brother-in-law, or levirate, marriage. (Genesis 38:8; Deuteronomy 25:5-6) Levirate marriage provided for widows who had no adult children to care for them; it also preserved the family name of the deceased, who would be the legal father of the first son of the second marriage.

[1064] According to the Sadducees, the law of levirate marriage applied only to engaged virgins, not to married women. The Pharisees, on the other hand, applied the law also to widows. This distinction adds meaning to the Sadducees' riddle; according to them the woman could have become the wife of only the seventh brother. The Sadducees were attacking both the Pharisees' interpretation of levirate marriage and the teaching of a resurrection from the dead, which they apparently found to be incompatible with monogamy.

[1065] If the Sadducees had understood what God said in the Scriptures and his miraculous works, they would have believed in the resurrection.

[1066] Sadducees did not accept the existence of **angels**. (Acts 23:8) They also made the mistake of assuming that life in **the coming age** will be as it is in **this age**.—**Luke 20:34-35**; see 1 Corinthians 15:50-53.

[1067] Jesus knew the Sadducees accepted only Moses' writings as inspired.

[1068] Long after the patriarchs had died, Jehovah was still their God. HIs deceased servants are still "living from his standpoint," since his purpose to resurrect them is so sure of fulfillment.—Luke 20:38 footnote, *New World Translation*. See Romans 4:17.

[1069] Most scholars were Pharisees, who believed in the resurrection of the dead.—Luke 20:39; Acts 23:6-9.

[1070] "As we conceive it, among those who listened to the brief but decisive passage between Jesus and the Sadducees were some 'Scribes'—... or, as they are also designated, 'lawyers,' 'teachers of the Law,' experts, expounders, practitioners of the Jewish Law. One of them, perhaps he who exclaimed: Beautifully said, Teacher! hastened to the knot of Pharisees, whom it requires no stretch of the imagination to picture gathered in the Temple on that day, and watching, with restless, ever foiled malice, the Saviour's every movement. As 'the Scribe' came up to them, he would relate how Jesus had literally 'gagged' and 'muzzled' the Sadducees... [Matthew 22:34; Mark 12:28]. There can be little doubt that the report would give rise to mingled feelings, in which that prevailing would be, that, although Jesus might thus have discomfited the Sadducees, He would be unable to cope with other questions, if only properly propounded by Pharisaic learning. And so we can understand how one of the number, perhaps the same Scribe, would volunteer to undertake the office; and how his question was, as St. Matthew [22:35] reports, in a sense really intended to 'tempt' Jesus."—Edersheim, page 752.

[1071] Israel's God is the True God; no false gods can compare to him. (Exodus 15:11; Deuteronomy 3:24; 2 Samuel 7:22; 1 Kings 8:23; 1 Chronicles 16:25-26; Psalm 96:4-5) He is **one** God, and his worshipers' love for him must be undivided. (**Mark 12:29, 32**) God's love is expressed thoughtfully and actively; it involves commitment and actions, not just emotions and feelings. Humans who show such love do so as a deliberate choice in imitation of God. (Ephesians 5:1-2) That is why humans can be commanded to show love, as in the two greatest commandments. The terms **heart**, **soul** and **might** are not mutually exclusive; they are used in an overlapping sense, emphasizing in the strongest possible way the need for complete and total love for God.—**Deuteronomy 6:5**.

[1072] "Heart" figuratively refers to the whole inner person, including a person's thinking, feelings, attitudes and motivations. (Deuteronomy 29:4; Psalm 26:2; 64:6) For this reason, where the Hebrew text uses the word "heart," the *Septuagint* often uses the Greek equivalent for "mind." Ancient Hebrew did not have a specific word for "mind," but this concept was often included in the word for **heart**.—**Matthew 22:37**; **Mark 12:30**; **Luke 10:27**.

[1073] Or "strength," including both physical prowess and mental or intellectual ability. (Deuteronomy 6:5, *The Darby Bible*) Jesus included the concept of "mind" when he quoted the Greatest Commandment. Matthew 22:37 uses "mind" but does not use "strength" in the same quotation. Luke 10:27 uses "heart," "soul," "strength" and "mind" to express the three Hebrew concepts of the original quotation.

[1074] **Burnt offerings** were completely burned by fire on the altar and presented in their entirety to God, with no part of the animal (bull, ram, male goat, turtledove or young pigeon) being eaten by the worshiper. (**Mark 12:33**; see Exodus 29:18) Jesus, as a figurative burnt offering, gave himself wholly, fully.

[1075] Messiah sits at Jehovah's right hand, the preeminent place of honor. Illustrating this relationship, the king's palace in Jerusalem was located to the right of the Temple.

[1076] Or "under your feet," that is, under Messiah's authority.—Psalm 110:1, *The Bible in Basic English.*

[1077] Jesus' countrymen were hoping for a human descendant of David to liberate them from Roman domination. Drawing on David's words, Jesus showed that the Messiah was David's Lord, more than a human ruler. After sitting at God's right hand, the Messiah will exercise his royal power. (1 Corinthians 15:24-25; Hebrews 10:12-13) At that time, everyone—David included—will confess Jesus as Lord.—Philippians 2:11.

[1078] These teachers of the Law were often dependent on people's gifts for their support. Some flaunted their position of respect and trust and took material advantage of their supporters, including widows.—Matthew 23:14; Mark 12:38, 40; Luke 20:46-47.

[1079] Instructions from scholars and Pharisees were to be obeyed because they took the Scriptures at face value. They valued more highly, however, their manufactured customs and expected everyone to follow them. Jesus warned people not to imitate the scholars and the Pharisees. Their actions appeared righteous, but their hearts were filled with unrighteousness.

[1080] The tassels on the Israelites' garments were a visual reminder of their sanctification to the True God. (Numbers 15:38-40; Deuteronomy 22:12) A phylactery is a small leather case containing strips of parchment on which four passages of Scripture are written: Exodus 13:1-10, 11-16; Deuteronomy 6:4-9; 11:13-21. After their exile in Babylon, Israelite males began to wear phylacteries on the left arm and forehead during morning prayer (except on festival days and the Sabbath). This practice had its origin in a literal interpretation of Exodus 13:9, 16 and Deuteronomy 6:8; 11:18. The Pharisees should have known, however, that more than outward adornment was intended. (See Proverbs 3:3; 6:20-21; 7:2-3) To give an impression of zeal for God's law, Pharisees enlarged their **phylacteries**, attaching superstitious reverence to them. They also made the **tassels** on their robes longer than anyone else's.—**Matthew 23:5**.

[1081] The front seats in the synagogue were apparently reserved for prominent individuals. These **places of honor** may have been located on or near the speaker's platform in full view of the congregation. (**Matthew 23:6**) Seating along the wall may have been occupied by people with status in the community, whereas others might have sat on mats on the floor. The seating arrangements in the synagogue were a constant reminder to those in attendance that some had greater status than others.

[1082] Literally meaning "my great one," **Rabbi** in common usage meant "Teacher." (**Matthew 23:7-8**; *The New Bible Dictionary*—2nd edition, page 1006; see John 1:38) Some learned men, scholars and Law teachers demanded to be addressed by this honorary title and punished those who neglected to do so.

[1083] Or "brothers."—Matthew 23:8, *Catholic Public Domain Version.*

[1084] Jesus prohibited applying the term **Father** as a formalistic or religious title of honor to humans.—**Matthew 23:9**.

[1085] A **Master**, or "Teacher," is a spiritual leader, one who provides guidance and instruction. (**Matthew 23:10**, *Catholic Public Domain Version)* Since no imperfect human can be the spiritual Master of true Christians, Jesus is the only one rightly bearing this title.

[1086] Referring to a Gentile convert to Judaism, a "proselyte."—Matthew 23:15, *King James Version.*

[1087] "The purpose of oaths of the type described was to guard against the profaning of the holy sanctuary or altar (and, ultimately, the name of God) by broken oaths; compare [Matthew] 5.33-37."—M. Jack Suggs: Matthew 23:16-22 footnote,

The New English Bible.

[1088] Under the Mosaic Law, the Israelites were to pay the tithe—one tenth—of their crops. (Leviticus 27:30; Deuteronomy 14:22) This was a tax that supported priests and Levites. Jesus did not contradict the tradition of tithing herbs, although the Law did not explicitly command it. The religious leaders focused on such minor details instead of promoting underlying principles of the Law, such as justice, mercy and faithfulness. (Micah 6:8) For those hypocrites, tithing was a duty carried out legalistically but without piety.

[1089] The gnat and the camel were unclean creatures to the Israelites. (Leviticus 11:4, 21-23) Religious leaders filtered their beverages so as not to be ceremonially defiled by a tiny gnat, while they completely disregarded the weightier matters of the Law, an action comparable to swallowing a much larger camel.

[1090] It was a custom in Israel to whitewash graves so that those passing by would not accidentally become ceremonially defiled through contact with a burial place. (Numbers 19:16) This whitewashing was done annually, one month before Passover.

[1091] Or "inwardly you are full of hypocrisy and far from *Torah*." (Matthew 23:28, *Complete Jewish Bible)* The Greek word for **lawlessness** includes the idea of violation of and contempt for laws, especially God's laws. (**Matthew 23:28**; 1 John 3:4) While the Pharisees were scrupulous when it came to ceremonial cleanness and outward appearance, they neglected their inner person.

[1092] Jesus used irony in foretelling that his enemies would kill him, as their ancestors killed God's prophets of former times.

[1093] These religious leaders were spiritual poison to those who were influenced by their wickedness.—Matthew 3:7; 12:34.

[1094] Jesus' statement embraced all the martyrs mentioned in the Old Testament, **from Abel**, listed in the first book Genesis (4:8), **to Zechariah**, mentioned in 2 Chronicles (24:20-21), that being the last book in the traditional Hebrew canon.—**Matthew 23:35**.

[1095] In A.D. 70 Roman armies destroyed Jerusalem and many thousands of Israelites perished. Jesus held these religious leaders accountable because they had the same murderous disposition as their ancestors. Compare Revelation 18:24.

[1096] Jesus painted a touching word picture, likening his concern for the people of Jerusalem to the protectiveness of a mother bird that is sheltering her young with her wings. (Luke 13:34) God cared for his ancient people "just as an eagle ... hovers over its fledglings, spreading out its wings." (Deuteronomy 32:11, *New World Translation*; also, Ruth 2:12; Psalm 17:8; 36:7; 61:4; 63:7; 91:4; Isaiah 31:5; Malachi 4:2) Jesus offered to his contemporaries similar motherly care, but Israel rejected him.

[1097] Or "And so your Temple will be abandoned and empty."—Matthew 23:38, *Today's English Version*. Compare Jeremiah 12:7; 22:5.

[1098] "Psalm 118 reflects the greeting of a priest to a group entering the temple. Jesus used the language of this psalm to illustrate God's greeting to Him." (Luke 13:35 footnote, *The Nelson Study Bible*. Copyright © 1997 by Thomas Nelson, Inc. Used with permission) Two days earlier, when the jubilant crowd was accompanying Jesus on his royal ride into Jerusalem, they quoted **Psalm 118:26** but Jerusalem's leaders did not accept Jesus as **the One coming in the name of Jehovah**. (Matthew 21:9, 15; Mark 11:10; Luke 19:37-39; John 12:12-13, 19) Therefore, Jesus would not present himself again in the flesh to them as the rightful heir of David at Jerusalem. And yet the day would arrive when he would come into the Kingdom and sit on the throne at God's right hand. (Hebrews 10:12-13) Then those who would discern the evidence of his presence would see him with eyes of faith and say, "Blessed is he who has come in the name of THE LORD JEHOVAH."—Matthew 23:39, *Aramaic Bible in Plain English*.

[1099] Those who heard Jesus condemn people who symbolically blew a trumpet when making charitable contributions may have been reminded of the noise that coins made as they were dropped into these trumpet-shaped treasury chests. (Matthew 6:2) The treasury was apparently located in the area called the Court of the Women. It is believed that the Temple also contained a major treasury where the money from the treasury chests was brought.

[1100] The widow contributed two lepton coins (called "mites" in the *King James Version* [Mark 12:42; Luke 21:2]). One lepton equaled 1/128 of a denarius (or six minutes of a day's wage) and was evidently the smallest copper or bronze coin used in Israel. For eight lepta (or one assarion coin) a person could purchase two sparrows, which were among the cheapest birds used for food. (Matthew 10:29) This widow had only half the amount needed to buy one sparrow, hardly enough for a single meal.

[1101] Josephus compared Herod's temple to a beautiful snowcapped mountain. According to Nelson, the "beautiful white marble stones with gold ornamentation reached one hundred feet high. Surrounding [the Temple] were colonnaded walkways, courtyards, and stairways that filled 20 acres of the most prominent landscape in all Jerusalem." The dedicated gifts decorating the Temple "included gold and silver-plated gates, grapevine clusters, and Babylonian linen tapestries which hung from the temple veil." (Mark 13:1-2 footnote; Luke 21:5 footnote, *The Nelson Study Bible.* Copyright © 1997 by Thomas Nelson, Inc. Used with permission) Jesus' apostles praised the splendid structure, its massive stones and rich offerings with which it was adorned, seemingly forgetful of his recent prediction of the Temple's desolation.—Matthew 23:37-39.

[1102] In A.D. 70 the Romans demolished Jerusalem and its Temple. Apart from a few sections of its wall, the city was completely leveled. So thorough was the devastation that the exact location of the sanctuary is unknown today. "This catastrophe is itself a symbol of the end of the world and in one sense a coming of Christ in power and judgment."—Robertson, page 173.

[1103] A chain of rounded limestone hills is located on the eastern side of Jerusalem and separated from the city by the Kidron Valley. The summit across from the Temple mount—the one generally referred to in the Bible as the Mount of Olives—is about 2,664 feet (812 m) at its highest point. Here Jesus gave what is known in scholarly circles as the Olivet Discourse.

[1104] The Gospel of Mark, evidently written primarily for the Romans, gives extra information about geographic locations that would not be needed by Jewish readers (for example, the visibility of the Temple from the Mount of Olives; 13:3). See "The Gospel According to..."

[1105] Jesus had earlier connected the desolation of the Temple with his absence, adding that Jerusalem would not see him again until she acknowledged him as the One coming in God's name. (Matthew 23:37-39) "Between the desolation of the House and their new welcome to Him, would intervene a period of indefinite length, during which they would not see Him again." (Edersheim, page 773) This, in the apostles' view, referred to his second presence and the "end of the age," prompting their twofold question: "When shall these [things] be? and what is the sign of thy presence, and of the full end of the age?" (Matthew 24:3, Young's *Literal Translation)* "These things" presupposes that more than the Temple's destruction is in view.

[1106] The apostle's question(s) assumed that the Temple's destruction would signal the end of the Jewish age and the inauguration of Messiah's rule. They did not understand that Jerusalem's destruction was not necessarily indicative of the end's nearness. (Luke 19:11-27; Acts 1:6-7) Appropriately, Jesus began his answer with a warning against being misled. In the first century of the Christian Era, some who claimed to be prophets or liberators arose, promising relief from Roman oppression. These may have been viewed by their followers as political Messiahs. Acts of Apostles (5:36-37; 8:9-11; 21:38) suggests the appearance of many such seducers. Also see Josephus' *Wars of the Jews* (Book 6, paragraph 54).

[1107] Between Jesus' ascension to Heaven and Jerusalem's destruction occurred the Parthian wars in southwest Asia, uprisings in the Roman provinces of Gaul and Spain, risings of Jews against other nationalities and risings of other neighboring nationalities against the Jews involving the Syrians and Samaritans.

[1108] Like birth pangs, the foretold troubles and suffering will increase in frequency, intensity and duration until the new age is born.

[1109] There was an earthquake on the island of Crete during the reign of Claudius Caesar, another in Smyrna, others in Hierapolis, Colossae, Chios, Miletus and Samos. A quake overthrew the city of Laodicea during the reign of Emperor Nero. There was even one in Rome, as reported by the Latin historian, Tacitus. Josephus, in his *Wars of the Jews,* mentioned a dreadful earthquake in Judea.

[1110] The Christian prophet Agabus foretold the famine that occurred during the reign of Emperor Claudius. (Acts 11:27-28) Reportedly, many in Jerusalem died in this famine. Due to lack of proper nourishment, people succumbed to sicknesses, and pestilences broke out. *Webster's New International Dictionary* defines pestilences, or plagues, as "malignant and contagious or infectious epidemic diseases which are deadly and devastating." (quoted in *The Amplified Bible—Classic Edition*, Luke 21:11) Only the physician's gospel mentions this feature of the "sign."—Luke 21:7; Colossians 4:14; see "The Gospel According to..."

[1111] Preaching was to be every disciple's responsibility, for by means of it the Christian congregation would be established. Although the gospel of God's kingdom would be "proclaimed in all the inhabited earth," the purpose of doing so was not to convert all nations to Christianity, but to give them opportunity to hear the testimony.—Matthew 24:14, *The Emphasized Bible;* compare Acts 1:8.

[1112] Those who endure suffering and persecution are blessed with the opportunity to witness about God's kingdom. (Matthew 5:10-12). Jesus promised that God's spirit would assist his followers to give testimony. See Acts 4:8-12; 7:55-56.

[1113] Christians can be confident in God's protection from spiritual or eternal harm and in his power to resurrect them from the dead.—Matthew 10:30, 39; Luke 12:7.

[1114] **Endurance** is courageous, patient steadfastness that does not lose hope in the face of obstacles, persecutions, trials or temptations.—**Luke 21:19**.

[1115] Or "your future lives; your real life." (Note on Luke 21:19, *New World Translation—Study Edition;* compare 1 Timothy 6:19) In this context, the Greek word traditionally rendered "soul" refers to a person's present or future life. See Luke 21:19 in the *King James Version*.

[1116] Jesus' name stands for the authority and position that his Father has given him. (Matthew 28:18; Philippians 2:9-11; Hebrews 1:3-4) Christ's followers would be hated because of what his name represents, that is, his position as God's appointed Ruler, the "King of kings," the one to whom all people should bow in submission in order to gain life.—Matthew 5:10-12; John 15:20-21; Revelation 19:16.

[1117] Or "be led into sin." (Matthew 24:10, *Lexham English Bible)* Passages such as Matthew 24:10 suggest that the end times will be characterized by exceptionally severe apostasy. See also Matthew 13:20-21; Mark 4:16-17; Luke 8:13.

[1118] Not just people in general but the majority of those who have been influenced by false prophets and **lawlessness**— disregard for law and order but God's laws in particular.—**Matthew 24:**11-**12**; 1 John 3:4.

[1119] In this context, perseverance means to stand one's ground as a Christian despite opposition and trials. See also Matthew 10:22; Romans 12:12; Hebrews 10:32; James 5:11.

[1120] In A.D. 66 Roman armies surrounded Jerusalem. For reasons lost to history, the troops withdrew. Afterward, Christians fled to the mountains. The Romans eventually returned to Jerusalem and desolated the city.—Luke 19:43-44.

[1121] Winter weather would make it difficult to travel and to find food and shelter. (Ezra 10:9, 13) On the sabbath day in Israel, less than a mile from the city gate was permitted. (Acts 1:12) Such a short flight would be of little value in escaping the vengeance of destroying armies.

[1122] Referring to "Gentiles," non-Jewish nations.—Luke 21:24, *King James Version*.

[1123] The destructive conquest of Israel's "holy city," including its Temple, proved to be "tribulation" far greater than any previously experienced. (Matthew 4:5; 24:21, *King James Version)* Over a million people were killed, nearly 100,000 captured, and a centuries-old system of worship was brought to an end.

[1124] Signs of distress in the spiritual realm or to the heavenly bodies themselves.—Matthew 24:29; Mark 13:24-25; Luke 21:25-26; compare Isaiah 13:10; 34:4; Ezekiel 32:7-8; Joel 2:10, 30-31; 3:15.

[1125] Referring to complete discouragement and loss of hope.

[1126] This sign relates to the coming of the Son of Man as Judge to pronounce and execute judgment during the Great Tribulation; it is not the same as the sign of Jesus' second presence. (Matthew 24:3; Mark 13:4; Luke 21:7) No one will need to point out the coming of the Son of Man in power because it will be sudden and obvious.

[1127] Or "beat the breast." (Matthew 24:30, *A Conservative Version)* Repeatedly beating the hands against the chest expressed grief, guilt or remorse.—Luke 23:48.

[1128] Clouds tend to obstruct vision (Acts 1:9) but observers can "see" with eyes of understanding.—Matthew 24:30; Mark 13:26; Luke 21:27; Ephesians 1:18.

[1129] The Son of Man 'comes' to pronounce and execute judgment during the Great Tribulation.—Matthew 24:30, 42, 44, 46; 25:13, 31.

[1130] Or "from the four winds," an idiom referring to the four directions of the compass—east, west, north and south. (Matthew 24:31; Mark 13:27, *King James Version*; compare Jeremiah 49:36; Ezekiel 37:9; Daniel 8:8; Zechariah 2:6) **The Son of Man** will share rulership with **his chosen ones.**—**Matthew 24:30-31**; **Mark 13:26-27**; Daniel 7:13-14, 27; Revelation 2:26-27.

[1131] In Israel, the first fruit buds typically appear on the branches of the fig tree in February and the leaves appear in the final part of April or in May, indicating the approach of summer.

[1132] Or "coming," Matthew 24:37, *King James Version*. The Greek word commonly translated "coming" "means 'presence' and in the Graeco-Roman world was used for official visits by royalty"; it refers to a period of time rather than an arrival. (Matthew chapter 24 note b, *The Jerusalem Bible:* Edited by Alexander Jones) In verse 3 of Matthew 24 "the end of the age" parallels Jesus' second "presence"; in verses 37-39 Jesus compared his future royal presence to the days of Noah, that is, to a period of time.—*The Emphasized Bible.*

[1133] As **the days of Noah** covered a period of years, **the presence of the Son of Man** would likewise cover a period of years. Like Noah's days, the days of the Son of Man would climax in the destruction of those who do not seek deliverance.—**Matthew 24:37, 39**; Luke 17:26-27.

[1134] One type of mill used in Bible times was a rotary hand mill. Two women sat facing each other, each placing one hand on the handle to turn the upper stone. With her free hand, one woman fed grain in small amounts into the filler hole of the upper stone while the other woman gathered the flour as it emerged from the rim of the mill and fell to the tray, or the cloth spread beneath the mill. Women ground grain every day, rising early in the morning to prepare the flour needed for that day's bread.

[1135] "As in the days of Noah the long delay of threatened judgment had led to absorption in the ordinary engagements of life, to the entire disbelief of what Noah had preached, so would it be in the future. But that day would come certainly and unexpectedly, to the sudden separation of those who were engaged in the same daily business of life, of whom one might be taken up ..., the other left to the destruction of the coming Judgment."—Edersheim, page 786. See 2 Peter 2:5.

[1136] Although Jesus' prophecy was fulfilled in some respects prior to and during the destruction of Jerusalem, he also pointed to developments that would affect the whole world. For example, Jesus said that Christians would be hated by all nations, and that the gospel would be proclaimed worldwide as a testimony to all nations.—Matthew 24:9, 14; Mark 13:10.

[1137] Standing before someone in authority indicates that an individual or a group holds a favored or approved position with that authority.—Proverbs 22:29; Luke 1:19; Revelation 7:9.

[1138] Jesus made clear that he would come again unexpectedly. If the **day and hour** of his return could be timed, his admonition to be watchful would have no meaning—**Matthew 24:36**; **Mark 13:32**.

[1139] In ancient times, doorkeepers, or gatekeepers, served at entrances to cities, temples and sometimes private homes. Besides ensuring that gates and doors were shut at night, these individuals also served as watchmen. (2 Samuel 18:24, 26; 2 Kings 7:10-11; Esther 2:21; 6:2; John 18:17) By likening a Christian to a doorkeeper of a house, Jesus emphasized the need for Christians to be alert and watchful concerning his future coming to execute judgment.

[1140] Or "at the cockcrowing." (Mark 13:35, *King James Version)* The third watch of the night, according to the Greek and Roman division, ran from midnight to about 3:00 a.m. Rooster-crowing has long been and still is a time indicator in lands east of the Mediterranean.

[1141] Like the parable of the faithful and wise servant, the parable of the bridesmaids illustrates the need for spiritual preparation. (Matthew 24:42, 44; 25:13) Spiritual vigilance is vital for Christians. (Mark 13:33; Luke 21:36; Romans 13:11; 1 Thessalonians 5:5-9; 1 Peter 5:8; Revelation 16:15) Without it, "the sign of [Jesus'] appearance, and of the end of the age" cannot be understood.—Matthew 24.3, *The New Testament in an Improved Version Upon the Basis of Archbishop Newcome's New Translation* (1808).

[1142] "Virgins" or "maidens."—Matthew 25:1, 7, 10-11, *King James Version; Revised Standard Version.*

[1143] Or "prudent," that is, wise in a practical sense.—Matthew 25:2, *New English Bible.*

[1144] The foolish bridesmaids were neglectful, not forgetful. They were foolish for not being prepared.

[1145] Putting the **lamps in order** would include trimming the wicks and adding oil so that the lamps would burn brightly.—**Matthew 25:7**.

[1146] Although professing to be bridesmaids, the five foolish virgins had not been in the bridal procession. In truth, therefore, the bridegroom could only answer, **I don't know you**.—**Matthew 25:12**; compare Matthew 7:21-23; Luke 13:25-27.

[1147] It is unnecessary to attach to the number 10 any symbolic significance. According to Edersheim, "it was the custom in the East to carry in a bridal procession about ten such lamps. ... ten was the number required to be present at any office or ceremony, such as at the benedictions accompanying the marriage-ceremonies."—page 788.

[1148] A Greek "talent" was, not a coin, but a unit of weight equal to 75 pounds (34 kg). A silver talent was worth approximately 6,000 drachmas or Roman denarii—about 20 years' wages for a common laborer. In Jesus' parable, the talent symbolizes everything entrusted to a Christian—time, money, opportunities, talents, education—to further the progress of Christ's Kingdom. "And to each of us He gives according to our capacity for working—mental, moral, and even physical—to one five, to another two, and to another one 'talent.' This capacity for work lies not within our own power; but it is in our power to use for Christ whatever we may have."—Edersheim, page 791.

[1149] The large quantities of valuables and coins unearthed by archaeologists and farmers in Bible lands give evidence of this practice.

[1150] "The first two servants received the same reward, even though they had received different amounts of money. The reward was based on faithfulness, not on the size of their responsibilities. The smallest task in God's work may receive a great reward if we are faithful in performing it ([Matthew] 10:42)." (Matthew 25:23 footnote, *The Nelson Study Bible*. Copyright © 1997 by Thomas Nelson, Inc. Used with permission) Sharing the Master's joy implies more than advancement from the position of a servant to that of a friend (John 15:15); it includes "satisfied heart-sympathy with the aims and gains of his Master, and participation in them, with all that this conveys."—Edersheim, page 792.

[1151] The servant's admitted dereliction of duty "was also an insult and a mendacious pretext. He had been idle and unwilling to work for his Master. If he worked it would be for himself. He would not incur the difficulties, the self-denial, perhaps the reproach, connected with his Master's work. ... The falseness of the excuse, that he was afraid to do anything with it ... lest, peradventure, he might do more harm than good, ... proceeded from a want of knowledge of Him, as if He were a hard, exacting Master, not One Who reckons even the least service as done to Himself; from misunderstanding also of what work for Christ is, in which nothing can ever fail or be lost; and, lastly, from want of joyous sympathy with it."—Edersheim, page 793.

[1152] By the servant's own words his master judges him. (Compare Luke 19:22) Had the servant deposited his master's wealth in a bank where it could have earned interest, "he might, without incurring responsibility, or much labour *[sic]*, have been at least in a limited sense, faithful to his duty and trust as a servant."—Edersheim, page 793.

[1153] "Faithful use for God of every capacity will ever open fresh opportunities, in proportion as the old ones have been used, while spiritual unprofitableness must end in utter loss even of that which, however humble, might have been used, at one time or another, for God and for good."—Edersheim, p. 794. See Matthew 13:12; Mark 4:25; Luke 8:18; 19:26; 1 Peter 4:10.

[1154] Jesus, **the Son of Man,** comes to pronounce and execute judgment during the Great Tribulation.—**Matthew 25:31**, 34, 41; see Daniel 7:9-10, 13; Matthew 24:29-30.

[1155] Or "all nations," that is, the Gentile nations. (Matthew 25:32, *King James Version;* compare Isaiah 2:2-4) The parables of the Bridesmaids and the Talents concern the judgment on Israelites who were unprepared for the Messiah. The parable of the Sheep and the Goats focuses attention on judgment for all nations.

[1156] Sheep and goats commonly grazed together in the Middle East. (Genesis 30:32-33; 31:38) Sheep are easily led, whereas goats can be stubborn. Each animal represents a class of people in Jesus' parable.

[1157] Both positions can indicate honor and authority. (Matthew 20:21, 23; Mark 10:37, 40) In this parable, however, there is a clear contrast between the place of favor at the King's right hand and that of disfavor at his left. Compare Ecclesiastes 10:2.

[1158] To **inherit the Kingdom** means to receive the blessings of being ruled by God's kingdom and enjoying life within its realm. **The founding of the world** apparently refers to the conception and birth of children born to Adam and Eve; their son Abel was the first redeemable person of the world of humankind.—**Matthew 25:34**; Luke 11:50-51.

[1159] Or "not sufficiently dressed."—Matthew 25:36 footnote, *New World Translation;* compare James 2:15.

[1160] The righteous are rewarded by God because they serve him without thought of reward.

[1161] Or "the humblest of my brothers." (Matthew 25:40, *The New Testament in Modern English)* The Greek word for "brother" can be understood as a gender-neutral reference to a Christian.

[1162] "Since 'curse' is the opposite of 'blessing' ..., one cursed by God can expect blessing to be withdrawn, a diminishing of the enjoyment God yearns to provide his children. ... Since we have all sinned against God, we all lie under the curse of God. ... Those who stubbornly refuse to believe the Good News, however, continue to lie under the curse of God."—Verlyn D. Verbrugge: *The NIV Topical Study Bible,* page 216. See 2 Thessalonians 1:8.

[1163] The Bible warns against losing the inheritance of eternal life through disobedience. (John 3:36) That inheritance can be lost also due to lack of obedience. The "goats" lose their inheritance, not for anything they did, but for what they failed to do.

[1164] Literally, "lopping off," as in pruning dead branches from trees. (Matthew 25:46, *Kingdom Interlinear Translation of the Greek Scriptures)* The "goats" are forever cut off from life.

[1165] "On the day before the unfermented cakes the disciples came up to Jesus, saying: 'Where do you want us to prepare for you to eat the Passover?'" (Matthew 26:17 footnote, *New World Translation of the Holy Scriptures—with References)* The original Greek, as well as Jewish custom, allows for the disciples' question to have been asked of Jesus on Nisan 13, "at the onset of" the festival.—Matthew 26:17, *Orthodox Jewish Bible.*

[1166] Bitter greens evidently reminded the Israelites of their bitter slavery in Egypt.

[1167] "Probably they had not yet fixed on any definite plan. Only at this conclusion had they arrived—probably in consequence of the popular acclamations at His Entry into Jerusalem, and of what had since happened—that nothing must be done during the Feast, for fear of some popular tumult. They knew only too well the character of [Governor Pontius] Pilate, and how in any such tumult all parties—the leaders as well as the led—might experience terrible vengeance."—Edersheim, page 802. See "Biographical Sketch: Pontius Pilate."

[1168] Actually, leaders of the Temple guards, these 'policemen' may have been included in the discussion with Judas to make the planned arrest of Jesus appear legal. (Luke 22:4, 52; Acts 4:1; 5:24, 26) "There had previously been a similar gathering and consultation, when the report of the raising of Lazarus reached the authorities of Jerusalem (John 11:47, 48). The practical resolution adopted at that meeting had apparently been, that a strict watch should henceforth be kept on Christ's movements, and that every one of them, as well as the names of His friends, and the places of His secret retirement, should be communicated to the authorities, with the view to His arrest at the proper moment (John 11:57)."—Edersheim, page 802.

[1169] With Judas involved in the plot the religious leaders "could arrest Jesus secretly and later claim that the driving force to stop Him came from within His own group of disciples." (Luke 22:4 footnote, *The Nelson Study Bible.* Copyright © 1997 by Thomas Nelson, Inc. Used with permission) "It was in literal fulfilment *[sic]* of prophecy (Zech. 11:12), that they 'weighed out' to him from the very Temple-treasury those thirty pieces of silver .... And yet it was surely as much in contempt of the seller as of Him Whom he sold, that they paid the legal price of a slave." Significantly, the betrayal of Jesus was "paid for out of the Temple-money, which was destined for the purchase of sacrifices, and ... He, Who took on Him the form of a servant (Phil. 2:7), was sold and bought at the legal price of a slave (Exod. 21:32)."—Edersheim, page 803.

[1170] Or "an earthenware vessel of water." (Mark 14:13; Luke 22:10, *New World Translation of the Holy Scriptures—with References)* Water jars were usually carried by women so a man with one would have stood out to Peter and John.—Genesis 24:15; Ruth 2:8-9; John 4:28.

[1171] It is reasonable to assume that the owner was a disciple. Would a stranger have given up his best room in answer to such a mysterious message without further questioning? Also, it would make sense for Jesus to presume upon the hospitality of a follower at a time when accommodations in the city could be difficult to find. (Jerusalem's homeowners customarily provided rooms to pilgrims who, in obedience to Deuteronomy 16:16, came to the city to celebrate Passover.) Edersheim speculates that this house belonged to the family of the disciple and evangelist John Mark, suggesting that "the traitor may have first brought the Temple-guards, who had come to seize Christ, to the house of Mark's father, where the Supper had been held, and that, finding Him gone, they had followed to Gethsemane, for 'Judas knew the place, for Jesus ofttimes resorted thither with His disciples' (John 18:1, 2)—and how Mark, startled from his sleep by the appearance of the armed men, would hastily cast about him his loose tunic and run after them; then, after the flight of the disciples, accompany Christ, but escape intended arrest by leaving his tunic in the hands of his would-be-captors." This, Edersheim believes, would be "the most obvious explanation of the introduction by St. Mark alone of such an incident as that about the young man who was accompanying Christ as He was led away captive, and who, on fleeing from those that would have laid hold on him, left in their hands the inner garment which he had loosely cast about him, as, roused from sleep, he had rushed into Gethsemane, is, that he was none other than St. Mark himself."—page 809; Mark 15:51-52. See Acts 12:12.

[1172] "... the expression 'furnished,' no doubt, refers to the arrangement of couches all-round the Table, except at its end, since it was a canon, that the very poorest must partake of that Supper in a reclining attitude, to indicate rest, safety, and liberty; while the term 'ready' seems to point to the ready provision of all that was required for the feast." (Edersheim, page 808; Matthew 26:19; Mark 14:15-16; Luke 22:12-13) According to tradition this upper room was where over a hundred believers would meet the following day of Pentecost.—Acts 1:13.

[1173] The necessary purchases would have been made on the previous afternoon. On Passover Day there would have been no time to subject the Paschal lamb to Levitical scrutiny and pass inspection. "... if Judas had made this purchase, we perceive not only on what pretext he may have gone to Jerusalem on the previous afternoon, but also how, on his way from the Sheep-market to the Temple, to have his lamb inspected, he may have learned that the Chief-Priests and Sanhedrists were just then in session in the Palace of the High-Priest close by." (Edersheim, page 810) It is also possible that the owner of the house procured the lamb.

[1174] Jesus knew the significance of the events soon to take place. Also, he had much to tell his apostles before he died, instilling courage in them to remain loyal.

[1175] "[A]s in the Paschal Supper all Israel were gathered around the Paschal Lamb in commemoration of the past, in celebration of the present, in anticipation of the future, and in fellowship in the lamb, so has the Church been ever since gathered together around its better fulfilment *[sic]* in the Kingdom of God." (Edersheim, page 814) Jesus' last Passover pointed forward to "the marriage supper of the Lamb" at the final consummation of his Kingdom.—Revelation 19:9, *King James Version.*

[1176] This was probably the first of four cups of wine traditionally shared during the Passover meal.

[1177] Wine can symbolize joy. (Psalm 104:15; Ecclesiastes 9:7; 10:19) The ultimate joy for Jesus and his apostles will be when they are together in the heavenly Kingdom.—Matthew 26:29.

[1178] After the cup of wine had been blessed and passed around, the next part of the ceremony was for "the Head of the Company to rise and 'wash hands.' It is this part of the ritual of which St. John (John 13) records the adaptation and transformation on the part of Christ. The washing of the disciples' feet is evidently connected with the ritual of 'handwashing.' ... And so, 'during Supper,' which had begun with the first cup, 'He riseth from Supper.' [John 13:4] The disciples ... must have wondered as they saw Him put off His upper garment, gird Himself with a towel, and pour water into a basin, like a slave who was about to perform the meanest service." (Edersheim, pages 818-19; compare 1 Samuel 25:41) Hospitable hosts in ancient Israel made sure that their guests' feet were washed. (Luke 7:44) The towel Jesus used would have been a piece of linen cloth, long enough to wrap around his waist and still have a free end for wiping the apostles' feet.

[1179] Or "You are not in fellowship with me." (John 13:8, *New English Bible)* "Jesus washes his disciples' feet to symbolize the humiliation of his death, which is the sole source of forgiveness of sins and of fellowship with him ([John 13] v. 8)." (David M. Stanley: John 13:3-5 footnote, *The New English Bible)* The bare act of washing did not give Peter fellowship in Christ. But refusal to submit to it would have deprived him of fellowship. "... to share in this washing, was, as it were, the way to have part in Christ's service of love, to enter into it, and to share it."—Edersheim, page 819.

[1180] "According to the social customs of those times, once a person had bathed his entire body, he needed only to wash his feet before partaking of a meal. ... Just as those who have bathed need only to wash their feet, so believers who have been bathed by the Lord through His word and the Spirit (see [John] 15:3; Eph. 5:26; Titus 3:5) need only to wash themselves daily from the filth and defilement they accumulate by their contact with the world."—*The Nelson Study Bible,* page 1791. Copyright © 1997 by Thomas Nelson, Inc. Used with permission.

[1181] Like the other apostles, Judas Iscariot was physically clean. Like the scholars and the Pharisees, Judas was spiritually unclean. (Luke 11:39) Since Jesus could discern the thinking and attitudes of others (Matthew 9:4; Mark 2:8; Luke 6:8; John 2:24-25; Revelation 2:23), Judas clearly did not have a treasonous spirit when he was selected to be an apostle. When Judas began to develop a bad attitude, Jesus detected it and was able to identify his betrayer. (John 6:64, 70) Despite knowing that Judas would betray him, Jesus washed the traitor's feet.

[1182] Jesus' example was one of showing humble concern for the physical and spiritual needs of others. He wanted the apostles to imitate him by serving one another in humility and not seek preeminence over one another. (1 Peter 5:5) Also in imitation of Jesus, they could help one another to keep clean from daily temptations and worldly entanglements that might contaminate them.—Galatians 6:1-2; Hebrews 10:22.

[1183] Psalm 41:9, *New Life Version.* David was betrayed by one of his closest friends, his adviser Ahithophel.—2 Samuel 15:12.

[1184] Jesus had told his apostles that he would die in Jerusalem, but this revelation of betrayal was new to them.—Matthew 16:21; 20:18-19; Mark 10:33-34.

[1185] Five times the Gospel of John mentions a certain disciple of whom Jesus was especially fond. (John 13:23; 19:26; 20:2; 21:7, 20) Although that man is not named, it may have been the apostle John, the son of Zebedee and the brother of James. (Matthew 4:21; Mark 1:19; Luke 5:10) The apostle John is not referred to by name in this gospel (except for the mention of "the sons of Zebedee" at 21:2). At John 21:20-24, the beloved disciple is connected with the writer of this gospel; and Jesus suggested that this apostle would outlive the others, a description that fits John. See "The Gospel According to..."

[1186] At a dining table in Jesus' time, guests reclined on their left side with a cushion supporting the elbow. A guest could lean back on the bosom, or chest, of a friend reclining next to him and engage in a confidential conversation. John was literally "in Jesus' bosom," a position suggesting a special relationship of favor and close fellowship. (John 13:23, *American Standard Version;* see also Luke 16:22-23; John 1:18) This custom suggests some things about the seating arrangement at the last supper. "It is entirely possible that Judas was seated to Jesus' left. Matt 26:25 seems to indicate that Jesus could speak to him without being overheard by the rest of the group. Judas is evidently in a position where Jesus can hand him the morsel of food ([John] 13:26)." On the other hand, "it is not clear where *Simon Peter* was seated. If he were on Jesus' [left] side, it is difficult to see why he would not have asked the question himself. It would also have been difficult to beckon to the beloved disciple, on Jesus' right, from such a position. So apparently Peter was seated somewhere else.—John 13:24 footnote, *The NET Bible*.

[1187] "The point of Jesus' comment here is not to identify the specific individual per se, but to indicate that it is one who was close to him—somebody whom no one would suspect. His comment serves to heighten the treachery of Judas' betrayal."—Luke 22:21 footnote, *The NET Bible*.

[1188] **Going**, that is, to his death.—**Matthew 26:24**; **Mark 14:21**; **Luke 22:22**.

[1189] Or "You said it," a Hebrew idiom used to affirm the truth of a statement made by a questioner. (Matthew 26:25, *World English Bible)* Jesus was, in effect, saying: 'You have said so, and what you say is true.' Judas' own words were an admission of responsibility for Jesus' betrayal.

[1190] In Jesus' time and culture, people usually ate food with their fingers, using a piece of bread—a "sop"—somewhat like a spoon. (John 13:26-27, *King James Version)* The sop consisted of flesh of the Paschal Lamb, a piece of unleavened bread, and bitter herbs all wrapped together. "This, we believe, was 'the sop,' which Jesus, having dipped it for him in the dish, handed first to Judas, as occupying the first and chief place at Table. But before He did so, probably while He dipped it in the dish, Judas, who could not but fear that his purpose might be known, reclining at Christ's left hand, whispered into the Master's ear, 'Is it I, Rabbi?' [Matthew 26:25] It must have been whispered, for no one at the Table could have heard either the question of Judas or the affirmative answer of Christ (John 13:28)."—Edersheim, page 824.

[1191] At this point Judas came under the influence of Satan even more completely and finally; it marks the end of a process which, as Luke 22:3 indicates, had begun earlier.—John 13:2, 27.

[1192] Judas "was the treasurer and administrator of the small common stock of Christ and His disciples." To be appointed to an office of trust, he must have been prudent, a good administrator and respected by the other apostles. Why, though, would Jesus allow a thieving hypocrite to continue in a trusted position? (John 12:5-6) Edersheim speculates, "To engage in that for which a man is naturally fitted is the most likely means of keeping him from brooding, dissatisfaction, alienation, and eventual apostasy. On the other hand, it must be admitted that, as mostly all our life-temptations come to us from that for which we have most aptitude, when Judas was alienated and unfaithful in heart, this very thing became also his greatest temptation, and, indeed, hurried him to his ruin. But only after he had first failed inwardly. And so, as ever in like circumstances, the very things which might have been most of blessing become most of curse, and the judgment of hardening fulfils *[sic]* itself by that which in itself is good. Nor could 'the [money] bag' have been afterwards taken from him without both exposing him to the others and precipitating his moral destruction. [John 13:29] And so he had to be left to the process of inward ripening, till all was ready for the sickle."—page 800.

[1193] From the meal Judas rushed into the dark night. Even this had symbolic meaning. Daytime was over; night had arrived. (John 9:4-5; 11:9; 12:35-36) Judas had become one of those who walked by night and stumbled, because the light was not in him. (John 11:10) A comparison of Matthew 26:20-29 and Mark 14:17-25 with John 13:21-30 shows that Judas departed before Jesus instituted the observance of the Lord's Evening Meal with his faithful 11 apostles. Luke 22:21-23 evidently does not follow in strict chronological order.—Luke 22:28-30.

[1194] In the Middle East loaves were thin and, if unleavened, brittle. Breaking the bread was the normal way to divide that type of loaf, although some spiritual significance may be seen therein.

[1195] Literally, "is," in the sense of signifying. (Matthew 26:26; Mark 14:22; Luke 22:19, *King James Version)* The bread "represents" Jesus' body. *(The Christian's Bible—New Testament* by George N. LeFevre) Because the Lord's Evening Meal is a memorial ceremony, the emblems of bread and wine represent Christ—they are not his literal body and blood, as the doctrine of transubstantiation holds.

[1196] "According to the Jewish ritual, the third Cup was filled at the close of the [Paschal] Supper. This was called, as by St. Paul (1 Cor. 10:10), 'the Cup of Blessing,' partly, because a special 'blessing' was pronounced over it. It is described as one of the ten essential rites in the Paschal Supper. ... But we can have little doubt, that the Institution of the Cup was in connection with this third 'Cup of Blessing.'"—Edersheim, page 827.

[1197] Or "ratified by"; "sealed with." (Luke 22:20, *The New Testament in Modern Speech*; *Today's English Version)* Only Luke mentions a "new covenant," an allusion to Jeremiah 31:31-33; 32:40 and Ezekiel 34:25; 37:26. As the blood of bulls and goats validated the Law covenant between God and the nation of Israel, Jesus' blood validated **the new covenant** that God would make with spiritual Israel—the Christian congregation.—**Luke 22:20**. See Exodus 24:8; Hebrews 8:10; 9:13-15, 19-21.

[1198] "The word *many* looks back to [Matthew] 20:28 and anticipates the command to preach the Good News to all the world in 28:19, 20."—Matthew 26:28 footnote, *The Nelson Study Bible*. Copyright © 1997 by Thomas Nelson, Inc. Used with permission.

[1199] The Lord's Evening Meal will call to remembrance what Jesus and his Father have done to enable faithful ones to escape from the condemnation of sin and death.

[1200] According to Luke 22:23-24, the apostles' argument grew out of their discussion about the identity of Jesus' betrayer. Edersheim suggests that the argument started earlier and was associated with Judas claiming "the chief seat at the table next to the Lord. ... We know from the Gospel-narrative that John occupied the place on His right, at that end of the divans—as we may call it—at the head of the table. But the chief place next to the Master would be that to His left, or above Him. In the strife of the disciples, which should be accounted the greatest, this [place] had been claimed, and we believe it to have been actually occupied, by Judas. This explains how, when Christ whispered to John by what sign to recognise the traitor (John 13:26), none of the other disciples heard it. It also explains, how Christ would firsthand [to] Judas the sop, which formed part of the Paschal ritual, beginning with him as the chief guest at the table, without thereby exciting special notice. Lastly, it accounts for the circumstance that, when Judas, desirous of ascertaining whether his treachery was known, dared to ask whether it was he, and received the affirmative answer (Matt. 26:25), no one at [the] table knew what had passed. But this could not have been the case, unless Judas had occupied the place next to Christ; in this case, necessarily that at His left, or the post of chief honour [sic]."—pages 815, 816; John 13:2.

[1201] **Benefactor** was an honorary title for princes or distinguished people, especially those recognized for their civic contributions. (**Luke 22:25**) Even tyrants could be called Benefactors. Those who take the lead among their fellow believers should not consider themselves to be "benefactors" to whom other Christians are somehow indebted, for they are not to be like the rulers of this world.—Hebrews 13:7, 17, 24.

[1202] Jesus demonstrated this example earlier by washing his apostles' feet. (John 13:12-17) He is the foremost example of the servant-leader. "Jesus wants us to serve him by serving others, recognizing that whatever we do for one of God's children we do for him. In our service we are to have the same humble, gentle, giving attitude that characterized Jesus."—Verlyn D. Verbrugge: *The NIV Topical Study Bible*, page 790. See Matthew 25:40.

[1203] Or "I covenant unto you—As my Father hath covenanted unto me—a kingdom." (Luke 22:29, *Emphasized Bible)* Jesus refers to two covenants, one between him and his Father, and one between him and all spirit-begotten conquerors. (Revelation 3:21) The latter covenant was inaugurated on Pentecost by the anointing with God's spirit; it remains operative between Christ and his corulers forever.—Acts 2:1-4, 33; Revelation 20:4, 6; 22:5.

[1204] To share a meal with someone signified friendship and peace between the diners. One who was privileged to eat regularly at a king's table was specially favored and enjoyed a very close bond with the monarch. (1 Kings 2:7) This is the kind of relationship that Jesus promised his faithful followers. See also Luke 13:29; Revelation 19:9.

[1205] Or "judging." (Luke 22:29, *King James Version*) The world of humankind will be judged by a royal priestly class, according to 1 Corinthians 6:2 and Revelation 20:4.—Matthew 19:28; 2 Timothy 2:12.

[1206] This affectionate expression occurs nine times in the New Testament and is always used in a figurative sense, referring to disciples.—Galatians 4:19; 1 John 2:1, 12, 28; 3:7, 18; 4:4; 5:21.

[1207] Israel's law called for neighbor love but not necessarily for self-sacrificing love. (Leviticus 19:18) Jesus provided his followers a perfect model of living and loving unselfishly—the kind of love that would move a person to die for others. Jesus' life and death exemplified the love called for by this **new** (or unprecedented) **commandment**. (**John 13:34**; 15:13) Love, therefore, is the key test of Christian discipleship and the greatest of all Christian virtues, even greater than faith and hope.—1 Corinthians 13:13.

[1208] After it had been threshed and winnowed, wheat was sifted, or shaken vigorously to pass through a sieve. Sifting separated the straw and chaff from the grain. Jesus likened tests of faith to the sifting of wheat. Satan wanted to separate the apostles from Jesus and from one another.

[1209] Except for Judas Iscariot, all the apostles were from Galilee. Perhaps that was why Christ intended to meet them there. Then, too, he may have wanted to take up the work of shepherding his flock where he had ministered to them before. Away from opposition in Jerusalem, Galilee might have been the most effective setting for the Great Commission.—Matthew 4:12-16; 28:19-20.

[1210] "Intercession is prayer offered by one person on behalf of another. ... Christ is the great Intercessor. While on earth he prayed for both friends and enemies, and he is now in the presence of the Father, bringing our hurts and sorrows and weaknesses to the Father."—Verlyn D. Verbrugge: *The NIV Topical Study Bible*, page 295.

[1211] The confidence Peter displays in private will wither in public under peer pressure. And when all the apostles see the one whom they believe to be the triumphant Messiah passively yield to his enemies, their faith will be severely tested.

[1212] Here Jesus referred to Peter's recovery from his fall that would be caused largely by haughty overconfidence combined with a fear of man.—Proverbs 16:18; 29:25.

[1213] All four Gospels mention this statement, but Mark adds the detail of how many times the rooster would crow (a detail that doubtless remained vivid in Peter's mind when he related these events to Mark). Because rabbinic law forbade keeping fowls in Jerusalem (on account of possible Levitical defilements through them) Edersheim proposes that "Peter might have heard the cock crow from Fort Antonia, occupied by the Romans, or else that it might have reached thus far in the still night air from outside the walls of Jerusalem." (page 844 note 4) The Mishnah indicates that roosters were bred in Jerusalem in Jesus' day, lending support to the Bible account.

[1214] Jesus quoted, in part, Isaiah 53:12, which said that Messiah would be put to death alongside criminals. (Luke 22:37) Thereafter, his followers would face persecution.

[1215] Jesus knew that his disciples would soon be persecuted. Even persons favorable to their message might be afraid to assist them because of official opposition. Also, Jesus' followers would soon be carrying gospel truth to Gentile lands. These circumstances would require them to be prepared to care for themselves materially.

[1216] According to Edersheim, Galilean men carried short swords concealed under their outer garments. The fact that the apostles possessed swords would soon afford Jesus an opportunity to teach an important lesson: though they would come into circumstances that could easily provoke armed resistance, he did not intend to resort to the sword but would give himself up voluntarily in harmony with God's will.—John 18:10-11.

[1217] There are many "abodes" or "dwellings" in Heaven. (John 14:2, *The Holy Bible in Modern English—Revised Edition; The Emphasized Bible*; compare verse 23) It was a "very common Jewish idea," says Edersheim, "that those in glory occupied different abodes, corresponding to their ranks. If the words of Christ, about the place whither they could not follow Him, had awakened any such thoughts, the explanation which He now gave must effectually have dispelled them. ... It was His Father's House of which they were thinking, and although there were 'many mansions,' or rather 'stations,' in it—and the choice of this word may teach us something—yet they were all in that one House." (page 829; John 14:2, *King James Version)* Some understand the phrase **my Father's house** as a reference to Jesus' body, suggesting the believer's relationship as an adopted child of God who remains in the Father's household forever.—**John 14:2**. See John 2:19-22; 8:35; Ephesians 1:3-5.

[1218] Jesus had spoken of his destination previously, but the apostles did not understand at the time. (John 12:32-33; 13:33) For Jesus the way back to the Father was by means of a sacrificial death. For his apostles **the way** to where he was going was Jesus himself. (**John 14:6**) The object of Jesus' going was to prepare by his death and resurrection a place for the disciples. Such preparation would involve Jesus' validating or inaugurating the new covenant by appearing before God and presenting to Him the value of his blood, after which humans could follow him to Heaven. (Hebrews 9:12, 24; 12:24) "Not final separation, then, but ultimate gathering to Himself, did His present going away mean. 'And whither I go, ye know the way' (John 14:1-4)."—Edersheim, pages 829-30.

[1219] Jesus is **the way** for humans to be reconciled to God, and the only means of approach to God in prayer. Jesus spoke and lived in harmony with truth and is therefore **the truth**. Also, he fulfilled scores of prophecies. Jesus is **the life** because the sacrifice of his life made eternal life possible.—**John 14:6.** See John 3:16; 16:23; Acts 10:43; 2 Corinthians 1:20; Ephesians 4:21; Colossians 1:19-20; 1 Peter 3:18.

[1220] "If they had spiritually known Him as the way, they would also have known the goal, the Father, and now, by having the way clearly pointed out, they must also know the goal, God; nay, He was, so to speak, visibly before them—and, gazing on Him, they saw the shining track up to heaven, the Jacob's ladder at the top of which was the Father (John 14:7)."—Edersheim, page 830.

[1221] Perhaps Philip wanted Jesus to provide a visible manifestation of God, such as was seen in visions by Moses, Elijah and Isaiah. (Exodus 24:9-10; 1 Kings 19:9-12; Isaiah 6:1-5) In such visions, God's servants saw symbolic representations of God, not God himself. (Exodus 33:20; John 1:18; 6:46; 1 John 4:12) Philip and the other apostles had seen something better than such a vision. They had seen the Father by perceiving God's personality, will and purpose through what Jesus said and did.—Matthew 11:27; Luke 10:22. See "Seeing Me Is Like Seeing the Father Himself!"

[1222] Jesus' words and his works revealed who he was but, as the saying goes, actions speak louder than words.

[1223] Jesus expected his followers to continue his work and acknowledged that the scope of their ministry would be greater than his. On the day of Pentecost more believers were added to the Christian congregation than had become followers of Jesus during his entire earthly ministry. (Acts 2:41) And the message went forth not just in Jerusalem, Judea and Samaria, but to "the ends of the earth."—Acts 1:8; *Catholic Public Domain Version*.

[1224] Or "advocate"; "intercessor"; "counsellor" *[sic]*; "protector"; "support." (John chapter 14 note i, *The Jerusalem Bible)* The disciples already had a "helper" in Jesus. (1 John 2:1) But Jesus promised that God's spirit would provide further help after his departure from the earthly scene.

[1225] Never had God required that people pray in someone's name. Jesus introduced a new feature to prayer, mentioning the expression 'ask in my name' four times. (John 14:13-14; 15:16; 16:23) Jesus is "the way," the only channel of approach to God. (John 14:6; Hebrews 4:14, 16) To pray in Jesus' name is to acknowledge the vital role he plays.

[1226] Or "fatherless." (John 14:18, *The Holy Bible in Modern English—Revised Edition)* Jesus is promising his "children" that he will not leave them abandoned, helpless or unprotected.—Mark 10:24; John 13:33; 21:5.

[1227] On the next Day of Pentecost, Jesus 'returns' and pours out God's spirit on his followers.

[1228] Jesus will appear to his followers after his resurrection and, in time, resurrect them to be with him in Heaven. Once Jesus ascends to Heaven, **the world** of unbelievers will have seen the last of him.—**John 14:19**. See John 7:34; 8:21.

[1229] This would be contrary to all Jewish ideas about the Messiah's future manifestation. Israelites expected Messiah to deliver their country from Rome and its own corrupt priesthood.

[1230] Or "make our abode with."—John 14:23, *King James Version*; compare verse 2.

[1231] Jesus foresaw the role God's spirit would play in writing portions of the New Testament. The gospels of Matthew and John, the letters of John and Peter and the Revelation were written by apostles. (The Gospel of Mark was written at Peter's dictation, according to tradition.)—2 Timothy 3:16.

[1232] More than just the absence of conflict, peace is safety, wholeness, completeness and well-being in all relationships of life. Christians have a special responsibility to live at peace with others. True **peace** is a gift from God to his people, a kind of peace not experienced by the wicked **world**. (**John 14:27**) When the "Prince of Peace" rules the Earth, "there will be no end to his peace."—Isaiah 9:6-7, *Catholic Public Domain Version*.

[1233] The events of that evening and the next day—Jesus' arrest, trials, execution and death—will cause his disciples extreme emotional distress.

[1234] After Jesus goes to the Father and is glorified by Him, the apostles will be glorified as well. (John 17:5, 24) A cause for rejoicing indeed!

[1235] Satan and his demons rule the "world" of human society alienated from God, people whose behavior is out of harmony with His will. (John 12:31; 16:11; Ephesians 6:11-12; 1 John 5:19) Jesus had no imperfection or wrong desire that **the ruler of the world** could exploit.—**John 14:30**-31.

[1236] The institution of the Lord's Evening Meal was followed by the discourse recorded in John chapters 14-16. The meeting concluded with prayer and hymns, after which Jesus and the apostles left the upper room.—Matthew 26:30; Mark 14:26; John 17:1-18:1.

[1237] **Barren branch** may refer to an unfaithful (disobedient) Christian, or to a professed Christian who does not truly belong to Jesus.—**John 15:2**. See Matthew 7:21-23; 1 John 2:19.

[1238] Once fruit is on the vine, the vinedresser **prunes**, or cleanses, the fruit of bugs and diseases. Spiritual pruning is done through Jesus' **teaching**.—**John 15:2-3**.

[1239] A Christian could produce no fruit without a relationship with Jesus. Key to this, as Jesus went on to explain, is obedience.—John 15:10; 1 John 3:24.

[1240] Burning up means loss through trials or judgment. (Deuteronomy 32:22; Isaiah 33:14; Jeremiah 7:20; Ezekiel 15:6-7; 1 Peter 1:7; 4:12) This is a warning to Christians who cut themselves off from Christ.—1 John 2:19.

[1241] Earlier, Jesus promised the apostles that anything they asked in his name would be done for them. (John 14:13-14) That promise is conditioned on remaining united with Jesus and keeping his teaching.

[1242] "[Christian] joy is made possible by the death and resurrection of Jesus Christ. It is the joy that lodges deep within the human heart and is not necessarily related to one's personal circumstances. The early Christians, for example, experienced joy in the midst of persecution and suffering. The ultimate joy the Christian anticipates is the joy of the new heaven and the new earth and the celebration at the wedding feast of the Lamb."—Verlyn D. Verbrugge: *The NIV Topical Study Bible*, page 748. See Matthew 5:12; Acts 5:41; Colossians 1:11; Hebrews 10:34; James 1:2-3; 1 Peter 1:3, 8; 4:13; Revelation 19:7; 21:1-2.

[1243] **Love one another as I have loved you** was Jesus' "new commandment." (**John 15:17**; also 13:34) Like Jesus' love for his followers, the love among Jesus' followers must include a self-sacrificial willingness to die for one another.—1 John 3:16.

[1244] Or "slaves." (John 15:15, 20, *New American Bible)* Jesus called the apostles his friends; however, he redeemed them from sin, and they became his slaves.—1 Corinthians 6:20; 7:22-23; Galatians 3:13.

[1245] "It appears that as the imagery of the vine and the branches develops, the 'fruit' which the branches produce shifts in emphasis from qualities in the disciples' own lives in John 15:2, 4, 5 to the idea of a mission which affects the lives of others in John 15:16. The point of transition would be the reference to fruit in 15:8."—John 15:16 footnote, *The NET Bible*. See "I Am the True Vine."

[1246] This **world** refers to humankind apart from God's servants, the unrighteous human society alienated from God. (**John 15:19**; 17:15) The union between Christ and his congregation and the communion of Christ with his followers and of his followers among themselves means disunion with, or separation from, the world. For this separation from itself the world hates Christians. Christians are in the world but because Jesus chooses them out of the world, they no longer belong to it.—John 17:14-16; 1 John 4:5-6.

[1247] Or "my name." (John 15:21, *The Darby Bible)* Jesus' name means "Jehovah Is Salvation." *(The New Compact Bible Dictionary*, page 106) Knowing God would help unbelievers to understand and acknowledge what Jesus' name stands for. (John 17:3; Acts 4:12) Sharing that knowledge with the world is a Christian responsibility, which may provoke persecution similar to what Jesus experienced.

[1248] To reject the only cure for a fatal illness would mean certain death. Similarly, to reject Jesus—the only cure for sin—would mean eternal death. Compare John 9:41.

[1249] Jesus' agony over unwarranted hatred for him and his Father fulfilled a prophecy of David, in which the king reflected on the agony of his own persecution.—Psalm 35:19; 69:4; compare John 13:16.

[1250] Or "so that you would not stumble"; "be offended." (John 16:1, *Catholic Public Domain Version; King James Version)* To preserve their faith from shock, Jesus forewarned his apostles of coming trials. (John 13:19) "There may have been a tendency for the disciples to expect immediately after Jesus' victory over death the institution of the messianic kingdom, particularly in light of the turn of events recorded in the early chapters of Acts. Jesus here forestalls such disillusionment for the disciples by letting them know in advance that they will face persecution and even martyrdom as they seek to carry on his mission in the world after his departure."—John 16:1 footnote, *The NET Bible*.

[1251] Because much of Jewish life revolved around the synagogue, excommunication would have severe social and economic consequences.—John 9:22; 12:42.

[1252] Although Jesus had earlier said that the world would hate his followers, this was the first time he directly said that some of them would be killed. The first martyr for Christ, Stephen, was stoned by the Sanhedrin. (Acts 7:58-59) Those religious leaders thought they were rendering **sacred service to God.**—**John 16:2**.

[1253] After Jesus' departure, believers would have God's spirit and through that spirit the potential of full joy, the possibility of further knowledge and the privilege of peace.

[1254] Jesus foretold the spirit's involvement with the progressive revelation of truth to Christians.—John 14:26; Ephesians 3:3-5; Revelation 1:1-4; compare John 8:31-32; 2 Timothy 3:16.

[1255] Or "convict the world in respect of ..." (John 16:8, *American Standard Version)* God's spirit will expose the world's failure to demonstrate faith in Jesus. Jesus' ascension to Heaven proved that the world was wrong about him and vindicated him as righteous. God's spirit would also demonstrate why Satan, this world's ruler, deserves his adverse judgment. Some take the word "convict" to mean "convince" *(Free Bible Version)* or "reprove" *(King James Version)*, understanding Jesus to mean that God's spirit convinces or reproves unbelievers through the witness of believers.—John 15:26-27.

[1256] When Jesus is killed the next afternoon, his enemies rejoice but his disciples grieve. That grief becomes joy when Jesus is resurrected, and he pours out upon the disciples God's spirit.

[1257] Birth pangs are the "traditional biblical metaphor for the sufferings which will herald the new, messianic age." (John chapter 16 note j, *The Jerusalem Bible:* Edited by Alexander Jones) The **world** into which the child is born is the organized human society or sphere of human life and circumstances. (**John 16:21**; contrast verse 33) For similar use of "world" see Matthew 16:26; Mark 8:36; Luke 9:25; 1 Corinthians 14:10; 1 Timothy 6:7.

[1258] Jesus' words allude to Isaiah 66:7-14, which refers to the institution of Messiah's kingdom. Even now, Christians can "rejoice with joy unspeakable," anticipating "the salvation of [our] souls."—1 Peter 1:8-9, *King James Version.*

[1259] In addition to the subjects of Jesus' model prayer, the Scriptures mention a wide range of circumstances that affect God's worshipers and that are appropriate subjects for prayer. (Matthew 6:9-13) Personal prayers may embrace virtually every facet of life.—Philippians 4:6; James 1:5; 1 John 3:22; 5:14.

[1260] Or "have believed that I came forth from the Father."—John 16:27, *American Standard Version.*

[1261] Jesus had read the apostles' hearts and answered their questions. (John 16:19) This supernatural knowledge, they concluded, proved that he was who he claimed to be. Compare John 4:39.

[1262] Or "through union with me."—John 16:33, *The New Testament in the Language of the People* by Charles B. Williams.

[1263] Jesus conquered the "world" of unrighteous human society alienated from God. (John 12:31; 15:18-19; 17:6, 9, 14-16, 25; 18:36; James 4:4; 2 Peter 2:5; 3:6; 1 John 2:15-17; 5:19) On the whole, the behavior and attitudes of people of this "world" are out of harmony with God's will as expressed in the Scriptures. Jesus **conquered the world** by not permitting the unrighteous thinking and actions of society to influence him in any way. (**John 16:33**; compare Romans 12:2) By his faith, loyalty and integrity, Jesus proved that "the ruler of the world," Satan, had "no power" over him.—John 14:30; see 1 John 5:4-5.

[1264] Jesus' **time** began with the conclusion of his public ministry and ended with returning to the Father through death, resurrection and exaltation.—**John 17:1**; see John 12:23; 13:1.

[1265] In John chapter 17 Jesus prays for himself, for his disciples and for all believers. "In its three parts (vv. 1-5; 6-19; 20-26) it seems almost to look back on the teaching of the three previous chapters, and convert them into prayer."—Edersheim, page 839.

[1266] The benefits of Jesus' sacrificed life are for those who know the Father and the Son and who are known by the Father and the Son. (John 10:14-15) Eternal life "is not just unending life in the sense of prolonged duration. Rather it is a quality of life, with its quality derived from a relationship with God." John 17:3 defines eternal life "as knowing (being in relationship with) the Father and the Son. The only way to gain this eternal life, that is, to obtain this knowledge of the Father, is through the Son (cf. [John] 14:6)." (John 17:3 footnote, *The NET Bible)* Coming to know God and Jesus is a continuous process (the Greek verb for **knowing** at **John 17:3** is in the present tense). This process involves knowing and accepting their values and standards.—1 John 2:3; 4:7-8.

[1267] The **work** given to the Son by the Father involved Jesus' mission to be the world's savior, accomplished specifically through his sacrificial death.—**John 17:4**; see John 4:34; 19:30.

[1268] Jesus asked to be restored to heavenly glory (implying his pre-human existence; John 1:1-14) by means of a resurrection. (Philippians 2:9-11) At **John 17:5** & 24 Jesus apparently referred to the **world** of humankind.

[1269] Or "I have given knowledge of your name." (John 17:6, *The Bible in Basic English;* also verse 26) In the Bible, making known someone's name may involve revealing the name itself as well as what the name stands for—the person's reputation and all that one declares himself or herself to be. (Matthew 6:9; Revelation 3:4) Jesus gave to his followers knowledge of the Father's name.

[1270] The **ones ... out of the world** specifically were the 11 faithful apostles. Jesus apparently meant the world of people alienated from God and separate from the true followers of Christ, his congregation.—**John 17:6**, 9, 14-16, 25; also, John 15:19.

[1271] The expression **Holy Father** occurs in the Bible only at **John 17:11** and is used as a form of address with reference to God; it is never used in reference to a human. See also Matthew 23:9.

[1272] Or "the son of destruction." (John 17:12, *Emphasized Bible)* The expression "son of" can refer to the judgment or outcome that results from following a certain course or displaying a certain characteristic. (2 Thessalonians 2:3) Jesus protected his disciples, but Judas Iscariot, who destroyed his own prospects for eternal life, **chose to be lost**.—**John 17:12**; 18:9.

[1273] Or "Make them holy"; "Set them apart," that is, for sacred service to God. (John 17:17, *The Holy Bible in Modern English; New English Translation;* see Exodus 40:13; 2 Chronicles 5:11; Jeremiah 1:5) Because the 11 faithful apostles continued in Jesus' teaching and knew the truth about his identity and mission (John 8:31-32; 17:8), Jesus could ask the Father to **sanctify them through ... Truth**—as he was sanctified through Truth—so that they might continue his work.—**John 17:17**.

[1274] God's **word** basically refers to communication with his people. (**John 17:17**) Much of what God communicated through prophets and others was written down and became Scripture inspired. God's word of truth shows what is required for a believer to be sanctified (or set apart) by God for His service, and then to remain in a sanctified state. When Jesus' followers obey God's word of truth, they become sanctified, or "purified." (1 Peter 1:22, *King James Version)* Christians live in a world ruled by Satan and so must keep themselves holy by living according to God's word of truth.

[1275] Or "setting myself apart"; "sanctifying myself." (John 17:19, *Complete Jewish Bible; Holy Bible from the Ancient Eastern Text)* From birth Jesus was holy and remained so throughout his life on Earth. (Luke 1:35; John 10:36; Acts 4:27; Hebrews 7:26) Jesus' blameless life course—including his sacrifice—made it possible for his followers to be sanctified, made holy, set apart for God's service. Therefore, Jesus could say that he was sanctifying himself for them. Jesus' followers are **sanctified through the truth** if they follow his footsteps closely and live by the truths he taught and the truths found in the Word of God, the Bible. (**John 17:19**; 2 Timothy 2:20-21; Hebrews 12:14; 1 Peter 2:21) Even so, Christians are not sanctified through personal merit, but sanctification comes through Jesus Christ.—Romans 3:24-26; Hebrews 10:10.

[1276] Some of the apostles will write inspired works that will become part of God's "word" that can help to sanctify a person. In time, others will accept this "truth."—John 17:17; Romans 10:13-15.

[1277] Jesus and his Father agree on all things. (John 10:30) Jesus prays that his followers similarly be **one**, unitedly working together for the same purpose, demonstrating cooperation and unity of thought. (**John 17:11, 21-23**; 1 Corinthians 3:6-9) First-century Christians were unified in action, belief and teaching. (Romans 15:5-6; 1 Corinthians 1:10; 2 Corinthians 13:11; Ephesians 4:3; Philippians 1:27; 2:2; 1 Peter 3:8) Jesus connected perfect unity with being loved by the Father. The love that true Christians have for one another identifies them as Jesus' disciples.—John 13:35; Colossians 3:14.

[1278] Jesus' apostles saw his **glory** in his words and works. (**John 17:22**) Jesus prayed for the future glorification of believers in Heaven.—Romans 8:17.

[1279] **The founding of the world** of humankind is associated with Abel, apparently the first redeemable human.—**John 17:24**; compare Luke 11:50-51.

[1280] Or "I have given to them knowledge of your name." (John 17:26, *The Bible in Basic English;* compare verse 6) Jesus could explain the Father—His purposes, activities and qualities—in a way that no one else could. (Matthew 11:27; John 1:18) Jesus helped his apostles to come to know the Father, the role of his Son and the things Jesus taught. Jesus said he had made known God's name and would continue to do so. Thus, God's name would continue to take on greater meaning to Jesus' followers.

[1281] Jesus and the apostles "apparently sang the hymn (probably one of the Psalms) as they rose to leave the Upper Room (John 14:31). Hence the passage in John 15 to 17 comes in between singing the hymn and reaching Gethsemane." (Robertson, page 201) According to tradition, the Hallel Psalms (113-118) were sung, or recited, during the Passover meal and at its conclusion; they contain prophecies about the Messiah. (Psalm 118:22-23; compare Matthew 21:42-44; Mark 12:10-11; Luke 20:17-18; Acts 4:11; 1 Peter 2:7-8) "The last Discourses had been spoken, the last Prayer, that of Consecration, had been offered, and Jesus prepared to go forth out of the City, to the Mount of Olives. The streets could scarcely be said to be deserted, for, from many a house shone the festive lamp, and many a company may still have been gathered; and everywhere was the bustle of preparation for going up to the Temple, the gates of which were thrown open at midnight."—Edersheim, page 842.

[1282] The Kidron Valley (Nahal Qidron), mentioned only at John 18:1 in the New Testament, separates Jerusalem from the Mount of Olives; it runs along the eastern side of the city, starting some distance to the north of Jerusalem's walls. At first, it is broad and shallow, but then it begins to narrow and deepen. Opposite the southern end of the former Temple area, it is approximately 100 feet (30 m) deep and 390 feet (120 m) wide, though it was evidently deeper in Jesus' time. The valley continues through the Judean wilderness to the Dead Sea. Also called the Winter Torrent of Kidron (the Greek word for "valley" literally means "a winter torrent"), the Kidron Valley was usually waterless even in winter, except in the case of an especially heavy rain.—Note on John 18:1, *New World Translation* Study Edition.

[1283] Tradition identifies Gethsemane with an orchard located at the foot of the Mount of Olives, at the fork of the road on its western slope. "It was a small property enclosed ..., 'a garden' in the Eastern sense, where probably, amidst a variety of fruit trees and flowering shrubs, was a lowly, quiet summer-retreat, connected with, or near by *[sic]*, the 'Olive-press.'" (Edersheim, page 842) The garden's name means "Oil Press." Here, "in the place where olives were crushed and ground, the One anointed with oil was crushed and rent."—Matthew 26:36 footnote, *The Nelson Study Bible*. Copyright © 1997 by Thomas Nelson, Inc. Used with permission.

[1284] "They had now reached the entrance of Gethsemane. It may have been that it led through the building with the 'oil-press,' and that the eight Apostles ... were left there. Or they may have been taken within the entrance of the Garden, and left there, while, pointing forward with a gesture of the Hand, He went 'yonder' and prayed (Matt. 26:36). According to St. Luke, He added the parting warning to pray that they might not enter into temptation." (Edersheim, page 845) The **temptation** to defect from Jesus had already overreached Judas and would temporarily snare Peter.—**Luke 22:40**.

[1285] The same three apostles who were present for the raising of Jairus' daughter and the Transfiguration. (Matthew 17:1; Mark 5:37; 9:2; Luke 8:51; 9:28) "If in that last contest His Human Soul craved for the presence of those who stood nearest Him and loved Him best, or if He would have them baptized with His Baptism, and drink of His Cup, these were the three of all others to be chosen."—Edersheim, page 845; Matthew 20:22; 26:33; Mark 10:38; 14:29.

[1286] Or "stay awake; be alert." (Matthew 26:38; Mark 14:34, *Expanded Bible)* At Matthew 26:41 Jesus linked staying awake spiritually with persevering in prayer. See also Matthew 24:42; 25:13.

[1287] In the Bible, several postures for prayer are mentioned, including standing and kneeling. However, a person in fervent prayer might lie face down with the body outstretched.—Numbers 16:22; 1 Kings 8:54; 1 Chronicles 21:16-17; Nehemiah 8:6; Daniel 6:10; Mark 11:25; Acts 9:40; 20:36; 21:5.

[1288] A Hebrew or Aramaic word (transliterated into Greek) meaning "father." *(The New Compact Bible Dictionary*, page 12; Romans 8:15; Galatians 4:6) Informal yet respectful, ***Abba*** combines some of the intimacy of "papa" with the dignity of "father." (**Mark 14:36**) It was among the first words a child learned to speak and an endearing form of address to one's father. Jesus' use of this expression shows the close, trusting relationship he had with his Father.

[1289] In the Bible, **cup** is often used figuratively of God's will for a person or persons. (**Matthew 26:39, 42**; **Mark 14:36**; **Luke 22:42**; see also Psalm 11:6; 16:5; 23:5; 75:8; Isaiah 51:17, 22; Jeremiah 25:15; Matthew 20:22; Mark 10:38; John 18:11) The reproach on his Father's name that Jesus' death as one charged with blasphemy and sedition could bring, along with the physical suffering of execution, would be a bitter drink, indeed.—2 Corinthians 5:21; Galatians 3:13; Hebrews 12:2; 1 Peter 2:24.

[1290] If Jesus feels the full force of the human fear of death and the instinctive urge to escape it, he gives expression to it but then stifles it by accepting his Father's will. God's will is God's law, and doing God's will is a choice proven with obedience. (Romans 12:2) Jesus chose to obey God's will, despite the suffering it brought upon him. In some cases, God's will refers to whatever God permits, including pain and suffering. In imitation of Jesus, we ought to accompany our prayers to God with **let your will ... be done**.—**Matthew 26:39, 42**; **Mark 14:36**; **Luke 22:42**.

[1291] Jesus may have been sweating blood metaphorically, or the physician's gospel could be describing a medical phenomenon. A condition known as hematidrosis refers to perspiration mingled with blood—literal sweating blood. This rare condition occurs in highly emotional states. See "The Gospel According to..."

[1292] Or "You want to do what is right, but you are weak." (Matthew 26:41, *Contemporary English Version)* Jesus knew that imperfect human beings often struggle to do what is right and resist temptation.—Matthew 6:13; Luke 11:4; compare Romans 7:18-19.

[1293] The day's events had evidently taken a toll on the apostles. They had prepared for Passover and celebrated it that evening. After Jesus instituted the Memorial of his death, he had a long talk with the apostles. Then they walked some distance through the narrow streets of Jerusalem, arriving at Gethsemane. By then it may have been well past midnight.

[1294] "Prayer consumed much time and energy in Jesus' earthly work. It crowned both the beginning (Luke 3:21) and ending (Luke 24:50, 51) of His public ministry. When necessary, He would take extraordinary measures to ensure privacy in order to pray ([Mark] 6:46; Matt. 14:22, 23; John 6:14, 15). Though the Lord Jesus did praise God (Luke 10:21) and thank the Father ([Mark] 8:6, 7) in His praying, most of His recorded prayers were petitions and intercessions."—Mark 14:32-42 footnote, *The Nelson Study Bible.* Copyright © 1997 by Thomas Nelson, Inc. Used with permission.

[1295] Or "You can sleep on now and take your rest." (Matthew 26:45; Mark 14:41, *Jerusalem Bible)* This sentence can be a question or a command. With gently ironical reproach, Jesus might have been saying, 'The time that you should have stayed awake with me has passed. You may as well go on sleeping.'

[1296] Evidently, when dismissed from the Passover meal, Judas went directly to the chief priests. (John 13:27) These immediately assembled their own officers—the Temple police—as well as a band of Roman soldiers. During Passover "the Temple itself was guarded by an armed Cohort, consisting of from 400 to 600 men, so as to prevent or quell any tumult among the numerous pilgrims. It would be to the captain of this 'Cohort' that the Chief Priests and leaders of the Pharisees would, in the first place, apply for an armed guard to effect the arrest of Jesus, on the ground that it might lead to some popular tumult." (Edersheim, pages 847-48; John 18:3, 12, *Catholic Public Domain Version)* "With a huge crowd of pilgrims in Jerusalem for the Passover, the Romans would have been especially nervous about an uprising of some sort. No doubt the chief priests and Pharisees had informed Pilate that this man Jesus was claiming to be the Messiah, or in the terms Pilate would understand, king of Israel. ... These Roman soldiers must have been ordered to accompany the servants of the chief priests and Pharisees by Pilate, since they would have been under the direct command of the Roman prefect or procurator." (John 18.3 footnote, *The NET Bible)* "This also explains not only the apparent preparedness of Pilate to sit in judgment early next morning, but also how Pilate's wife may have been disposed for those dreams about Jesus which so affrighted her." (Edersheim, page 848) Judas had perhaps first led the mob to where Jesus and his apostles had celebrated the Passover. Discovering that they had left, the mob followed Judas to Gethsemane, where Jesus and the apostles had often stopped as they traveled between Bethany and Jerusalem during the previous week.

[1297] According to Mark 14:44, Judas stipulated that Jesus be led away "safely." *(King James Version)* Judas may have already been feeling remorse and regret for his despicable actions. (Matthew 27:3) Otherwise, Judas may have been saying, 'lead him away so diligently, that he escape not out of your hands.'—Mark 14:44 footnote, *Geneva Bible 1599 Edition.*

[1298] In Jesus' day and culture, it was common for a disciple to greet his master with a kiss. According to the intensive form of the Greek verb for "kissed," Judas the hypocrite kissed Jesus repeatedly, loudly, effusively—literally covered Him with kisses. (Matthew 26:49; Mark 14:45; compare Proverbs 27:6) Luke 15:20 uses the same verb form to describe the father's welcome of his prodigal son.

[1299] From Jesus' unexpected advance the men in front recoiled, bumping into those behind them, causing them to stumble and fall.

[1300] Perhaps intending to behead Malchus, Peter may have swung the sword wildly, only wounding the servant. Mark (14:47) and John (18:10) both use a double diminutive to describe what was cut off, and this may indicate that just a part of the ear (for example, the earlobe) was severed.

[1301] Following his own teaching, Jesus showed kindness to those who hated him.—Luke 6:27.

[1302] Literally, "12 legions." (Matthew 26:53, *King James Version)* A legion was the principal unit of the Roman army, consisting of some 6,000 soldiers. Considering the power of just one angel, the power of 72,000 is beyond human comprehension.—2 Samuel 24:15-16; 2 Kings 19:35; 1 Chronicles 21:14-15; 2 Chronicles 32:21.

[1303] Although Jesus did not resist arrest he shamed His captors for their cowardice. The swarms of soldiers, the secluded location, the cover of night, the weapons—all suggested that Jesus was some violent **outlaw** (the same word used to describe Barabbas and the two men who were executed with Jesus) instead of the peaceful teacher he was.—**Mark 14:48**; 15:27; John 18:40.

[1304] Or "the power of darkness," that is, spiritual darkness. (Luke 22:53, *King James Version)* Satan exercised his power by influencing human agents to carry out the works of darkness that led to the execution of Jesus.—Acts 26:18; compare Colossians 1:13.

[1305] Literally, "the scriptures," meaning the Old Testament. (Matthew 26:54, 56, *King James Version)* Had Jesus applied for angelic aid, prophecies concerning his death and resurrection would not have been fulfilled.

[1306] "But there was one there who joined not in the flight, but remained, a deeply interested onlooker. When the soldiers had come to seek Jesus in the Upper Chamber of his home, Mark, roused from sleep, had hastily cast about him the loose linen garment or wrapper that lay by his bedside, and followed the armed band to see what would come of it. He now lingered in the rear, and followed as they led away Jesus, never imagining that they would attempt to lay hold on him, since he had not been with the disciples nor yet in the Garden. But they, perhaps the Jewish servants of the High-Priest, had noticed him. They attempted to lay hold on him, when, disengaging himself from their grasp, he left his upper garment in their hands, and fled."—Edersheim, pages 849-50.

[1307] Under Israel's law, the high—or "chief"—priest represented Israel before God and supervised other priests. (2 Chronicles 26:20; Ezra 7:5, *King James Version)* During the Roman occupation of Israel, Rome's rulers had authority to appoint and to depose the high priest. Changes in high priests by Roman authorities were not always recognized by the Israelites because the high priest held his office for life when Israel functioned as an independent nation. (Numbers 35:25, 28) This may explain why Jesus was taken to Annas. Appointed in A.D. 6 or 7 by Quirinius, the Roman governor of Syria, Annas served until his removal by prefect Valerius Gratus about A.D. 15. Even after the Romans deposed him, Annas was a powerful high priest emeritus, particularly influential with the relatives who succeeded him. His five sons and son-in-law Caiaphas also held the office of high priest. See Acts 4:6.

[1308] "The nature of this hearing seems to be more that of a preliminary investigation; certainly, normal legal procedure was not followed, for no indication is given that any witnesses were brought forth at this point to testify against Jesus." (John 18:15 footnote, *The NET Bible)* Of greater concern to Annas than the veracity of Jesus' teaching was how influential Jesus had become and how large a following he had gathered.

[1309] In Jesus' day and culture, striking the right cheek with the back of the hand was the most insulting of all physical blows. For inflicting such a slap, one could be fined 400 denarii—more than a year's wages for an agricultural worker.

[1310] According to tradition, Annas and Caiaphas resided in different wings of the same palace, sharing a common courtyard through which Jesus would have been led from Annas' residence to that of Caiaphas. "[T]he trial, and sentence of Jesus in the Palace of Caiaphas would ... have outraged every principle of Jewish criminal law and procedure." (Edersheim, page 858; see "The Sanhedrin—Theocracy's High Court.") Cases could be tried, and capital sentences pronounced, only in the Sanhedrin Hall. Furthermore, no trial could begin at night or be held on the Sabbath or on a Feast Day (or on the eve thereof).

[1311] At John 18:15 the author of the fourth gospel refers to himself as "another disciple." But how could a humble fisherman like the apostle John be acquainted with Jerusalem's most powerful family? Unable to answer that question, E.A. Tindall identified Peter's unnamed associate as Nicodemus. As a member of the Sanhedrin, Nicodemus would have had access to the high priest's palace. Another scholar, E.A. Abbott, proposed that the anonymous disciple was Judas Iscariot, the one apostle who was known to have had dealings with the high priest. These suggestions are, at best, speculative. In fact, the Scriptures suggest that John came from a well-to-do family whose members—including the apostle himself—were concerned with position and prestige. (Matthew 20:20-21; Mark 1:20; 10:35-37) Was theirs a priestly family, as Bishop Polycrates of Ephesus (c. 130 - 196) claimed? If they were, one can understand how John could be known to Caiaphas. See *The Ecclesiastical History of Eusebius Pamphilus:* Book 3, Chapter 31.

[1312] According to Edersheim, "the High-Priest's Palace was built on the slope of the hill, and ... there was an outer court, from which a door led into the inner court." He speculates that "Peter had followed as far as that inner door, while John had entered with the guard. When he missed his fellow-disciple, who was left outside this inner door, John 'went out,' and, having probably told the waiting-maid that this was a friend of his, procured his admission. [John 18:16] While John now hurried up to be in the Palace, and as near Christ as he might, Peter advanced into the middle of the court, where, in the chill spring night, a coal fire had been lighted. ... It was a chill night when Peter, down 'beneath' (Mark 14:66), looked up to the lighted windows. There, among the serving-men in the court, he was in every sense 'without' (Matt. 26:69). He approached the group around the fire. He would hear what they had to say; besides, it was not safe to stand apart; he might be recognised as one of those who had only escaped capture in the Garden by hasty flight."—page 854.

[1313] The Sanhedrin was made up of chief priests (including the high priest and his predecessors), elders ("heads of leading families in the community") and scholars ("experts and teachers of the commandments of God as well as the traditions of men").—Mark 14:53 footnote, *The Nelson Study Bible.* Copyright © 1997 by Thomas Nelson, Inc. Used with permission. See Mark 15:1; Luke 22:66.

[1314] Accusing Jesus "of being a fanatical seducer of the ignorant populace, who might lead them on to wild tumultuous acts"—such as destroying the Temple—would be an effective charge before Governor Pilate. (Edersheim, pages 859-60) But the witnesses misunderstood Jesus and misquoted him.—John 2:19-21.

[1315] The law of Israel required two or three witnesses to convict anyone and forbade false testimony. (Exodus 20:16; Deuteronomy 17:6; 19:15) Through the disagreement of the two witnesses, the charges against Jesus began to break down.

[1316] Or "of power." (Matthew 26:64; Mark 14:62, *KIng James Version)* The word "power" may be understood to refer to God himself; it may also imply that Jesus would be infused with power, or authority. To be on a ruler's right-hand means being in "the place of power."—Luke 22:69, *The Message.* See Hebrews 1:3; 8:1; 12:2; 1 Peter 3:22.

[1317] "At this critical moment Jesus abandons his policy of the 'messianic secret', ... and unequivocally acknowledges—as he had already acknowledged to his intimates...—that he is the Messiah. But he goes further and reveals himself not as the human Messiah of traditional expectation but as the Lord of Ps 110, ... and the mysterious personage of heavenly origin whom Daniel had seen in vision... [7:13-14]. Henceforth the Jews will not see him except in his glory which will be manifested ... in the victory of the resurrection... ."—Matthew chapter 26 note u, *The Jerusalem Bible:* Edited by Alexander Jones. See Matthew 16:27; 23:39; 24:30; 25:31; 26:64; Mark 8:38; 13:26; 14:62; Luke 9:26; 21:27.

[1318] A gesture expressing indignation. "[A]s the Law directed when blasphemy was spoken, the High Priest rent both his outer and inner garment, with a rent that might never be repaired...."—Edersheim, page 861.

[1319] "Blasphemy refers to any insulting of God, whether directly or indirectly, whether in speech or in actions. ... Both the Old Testament and the New Testament prohibit this sin and prescribe severe punishments for it. ... When [Jesus] claimed to be the exalted Son of God, [the Sanhedrin] judged his claim to be a mockery of God, the ultimate blasphemy, and therefore punishable by death."—Verlyn D. Verbrugge: *The NIV Topical Study Bible*, page 904. See Leviticus 24:15-16; Matthew 12:31; Mark 3:29; Luke 12:10.

[1320] Another of the many irregularities of this show trial, as Edersheim points out: "... the formal sentence of death, which, if it had been a regular meeting of the Sanhedrin, must now have been spoken by the President..., was not pronounced."—page 861.

[1321] Israel's law concerning cities of refuge stated that the accused was to be shielded from mistreatment. (Numbers chapter 35) Jesus was not afforded such protection.

[1322] Peter was quiet but restless. He sat down with the servants (Matthew 26:69; Mark 14:54; Luke 22:55) then stood up among them (John 18:25). This restlessness of attempted indifference attracted the attention he sought to avoid.

[1323] Peter invoked a curse on himself, saying, in effect, that he wished to be cursed if he was lying. By swearing that he did not know Jesus, he took an oath that his denials were true.

[1324] Peter's Galilean dialect or accent may have reflected regional vocabulary or pronunciation that differed from the Hebrew spoken in Judea. "Although the Judaean or Jerusalem dialect was far from pure," Edersheim comments, "the people of Galilee were especially blamed for neglecting the study of their language, charged with error in grammar, and especially with absurd mispronunciation, sometimes leading to ridiculous mistakes." (page 156) The distinct Galilean accent or vocabulary may have been due to foreign influence.

[1325] The crowing heard by Peter likely occurred during the third watch of the night, from midnight to about 3:00 a.m. (Mark 13:35) All four gospels mention this event, but only Mark (14:72) adds the detail that the rooster crowed twice. After the crowing, "the Lord turned and looked at Peter," according to Luke 22:61 *(The Emphasized Bible)*. At that point, Jesus was looking through a window that opened into the courtyard or was on a balcony overlooking the courtyard.

[1326] The "Sanhedrin" can refer to the people making up the court or to the building or location of the court. From John 18:28 it would appear that members of the Sanhedrin met again at Caiaphas' residence, not in their council chamber. Because "the hate of the Sanhedrin for Jesus [had] made them violate their own rules of legal procedure," Robertson suggests, "this ratification of the condemnation after dawn was an effort to make the action legal." (page 215) "It is not unreasonable to suppose," Edersheim posits, "that some who would not take part in deliberations which were virtually a judicial murder might, once the resolution was taken, feel ... absolved from guilt in advising how the informal sentence might best be carried into effect. It was this, and not the question of Christ's guilt, which formed the subject of deliberation on that early morning." (page 864) This session nevertheless "violated various Jewish legal rules given in later sources: meeting on the morning of a feast; meeting at Caiaphas's home; trying a defendant without defense; and reaching the verdict in one day instead of the two days that were required for capital cases."—Luke 22:66 footnote, *The Nelson Study Bible*. Copyright © 1997 by Thomas Nelson, Inc. Used with permission.

[1327] Or "on the right hand of the power of God." (Luke 22:69, *King James Version)* For the second time, Jesus courageously identified himself as the foretold Son of Man. (Matthew 26:64; Mark 14:62; Daniel 7:13-14. See "Jesus, A.K.A. ...") Where the Son of Man is seated implies that Jesus would be infused with power, or authority.—1 Peter 3:22.

[1328] In the court's eyes, Jesus' answer sufficed as an admission of blasphemy deserving of death. Claiming to be the Messiah was not blasphemous; claiming to be God's judge of his people, however, was.

[1329] As Rome's representative, Pilate had to confirm and carry out any sentence pronounced by the Israelites.

[1330] While Judas may have felt remorse or regret, his actions—returning to the very men he had conspired with and then committing suicide—show he was not repentant. The basic difference between remorse and repentance is that positive change accompanies repentance.—Acts 3:19.

[1331] According to Matthew 27:5 Judas hanged himself. Acts 1:18 reports that Judas died as the result of a fall. Apparently, the tree branch to which Judas tied the rope (or the rope itself) broke and he fell. Whether it was the fall that killed him, or he was already dead from a broken neck when his body struck the ground cannot be known.

[1332] Or "the price of blood." (**Matthew 27:6**, *King James Version*) The priests saw the wrong in donating **blood money** to God's temple. (Deuteronomy 23:18) But they saw nothing wrong with paying "the price of blood" for the betrayal of God's son!

[1333] Since the fourth century, the Field of Blood has been identified with a location on the southern slope of the Hinnom Valley, just before it joins the Kidron Valley. This seems to have been an area where potters pursued their craft. According to Matthew 27:9-10 the field's purchase fulfilled a prophecy: "They took the thirty pieces of silver, the cost of him whom they so valued, as a price from the sons of Israel, and they bought a potter's field with them, just as Jehovah had instructed." *(21st Century New Testament* by Vivian Capel) Matthew paraphrased the words of Zechariah 11:12-13 but attributed them to Jeremiah. In the Hebrew canon, Jeremiah was placed first among the prophetic books so his name may have applied to the whole collection of Prophets, which included Zechariah; or Zechariah recorded a prophecy spoken by Jeremiah.

[1334] Christ's accusers were early on the governor's doorstep that morning because a Roman court could convene immediately after sunrise. The Sanhedrin's leaders or their representatives (neither Annas nor Caiaphas seems to have been present) handed over Jesus to Pilate. (Matthew 27:1-2; Mark 15:1; Luke 22:66; 23:1) Jesus had foretold that he would be executed by foreigners ("lifted up" as opposed to Israel's method of execution, stoning; John 3:14; 8:28; 12:32-33) on charges brought against him by his own countrymen.—Matthew 20:18-19; John 18:31-32.

[1335] The governor's official residence was called a praetorium; its traditional location is the tower-fortress of Antonia, on the east hill north of the Temple area. The palace of Herod, situated in the northwest corner of the upper city (that is, of the southern part of Jerusalem) near the present Jaffa Gate, is another possibility. The governor stayed in Jerusalem only on certain occasions, such as festivals, since there was a potential for unrest. (His usual residence was in Caesarea.—Acts 23:33, 35) Jesus' accusers refused to enter Pilate's palace, knowing that contact with Gentiles would disqualify them from eating the Passover. (See Acts 10:28) Although the main meal had taken place, there remained ceremonial meals that lasted throughout the week.

[1336] Pilate was not professing ignorance of the charge, only requesting that it be formally stated. Since Pilate had cooperated with them in Jesus' arrest by providing Roman soldiers, Israel's authorities might have expected Pilate to grant them permission to carry out the death sentence. Pilate's question, however, indicated that he was going to try the prisoner personally. He regarded Jesus' appearances before the Sanhedrin as inquiries only and their decision as merely an accusation.

[1337] The Sanhedrin may have had the authority to execute a person for religious reasons, but not for civil offenses. (John 18:31; see "The Sanhedrin—Theocracy's High Court.") If the Sanhedrin could get Pilate to execute Jesus on a political charge it would tend to absolve them of responsibility before the people.

[1338] No one could rule in the Roman Empire without Caesar's consent. Anyone who declared themselves a king in opposition to Caesar would be guilty of sedition. (The charge of opposition to taxation was an outright lie.—Matthew 22:21; Mark 12:17; Luke 20:25.) The charges were a direct challenge to the authority of Rome; her representative (Pilate) had to act upon them.

[1339] Or "king of the Jews." (John 18:33, *King James Version;* compare John 1:49) Seemingly with sarcasm and an attitude of incredulity Pilate asked, 'So you're the king of the Jews, are you?' But it is also possible that Pilate was impressed by Jesus' regal disposition and dignity and asked sincerely, 'Are you really the king of the Jews?'

[1340] Though Jesus confessed to Pilate that he was a king, his kingship was not what Pilate imagined. Jesus made clear that he was "not a king in this world" and therefore no threat to Caesar.—John 18:36, *The Bible in Worldwide English.*

[1341] By word and deed, Jesus bore witness to the truth regarding God's promises. (2 Corinthians 1:20) The expression **came into the world** seems to refer primarily to Jesus' going out among people at the time of his baptism.—**John 18:37**; compare John 1:9; 3:19; 9:39; 12:46.

[1342] Pilate apparently referred to truth in general or as an abstract concept. His question was rhetorical, asked in cynical disbelief. A sincere question Jesus would have answered. Regardless of the spirit in which the question was asked, the answer had already been given. See John 14:6.

[1343] This charge of stirring up rebellion against Rome pressured Pilate to act. The governor could not risk being found derelict in his duty by releasing Jesus.

[1344] While in Jerusalem for the Festival (an obligation that even a nominal Jew like Herod would fulfill), Herod "occupied the old Maccabean Palace, close to that of the high priest," according to Edersheim. From its halls one could see into the city, and even into the Temple. "We know not which of the Maccabees had built this palace. But it was occupied, not by the actually reigning prince, who always resided in the fortress (Baris, afterwards Antonia), but by some other member of the family. From them it passed into the possession of Herod."—pages 868-69, 83-4.

[1345] Hearing of Jesus' miracles, Herod was concerned that Jesus might be John—whom he beheaded—raised from the dead. Unsure, Herod wanted to see Jesus.—Luke 9:7-9; see "Biographical Sketch: Herod Antipas."

[1346] Herod might have taken one of his own splendid royal garments to dress up Jesus before sending him back to Pilate. This is a different garment from the scarlet (or purple) robe with which Pilate's soldiers later clothed Jesus at the governor's residence. (Matthew 27:28, 31; Mark 15:17; John 19:2, 5) Herod, Pilate and the Roman soldiers apparently had the same intention when clothing Jesus with these two different garments—to mock him as the so-called King of the Jews.—John 19:3.

[1347] Herod had leveled certain accusations against Pilate, who had experienced trouble with the Galileans. (Luke 13:1; see "Biographical Sketch: Pontius Pilate.") But Herod was pleased with Pilate's decision to send Jesus to him. Although disappointed in Jesus, Herod agreed with Pilate that the charges against Jesus were baseless.—Luke 23:14-15.

[1348] Pilate's judgment seat was probably a chair on a platform, approached by steps, from which he addressed crowds and announced decisions.—Matthew 27:19; John 19:13; see also Acts 12:21; 25:6, 10, 17.

[1349] The dream of Pilate's wife, to whom tradition has given the name Procula, was evidently of divine origin. On the previous evening, after granting the Roman guard for arresting Jesus, Pilate may have spoken of this to his wife. This could explain both her dream and his reluctance to condemn Jesus. An apocryphal gospel describes Procula as a convert to Judaism. The Greek Church places her in its Catalog of Saints.

[1350] Romans released prisoners to please the crowds, but this tradition originated with the Israelites. (John 18:39) By releasing Jesus on account of the custom rather than acquitting him, Pilate would avoid insulting Israel's leaders, who had already found Jesus guilty.

[1351] "[I]f the stream of popular sympathy might be diverted to Bar-Abbas, the doom of Jesus would be [all] the more securely fixed. On the present occasion it might be [all] the easier to influence the people, since Bar-Abbas belonged to that class, not uncommon at the time, which, under the colourable pretence *[sic]* of political aspirations, committed robbery and other crimes. But these movements had deeply struck root in popular sympathy." (Edersheim, pages 871-72) Barabbas had been convicted of, among other things, insurrection—a crime of which Jesus had been accused.—Luke 23:18-19.

[1352] Or "So I will have him scourged, and then release him." (Luke 23:22, *Open English Bible)* "Scourging was a life-threatening punishment. Evidently this was an attempt by Pilate to punish Jesus so severely that the people would have pity and say, 'It is enough; release him' (see John 19:4, 5)."—Matthew 27:26 footnote, *The Nelson Study Bible.* Copyright © 1997 by Thomas Nelson, Inc. Used with permission.

[1353] Three times Pilate asked the crowd questions regarding Jesus and three times (at least) the crowd called for Jesus' execution. (Mark 15:9, 12, 14; Luke 23:18-23) If anyone raised their voice for Jesus they were not heard. All of his apostles seem to have scattered.—Matthew 26:31, 56; Mark 14:27, 50; John 16:32.

[1354] The religious authorities, who wanted to avoid a riot earlier, now used one to accomplish their goal. "The tenure of Pilate had been rocked by conflicts with the Jews from the very beginning. He could scarcely have afforded another one on his record."—Matthew 27:24 footnote, *The Nelson Study Bible.* Copyright © 1997 by Thomas Nelson, Inc. Used with permission. See "Biographical Sketch: Pontius Pilate."

[1355] Or "The responsibility for killing him will rest on us and our children." (Matthew 27:25, *GOD'S WORD Translation)* The words recall the rite prescribed to mark the freedom from guilt of the elders of a city where untracked murder had been committed. (Deuteronomy 21:6-9; compare Psalm 26:6, 73:13) "The Mishnah tells us, that, after the solemn washing of hands of the elders and their disclaimer of guilt, priests responded with this prayer: 'Forgive it to Thy people Israel, whom Thou hast redeemed, O Lord, and lay not innocent blood upon Thy people Israel!'" (Edersheim, pages 872-73) As one who administered justice in Israel, Pilate must have been aware of this rite.

[1356] The punishment of scourging (flogging) usually preceded execution. The victim was stripped of his clothes and bound to a post with his hands fastened above him (or sometimes he was thrown to the ground). Guards standing on either side of the victim would incessantly beat him with a flagellum. This instrument consisted of a handle into which several cords or knotted leather thongs were fixed. Sometimes the thongs were weighted with jagged pieces of bone or metal to make the blows more painful. Each blow cut deeper and deeper, tearing into subcutaneous tissue and muscle. While the Israelites allowed only 39 lashes, the Romans had no limit; many people died of such a beating.

[1357] "The soldiers were, as mostly in the provinces, chiefly provincials—in this case, probably Syrians. They were all the more bitterly hostile to the Jews."—Edersheim, page 873 note 35.

[1358] The plant from which the wreath was fashioned may have been the Christ-thorn, a shrub with flexible branches and stiff thorns. "In placing the crown of *thorns* on his head, the soldiers were unwittingly symbolizing God's curse on humanity (cf. Gen 3:18) being placed on Jesus. Their purpose would have been to mock Jesus' claim to be a king; the crown of thorns would have represented the 'radiant corona' portrayed on the heads of rulers on coins and other artifacts in the 1st century."—Matthew 27:29 footnote, *The NET Bible.*

[1359] According to Matthew 27:28 the soldiers draped Jesus with a scarlet robe. Mark 15:17 and John 19:2 & 5 say that the garment was purple. The robe was probably a military garment called a *sagum;* being red it suggested the royal purple to the soldiers. This short cloak was usually made of wool; in more costly form and material it was presented to foreign kings. Along with the robe, Jesus was given other mock attributes of royalty—thorns for a crown and a reed for a scepter.

[1360] The soldiers hailed Jesus as they would have hailed Caesar, evidently to ridicule the claim that he was a king.

[1361] This contemptuous treatment of Jesus fulfilled his own words as well as prophecy regarding the Messiah.—Mark 10:34; Isaiah 50:6.

[1362] The Latin *Vulgate* rendering of Pilate's words, *ecce homo,* has been the theme for many artists. (John 19:5) Those who heard Pilate and were familiar with the Scriptures may have remembered a prophetic description of the Messiah: "Thus speaks Jehovah of hosts, saying, Behold, the man whose name is the Branch." (Zechariah 6:12, *A Conservative Version)* Unknowingly (and ironically) Pilate presented Jesus to the nation under a messianic title.

[1363] In Rome, claiming to be **the Son of God** was a serious offense. (**John 19:7**) After the posthumous deification of Julius Caesar, his adopted son and successor Octavian was declared *divi filius*—"Son of God." This designation became a title of emperors, inscribed on Roman altars, temples, statues and coins. When the chief priests and their accomplices charged Jesus with claiming to be the Son of God, they were essentially accusing him of assuming an official title, which was tantamount to treason. This charge was new to Pilate, and it concerned him greatly. At the time, Tiberius held the title *divi filius* and his reputation for killing enemies—real or imagined—put the fear of "God" in Pilate.

[1364] God grants authority to human rulers to administer earthly affairs. Pilate was not personally put in his position by God; his life-and-death authority over Jesus was by God's permission. "The higher powers," of which Pilate was part, exercise authority by divine tolerance.—Romans 13:1, *King James Version.*

[1365] Or "So those [literally, "he"] who brought me to you have the greater sin." (John 19:11 & footnote, *The Living Bible)* Several culpable men were involved in the events leading up to Jesus' appearance before Pilate: Judas Iscariot, Caiaphas and the entire Sanhedrin, and even the crowds that were persuaded to ask for the release of Barabbas. (Matthew 26:47-48, 59; 27:1, 20, 24-25; Mark 14:43-44, 55; 15:11, 15; Luke 22:47-48; 23:23-25; John 18:3-5, 14; 19:14-16; Acts 3:13-15) Jesus likely had in mind all those who shared in the sin of killing him. Pilate did not act out of calculated malice, unlike Jesus' religious and civic enemies. Theirs was the **greater guilt**; Pilate's less-so.—**John 19:11**.

[1366] The honorary title **Friend of Caesar** was often bestowed on provincial governors in the Roman Empire. (**John 19:12**) Pilate would have been eligible to receive such an honor. "It also appears that the powerful Sejanus was his patron in Rome, and Sejanus held considerable influence with Tiberius. ... Thus, it is possible that Pilate held this honor. Therefore, it appears that the Jewish authorities were putting a good deal of psychological pressure on Pilate to convict Jesus."—John 19:12 footnote, *The NET Bible.*

[1367] If Pilate had acquitted Jesus, Israel's authorities could have complained to Rome that Pilate had released a traitor. Tiberius Caesar had broadened the law of injured majesty to include virtually any insult against the emperor and he was infamous for executing any whom he considered disloyal—even high-ranking officials. Pilate had already irritated the Judeans and could not risk an accusation of treason. (See "Biographical Sketch: Pontius Pilate.") He allowed his fear of a jealous emperor to influence him when he pronounced the death sentence on Jesus, a man he knew to be innocent.

[1368] In Rome there was an interval of two days between sentencing and execution. Perhaps Pilate was anxious to be finished with the matter and sidestepped the rule (assuming it applied in the provinces).

[1369] Simon took over after Jesus' strength gave out. (Roman authorities could demand compulsory service from a citizen.) Simon was from Cyrene, a city located near the North African coast, south-southwest of the island of Crete, where Tripoli is today. According to Edersheim, a "large colony of Jews ... had settled in Cyrene. He ... seems to have been well known, at least afterwards, in the Church—and his sons Alexander and Rufus even better than he (Mark 15:21)."—page 878; Romans 16:13.

[1370] "From the ancient Palace of Herod [the procession] descended, and probably passed through the gate in the first wall, and so into the busy quarter of Acra. As it proceeded, the numbers who followed from the Temple, from the dense business-quarter through which it moved, increased. Shops, bazaars, and markets were, indeed, closed on the holy feast-day. But quite a crowd of people would come out to line the streets and to follow; and, especially, women, leaving their festive preparations, raised loud laments, not in spiritual recognition of Christ's claims, but in pity and sympathy (St. Luke)." (Edersheim, page 877) The **daughters of Jerusalem** could have been professional mourners appointed by custom. (**Luke 23:28**) However, from Luke 23:37, it seems that the mourning for Jesus was sincere, not *pro forma*.

[1371] Birth was a sign of blessing; barrenness a sign of judgment. Jesus' reversal of imagery indicated that something was wrong.

[1372] There would be no hiding place for those who stayed in Judea when Rome invaded in A.D. 70. Even when people fled to the mountaintop citadel of Masada, they could not escape God's judgment. Rather than endure divine wrath, they desired the relief of death. See Hosea 10:8; compare Revelation 6:15-17.

[1373] Or "If these things are done to me, the living tree, what will happen to you, the dry tree?" (Luke 23:31 footnote, *New Living Translation)* Israel was like a dying tree that still had some moisture left, for Jesus was present and so were a number of Israelites who believed in him. However, Jesus would soon be executed, and the nation would be spiritually dead, resembling a dried-up tree. (Matthew 21:43) When Israel's people and her leaders demanded death for Jesus, they pronounced a sentence of death upon themselves.—Matthew 27:25.

[1374] In fulfillment of prophecy, Jesus was "counted with criminals." (Isaiah 53:12, *The Bible in Living English;* Luke 22:37) Luke (23:32-33, 39) refers to the two men generically as "evil-doers"; Matthew (27:38) and Mark (15:27) are more specific, calling them "robbers." Barabbas is similarly described by John (18:40); according to Luke (23:19) he was in prison for sedition and murder.—Young's *Literal Translation.*

[1375] The names Golgotha and Calvary come from the words for "skull" in Hebrew and Latin, respectively. The name "implies a bald, round, skull-like mound or hillock." *(The New Compact Bible Dictionary,* page 202) Whereas the gospels identify Calvary merely as a "place," tradition describes the location as a mountain or hill. (Matthew 27:33; Mark 15:22; Luke 23:33; John 19:17) Perhaps it was from such an elevation that some were able to view Jesus' execution from a distance. Although the exact location of Golgotha is uncertain, the traditional site where the Church of the Holy Sepulchre now stands is a reasonable possibility.

[1376] "Ordinarily, the [death sentence] procession was headed by the centurion, or rather, preceded by one who proclaimed the nature of the crime, and carried a white, wooden board, on which it was written. Commonly, also, it took the longest road to the place of execution, and through the most crowded streets, so as to attract [the] most public attention." However, "this long circuit and the proclamation of the herald ... are not hinted at in the text, and seem incongruous to the festive season, and the other circumstances of the history."—Edersheim, pages 875-76.

[1377] It was evidently customary for executioners to keep the clothes of the condemned. Criminals were stripped of their clothing and possessions before being executed, making the ordeal even more humiliating. Israelite males typically wore an inner garment (a shirt-like tunic with long sleeves or half sleeves, reaching to the knees or ankles) and an outer garment (a loose robe or coat, or just a simple rectangular piece of material). "At a distance of six feet from the place of execution the criminal was undressed, only the covering absolutely necessary for decency being left.... In the case of Jesus, we have reason to think that, while the mode of punishment to which He was subjected was un-Jewish, every concession would be made to Jewish custom, and hence we thankfully believe that ... He was spared the indignity of exposure."—Edersheim, page 876.

[1378] Completely seamless garments were unique, a rare and desirable possession.

[1379] Lots were pebbles or small bits of wood or stone gathered into the folds of a garment or into a vessel and then shaken. The lot that fell out or was drawn out was the one chosen. (Joshua 18:6; Nehemiah 11:1; Proverbs 16:33; 18:18) In Scripture the term "lot" is also used figuratively with the meaning "share or inheritance."—Deuteronomy 32:9; Psalm 16:5; *The New Compact Bible Dictionary*, page 328.

[1380] Since the Last Supper Jesus had tasted neither food nor drink. The hours following were filled with emotional agony and physical torment. And yet, Jesus refused the pain-dulling potion, evidently wanting to have full possession of all his faculties during this test of his faith. Women of Jerusalem customarily gave bitter-tasting narcotic drinks to condemned criminals.

[1381] Tied to a stake, the condemned person might live for several days before dying from pain, thirst, hunger and exposure. In the case of Jesus, the Romans nailed his hands and feet to a stake. (John 20:25; compare Psalm 22:16) The Greek word traditionally translated "cross" "means primarily an upright stake or beam, and secondarily a stake used as an instrument for punishment and execution."—J.B. Torrance: *The New Bible Dictionary*—2nd edition, page 253.

[1382] Ignorant of who Jesus really was, the Roman soldiers did not appreciate the gravity of their actions. Jesus may also have had in mind the crowd who called for his execution, some of whom repented a short time later.—Acts 2:36-42.

[1383] Or "the king of the Jews." (John 19:19, Young's *Literal Translation*) The Romans customarily posted a sign stating the crime of the condemned criminal. Israel in Jesus' day was a multilingual environment. The charge against Jesus was written in official Latin (John 19:20 contains the only specific mention of the Latin language in the Bible.) and in Hebrew and Greek (Koine). The chief priests objected to the sign's wording, insisting it should read, "he said, I am King of the Jews." Pilate answered, "What I have written I have written." (John 19:21-22, *King James Version*) Placing the title "King of the Jews" over Jesus' head may have been Pilate's response to the Jewish authorities who pressured him into executing an innocent man.

[1384] This gesture expressed derision, contempt or mockery. The passersby inadvertently fulfilled a prophecy about the Messiah: "All those who see me mock me. They insult me with their lips. They shake their heads, saying, 'He trusts in JEHOVAH; let him deliver him. Let him rescue him, since he delights in him.'"—Psalm 22:7-8, *New Heart English Bible*: Jehovah Edition.

[1385] This criminal was not a conqueror of the world with Christ, nor had he been born again. (John 3:5; 16:33; Revelation 2:7) He was, however, an Israelite (his beliefs in one God and the resurrection were uniquely Jewish; Luke 23:40, 42) and would have known about the Garden of Eden, humankind's original home. (In Biblical Hebrew the word for paradise is used for a choice garden.—Ecclesiastes 2:5) Translations of the New Testament into Hebrew by Delitzsch, Salkinson & Ginsburg and United Bible Societies render Luke 23:43: "You will be with me in the garden of Eden." God's prophets foretold the restoration of Edenic paradise on Earth. (Isaiah 51:3; Ezekiel 36:35) With the hope of being resurrected into that paradise the penitent thief died.—Acts 24:15.

[1386] This imagery has parallels to the Day of the Lord. (Joel 2:10-11; Amos 8:9; Zephaniah 1:14-15) Solar eclipses last for less than eight minutes and are astronomically impossible when the moon is full (it was Passover season). This miraculous darkness was caused by God.

[1387] Salome's name means "peace." (*The New Bible Dictionary*—2nd edition, page 1056) She was the mother of the apostles James and John and the fleshly sister of Mary, Jesus' mother. Salome was among the women who accompanied Jesus and ministered to him from their belongings.—Matthew 27:55-56; Mark 15:40-41; John 19:25.

[1388] Unnamed in the gospel account, Jesus' specially loved disciple is believed to be the apostle John.—John 13:23; 19:26; 20:2; 21:7, 20.

[1389] Mary's oldest son must have been concerned with his (probably widowed) mother's physical and material needs and especially with her spiritual welfare. John had proved his faith, whereas it is unclear whether Jesus' fleshly brothers were as yet believers.—John 7:5.

[1390] Jesus' words are usually considered to be Aramaic, perhaps of a Galilean dialect. As to whether Jesus would have spoken Hebrew or Aramaic, opinion is divided. The Greek transliteration of Jesus' words does not allow for a positive identification of the original language.

[1391] Jesus senses that his Father has, as it were, withdrawn his protection so that his Son's integrity might be tested to the limit. Jesus' cry is one of distress but not despair; it may have brought to hearers' minds the many things prophesied about Messiah in Psalm 22—that he would be mocked, derided and attacked in his hands and feet and that his garments would be divided by lot. (verses 1, 7-8, 16, 18) "[T]his lament which Jesus takes from the scriptures is a prayer to God and is followed in the Psalm by an expression of joyful confidence in final victory."—Matthew chapter 27 note s, *The Jerusalem Bible:* Edited by Alexander Jones.

[1392] From Jesus' accusers and the infuriated mob Roman soldiers present had learned snatches of a distorted story of the Messiah. They must have been the ones who misunderstood who Jesus was calling. An Israelite would not have mistaken "Eli" for "Elijah" or misinterpreted a quotation of Psalm 22:1 as a call for that prophet. It is also possible that dehydration made Jesus' speech somewhat unintelligible.

[1393] Jesus, the source of "living water," expressed his thirst in fulfillment of Psalm 22:15 and 69:21—John 4:10; 7:38, *King James Version*.

[1394] This beverage was not the drugged wine previously refused by Jesus. (Matthew 27:34, 48; Mark 15:23, 36; Luke 23:36; compare Psalm 69:21) Wine vinegar was a cheap drink of the lower class, including slaves and soldiers.

[1395] Hyssop might have been available when Jesus was executed because of its use in the Passover celebration. (Exodus 12:21-22; John 19:29) The original language terms rendered "hyssop" in many Bible translations may embrace several different kinds of plants. Marjoram, for instance, is common in the Middle East. However, because marjoram might not have been long enough to carry the stalk to Jesus' mouth (under favorable conditions, it attains a height of 1.5 to 3 feet [0.5 to 0.9 m]), the hyssop may have been a bunch of marjoram attached to a reed and held to Jesus' mouth.—Matthew 27:48; Mark 15:36.

[1396] Or "to your hands I commit my spirit." (Luke 23:46, *World English Bible)* Jesus committed his life force to God for safe keeping, with confidence that it would be restored to him. Jesus quoted from Psalm 31:5.

[1397] Israelites usually buried their dead in caves or vaults cut into the rock. These tombs were customarily located outside the cities, an exception being the tombs of the kings.

[1398] There have been similar incidents in modern times. An earthquake in Ecuador in 1949 broke open burial vaults, ejecting many bodies. In Sonson, Colombia, in 1962, 200 corpses in the town cemetery were thrown out of their tombs by a violent tremor. After a quake in Guatemala in 1976 mourners who went to bury their dead in family plots found that the coffins of long-dead relatives had been uncovered. An earthquake in Popayán, Colombia, in 1983 struck with such force that the walls of mausoleums crumbled, spilling caskets.

[1399] This catastrophe betokened the impending destruction of the Temple. "The Veils before the Most Holy Place were 40 cubits (60 feet) long, and 20 (30 feet) wide, of the thickness of the palm of the hand, and wrought in 72 squares, which were joined together; and these Veils were so heavy, that, in the exaggerated language of the time, it needed 3000 priests to manipulate each. ... [A]lthough the earthquake might furnish the physical basis; the rent of the Temple-Veil was—with reverence be it said—really made by the Hand of God." (Edersheim, page 894) Only God could have torn the curtain "from the top to the bottom." (Matthew 27:51; Mark 15:38, *King James Version)* This not only manifested God's wrath against his Son's killers but also signified the possibility of entry into Heaven "through the veil, that is to say, [Jesus'] flesh."—Hebrews 10:19-20, *King James Version*. See John 3:13.

[1400] The officer was a centurion, one in command of about 100 soldiers in the Roman army. He may have been at Jesus' trial before Pilate and heard the charge that Jesus claimed to be the Son of God. (Matthew 27:27; John 19:7) "Whatever a Roman soldier might mean by *a son of God* (perhaps, 'divine hero' ...), the Gospel writer probably understood the words as a Christian confession."—M. Jack Suggs: Matthew 27:54 footnote, *The New English Bible*.

[1401] Normally, Romans would let bodies hang as a warning to would-be offenders. In this case, however, Israel's authorities asked Pilate to order the legs of Jesus and the two criminals to be broken and their bodies removed before the Sabbath began at sundown. (How ironic that the perpetrators of judicial murder should be concerned with upholding ceremonial law!) A person hanging with arms raised above the head would have difficulty breathing. Broken legs could not raise the body to relieve pressure on the lungs, resulting in suffocation. The bones were broken with a club or a hammer. "This would not itself bring death, but the breaking of the bones was always followed by a coup de grace, by sword, lance, or stroke ..., which immediately put an end to what remained of life. Thus the 'breaking of the bones' was a sort of increase of punishment, by way of compensation for its shortening by the final stroke that followed."—Edersheim, page 895; John 19:31.

[1402] As a matter of anatomy, the sword probably pierced Jesus' pericardium, a membrane surrounding the heart. From the pericardium would flow red clotted matter and serum, resembling **blood and water**. (**John 19:34**) Some theologians interpret the blood and water as symbols of sacrifice and grace; others see the blood and water as symbolizing baptism or the gift of God's spirit.—John 7:38-39; 1 John 5:6-8.

[1403] God commanded regarding the Passover sacrifice that the animal's bones are not broken. (Exodus 12:46; Numbers 9:12) True to that pattern, none of Jesus' bones were broken. (1 Corinthians 5:7) Although the Israelite authorities and Roman soldiers did "look on him whom they pierced," John 19:37 *(King James Version)* alludes to Christ's second presence. Compare Revelation 1:7.

[1404] Joseph was probably not present at the trial, since Mark 14:64 indicates that all the council members condemned Jesus to death. It may be that he "had gone into hiding for fear of the Jews."—John chapter 19 note m, *New English Bible*.

[1405] Joseph wanted to give Jesus an honorable burial. This brave act openly identified Joseph, a member of the Sanhedrin, with the man it condemned.

[1406] It seems that Joseph was present when Jesus died; he knew of Jesus' death before Pilate did.—Mark 15:43-45.

[1407] Linen varied in quality, the superior kind being worn by kings, the wealthy and men in high governmental positions. (Genesis 41:42; Exodus 28:39-42; 2 Samuel 6:14; 1 Chronicles 15:27; Esther 8:15; Luke 16:19) The cleanliness and purity of white linen symbolizes righteousness. (Revelation 19:8, 14) "It seems as if the 'clean linen cloth' in which the Body had been wrapped, was now torn into 'cloths' or swathes, into which the Body, limb by limb, was now 'bound,' no doubt, between layers of myrrh and aloes, the Head being wrapped in a napkin." (Edersheim, page 899; Matthew 27:59; John 19:39-40) Myrrh is an aromatic gum resin obtained from a variety of thorny shrubs or small trees; it was one of the ingredients of the holy anointing oil. (Exodus 30:23-25) In addition to preparing bodies for burial, myrrh was used to scent such things as garments or beds, and it was added to oil for massages and body lotions. (Proverbs 7:17) The aloes brought by Nicodemus were likely the same as the aloeswood product referred to in the Old Testament. (Psalm 45:8; Song of Solomon 4:14) The aloe tree of the Bible may be the eaglewood tree, now found principally in India and neighboring regions. The inner core of the trunk and the branches is impregnated with resin and a fragrant oil, from which comes the highly prized perfume. Apparently at its most aromatic when in a state of decay, the wood is sometimes buried in the ground to hasten the process. The decayed wood was ground into a fine powder and then sold as "aloes." In preparing a body for burial, aloe powder and myrrh were used to overpower the smell of decomposition.

[1408] The Israelites usually buried their dead in caves or vaults cut into soft rock. These tombs were customarily located outside the cities (except for the tombs of the kings). Such tombs often contained benchlike shelves or niches where bodies could be laid. "[A]t the entrance to 'the tomb'—and within 'the rock'—there was 'a court,' nine feet square, where ordinarily the bier was deposited, and its bearers gathered to do the last offices for the Dead." (Edersheim, page 898) Joseph's vault had never been used, which suggests that he had recently moved from Arimathea to Jerusalem and that he expected to use this property as his family burial site. Burying Jesus in Joseph's own future tomb was a generous gesture and fulfilled the prophecy: "they made his grave ... with a rich man in his death."—Isaiah 53:9, *American Standard Version.*

[1409] "The tomb of Jesus was sealed with two stones - a great stone, ... covering the entrance and then laid against it, another smaller stone ... . It was at the area where one stone laid against the other that a seal was placed by the Roman authorities so that the slightest disturbance might become apparent." (https://www.anushjohn.com/the-millennium) "The **stone** used to cover the opening of the tomb may not have been more than four feet in diameter, since tomb openings were not usually as tall as doorways."—**Mark 15:46** footnote, *The Nelson Study Bible.* Copyright © 1997 by Thomas Nelson, Inc. Used with permission.

[1410] The day Jesus died ended at sundown of what is today called Friday, at which time the Sabbath would begin. (Mark 15:42; Luke 23:54) On Preparation Day (Nisan 14 in this case), the day before the Sabbath, observants prepared extra meals and finished work that could not wait until after the Sabbath. (Deuteronomy 5:12-14) The first day of the seven-day Festival of Unleavened Bread was always a Sabbath. (Leviticus 23:5-7) This time that first day coincided with the weekly Sabbath, the seventh day. At sunset, then, a double, or "great," Sabbath began.—John 19:31, *The Emphasized Bible.*

[1411] Of all the witnesses to Jesus' execution, only these two women witnessed his burial. "It would scarcely have been in accordance with Jewish manners, if these women had mingled more closely with the two Sanhedrists and their attendants. From where they stood they could only have had a dim view of what passed within the court, and this may explain how, on their return, they 'prepared spices and ointments' (St. Luke [23:56]) for the more full honours *[sic]* which they hoped to pay the Dead after the Sabbath was past."—Edersheim, page 899.

[1412] Jesus' adversaries apparently knew that if Jesus were to be resurrected, his claim to be the Messiah (the alleged first deception) would be proved true.

[1413] Pilate evidently provided a guard of Roman soldiers. Had the guards been Temple police, the Judean authorities would not have had to consult Pilate. Also, the priests promised to set matters right with the governor if he heard of the disappearance of Jesus' body.—Matthew 28:14.

[1414] At verse 8 in Mark chapter 16 "some of the most ancient witnesses bring the book to a close; others continue with verses 9-20."—M. Jack Suggs: Mark chapter 16 note y, *The New English Bible.*

[1415] Matthew identifies Mary Magdalene and Mary the mother of James the Less and Joses—called "the other Mary"—at the tomb. (28:1) To that pair Mark adds Salome and Luke adds Joanna. John speaks only of Mary Magdalene. "It may have been," Edersheim suggests, "that there were two parties, starting from different places to meet at the Tomb, and that this also accounts for the slight difference in the details of what they saw and heard at the Grave. At any rate, the mention of the two Marys and Joanna is supplemented in St. Luke (Luke 24:10) by that of the 'other women with them,' while, if St. John speaks only of Mary Magdalene (John 20:1), her report to Peter and John: 'We know not where they have laid Him,' implies, that she had not gone alone to the Tomb." (Joh 20:2) Another possibility: Mary Magdalene went by herself to Jesus' grave, as John suggests, and found it empty; then, "while the Magdalene hastened, probably by another road, to the abode of Peter and John, the other women also had reached the Tomb, either in one party, or, it may be, in two companies."—pages 907, 908.

[1416] Jesus' body had already been prepared for burial according to Jewish custom. (John 19:39-40; compare 2 Chronicles 16:14) The preparation, however, must have been done hastily since Jesus died just a few hours before the Sabbath started. (Matthew 27:45, 50) On the first day after the Sabbath, women intended to add more spices and oils, perhaps as a means of preserving the body for a longer period. (Luke 23:55-24:1) Likely, they would have applied the spices and oils over the wrapped body.

[1417] "The first day of the week" was Sunday, the day after the Sabbath. (Matthew 28:1, *King James Version)* Jesus rose from death at early dawn. He was buried shortly before sunset on Friday, "so he lay in the tomb a small part of Friday, all of Saturday, and 10 or 11 hours of Sunday. This corresponds exactly with the seven times repeated statement that he would or did rise 'on the third day,' which *could not possibly* mean after 72 hours."—Robertson, page 240; Matthew 16:21; 17:23; 20:19; 27:63; Luke 9:22; 18:33; 24:7, 21, 46; Acts 10:40; 1 Corinthians 15:4.

[1418] "*Mary Magdalene* is always noted first in the appearance lists in the gospels. It is unusual that the first appearance would involve women as in this culture their role as witnesses would not be well accepted. It is a sign of the veracity of the account, because if an ancient were to create such a story he would never have it start with women."—Luke 24:10 footnote, *The NET Bible.*

[1419] Such brilliance is characteristic of angels.—Acts 1:10; Revelation 19:14.

[1420] These women are the first followers to be told of Jesus' resurrection and also the ones instructed to inform the others. Tellingly, the men did not believe the women. (Luke 24:11) A woman's testimony was not permissible in Israel's courts of law. By contrast, God's angel dignified the women by giving them this joyful assignment.

[1421] The disciple of whom Jesus was particularly fond is not named in the fourth gospel but believed to be the apostle John. (John 13:23; 19:26; 20:2; 21:7, 20) "Hastening from the Tomb, [Mary Magdalene] ran to the lodging of Peter and to that of John—the repetition of the preposition 'to' probably marking, that the two occupied different, although perhaps closely adjoining, quarters."—Edersheim, page 909; John 20:2.

[1422] Although age is not always directly correlated with running speed, the fact that John made it to the tomb first (combined with the tradition that he was the last apostle to die) suggests he was a young man, probably younger than Peter.

[1423] By the time John reached the tomb there was presumably enough daylight to penetrate the low opening and illuminate the interior sufficiently for him to see the wrappings lying where the body had been. "The most probable configuration for a tomb of this sort would be to have a niche carved in the wall where the body would be laid lengthwise, or a low shelf like a bench running along one side of the tomb, across the back or around all three sides in a U-shape facing the entrance. Thus, the graveclothes would have been lying on this shelf or in the niche where the body had been."—John 20:5 footnote, *The NET Bible.*

[1424] The *sudarium* "was a small towel used to wipe off perspiration (the way a handkerchief would be used today). This particular item was not mentioned in connection with Jesus' burial in John 19:40, probably because this was only a brief summary account. A face cloth was mentioned in connection with Lazarus' burial (John 11:44) and was probably customary. R. E. Brown speculates that it was wrapped under the chin and tied on top of the head to prevent the mouth of the corpse from falling open (*John* [AB], 2:986), but this is not certain." (*The NET Bible,* John 20:7 footnote) The presence of the graveclothes was strong circumstantial evidence that Jesus' body had not been stolen. What graverobber would unwrap the body and leave the clothes behind neatly folded up?

[1425] Certain prophecies—particularly those dealing with the Messiah's rejection, suffering, death and resurrection—were not immediately understood, even by Jesus' apostles.—Mark 9:31-32; Luke 9:44-45.

[1426] Who would believe a Roman soldier's claim to have slept on duty, a dereliction for which he could be put to death? (Compare Acts 16:27) Furthermore, how could he testify to something that supposedly happened while he was asleep? He would obviously be lying to cover up the bigger lie that Jesus' followers stole his body. Nevertheless, in the first century "the charge of the stolen body was used to counter the proclamation of Jesus' resurrection."—M. Jack Suggs: Matthew 28:15 footnote, *The New English Bible.*

[1427] In his post-resurrection appearances, Jesus was not always immediately recognizable. His voice, though, was unmistakable. Mary did not know she was talking to Jesus until he spoke her name.

[1428] It appears that Mary Magdalene feared that Jesus was about to ascend to Heaven. Moved by her strong desire to be with her Lord, she was holding fast to Jesus, not letting him go. To assure her that he was not yet leaving, Jesus instructed Mary to stop holding onto him and, instead, to go to his apostles and declare the news of his resurrection. Jesus called the apostles his **brothers** because of the spiritual relationship they shared.—**John 20:17**; see Matthew 12:49-50; 25:40; 28:10; Mark 3:34-35; Luke 8:21; Hebrews 2:11-12.

[1429] Edersheim describes Emmaus as "a sweet spot" for wandering on a spring day, and "a favourite *[sic]* resort of the inhabitants of Jerusalem for an afternoon." (page 913 note 21) Possibly, Emmaus was home to Cleopas and/or his unnamed companion. Some scholars identify Emmaus with El-Qubeiba, about 7 miles (11 km) northwest of Jerusalem. The location lends support to the view that this may be the Biblical village.

[1430] Edersheim suggests that the unnamed disciple is the evangelist Luke himself. "If so, then, ... each of the Gospels would, like a picture, bear in some dim corner the indication of its author: the first, that of the 'publican;' that by St. Mark, that of the young man, who, in the night of the Betrayal, had fled from his captors; that of St. Luke in the Companion of Cleopas; and that of St. John, in the disciple whom Jesus loved."—page 912.

[1431] Or "the chief priests and our rulers."—Luke 24:20, *King James Version*.

[1432] This is a metaphorical description of strong emotions, such as joy and pleasure, including the idea of intense interest and enthusiasm.

[1433] Before Jesus appeared to the apostles as a group, he appeared to Peter alone. (1 Corinthians 15:5) The details are unrecorded, but no doubt Jesus assured Peter that he had been forgiven for three times denying association with him.

[1434] The closed doors were no obstacle to the resurrected Jesus, whether they opened of their own accord before him, or he simply appeared in the middle of the room without passing through the doors at all.

[1435] Scripture suggests that a nail or nails pierced Jesus' feet, fixing them directly to the instrument of execution or to a small platform attached.—Psalm 22:16; John 20:25; Colossians 2:14.

[1436] Or "spirit." (Luke 24:39, *King James Version;* compare 1 Corinthians 15:45) Humans cannot see spirits, so the disciples evidently thought they were seeing a **vision** or an "apparition." (**Luke 24:37, 39**, *The New Testament in the Translation of Monsignor Ronald Knox*; compare Mark 6:49-50) As angels had done in the past, Jesus materialized to be seen by the disciples.—Genesis 19:1-3.

[1437] **The Law** refers to the first five Bible books—Genesis through Deuteronomy. **The Prophets** refers to the prophetic books, including the so-called Former Prophets (the books of Joshua through Kings). **Psalms** is the section containing the remaining books of the Old Testament and is called the Writings. The designation "Psalms" is used because it was the first book of the section.—**Luke 24:44.**

[1438] Or "You yourselves are to be witnesses to all this." (Luke 24:48, *Open English Bible)* This is one of the first times that Jesus tells his disciples to bear witness about his life and ministry, including his death and resurrection. (Compare John 15:27) Some 40 days later, Jesus repeated and emphasized their new assignment to be his witnesses.—Acts 1:8; 13:31.

[1439] That **power**, God's spirit (promised at Joel 2:28-29 and John 14:16-17, 26), would energize Jesus' disciples to serve as witnesses in all the world.—**Luke 24:49**; Acts 1:5, 8; 2:32-33.

[1440] Jesus' followers were to be baptized with God's spirit on the following festival day of Pentecost at Jerusalem, and their first witnessing about the repentance for forgiveness of sins through Christ was to be given to Pentecostal celebrators in that city.

[1441] The other disciples must have told Thomas that Jesus showed them his hands and his side.—John 20:20.

[1442] "Significantly, the expression 'for fear of the Jews' no longer occurs. That apprehension had for the present passed away."—Edersheim, page 918 note 37; John 20:19, 26.

[1443] The apostle Thomas was known by another Greek name, Didymus, which means "a twin." *(The New Compact Bible Dictionary*, page 133; John 11:16; 20:24: 21:2) In Thomas existed the opposite twin qualities of doubt and belief.

[1444] Whether Thomas touched Jesus' wounds is not stated. For Thomas, seeing was believing. He became convinced that Jesus was alive and confessed faith in him. See John 8:28.

[1445] See 1 Peter 1:8-9. The opportunity Jesus gave Thomas to allay his doubts, followed by a mild reprimand, encouraged the apostle and restored his faith. "This account ... invites belief which is not dependent on physical evidence."—David M. Stanley: John 20:24-29 footnote, *The New English Bible*. See 2 Corinthians 5:7.

[1446] Possibly, the two other apostles were Andrew, who was in the fishing business with his brother Peter (Matthew 4:18; 10:2; Mark 1:16, 29; 13:3; Luke 6:14; John 1:40-41, 44; 6:8), and Phillip, the close friend of Nathanael/Bartholomew (Matthew 10.3; John 1:45). Andrew and Phillip are mentioned together at John 6:7-8 and 12:22.

[1447] They were only 200 cubits, or 300 feet (90 m) from Jesus. According to Mark 16:12, he sometimes "manifested in another form" or "likeness" to his followers. *(American Standard Version; Wycliffe Bible)* The resurrected Jesus evidently materialized different bodies to suit the occasion. On at least two occasions he was recognizable to the disciples. (Luke 24:38-40; John 20:20-27) On other occasions—such as this one—"Jesus did not look the same as before he was killed"; "He looked like a different person."—Mark 16:12, *Easy-to-Read Version; Worldwide English (New Testament);* see Luke 24:15-16; John 20:14-16.

[1448] This endearing form of address, an affectionate expression of friendship, may indicate a fatherly interest as well.—Mark 10:24; John 13:33; 21:5.

[1449] The unnamed disciple of whom Jesus is particularly fond was one of the seven fishing apostles, among whom were Zebedee's sons. (John 21:2, 7, 20) He is generally believed to be the apostle John.—John 13:23; 19:26; 20:2.

[1450] Although some theologians attach symbolic significance to the number 153, this is merely a detail "indicative of an eyewitness account. ... Perhaps the reader is simply to understand this as the abundance which results from obedience to Jesus, much as with the amount of wine generated in the water jars in Cana at the beginning of Jesus' public ministry ([John] 2:6)."—John 21:11 footnote, *The NET Bible*.

[1451] Or "do you love me more than these?" (John 21:15, *World English Bible)* Jesus may have been asking the fisherman, 'Do you love me more than these fish?' In other words, 'Do you love me more than material things or pursuits?' What would Peter put first in his life—a career in the fishing business (represented by the fish) or the work of spiritually feeding Jesus' lambs, his followers? Grammatically, the phrase "more than these" can be understood in more than one way, however. According to a translation note in *The Expanded Bible*, "'these' probably refers to the other disciples ..., and [Jesus] could mean 'Do you love me more than you love your friends?' or 'Do you love me more than they love me?' The latter is more likely. This whole scene is the restoration of Peter after he had boasted of his loyalty to Jesus and then denied him." (Mark 14:29-30, 66-72) "Thus the semantic force of what Jesus asks Peter here amounts to something like 'Now, after you have denied me three times, as I told you would, can you still affirm that you love me more than these other disciples do?'"—John 21:15 footnote, *The NET Bible*.

[1452] Twice Jesus asked Peter: **Do you love me?** Both times Peter earnestly affirmed that Jesus was **dear** to him. Jesus allowed Peter to confirm his love for a third time and then entrusted him with responsibility to care for the sheep. In this way, Jesus dispelled any doubts that he had forgiven Peter for denying him three times. Each time Peter affirmed his love, Jesus emphasized that this love and affection should motivate Peter to **feed** and **shepherd** Jesus' disciples spiritually. (**John 21:15-17**) As Jesus told him to, Peter would feed, strengthen and shepherd his spiritual brothers.—Luke 22:32; 1 Peter 5:1-3.

[1453] Peter would submissively stretch out his hands to someone else who would take control of him; this one would bear Peter to a place where he did not want to go, a place of execution. Tradition has it that Peter was martyred, crucified upside down at his own request. See 2 Peter 1:13-15.

[1454] As John 21:20-24 shows, this unnamed disciple for whom Jesus had special affection is also the author of the Gospel According to John. The writer does not identify himself. However, by the second and third centuries, the fourth gospel was widely attributed to the apostle John. See "The Gospel According to..."

[1455] These words apparently gave the other apostles the impression that John would outlive them. In fact, he was likely the last apostle to die. In exile on the isle of Patmos near the end of his life, John received the Revelation with its prophetic signs of events that were to occur when Jesus would return. (Revelation 1:1, 9; 22:20; see "The Revelation of Jesus Christ") In a sense, then, John 'remained' until Jesus 'returned.'—John 21:22; compare Matthew 16:28-17:1; Mark 9:1-2; Luke 9:27-28.

[1456] God's kingdom was the main subject of Christ's teaching; it became the keynote of his apostles' preaching.—Matthew 4:17, 23; 9:35; 10:7; Mark 1:15; Luke 4:43; 8:1; 9:2, 11; 10:9; Acts 1:3; 8:12; 19:8; 20:25; 28:23, 31.

[1457] More than 500 followers attended this meeting in Galilee, including the women who were told by an angel that the resurrected Jesus would appear to them in Galilee. (Matthew 28:7; 1 Corinthians 15:6) Among the attendees were some with doubts, perhaps because Jesus had not yet appeared to them.—Matthew 28:17; Mark 16:11, 14; Luke 24:11, 41; John 20:24-29.

[1458] Or "disciple all the nations"; "teach all nations." (Matthew 28:19, *The Emphasized Bible; King James Version)* Before Jesus' ministry, Gentiles were welcomed to Israel if they came to serve the True God. (1 Kings 8:41-43) Before ascending to Heaven, Jesus commissioned his disciples to extend the gospel to Gentiles, revealing the worldwide scope of the Christian ministry. (Matthew 24:14; Mark 13:10; Revelation 14:6) Discipling would be an ongoing process, one that would include teaching what Jesus taught, applying his teaching and following his example.—John 13:17; Ephesians 4:21; 1 Peter 2:21.

[1459] Or "all the days, until the conclusion of the age," the period of time leading up to the end of the state of affairs dominated by Satan. (Matthew 28:20, *The Emphasized Bible)* "The conclusion of the age" runs concurrently with Christ's second presence. (Matthew 24:3) Through God's spirit Jesus keeps his promise to be with Christians.—Matthew 18:20; John 14:16-18.

[1460] Jesus was the first to be baptized with God's spirit. John the Baptist foretold that Jesus would baptize others with God's spirit.—Matthew 3:11, 16; Mark 1:8-11; Luke 3:21-22; John 1:32-34; Acts 1:5; 11:16; 1 Corinthians 12:13.

[1461] Or "the kingdom." (Acts 1:6, *King James Version)* Christ's words concerning baptism with God's spirit evidently triggered the apostles' concern regarding the kingdom's establishment. The connection was consistent with Jewish expectations. (Ezekiel 39:28-29) "The apostles still identified the messianic kingdom with the political restoration of David's dynasty."—Acts chapter 1 note g, *The Jerusalem Bible:* Edited by Alexander Jones.

[1462] Instead of correcting his disciples' views concerning the Kingdom, Jesus corrected their views concerning the timing of its rule. (He had sought to correct the same erroneous thinking with his parable of the minas.—Luke 19:11-27) The Great Timekeeper has reserved for himself the right to set "times" and "seasons" for the fulfillment of his purposes. (Acts 1:7, *King James Version)* Such knowledge was withheld from the ancient prophets. (1 Peter 1:10-12) Jesus said that even the Son did not know when the end would come; only the Father knew. (Mark 13:32) Christians, as stewards of every moment of time allotted, are to make the most of all opportunities to live for Christ.—Psalm 90:12; Ephesians 5:16.

[1463] Lucian writings present God's spirit "as a Power ... sent from God by Christ ... to broadcast the Good News." (Acts chapter 1 note i, *The Jerusalem Bible*: Edited by Alexander Jones; see Luke 1:35; 24:49; Acts 10:38) Acts of Apostles makes clear that the international Christian ministry could be accomplished only with the aid of God's spirit and power.—Acts 1:8; 4:33; compare Matthew 24:14; 28:19; Mark 13:10; Colossians 1:23; 1 Peter 1:12; Revelation 14:6.

[1464] Jesus' early disciples were already witnesses for the God of Israel, and they testified that He was the only true God. (Isaiah 43:10-12; 44:8) Now, though, the disciples were to be witnesses of both God and Jesus.

[1465] Jerusalem is the most important city in the Bible because it is where God chose to establish his name. (Ezra 6:12) Also, it was the center of the early Christian congregation, and from it the gospel spread worldwide. Jerusalem became a symbol of the congregation itself.—Revelation 3:12; 21:2, 9-10.

[1466] After his resurrection, Jesus had materialized fleshly bodies. Jesus dematerialized the body he used on this occasion and ascended to Heaven as a spirit being.—1 Corinthians 15:44, 50.

[1467] The "men" are angels.—Acts 1:9; compare Luke 24:4, 23.

[1468] Or "heaven." (Acts 1:11, *King James Version)* The Greek word that occurs three times in **Acts 1:11** can refer to the physical heavens (**the sky**) or to the spiritual heavens.

[1469] Jesus' departure was observed by only the apostles. His **return** would be in a **manner** (or "way," *Revised King James New Testament)* discernible only to Christians who recognize the sign of his second presence.—**Acts 1:11**; see Matthew 24:3; Revelation 1:7.

[1470] The apostles had been meeting behind locked doors for fear of their enemies. (John 20:19, 26) Strengthened by enlightenment from Jesus and witnessing his ascension to Heaven, they courageously came out in public, praising God.

[1471] During Jesus' ministry, his half-brothers did not demonstrate faith in him. (John 7:5) After Jesus' death and resurrection, however, they were changed men.—1 Corinthians 15:7.

[1472] Although an upstairs room was a typical meeting place (Acts 20:8), the "upper room" where Christians commemorated their first Pentecost together "could have been the room where Jesus spent the last Passover with His disciples, or the room in which He appeared to them after His resurrection (recorded in Luke 24). ... This room may have belonged to Mary, the mother of John Mark. Her house is mentioned in [Acts] 12:12 as a meeting place of disciples."—Acts 1:13 footnote, *The Nelson Study Bible*. Copyright © 1997 by Thomas Nelson, Inc. Used with permission.

[1473] It was not a wind, but it sounded like one. The noise attracted the attention of the many pilgrims.

[1474] The so-called tongues were, not of literal fire, but an observable manifestation upon each disciple that had the appearance and radiance of fire. (Acts 2:3) For other examples of fire symbolizing God's presence, see Exodus 3:2-4; 13:21; 19:18; Leviticus 9:24; Deuteronomy 4:33, 36; 1 Kings 18:38; 1 Chronicles 21:26; 2 Chronicles 7:1, 3; Psalm 50:3; 2 Thessalonians 1:7-8.

[1475] Many who heard the disciples may have spoken an international tongue, perhaps Greek. Being devout worshipers of Israel's God, they may also have been able to understand the services in Hebrew at the Temple. But hearing something in the language they had known from childhood caught their attention. "[T]he apostles speak a universal language; the unity lost at Babel is restored. This symbolizes and anticipates the apostles' worldwide mission."—Acts chapter 2 note f, *The Jerusalem Bible:* Edited by Alexander Jones. See Genesis 11:1-9.

[1476] Peter also explained how this event fulfilled prophecy. Joel foretold the outpouring of God's spirit; David prophesied concerning the resurrection of Jesus.—Psalm 16:8-10; 110:1; Joel 2:28-32; Acts 2:16-21, 25-28, 34-35.

[1477] Jesus' preaching to a Samaritan woman may have laid the foundation for many more Samaritans to later put faith in him. (John 4:39-42) Only the power of God's spirit could have united Samaritans and Israelites.—Acts 8:5-8, 14-17.

[1478] Cornelius and his family, none of whom were Jews, became Christians with Peter's assistance.

[1479] Paul is introduced in Acts of Apostles by his Hebrew name, Saul. He was of the tribe of Benjamin but also a Roman citizen from birth. (Acts 22:25-28; Philippians 3:5) "Saul" was a traditional name among Benjaminites because the first king over all Israel was a Benjaminite by that name. (Acts 13:21) Perhaps Saul was named after his father, which was customary. (Luke 1:59) His Hebrew parents may have given him the Roman name Paulus. From childhood, he likely had both names. When among fellow Israelites—and especially when studying to be a Pharisee and living as one—Saul would have used his Hebrew name. (Acts 22:3) For over a decade after becoming a Christian, he continued to be known as Saul.—Acts 13:9.

[1480] When Paul was converted to Christianity, the resurrected Jesus chose Paul to be "an apostle [meaning "one sent forth"] to the [Gentile] nations."—Acts 26:17-18; Romans 11:13; 15:16-18; Galatians 2:2, 8; Ephesians 3:8; 1 Timothy 2:7; *The New Compact Bible Dictionary*, page 48.

[1481] According to 1 Maccabees 15:21 Rome recognized the high priest's jurisdiction—including the right of extradition—over Jewish communities outside Palestine. See "The Sanhedrin—Theocracy's High Court."

[1482] The journey from Jerusalem to Damascus would have been about 150 miles (240 km). The capital of modern-day Syria, Damascus is one of the world's oldest continuously inhabited cities. In the first century, Damascus was part of the Roman province of Syria and an important trade center. Saul may have targeted Christians in Damascus because the city was situated at the crossroads of important travel routes from which Christianity could quickly spread. But instead of arresting the Christians, Saul became one of them. He began his career as a gospel preacher in the synagogues of Damascus.—Acts 9:20-22.

[1483] Jesus identified himself with the congregation that Paul was persecuting. Compare Luke 10:16.

[1484] In his epistles, Paul shared personal feelings about his past as a persecutor of Christians and how Christ stopped him in his tracks.—Galatians 1:13-16; Philippians 3:4-8; 1 Timothy 1:12-16.

[1485] "To be an apostle required having seen the risen Christ and received a commission from him, though other signs were important as well. Paul's apostleship was distinctive and was disputed by some in the early church. He was directly appointed by Christ and was able to bear witness to the resurrection because his call came from the risen Christ. Another outstanding feature of his apostleship was his call to serve as the apostle to the Gentiles. Paul valued the gift of apostleship so highly that he occasionally went to great lengths to prove its validity."—Verlyn D. Verbrugge: *The NIV Topical Study Bible*, page 1298. See 1 Corinthians 9:1; 15:3-8.

1486[1486] Christianity was widely known throughout the Roman Empire and beyond by the time Paul wrote his letter to the Colossians. (Romans 1:8; Colossians 1:5-6) Jews and proselytes who received God's spirit at Pentecost carried the gospel to Parthia, Elam, Media, Mesopotamia, Arabia, Asia Minor, the parts of Libya toward Cyrene, and Rome—encompassing the world known to Paul's readers. Gospel Truth had not literally reached every land around the globe, however. Paul himself said that Spain was then untouched territory.—Romans 15:23-24.

1487[1487] Hyperbolically speaking, "the world" would not have room for all "the books" (or "scrolls," the book style then used) needed to record an exhaustive account of Jesus' words and works. (John 21:25; *King James Version; New World Translation;* compare Ecclesiastes 12:9-12) The Greek term John used for "world" could have been understood in the broad sense of the whole human society (with its then existing libraries), though it was sometimes used in secular Greek writings to refer to the whole universe, that is, the greatest space conceivable. (Acts 17:24) Much more about Jesus could have been written, but there is enough in John's 'book' and the other gospels to prove beyond doubt that Jesus is the Messiah, the Son of God.

www.ingramcontent.com/pod-product-compliance
Lightning Source LLC
Chambersburg PA
CBHW051258120626
46547CB00015B/1988
* 9 7 8 1 9 6 0 9 0 3 6 6 2 *